FREEDOM
of RELIGION
the FIRST
AMENDMENT
and the SUPREME
COURT

FREEDOM
of RELIGION
the FIRST
AMENDMENT
and SUPREME
the
COURT

How the Court Flunked History

BARRY ADAMSON

PELICAN PUBLISHING COMPANY
GRETNA 2008

*The word "Pelican" and the depiction of a pelican
are trademarks of Pelican Publishing Company, Inc.,
and are registered in the U.S. Patent and Trademark Office.*

Library of Congress Cataloging-in-Publication Data

Adamson, Barry.
　　Freedom of religion, the First Amendment, and the Supreme
Court : how the Court flunked history / Barry Adamson.
　　　　p. cm.
　　Includes bibliographical references and index.
　　ISBN 978-1-58980-520-0 (hardcover : alk. paper)
　　1. Freedom of religion—United States—History. 2. Church and
state—United States—History. 3. United States. Constitution. 1st
Amendment—History. 4. United States. Supreme Court—History. I.
Title.
　　KF4783.A934 2008
　　342.7308'52—dc22

2007038063

Printed in the United States of America

Published by Pelican Publishing Company, Inc.
1000 Burmaster Street, Gretna, Louisiana 70053

Contents

Preface: How Clear the Lens of Historical Reality

Two fortuitous events spawned all that follows.

In the spring of 2002, I chanced to hear Darrell Scott speak of his certainty that his daughter Rachel might not have been gunned down by a fellow student on April 20, 1999, at Columbine High School in Littleton, Colorado, had our nation's public education system not been so persistent with its crusade to rid the educational process of any hint of faith-based influences such as character, values, integrity, truth, and non-variable morals. Irony of ironies, the fellow student who thrust his gun in Rachel's face that morning asked Rachel whether she believed in God; she said "yes," and in the next instant became the first victim, shot point blank.

Darrell posed this question to his audience: "How many of you can recite the first ten words of the First Amendment?" I can still recall the jolt of two emotions as he asked that question: the giddy elation of sensing that, as a graduate of the UCLA School of Law, I had an inherent advantage over other listeners, followed by an overwhelming discomfiture as, stunned, I realized that I had no recollection of having ever learned the precise wording of the First Amendment. Something to do with speech, or the press, I thought. Not even close; the first ten words of the Constitution's First Amendment—actually the first "right" implemented in the Bill of Rights—form the Establishment Clause: "Congress shall make no law respecting an establishment of religion[.]"[1]

Darrell asked more humbling questions: "How many of you have heard the expression 'separation of church and state'?" It seemed that all hands shot up, including mine. "How many of you think that phrase appears in the Constitution?" Hands started upward, then hesitated, as many folks suddenly found themselves wondering why he would ask the obvious, unless . . . then it dawned on them. I recall thinking that, although I knew the phrase "separation of church and state" appeared nowhere in the Constitution, I believed that the United States Supreme Court authored those words, and that the phrase summarized the historical meaning of the Establishment Clause. Wrong; so wrong.

Within a couple of months of Darrell Scott's piercing illumination of my ignorance, one of the most singularly dumb moments in United States history occurred: in June 2002 the United States Ninth Circuit Court of Appeals declared a portion of the Pledge of Allegiance unconstitutional because, according to the Court, the words "under God" ran afoul of the Establishment Clause.[2] I simply could not fathom how that could be.

I concluded at that point that I must have no idea what the Establishment Clause really means, because the Pledge of Allegiance's mere reference to "God" surely seems innocent enough. I also decided that simply reading what the United States Supreme Court had to say about it would simply not suffice, because even it had to start somewhere. So I began at the beginning—the *true* beginning.

I have now learned, as will you, that the Supreme Court has never had any idea what the words in the Establishment Clause actually mean, and has cared little about the reality that history so plainly reveals. And worse, the Court seems quite content to allow that predicament to endure.

I began my research with some unremarkable premises.

First, words have meaning only within a specific, singular, idiosyncratic context. In fact, words have no meaning otherwise. Correlatively, words relinquish "meaning" when divorced from the unique contextual framework within which their author(s) assembled them.

Second, authors mean what they say when they say it, and they write with neither the apprehension nor the expectation that the meaning of their published words will or might change over time. Hence, the meaning of published words necessarily remains constant over time, else "meaning" ceases to exist. Even those who disagree with this premise invariably—not to mention hypocritically—voice their disagreements in conformance with the very premise with which they purport to disagree. In other words, they certainly do not anticipate that their objections will change in meaning over time.

Third, the "intent" of an author to convey a particular thought, message, idea, or concept plays no role in the determination of "meaning"; only the words themselves and their unique historical context can determine "meaning." If an author successfully conveys "intent" via specific words used within a specific context, then "intent" becomes a superfluous and inconsequential consideration. And if an author fails in that effort, *viz.,* "intent" remains ineffectively expressed (or entirely unexpressed), then the author's unexpressed "intent" likewise remains irrelevant because it remains hidden.

Fourth, the opinions of others as to the "meaning" of an author's work never create a new "meaning."

And *fifth,* truth really does matter.

The narrative that follows offers none of the usual distractions and diversions:

> • no psychic delving into the minds or elusive "intention" of the 1789 Congress;
> • no scholarly excursions through perceived grammatical abstrusities among the words in the ten-word phrase "Congress shall make no law respecting an establishment of religion";
> • no academic ramblings about the nature of constitutions and why, according to some, words written in constitutions fluctuate or ebb and flow with time; and,
> • no treks along the interminable trails of the "what ifs."

Abiding the advice that "the right answer depends on the right question,"[3] the research that follows tracks two questions to a definitive conclusion: *First,* what did the word "establishment" and the phrase "an establishment of religion" mean on September 25, 1789, when Congress authored the text of the Establishment Clause? *Second,* has the United States Supreme Court abided by that historical meaning? Let the answers fall where they may.

1

The Historical Purpose and Meaning of the First Amendment's Establishment Clause

If you cannot understand that history can be objectively known, then you will believe that history bears no certainty. If you cannot understand that specific words used within a specific context convey a specific meaning, then you will believe that words can mean anything you want. And if you cannot understand that truth and reality remain constant, then you will believe that "truth" and "reality" will be relative to your personal expectations. Read on, and you *will* understand.

Americans have better odds of finding pearls in their cornflakes than they have of finding an evenhanded, "let-the-answers-fall-where-they-may" chronicling of the historical events that supply an objective meaning to four of this nation's most ill-understood words: "an establishment of religion." History confirms that the meaning of those words remains straightforward, but that reality has been obliterated by a Supreme Court that in 1947 decided to, in effect, concoct its own version of reality on its own say-so.

The United States Constitution's First Amendment—indeed, the historic Bill of Rights itself (the first set of constitutional amendments written by the inaugural 1789 Congress)—begins not with any reference to "speech" or "press" but with the following ten words, known as the "Establishment Clause":

> Congress shall make no law respecting an establishment of religion . . . [.][1]

The Establishment Clause and the very next clause in the First Amendment—the Free Exercise Clause ("Congress shall make no law . . . prohibiting the free exercise [of religion]")—comprise the First Amendment's religion clauses. All other First Amendment rights follow the religion clauses.[2]

The average American's need for a book about the history and

13

meaning of the Constitution's Establishment Clause became all too apparent at the moment that three realities collided:

• Thomas Jefferson's figurative "wall of separation" represents the sum total of what our nation's citizenry knows about the Constitution's relationship to "religion";

• the Supreme Court has demonstrated repeatedly—for decades—that it knows Establishment Clause history in the same way it knows rocket science; and,

• the average reader—you or your next-door neighbor—cannot locate a straightforward, readable, objective, accurate, historical chronicle of the Establishment Clause within a local bookstore or library.

Indeed, the public's unfamiliarity with the Supreme Court's mangling of one of the most important provisions in our nation's Bill of Rights prompted this book. Because of that unfamiliarity, the average American . . .

• cannot recite the first ten words of the First Amendment in our nation's Bill of Rights ("Congress shall make no law respecting an establishment of religion . . . "—the Establishment Clause);

• has no idea what the phase "an establishment" has always meant in the context of religion, or what the phrase "establishment of religion" meant when Congress wrote the First Amendment in 1789;

• believes that our nation's Constitution speaks of "separation of church and state";

• has never been informed that the source of the "separation" colloquialism—Thomas Jefferson—concocted his figurative "wall" almost thirteen years *after* Congress wrote the Establishment Clause (something that Jefferson had nothing to do with), and that he merely objected to a predominant institutional "state church" or a European-type "church-state"; and,

• remains woefully uninformed of the reality that the Supreme Court has flunked First Amendment history miserably and declared a nonsensical meaning for the first ten words in our nation's Bill of Rights that their author would find simply incomprehensible.

But the average American *wants* to know . . . to know why the "Pledge of Allegiance" has suddenly become vulnerable to challenge by a single person, to know why our nation's schools shudder at the mention of God or a Christmas holiday, to know why longstanding public displays of historical symbols of our nation's religious heritage may well be endangered, to know why a recurring holiday display on public property may include a Hanukkah menorah but not a crèche depicting the Christian nativity scene, to know how the phrase "wall of separation" became part of our vernacular.

"Congress shall make no law . . ." The first five words in the First Amendment bear no contextual uncertainty. Nonetheless, the Supreme Court has declared that, notwithstanding its uncomplicated and unambiguous limitation to "Congress," the Establishment Clause applies to the states as well—an oddity explained in Chapter 12.[3]

". . . respecting an establishment of religion." These five words incorporate both a compromise dictated by the language of 1789 politics and a well-understood term of art among the states in the 1700s, yielding a historically and contextually plain purpose, function, and meaning. The 1789 Congress, which crafted those ten words during August and September 1789, aimed to thwart a *single* government-*preferred,* government-*sanctioned,* government-*financed* ecclesiastical institution (or religion, church, denomination, faith, sect, creed, or religious society) from usurping or assuming governmental functions, but nothing more. Unfortunately, the Supreme Court's confounding incapacity to read historical text has promoted a freewheeling escapade of judicial *"ipse dixit-*isms" with respect to the Establishment Clause.

(The Latin term *ipse dixit* means, literally, "he himself said it."[4] More colloquially, it insinuates the truth of a declaration solely on the basis of the speaker having declared it. The Supreme Court has historically larded its opinions with instances of *"ipse dixit-*isms"— judicial peculiarities that endure only because the Court can say pretty much whatever it wants. As one of the Court's members once acerbically observed, "We are not final because we are infallible, but we are infallible only because we are final."[5] Less elegantly stated, Justice William J. Brennan, one of the most liberal justices on the Court during the mid-to-late twentieth century, once boasted to his law clerks that "you can do anything around here with five votes."[6])

Historical reality leaves it remarkably free from doubt that when Congress wrote the Establishment Clause in the summer of 1789, it knew full well the meaning of the term "an establishment" within the context of "religion," and history affords no justification for any dispute with that observation; the term "establishment" had long been a well-known concept as used in the Establishment Clause. (Within the "establishment" context, history reveals that the terms "religion," "church," "denomination," "faith," "sect," "creed," and "religious society" had been used interchangeably to reference a particular ecclesiastical institution.)

But when the United States Supreme Court imagines that the use of public funds for the provision of "field trip transportation" to students of nonpublic schools somehow implements an institutional ecclesiastical "establishment" on the order of a "state" church,[7] and when it conceives that a recurring Christmas display on public property, consisting of a crèche depicting the Christian nativity scene and a Hanukkah menorah, yields an institutional ecclesiastical "establishment" for the former but not the latter,[8] matters have come perilously close to a Lewis Carroll-like scenario in which black-robed Supreme Court justices leap through a hole into a dimensionless absurdity and expect everyone else to do the same.

> It might be a hilarious comedy routine to have a group of highly educated judges solemnly expounding on something that everybody knows to be utter nonsense. But it isn't nearly as funny when this solemn discourse about nonsense takes place on the Supreme Court of the United States—and when most people are unaware of what nonsense the learned justices are talking.[9]

Opinions proliferate, but impartial chronicles do not. During a 1994 political debate, the late four-term New York senator and former United Nations ambassador Patrick Moynihan framed the ultimate argument-ender with characteristic understated simplicity: "You're entitled to your own opinions. You're not entitled to your own facts."[10] Or your own reality.

Thus, you can, for instance, have your own opinion about the consequence or significance of historical reality, but in a rational society you cannot press your own version of historical reality as truth. Similarly, you can have your own opinion about the meaning of language, but in a rational society you cannot press your own belief about meaning as truth. And truth matters. Unfortunately, the United States Supreme Court's decisions betray an institutional spurning of the truth when it comes to the historical meaning of the first ten words of our Constitution's Bill of Rights.

Bearing in mind the Supreme Court's decades-old catchphrase that "a page of history is worth a volume of logic,"[11] the page after page after page of historical records that underlie the genesis of the Establishment Clause inform their readers of four paramount historical realities.

First, the First Congress designed the Establishment Clause—and confined it to "Congress"—to mimic at the federal level the correlative disestablishment assurances implemented within the various colonial constitutions in the 1770s and 1780s.

Second, the disestablishment aspect of the Establishment Clause meant in 1789—and thus means today—nothing more than its well-understood meaning throughout the 1600s and 1700s in the states within the context of religion, *viz.*

> a (1) *single,* dominant government-*recognized,* government-*preferred,* government-*mandated,* and government-*financed* ecclesiastical institution (or religion, church, denomination, faith, sect, creed, or religious society) that (2) functioned to the detriment of other, non-preferred, ecclesiastical institutions.

Third, the Supreme Court flunked First Amendment history when it opined that Jefferson's allegorical "wall of separation" may be accepted almost as an authoritative declaration of the scope and effect of the Establishment Clause. To say that the Court's view defies rational thought would be to shroud such a colossal gaffe in understatement. Jefferson's figurative "wall of separation" not only postdated the Establishment Clause by almost thirteen years, but Jefferson played no role in the genesis of the Establishment Clause—he lived in France from 1784 to late 1789, and his relationship to the 1789 congressional proceedings consisted of nothing beyond infrequent exchanges of letters with James Madison and others, none of which concerned the Establishment Clause. Might the offhand musings of the uninvolved ascribe "meaning" to someone else's words written years earlier? Never.

And *fourth,* the Supreme Court has flunked the First Amendment's Establishment Clause history miserably, rendering it problematic for our schools and public institutions to dare utter words like "God" or "Christianity" or even "religion."

The narrative that follows begins with an objective chronicling of pertinent historical events and concludes with an assessment of the meaning of the phrase "respecting an establishment of religion" wholly within that context. The historical genesis of the Establishment Clause reveals that, from any objective perspective, the Supreme Court has inexplicably disregarded history and has yet to arrive upon the readily discernible meaning of the words "respecting an establishment of religion" within the historical context in which their author crafted them.

(The notes that accompany the text throughout serve two purposes.

First, they demonstrate both the abundance and agreement of historical sources, thus assuring an enduring objectivity. *Second,* they furnish a wealth of additional historical details for those who enjoy roaming beyond the text.)

2

Religion and Government in the 1700s: The "Establishment"

The First Amendment's Establishment Clause speaks of "an establishment of religion," but few know what that expression means (and has meant for centuries). (Hint: It does *not* signify the erection of a building, or the creation of a system of beliefs, or the founding of a new "church.") The meaning of the constitutional command that "Congress shall make no law respecting an establishment of religion" depends, as always, upon the underlying context in which the author of those words—the 1789 Congress—used them. And that context yields but a single meaning.

When, in June 2005, the United States Supreme Court banned the display of the Ten Commandments from Kentucky courthouses as violative of the Establishment Clause, its opinion remarked that

> [t]he First Amendment contains no textual definition of "establishment," and the term is certainly not self-defining.[1]

As this chapter explains in detail, that assertion proves so contrived that it begs dismissal as inherently unbelievable. Not only did the Establishment Clause require no "textual definition" of the term "establishment" in 1789, but, when used within the context of religion in this country throughout the 1600s and 1700s, the term "establishment" had long borne a specific, well-known, universally understood meaning:

• A single, dominant ecclesiastical institution (or religion, church, denomination, faith, sect, creed, or religious society) that . . .

• enjoyed a government-*preferred,* government-*sanctioned,* government-*financed,* and government-*protected* status within a state, . . .

• and which represented an indistinguishable union with government and the preferred (or "established") ecclesiastical institution.[2]

Centuries later, we forget that in pre–Revolutionary America "establishment" churches dominated the religious landscape. An "establishment" (or "established" church) remains so far removed from contemporary experience and understanding that we need to be reminded of the pervasive role assumed by the state and local governments in the administration of church business. For example, government . . .

- required all citizens to attend the establishment church;
- compelled all citizens to contribute "tithes" to the established church in the form of taxes or other exactions, whether or not they actually attended the establishment church;
- mandated the public teaching of the establishment doctrine to the exclusion of others;
- prescribed the establishment church boundaries;
- sanctioned establishment clergy exclusively to perform marriages, baptisms, and other sacraments;
- paid for establishment church construction and the maintenance of establishment properties;
- funded the establishment clergy's salaries;
- hired and fired establishment preachers;
- suppressed anti–establishment dissent via imposition of civil disabilities; and
- limited government employment to establishment members.[3]

The various states—as the colonies described themselves with the advent of the Declaration of Independence and the Articles of Confederation[4]—never debated any perceived semantic or philosophical differences (assuming any) among the terms "religion," "church," "denomination," "faith," "sect," "creed," and "religious society" in the context of an "establishment." The institutional culprits could be readily identified as discrete entities by name, regardless of how anyone might choose to characterize them. And there exists no uncertainty but that an "establishment" represented a single, discrete, *institutional entity,* not merely a concept of "religion" in the sense of a belief system; "in the language of the day [an "establishment of religion"] connoted an *institution.*"[5]

The reality that any "establishment" constituted a *single,* dominant ecclesiastical institution explains why the First Amendment's Establishment Clause refers to "*an* establishment of religion"—in the singular—as opposed, for instance, to "*the* establishment of religion," a phrasing with an entirely different connotation.

The Supreme Court's purported bafflement concerning the

meaning of "an establishment" quoted at the outset of this chapter proves disingenuous from another perspective as well. The Court has consistently declared that, in the absence of a specific legislative (*viz.*, congressional) definition of a term or expression, the "normal" or "ordinary" meaning of that term or expression will apply.[6] That common-sense approach implements the reality that readers necessarily presume that authors say what they mean with words of a known meaning, and that the authors mean what they say. Readers likewise necessarily presume that the words themselves convey that meaning within the unique context in which the authors assemble them. And bear in mind that the Establishment Clause has always been a congressional work product.[7] Thus, the meaning of the Establishment Clause can readily be determined by resort to ordinary time-period-specific definitions.

A. "Establish" and "Establishment": Etymological History and Meaning

In general, the term "establish" appeared in use during the late "Middle English" period,[8] a language development era that etymologists generally view similarly.[9] As all of a host of authoritative dictionaries confirm, since the Middle Ages—and certainly during the 1600s and 1700s in the various states—the terms "establish," "established," and "establishment" *within the context of religion* invariably referred to a single, dominant ecclesiastical institution (or religion, church, denomination, faith, sect, creed, or religious society) that enjoyed a government-*preferred,* government-*sanctioned,* government-*financed,* and government-*protected* status, and represented an indistinguishable union with government.

The Oxford English Dictionary contains the following context-pertinent definitions which it identifies as having appeared in use as part of "Middle English," *viz.,* at some point between the fourteenth and sixteenth centuries:

> Establish: **7.** From 16th c[entury] often used with reference to ecclesiastical ceremonies or organization, and to the recognized national church or its religion; . . . Hence, in recent use: To place (a church or a religious body) in the position of a national or state church. [10]

> Established: used as part of the term "established church."[11]

> Establishment: **2.** The "establishing" by law (a church, religion,

form of worship). **a.** In early use, the settling or ordering in a particular manner, the regulating and upholding of the constitution and ordinances of the church recognized by the state. **b.** In 17th-18th c[entury] occasionally the granting of legal status to other religious bodies than that connected with the state.[12]

The New Oxford American Dictionary contains the following context-pertinent definitions which it identifies as having appeared in use as part of "late Middle English," *viz.*, the latter part of the time period between 1066 and 1474:

Established: **2.** (of a church or religion) recognized by the government as the national church or religion.[13]

Establishment: **1.** . . . the recognition by the state of a national church or religion[.] **4.** (the Establishment or the Church Establishment) the ecclesiastical system organized by law.[14]

The *Shorter Oxford English Dictionary* contains the following context-pertinent definitions which it identifies as having appeared during the times referenced:

Establish: give legal form and recognition to (a Church) as the official church of a country. [1350–1469][15]

Establishment: The ecclesiastical system established by law; the Established Church. [1730–69][16]

Establishment: The action of making a church an established Church. [1630–69][17]

The American Heritage Dictionary of the English Language contains the following context-pertinent definitions which it identifies as having appeared in use as part of "Middle English" (defined by that dictionary as the time period between 1100 and 1500[18]):

Establish: **6.** To make a state institution of (a church).[19]

Established church: A church that a government officially recognizes as a national institution and to which it accords support.[20]

Establishment: **[2.]c.** an established church.[21]

Random House Webster's Unabridged Dictionary contains the following context-pertinent definitions which it identifies as having appeared in use during the times referenced:

Establish: **7.** to make (a church) a national or state institution. [1325–75][22]

Established church (in use since at least 1650): a church that is recognized by law and sometimes financially supported, as the official church of a nation. [1650–60][23]

Establishment: **10.** the recognition by a state of a church as the state church. **11.** the church so recognized esp. the Church of England. [1475–85][24]

Random House Unabridged Dictionary contains the following context-pertinent definitions which it identifies as having appeared in use during the times referenced:

Establish: **7.** to make (a church) a national or state institution. [1325–75][25]

Established church: a church that is recognized by law, and sometimes financially supported, as the official church of a nation. [1650–60][26]

Establishment: **10.** the recognition by a state of a church as the state church. [1475–80][27]

Webster's Third New International Dictionary contains the following context-pertinent definitions which it identifies as having appeared in use as part of "Middle English" (which the dictionary defines as the time period spanning the twelfth to fifteenth centuries[28]):

Establish: **7.** to make a national or state institution of (a church).[29]

Established church: a church that is recognized by law as the official church of a nation, that is supported by civil authority, and that receives in most instances financial support from the government through some system of taxation—called also the state church.[30]

Establishment: **[1.]b.** established church[;] . . . **[2.]c.** the making of a church into an established church.[31]

Funk & Wagnalls Comprehensive Standard International Dictionary contains the following context-pertinent definitions, which that dictionary dates to "Old French" (or before 1400):

Establish: **7.** To appoint (a church) as a national or state institution.[32]

Established church: a church maintained by the state and receiving financial support out of public funds.[33]

Establishment: **8.** The act of recognizing a church as a state church. **9.** A church so recognized.[34]

Samuel Johnson expressly associated "establish" with "church" in his celebrated mid-eighteenth-century *Dictionary of the English Language:*

> Establish: (by way of example) "the Presbyterian sect was established in all its forms by an ordinance of the lords and commoners."[35]

The celebrated multivolume dictionary written and published in 1828 by Yale graduate and lawyer Noah Webster as our nation's first premier reference work[36] likewise defined "establishment" within the context of religion as "the act of establishing, founding, ratifying or ordaining . . . [t]he episcopal form of religion, so called, in England"[37]—and in England that has always meant the Church of England, the quintessential single, dominant ecclesiastical institution.

Even special etymological dictionaries date the terms "establish," "establishment," and "established church" to the Middle Ages; for instance, the term "establish" appeared in use by 1375,[38] the term "established church" appeared in use by 1660,[39] and the phrase "national church" appeared in use by 1655.[40] Another source reports that references to "the Establishment," with a capital "E," signified "the established church" at least by 1730.[41]

In his celebrated Memorial and Remonstrance published in opposition to Patrick Henry's 1784 legislative proposal to implement a state tax for the support of the Virginia Anglican Church,[42] constitutional (and Bill of Rights) architect James Madison used the term "establish," "establishment," or "establishments" no fewer than ten times:

> 3. . . . Who does not see that the same authority which can *establish* Christianity, in exclusion of all other Religions, may *establish* with the same ease any particular sect of Christians, in exclusion of all other Sects? [T]hat the same authority which can force a citizen to contribute three pence only of his property for the support of any one *establishment,* may force him to conform to any other *establishment* in all cases whatsoever? . . .

> 6. Because the *establishment* proposed by the Bill is not requisite for the support of the Christian Religion. . . .

> 7. Because experience witnesseth that ecclesiastical *establishments,* instead of maintaining the purity and efficacy of Religion, have had a contrary operation. During almost fifteen centuries has the legal *establishment* of Christianity been on trial. . . .

> 8. Because the *establishment* in question is not necessary for the support of Civil Government. . . . If Religion be not within the cognizance of Civil Government how can its legal *establishment* be necessary to Civil Government? . . .

> 9. Because the proposed *establishment* is a departure from that generous policy, which, offering an Asylum to the persecuted and oppressed of every Nation and Religion, promised a lustre [*sic*] to our country, and an accession to the number of its citizens. . . .[43]

In his June 21, 1785, letter to James Monroe concerning that very subject, Madison described Patrick Henry's proposal as a "Bill for *establishing* the Christian Religion in this state."[44] Indeed, Henry's proposal bore the following title: "A Bill *Establishing* a Provision for Teachers of the Christian Religion."[45] And in 1784 Virginia, the "Christian Religion" meant the Anglican Church (or the Church of England).

By the time the inaugural Congress assembled in 1789, the constitutions of New Jersey, Delaware, North Carolina, New York, Massachusetts, and New Hampshire actually incorporated religion-specific references to the terms "establishment" and "established"; the New Jersey, Delaware, and North Carolina constitutions included the phrase "no establishment,"[46] the New York constitution dis-"established" religion,[47] and the Massachusetts and New Hampshire constitutions declared that no preference (*viz.*, no preferred religion) shall be "established."[48]

Longtime early nineteenth-century United States Supreme Court justice, Harvard Law School professor, and constitutional law expert Joseph Story[49] summarized the meaning and import of the term "establishment" as well as anyone who lived during those times—and he specifically referenced the essential attribute of "preference":

> Now, there will probably be found few persons in this, or any other *Christian country*, who would deliberately contend, that it was unreasonable, or unjust to foster and encourage the Christian religion generally, as a matter of sound policy, as well as of revealed truth. In fact, *every American colony, from its foundation down to the revolution*, with the exception of Rhode Island (if, indeed, that state be an exception), *did openly, by the whole course of its laws and institutions, support and sustain, in some form, the Christian religion;* and almost invariably gave a peculiar sanction to some of its fundamental doctrines. And this has continued to be the case in some of the states down to the present period, *without the slightest suspicion that it was against the principles of public law, or republican liberty.*[50]

> Probably at the time of the adoption of the constitution, and of the

amendment to it, now under consideration [referencing the Establishment Clause], the general, if not the universal, sentiment in America was, that *Christianity ought to receive encouragement from the state,* so far as was not incompatible with the private rights of conscience, and the freedom of religious worship.[51]

Another celebrated nineteenth-century constitutional law expert, University of Michigan Law School professor and Michigan Supreme Court justice Thomas Cooley,[52] wrote similarly:

> By establishment of religion is meant the setting up or recognition of *a state church,* or at least the *conferring upon one church of special favors and advantages* which are denied to others. It was never intended by the Constitution that the government should be prohibited from recognizing religion.[53]

B. The Two Dominant "Establishments" in the States: The Anglicans (Or Church of England) and the Congregationalists (Or Puritans)

In England, both prior to and during the American colonial period, the Church of England "enjoyed the privileges of an exclusive legal union with the state,"[54] and, accordingly, the "[l]aw demanded that everyone support the official Church of England with taxes and regular attendance."[55] That reality did not disappear simply because English citizens emigrated to America; King James, for one, had specific intentions of implementing the Church of England in the colonies.[56]

> Myth persists that the seventeenth-century English colonists fled from religious persecution into a land of religious freedom. . . . [A]t the end of the seventeenth century, most colonies offered *less* religious toleration than did the mother country.[57]

Established churches dominated the colonies in the seventeenth and eighteenth centuries[58]; "established churches became the order of the day in early America."[59] Most of the colonies found themselves dominated by a particular established ecclesiastical institution:

• The Anglicans (or Church of England) became the established ecclesiastical institution in Virginia,[60] New York,[61] Maryland,[62] Georgia,[63] North Carolina,[64] South Carolina,[65] and, to a lesser extent and only in the early years, Pennsylvania[66] and New Jersey.[67]

• The Congregationalists (or Puritans) became the established ecclesiastical institution in Massachusetts,[68] Connecticut,[69] and New Hampshire.[70]

Even the United States Supreme Court has recognized as much:

> The Church of England was the established church of at least five colonies: Maryland, Virginia, North Carolina, South Carolina and Georgia. There seems to be some controversy as to whether that church was officially established in New York and New Jersey but there is no doubt that it received substantial support from those States. . . . In Massachusetts, New Hampshire and Connecticut, the Congregationalist Church was officially established.[71]

Establishment adherents in the states enjoyed broad civil rights that the establishment denied to others (such as excluding dissenters from universities and disqualifying non-adherents from public office), and the establishment effectively stifled and thwarted dissent by the imposition of civil disabilities enforced by the establishment government and magistrates.[72] The "established authority," which maintained "the traditional conviction that secular authority depended upon a religious establishment,"[73] represented nothing less than a merger of "minister and magistrate"[74] or an "exclusive legal union with the state."[75]

Wherever an established church existed, colonial law operated to prefer that single church at the expense of all others,[76] and the established church always remained dependent upon government taxes for financial support; "[a]lmost every colony exacted some kind of tax for church support."[77] In New England, for instance, the Congregationalists effectively dominated the civil authorities which, in turn, imposed uniformity in church government and passed legislation that compelled church attendance and payment of church taxes.[78] "By law every town had to sustain a church, supported by taxes levied on all the householders, whether [church] members or not,"[79] and "[t]heir magistrates and ministers cooperated in expelling dissenters, enforcing church attendance, limiting the electoral franchise to church members, and supporting the Congregational Church through taxation."[80]

Similarly, in Virginia and the other states in which the Anglicans (Church of England) had long been established, the Church acquired "preferred governmental status"[81] and had long been "characterized by public support, glebe lands,[82] compulsory church attendance, punishment of blasphemy, religious test oaths, and the suppression of dissenting views."[83] In practical effect, "[b]uttressed and safeguarded by many laws both local and English, [and] aided by a long tradition, the Anglican Church functioned as an arm of government."[84]

When Congress signed the Declaration of Independence in 1776, nine of the thirteen states still maintained established churches: Virginia, Maryland, North Carolina, South Carolina, Georgia, Connecticut, Massachusetts, New Hampshire, and Delaware—all except Pennsylvania, Rhode Island, New York, and New Jersey.[85] That situation did not long endure; Virginia (with its precedent-setting Declaration of Rights[86]), Maryland, and North Carolina became the first states to "disestablish" the Church of England,[87] and others soon followed.[88] By the time the 1787 Constitutional Convention convened in Philadelphia a decade later, the Anglicans remained the established church in only Georgia and South Carolina, while the Congregationalists remained the established church in only Massachusetts, Connecticut, and New Hampshire.[89] But memories—and fears—endured.

Only against that background can one understand and appreciate the significance of the host of colonial declarations of rights and constitutions adopted in the latter part of the eighteenth century that targeted the "establishment" and its attributes[90]—colonial enactments that eventually prompted the First Congress to craft the First Amendment's Establishment Clause as an "anti-establishment" assurance at the national level.

3

The States' Pre-Constitution Declarations of Rights

For reasons explained in the previous chapter, by the mid-to-late 1700s the states' dissatisfaction with the various preferential and punitive attributes of the existing establishments (*viz.*, the Anglicans and Congregationalists) had matured into a deep-rooted loathing; they despised . . .

- the merger of legislative and ecclesiastical authority;
- the deprivation of various civil rights—or "civil incapacitations"—as punishment for establishment opponents;
- the preferential reward of various honors and privileges (or "emoluments") to establishment supporters;
- the compelled allegiance to (and attendance of) the establishment; and
- the compelled financial support of the establishment via governmental taxes.

Inevitably, those animosities led to formal measures aimed to disestablish, or at least constrain to some extent, the colonial establishments.

Because it had endured an established church longer than any other state,[1] Virginia led the mid-1700s disestablishment movement with its historic 1776 Declaration of Rights and other disestablishment measures. In the Supreme Court's own words,

> Virginia, where the established church had achieved a dominant influence in political affairs and where many excesses attracted wide public attention, provided a great stimulus and able leadership for the [disestablishment] movement.[2]

Virginia's efforts spawned a host of similarly directed mid-1700s rights-based declarations in the various states. Ultimately, these various declarations served as the foundation for the First Congress's creation of the Establishment Clause in 1789.

A. Virginia's June 1776 Declaration of Rights

On May 10, 1776, the Continental Congress debated a resolution that would authorize the individual states[3] to proceed with plans to "adopt such government as shall, in the opinion of the representatives of the people" best suit their individual colonial needs—in other words, their own constitutions:

> Resolved, That it be recommended to the respective assemblies and conventions of the United Colonies, where no government sufficient to the exigencies of their affairs have been hitherto established, to adopt such government as shall, in the opinion of the representatives of the people, best conduce to the happiness and safety of their constituents in particular, and America in general.[4]

On May 15, 1776, the Congress approved the May 10 resolution—"the most important act of the Continental Congress"[5]—as well as a lengthy preamble.[6]

After the Continental Congress passed that resolution, a specially assembled Virginia Revolutionary Convention took two monumental steps. *First,* on May 15, 1776, the Convention resolved to craft Virginia's own "bill of rights" as well as a separate constitution (or what it characterized as a "plan of government").[7] *Second,* also on May 15, 1776, it instructed its congressional delegation to urge that the Continental Congress declare the nation's independence from Great Britain,[8] and the Virginia congressional delegation promptly did just that on June 7, 1776—a step that resulted in the Declaration of Independence a month later.[9] Thomas Jefferson's notes of the June 7, 1776, congressional proceedings read, in pertinent part:

> The delegates from Virginia moved in obedience to instructions from their constituents that the Congress should declare that these United colonies are and of right ought to be free and independent states, that they are absolved from all obedience to the British crown, and that all political connection between them and the state of Great Britain is and ought to be totally dissolved; that measures should be immediately taken for procuring the assistance of foreign powers, and a Confederation be formed to bind the colonies more closely together.[10]

To attend to the first of those two matters, the Virginia Convention selected Patrick Henry, George Mason, James Madison, and others to serve on the committee assigned to draft both a Declaration of Rights and a separate "Plan of Government" (or constitution) for Virginia.[11]

Just days later, on June 12, 1776, the Convention adopted Virginia's historic and precedent-setting Declaration of Rights,[12] and on June 29, 1776, the Convention adopted Virginia's—indeed, the states'— first constitution (or "Plan of Government").[13]

Mason drafted most of the 1776 Declaration of Rights[14] (not to be confused with the completely distinct 1788 rights proposal that Virginia submitted to Congress with its vote to ratify the Constitution[15]), and he included a groundbreaking proclamation of religious rights designed to assure religious freedom in establishment-dominated Virginia.[16]

Mason's initial draft of the Declaration provided, as unnumbered paragraph 9:

> That as religion, or the duty which we owe to our divine and omnipotent creator, and the manner of discharging it, can be governed only by reason and conviction, *not by force or violence;* and therefore that all men shou'd [*sic*] enjoy the fullest toleration in the exercise of religion, according to the dictates of conscience, *unpunished and unrestrained by the magistrate,* unless under colour [*sic*] of religion, any man disturb the peace, the happiness, or safety of society, or of individuals. And that it is the mutual duty of all, to practice Christian forbearance, love and charity towards each other.[17]

The emphasized text in Mason's draft passage posed a direct challenge to the core attributes of the longtime Anglican establishment in Virginia. When the committee reviewed Mason's draft, it embraced it almost verbatim, including it as paragraph 18 of the proposed Declaration:

> 18. That religion, or the duty which we owe to our Creator, and the manner of discharging it, can be directed only by reason and conviction, *not by force or violence;* and therefore, that all men should enjoy the fullest toleration in the exercise of religion, according to the dictates of conscience, *unpunished and unrestrained by the magistrate,* unless, under colour [*sic*] of religion, any man disturb the peace, the happiness, or safety of society. And that it is the mutual duty of all to practice Christian forbearance, love, and charity, towards each other.[18]

Madison, however, believed that neither Mason's wording nor the committee's version went far enough to disestablish Virginia's Anglicans. Invigorated by his disestablishment views (and disenchanted with the committee's verbiage), Madison crafted an alternative version of Mason's proposal:

> That Religion or the duty we owe our Creator, and the manner of discharging it, being under the direction of reason and conviction only, *not of violence or compulsion,* all men are equally entitled to the full and free exercise of it, according to the dictates of conscience; and therefore that *no man or class of men, ought, on account of religion, to be invested with peculiar emoluments or privileges, nor subjected to any penalties or disabilities under colour [sic] of religion,* [unless] the preservation of equal liberty and the existence of the State be manifestly endangered.[19]

The last half of Madison's revision more directly targeted the Virginia establishment's chief attributes—and duly alarmed the committee's establishment supporters.

However, Madison lacked sufficient status and influence at the time to introduce his own proposal to the full Convention; his participation in Virginia's 1776 Revolutionary Convention represented his inaugural effort in Virginia politics at the state level, and his first experience with public office came barely two years earlier in 1774, when his home county elected him to the County Committee.[20] Madison attended Virginia's Revolutionary Convention in 1776 as a county delegate[21] and, because of his intellectual capabilities rather than experience, the Convention promptly appointed him to the committee tasked with drafting the declaration of rights and the state constitution.[22]

Thus, Madison asked Patrick Henry to introduce his proposal.[23] However, the reality of Virginia politics in 1776 doomed Madison's revision, and it stood no chance from the outset; the Convention's establishment supporters rejected Madison's proposed wording, properly regarding it as a threat to the established Anglican Church.[24] "Since this clause, if adopted, would have wiped out the establishment of the Anglican Church, it alarmed enough men to cause its defeat."[25] Thus, when a Convention delegate pressed Henry whether, in fact, Madison's proposed verbiage served to disestablish the Anglicans in Virginia, Henry, reluctant to entangle himself in the debate and quick to realize his predicament if he confirmed Madison's intentions as his own, replied in the negative—dooming Madison's proposed revision.[26]

Madison promptly revised his proposal to remove the offending references[27] and submitted a more palatable version, which read:

> 16.That Religion, or the duty which we owe to our Creator, and the manner of discharging it, can be directed only by reason and conviction, not by force or violence; and, therefore, all men are equally entitled to

the free exercise of religion, according to the dictates of conscience, *unpunished and unrestrained by the magistrate, unless the preservation of equal liberty and the existence of the State are manifestly endangered;* and that it is the mutual duty of all to practise [*sic*] Christian forbearance, love, and charity, towards each other."[28]

The Convention deleted the emphasized text from Madison's work. But Madison's final effort, as amended slightly by the full Convention, ultimately became Article 16 of Virginia's 1776 Declaration of Rights:

> 16. That Religion, or the duty which we owe to our Creator, and the manner of discharging it, can be directed only by reason and conviction, not by force or violence; and, therefore, all men are equally entitled to the free exercise of religion, according to the dictates of conscience; and that it is the mutual duty of all to practise [*sic*] Christian forbearance, love, and charity, towards each other.[29]

The history of Virginia's 1776 Revolutionary Convention leaves it uncertain whether the Convention understood its historic Declaration of Rights to possess the stature of a constitution, as opposed, for instance, to a statute—or something else entirely. But the fact that a specially convened Convention adopted the Declaration, as opposed to the Virginia legislature having done so, suggests that the Declaration bore a status commensurate with the constitution that the same Convention adopted just days later.

Although the final wording of Article 16 fell short of disestablishing the Anglicans in Virginia at that juncture,[30] it nevertheless represented the states' first such declaration of religious rights in a constitution-like format.[31] And it secured a reputation for Madison in the political and legislative realm as well; Madison served in Virginia's inaugural post-constitution legislature in 1776–77,[32] and in 1777 the legislature elected him to the Governor's Council,[33] an honor for a comparatively inexperienced legislator.

The Virginia Declaration had an immediate impact in the other states:

> . . . [T]he Virginia Declaration became a model for similar documents as it became the Revolutionary fashion to affix a ["declaration of rights"] preamble to state constitutions . . . [.][34]

Ironically, George Mason's unsuccessful insistence a decade later at the 1787 Constitutional Convention in Philadelphia that the Constitution itself contain a similar Bill of Rights ("[it] would give great quiet to the people")[35] prompted objections from Mason prior to the final Convention vote,[36] and ultimately led him to refuse to sign the Constitution—one of only three delegates to do so.[37] On September 13, 1787,[38] Mason wrote the following on his copy of the September 12, 1787, draft of the Constitution:

> There is no Declaration of Rights, and, the laws of the general government being paramount to the laws and constitutions of the several States, the Declarations of Rights in the separate States are no security. Nor are the people secured even in the enjoyment of the benefit of the common law (which stands here upon no other foundation than its having been adopted by the respective acts forming the constitutions of the several States).[39]

The Virginia Declaration of Rights also had a monumental impact in a related—and more famous—historical proceeding, also energized by Virginia. On June 7,[40] 8,[41] 10,[42] and 11,[43] 1776, the Continental Congress debated the Virginia Congressional delegation's proposal that the states declare their independence from Great Britain, and it delegated the task of drafting a formal declaration of independence to a committee of five: John Adams, Benjamin Franklin, Roger Sherman, Robert Livingston, and Thomas Jefferson.[44]

Jefferson, "their cerebral young colleague,"[45] had by that time secured a reputation as an elegant and masterful writer whose "reputation had gone before him,"[46] so the other four on the committee promptly handed him the task.[47]

> Mr. Jefferson, though younger than Mr. Adams and Dr. Franklin, had been placed at its head, not less in deference to the leading position of Virginia than to his well-merited reputation for a matchless felicity in embodying popular ideas.[48]

Jefferson, reluctant to tackle an undertaking with such an intercontinental significance, tried to defer that task to others[49]—particularly John Adams—but Adams would hear none of it[50]; Adams counseled Jefferson that, given Virginia's status among the states, "a Virginian ought to appear at the head of the business," and he persuaded Jefferson with the self-deprecating observation that "[y]ou can write ten times better than I can."[51] Jefferson had a more modest recollection: "I consented; I drew it,"[52] and "[T]he committee for drawing the declaration of independence desired me to do it."[53] (One historian hints that the committee's selection of Jefferson on that basis had been somewhat of a pretense, aimed to disassociate the names of Adams, Franklin, Sherman, and Livingston from any such declaration in the event that matters did not turn out well.[54])

In late June 1776, Jefferson delivered; after seventeen days of drafting, Jefferson produced a draft "declaration" on June 28, 1776.[55] The Continental Congress debated Jefferson's draft for three days before accepting it (with some revisions[56]); although the initial vote proved less than unanimous, all of the voting congressional delegations ultimately approved it.[57] Thus, on July 4, 1776,[58] all but one of the state congressional delegations signed Jefferson's modified version[59] (New York's delegates abstaining for the time being, adding their signatures on August 2, 1776[60]), thus creating the Declaration of Independence.[61]

As finalized, the Declaration of Independence appeared to incorporate some of the core concepts of Virginia's Declaration of Rights. Madison, for one, appreciated that the Declaration of Independence certainly drew inspiration, if not some wording, from the Virginia Declaration of Rights.[62] Jefferson claimed to have relied on no specific document,[63] although he "insisted that his [draft] was not a particularly original composition, [and] that the truths he recited were so self-evident that he was merely a reporter rather than a formulator of any new doctrine."[64] Late in life Jefferson acknowledged the similarity between the 1776 Virginia Declaration of Rights and the Declaration of Independence.[65]

B. Jefferson's June 1779 Bill
for Establishing Religious Freedom

On June 12, 1779, then-Virginia governor Thomas Jefferson penned a proposed Bill for Establishing Religious Freedom that would have implemented in Virginia a disestablishment assurance of the kind that Madison had first proposed (albeit unsuccessfully) in the latter's revision of Article 16 of Virginia's 1776 Declaration of Rights:

> Well aware that the opinions and belief of men depend not on their own will, but follow involuntarily the evidence proposed to their minds, that Almighty God hath created the mind free, and manifested his Supreme will that free it shall remain, by making it altogether insusceptible of restraint[.]
> That all attempts to influence it by *temporal punishments or burthens,*

or by civil incapacitations, tend only to beget habits of hypocrisy and meanness, and are a departure from the plan of the holy author of our religion, . . . [.]

That the impious *presumption of legislators and rulers,* civil as well as ecclesiastical, who, being themselves but fallible and uninspired men, have assumed dominion over the faith of others, *setting up their own opinions and modes of thinking, as the only true and infallible, and as such, endeavouring [sic] to impose them on others, hath established and maintained false religions* over the greatest part of the world, and through all time[.]

That *to compel a man to furnish contributions of money* for the propagation of opinions which he disbelieves and abhors, is *sinful and tyrannical[.]*

That even the *forcing him to support this or that teacher* of his own religious persuasion, is depriving him of the comfortable liberty of giving his contributions to the particular pastor whose morals he would make his pattern, and whose powers he feels most persuasive to righteousness . . .[.]

That our civil rights have no dependance [*sic*] on our religious opinions, any more than on our opinions in physicks [*sic*] or geometry[.]

That therefore the proscribing any citizen as unworthy [of] the publick [*sic*] confidence, by laying upon him an *incapacity of being called to offices of trust and emolument, unless he profess or renounce this or that religious opinion,* is depriving him injuriously of those privileges and advantages to which, in common with his fellow citizens he has a natural right[.] . . .

We the General Assembly of Virginia do enact, that *no man shall be compelled to frequent or support any relig[i]ous Worship place or Ministry whatsoever,* nor shall be enforced, restrained, molested, or burthened in his body or goods, nor shall otherwise suffer on account of his religious opinions or belief, but that all men shall be free to profess, and by argument to maintain their opinions in matters of religion, and that the same *shall in no wise diminish, enlarge, or affect their civil capacities. . . .*[66]

The emphasized passages illustrate Jefferson's focus: the elimination of (1) the inherent relationship between the establishment and the government, (2) the compelled financial support, and (3) the punitive deprivations of various rights upon which the establishment had long relied to sustain its status in Virginia.

Jefferson introduced his proposal in the Virginia legislature the next day. But Jefferson's disestablishment efforts in Virginia in the 1770s had been "opposed by many influential men"[67]; thus for a variety of political reasons Jefferson's bill languished in the Virginia legislature for years until Madison reintroduced a revised version in the Virginia legislature in 1785, entitled an Act for Establishing Religious Freedom, *infra.*[68]

The bill proposed by Jefferson proved to be his final legislative initiative in Virginia for many years. In 1780, the Virginia legislature reelected Jefferson as its second governor[69] (a position he held until mid-1781), from late 1783 to mid-1784 he served as a Virginia delegate to the Continental Congress,[70] and in July 1784 he left for Paris for five years to replace Benjamin Franklin as the nation's representative (Jefferson sailed for Paris on July 5, 1784, and did not return to the United States until November 23, 1789).[71]

C. Madison's June 1785 Memorial and Remonstrance against Religious Assessments

As his stature rose in the Virginia legislature after his efforts in 1776 to disestablish the Anglican Church, James Madison battled Virginia's legislative efforts in the late-1700s to enlarge the establishment's ecclesiastical powers and to impose taxes dedicated for the support of particular institutional beneficiaries. For instance, he actively (albeit unsuccessfully) opposed the Virginia legislature's 1784 passage of legislation entitled Act for Incorporating the Episcopal [*viz.*, Anglican] Church.[72]

Madison also (successfully, this time) battled Patrick Henry's December 1784 legislative proposal entitled A Bill Establishing a Provision for Teachers of the Christian Religion.[73] Backed by Virginia's establishment protagonists, Henry designed his proposed legislation to (1) reverse the Virginia Assembly's 1779 measure that eliminated tax support for the state's Anglican ministers, and (2) authorize the state to levy a general tax assessment for the support of "minister[s]" and "teacher[s]" of "each religious society." The revealing reference to "establish" in the title of Henry's proposal confirmed the reality that the measure would enact an "establishment" tax for religious support; indeed, in a letter to James Monroe, Madison described Patrick Henry's proposal as a "Bill for *establishing* the Christian Religion in this state."[74] Henry's proposal ultimately prompted Madison to compose the subject of this very topic.

Henry's proposed legislation provided, in pertinent part:

Be it therefore enacted by the General Assembly, that for the *support of Christian teachers,* _____[75] per centum on the amount, or _____ in the pound on the sum payable for tax on the property within this Commonwealth, is hereby assessed, and shall be paid by every person chargeable with the said tax at the time the same shall become due; and *the Sheriffs of the several Counties shall have power to levy and collect the same* in the same manner and under the like restrictions and limitations, as are or may be prescribed by the laws for raising the Revenues of this State.

And be it enacted, That for every sum so paid, the Sheriff or Collector shall give a receipt, *expressing therein to what society of Christians the person from whom he may receive the same shall direct the money to be paid,* keeping a distinct account thereof in his books. . . . One of which lists, after being recorded in a book to be kept for that purpose, shall be filed by the Clerk in his office; the other shall be the Sheriff be fixed up in the Court-house [*sic*], there to remain for the inspection of all concerned. . . . And be it further enacted, that the money to be raised by virtue of this Act, *shall be by the Vestres, Elders, or Directors of each religious society, appropriated to a provision for a Minister or Teacher of the Gospel of their denomination, or the providing place of divine worship, and to none other use whatsoever;* except in the denominations of Quakers and Menonists, who may receive what is collected from their members, and place it in their general fund, to be disposed of in a manner which they shall think best calculated to promote their particular mode of worship. . . .[76]

Madison—and *not,* as some (including the Supreme Court) have incorrectly declared, Thomas Jefferson—launched an invigorated opposition to such an overt "establishment tax," and he debated Henry directly in the waning days of the 1784 legislative session.[77] (One writer oddly accords credit to Thomas Jefferson for opposing Henry's proposed tax, declaring that "Jefferson opposed the bill . . . , wielding quotes from portions of Jefferson's Notes on the State of Virginia."[78] And, perhaps not surprisingly, the United States Supreme Court has *twice* erred in the same manner.[79] Jefferson, however, would have been hard-pressed to have opposed Henry's proposed establishment tax, for at least two reasons. *First,* Patrick Henry introduced his legislative proposal in December 1784.[80] Yet Jefferson had been out of the country since July 1784, when he left for France to serve as the nation's representative; Jefferson left the United States in July 1784, and did not return until November 1789.[81] Thus, Jefferson had been abroad for four months *before* Henry even introduced his proposed tax. *Second,* Jefferson composed his *Notes on the State of Virginia* in

1781 ("The following Notes were written in Virginia in the year 1781, and somewhat corrected and enlarged in the winter of 1782 . . . [.]"[82]), three years *before* Henry introduced his proposed tax.)

As a result of Madison's vociferous opposition, on Christmas Eve 1784, the Virginia legislature postponed the requisite third reading of Henry's proposal until November 1785—the next year's legislative session—thus giving Madison and other adversaries an opportunity to mobilize public opposition.[83] (The postponement also fostered a political coup of sorts for disestablishment advocates; using the end-of-session adjournment to full advantage, Henry's political opponents managed to neutralize Henry's political influence by successfully engineering Henry's election as Virginia's governor between the 1784 and 1785 legislative sessions—thus ousting Henry and his celebrated oratory skills from legislative proceedings.)

Madison alerted others throughout Virginia to the establishment threat posed by Henry's legislative proposal. For instance: in a November 14, 1784, letter to James Monroe, Madison lamented Henry's proposed "General Assessment" establishment tax and any "more comprehensive" establishment in Virginia[84]; in a November 14, 1784, letter to Richard Lee, Madison lambasted Henry's proposed establishment tax and also expressed concerns about the Episcopal and Presbyterian supporters' efforts to secure a greater establishment[85]; and in a January 9, 1785, letter to Jefferson, Madison described the Virginia legislature's passage of an act to incorporate the Episcopal Church in Virginia as well as Henry's proposed establishment tax.[86]

Culminating his opposition efforts, on June 20, 1785, Madison wrote his celebrated (and highly publicized) Memorial and Remonstrance against Religious Assessments in which he urged the Virginia legislature to reject the kind of mandatory public financial support that Henry and other establishment devotees advocated. Scarcely concealing its underlying disestablishment passions, Madison's Memorial and Remonstrance employs the well-understood terms "establish," "establishment," or "establishments" no fewer than ten times in the course of a quintessential disestablishment treatise:

> To the Honorable the General Assembly of the Commonwealth of Virginia A Memorial and Remonstrance
>
> We the subscribers, citizens of the said Commonwealth, having taken into serious consideration, a Bill printed by order of the last

Session of General Assembly, entitled "A Bill establishing a provision for Teachers of the Christian Religion," and conceiving that the same if finally armed with the sanctions of a law, will be a dangerous abuse of power, are bound as faithful members of a free State to remonstrate against it, and to declare the reasons by which we are determined. We remonstrate against the said Bill,

1. Because we hold it for a fundamental and undeniable truth, "that Religion or the duty which we owe to our Creator and the manner of discharging it, can be directed only by reason and conviction, not by force or violence." [Virginia Declaration of Rights, § 16.] The Religion then of every man must be left to the conviction and conscience of every man; and it is the right of every man to exercise it as these may dictate. . . .

2. Because if Religion be exempt from the authority of the Society at large, still less can it be subject to that of the Legislative Body. . . . The preservation of a free Government requires not merely, that the metes and bounds which separate each department of power be invariably maintained[.] . . .

3. . . . Who does not see that the same authority which can *establish* Christianity, in exclusion of all other Religions, may *establish* with the same ease any particular sect of Christians, in exclusion of all other Sects? [T]hat the same authority which can force a citizen to contribute three pence only of his property for the support of any one *establishment,* may force him to conform to any other *establishment* in all cases whatsoever?

4. . . . As the Bill violates equality by subjecting some to peculiar burdens, so it violates the same principle, by granting to others peculiar exemptions. . . .

5. Because the Bill implies either that the Civil Magistrate is a competent Judge of Religious Truth; or that he may employ Religion as an engine of Civil policy. . . .

6. Because the *establishment* proposed by the Bill is not requisite for the support of the Christian Religion. . . .

7. Because experience witnesseth that ecclesiastical *establishments,* instead of maintaining the purity and efficacy of Religion, have had a contrary operation. . . .

8. Because the *establishment* in question is not necessary for the support of Civil Government. If it be urged as necessary for the support of Civil Government only as it is a means of supporting Religion, and it be not necessary for the latter purpose, it cannot be necessary for the former. If Religion be not within the cognizance of Civil Government how can its legal *establishment* be necessary to Civil Government? . . . Such a Government will be best supported by

protecting every Citizen in the enjoyment of his Religion with the same equal hand which protects his person and his property; by neither invading the equal rights of any Sect, nor suffering any Sect to invade those of another.

9. Because the proposed *establishment* is a departure from that generous policy, which, offering an Asylum to the persecuted and oppressed of every Nation and Religion, promised a lustre [*sic*] to our country, and an accession to the number of its citizens. . . .[87]

Madison based his Memorial, at least in part, on Virginia's 1776 Declaration of Rights,[88] and he acknowledged as much.[89]

Before the legislature ever had the opportunity for a final vote on Henry's proposed tax, Madison circulated his Memorial and Remonstrance throughout Virginia (with the assistance of others),[90] not merely as a political essay in opposition to public financial support for the established church, but, in addition, as the basis for petitions that Madison and others hoped would produce sufficient signatures as evidence of public opposition that the legislature would feel compelled to vote against the tax when the next legislative session began.

Copies of Madison's Memorial quickly circulated throughout Virginia during the summer of 1785 (with blank signature pages attached), and Madison and his fellow establishment opponents eventually delivered hundreds upon hundreds of signed petitions to the legislature prior to the legislature's final vote on Henry's proposed tax in the fall.[91] Faced with such a public outcry, the legislature ultimately abandoned Henry's proposal altogether. One ally reported to Madison that one copy of Madison's Memorial gathered 150 signatures in a single day in a single location, extraordinary for the times.[92] Madison described the Memorial's effect as having "'displayed such an overwhelming opposition of the people, that the plan of a general assessment was crushed under it.'"[93]

Madison promptly advised Jefferson (in Paris) of the political success in these brief sentences:

> The steps taken throughout the Country to defeat the Genl. [*sic*] Assessment, had produced all the effect that could have been wished. The table was loaded with petitions & remonstrances from all parts against the interposition of the Legislature in matters of Religion.[94]

Years later, Madison expounded more elaborately on the success of Virginia's groundbreaking disestablishment efforts:

> The Anglican hierarchy existing in Virginia prior to the Revolution

was abolished by an early act of the Independent Legislature. In the year 1785, a bill was introduced under the auspices of Mr. Henry, imposing a general tax for the support of "Teachers of the Christian Religion." It made a progress, threatening a majority in its favor. As an expedient to defeat it, we proposed that it should be postponed to another session, and printed in the meantime for public consideration. Such an appeal in a case so important and so unforeseen could not be resisted. With a view to arouse the people, it was thought proper that a memorial should be drawn up, the task being assigned to me, to be printed and circulated throughout the State for a general signature. The experiment succeeded. The memorial was so extensively signed by the various religious sects, including a considerable portion of the old hierarchy, that the projected innovation was crushed, and under the influence of the popular sentiment thus called forth, the well-known Bill prepared by Mr. Jefferson, for "Establishing Religious freedom," passed into a law, as it now stands in our code of statutes.[95]

(Madison's closing reference to Jefferson's June 1779 bill in that narrative—a proposal that the Virginia legislature actually never passed[96]—more accurately references Virginia's 1786 Act for Establishing Religious Freedom, a Madison work product that replicated much of Jefferson's earlier unsuccessful bill.[97])

After Madison defeated Henry's proposed establishment tax in the fall of 1785, he promptly introduced his celebrated Act for Establishing Religious Freedom[98]—the following topic.

D. Virginia's January 1786 Act for Establishing Religious Freedom

On October 31, 1785, as an integral part of his opposition to Patrick Henry's establishment tax proposal, James Madison introduced in the Virginia legislature a revised version of Thomas Jefferson's 1779 Bill for Establishing Religious Freedom,[99] titling it an Act for Establishing Religious Freedom.[100] Even six years after the fact, the Virginia legislature had yet to take any action on Jefferson's 1779 proposal.[101]

On January 16, 1786, the Virginia legislature passed Madison's act, which provided (in pertinent part):

I. Whereas Almighty God hath created the mind free; that all attempts to influence it by temporal punishments or burthens, or by civil incapacitations, tend only to beget habits of hypocrisy and meanness, and are a departure from the plan of the Holy author of our religion, who being Lord both of body and mind, yet chose not to propagate it by coercions on either, as was in his Almighty power to do; that the impious *presumption of legislators and rulers, civil as well as ecclesiastical, who being themselves but fallible and uninspired men, have assumed dominion over the faith of others, setting up their own opinions and modes of thinking as the only true and infallible,* and as such endeavouring to impose them on others, hath established and maintained false religions over the greatest part of the world, and through all time; *that to compel a man to furnish contributions of money for the propagation of opinions which he disbelieves, is sinful and tyrannical; that even the forcing him to support this or that teacher of his own religious persuasion,* is depriving him of the comfortable liberty of giving his contributions to the particular pastor . . . ; that our civil rights have no dependence on our religious opinions, any more than our opinions in physics or geometry; that therefore the proscribing [of] any citizen as unworthy [of] the public confidence by laying upon him an ,incapacity of being called to offices of trust and emolument, unless he profess or renounce this or that religious opinion, . . . tends only to corrupt the principles of that religion it is meant to encourage, by bribing with a monopoly of worldly honours [*sic*] and emoluments, those who will externally profess and conform to it; . . . :

II. Be it enacted by the General Assembly, That *no man shall be compelled to frequent or support any religious worship, place, or ministry whatsoever,* nor shall be enforced restrained, molested, or burthened in his body or goods, *nor shall otherwise suffer on account of his religious opinions or belief;* but that all men shall be free to profess, and by argument to maintain, their opinion in matters of religion, and that the same *shall in no wise [sic] diminish, enlarge, or affect their civil capacities. . . .*[102]

Madison's act finally achieved an enduring disestablishment impact of the kind that Madison had struggled unsuccessfully to implement years earlier. Later in 1786, Madison drafted and submitted to the Virginia legislature a Petition to Repeal the 1784 Incorporation of the Protestant Episcopal Church (*viz.,* the Church of England).[103] The following January, the Virginia legislature repealed the Church's incorporation act.[104]

Madison alone guided the 1786 act through the Virginia legislature[105]; Jefferson, in France from mid-1784 to late 1789, could not have had—and did not have—anything to do with it.

E. Pre-Establishment Clause (*viz.*, Pre-1789) State Constitutions and Declarations of Rights

Virginia's disestablishment accomplishments literally compelled the other states to follow. Virginia, the most populous colony from the mid-1600s to the mid-1700s[106] and the "oldest, largest, and most influential of the thirteen states,"[107] wielded a disproportionate political influence among the various states well into the eighteenth century. Although the New England population exploded from the late 1600s to the mid-1700s, Virginia nevertheless remained dominant.[108] By 1750, Virginia had become by far the most populous colony (260,000), followed by Massachusetts (230,000), Pennsylvania (150,000), Maryland (130,000), and Connecticut (100,000).[109] Perhaps contrary to popular assumption, even by the mid-1700s New York lagged far behind (75,000).[110]

By 1770, that hierarchy had not changed much: Virginia remained the most populous colony (450,000), followed by Massachusetts (299,000), Pennsylvania (275,000), North Carolina (230,000), Maryland (200,000), New York (185,000), Connecticut (175,000), South Carolina (140,000), New Jersey (110,000), New Hampshire (60,000), Rhode Island (55,000), and Georgia (26,000).[111]

A decade later, Virginia still dominated; by 1780, the states had the following estimated white populations (rounded):

- PA: 319,450[112] (increasing to 423,000 by 1790[113])
- VA: 317,425[114] (increasing to 442,000 by 1790[115])
- MA: 263,805[116] (increasing to 286,140 by 1784,[117] and to 373,000 by 1790[118])
- CT: 200,820[119] (increasing to 202,900 by 1782,[120] and to 231,000 by 1790[121])
- NY: 189,490[122] (increasing to 220,000 by 1786[123])
- NC: 179,135[124] (increasing to 288,000 by 1790[125])
- MD: 164,960[126] (increasing to 170,690 by 1782,[127] and to 209,000 by 1790[128])
- NJ: 129,170[129] (increasing to 138,935 by 1784[130])
- NH: 87,260[131] (increasing to 95,450 by 1786,[132] and to 141,000 by 1790[133])
- SC: 83,000[134] (increasing to 140,000 by 1790[135])
- RI: 50,275[136] (increasing to 65,000 by 1790[137])
- DE: 42,390[138] (increasing to 46,000 by 1790[139])
- GA: 35,240[140] (increasing to 58,000 by 1790[141])

In addition, Virginia's huge slave population—more than double that of any other state by the mid-1700s—had long rendered Virginia an economic powerhouse among the states.[142] Tobacco and other agricultural exports harvested with slave labor, coupled with extensive private land holdings, rendered Virginia the economic king among the states from the 1600s well into the 1700s.[143] By the mid-1700s, the value of exports from Virginia and Maryland alone almost equaled the combined export values of the two Carolinas and New England (*viz.*, New Hampshire, Connecticut, Massachusetts, and Rhode Island),[144] and the combined wealth of the southern states (Virginia, Maryland, North Carolina, South Carolina, and Georgia) dwarfed the combined wealth of all of the other states.[145] By 1789 (the year of the inaugural Congress), exports from Virginia and Maryland rivaled the combined export values from New England (*viz.*, New Hampshire, Connecticut, Massachusetts, and Rhode Island), the two Carolinas, New York, Pennsylvania, and Georgia.[146] Thus, whatever Virginia accomplished could scarcely be ignored.

In the political arena, Virginia boasted the states' first self-elected government[147] and constitution,[148] and, confirming Virginia's status, in 1774 the Continental Congress elected Virginian George Washington as commander of the Continental Army[149] (and, later, elected Washington president of the 1787 Constitutional Convention in Philadelphia and the nation's first president in 1789.)

Virginia's preeminence by the mid-to-late 1700s has long been confirmed in the Constitution itself; Article I, Section 2, Paragraph 3, of the Constitution provided in 1787 (and actually still provides) that

> . . . The number of representatives shall not exceed one for every thirty thousand, but each state shall have at least one representative; and until such enumeration shall be made, the state of New Hampshire shall be entitled to choose three, Massachusetts eight, Rhode-Island and Providence Plantations one, Connecticut five, New-York six, New Jersey four, Pennsylvania eight, Delaware one, Maryland six, *Virginia ten,* North Carolina five, South Carolina five, and Georgia three.[150]

Following Virginia's lead, the other states soon crafted a host of ecclesiastic-specific constitutional measures within a decade. And a number of those constitutional assurances incorporated specific disestablishment provisions. Thus, by the mid-1780s eleven states—all except Connecticut and Rhode Island—had adopted functional constitutions (and related bills of rights) that contained ecclesiastical-specific assurances.[151] (Connecticut operated under a 1662 charter until decades after the First Congress's inaugural proceedings in 1789.[152] Although Connecticut adopted a Constitutional Ordinance of 1776, that ordinance simply adopted Connecticut's 1662 Charter as Connecticut's "Civil Constitution."[153] Connecticut did not adopt its first true constitution until 1818.[154] And Rhode Island operated under a 1663 charter until decades after Congress first convened in 1789.[155] Rhode Island did not adopt its first true constitution until 1842.[156])

When the First Congress convened in 1789, the various states had already adopted the following legislative acts that incorporated various ecclesiastical-specific assurances (in chronological order):

• Virginia had its constitution-like 1776 Declaration of Rights[157] and its 1786 Act for Establishing Religious Freedom[158];

• New Jersey had its 1776 Constitution[159];

• Delaware had its 1776 Constitution[160] and a related, albeit separately adopted, 1776 Declaration of Rights[161];

• Pennsylvania had its 1776 Constitution (which incorporated a separate Declaration of Rights)[162];

• Maryland had its 1776 Declaration of Rights[163] and a related, albeit separately adopted, 1776 Constitution[164];

• North Carolina had its 1776 Constitution (which incorporated a separate Declaration of Rights)[165];

• New York had its 1777 Constitution[166];

• Georgia had its 1777 and 1789 Constitutions[167];

• South Carolina had its 1778 Constitution[168];

• Massachusetts had its 1780 Constitution (which incorporated a separate Declaration of Rights)[169]; and

• New Hampshire had its 1784 Constitution (which incorporated a separate Declaration of Rights).[170]

Although Vermont had its own constitution by 1789 (one adopted in 1777 and another in 1786[171]), it did not achieve statehood until March 4, 1791.[172]

Not every state adopted an independent Declaration of Rights; some incorporated their Declarations of Rights within a constitution, while others adopted only a constitution that incorporated assurances similar to those found in Declarations of Rights:

	Independent Constitution and Declaration of Rights	Constitution That Incorporated a Declaration of Rights	Constitution Only	Declaration of Rights Only
Virginia	✓ 2			
New Jersey			✓	
Delaware	✓ 1 and 2			
Pennsylvania		✓ 1 and 2		
Maryland	✓ 2			
North Carolina		✓ 1		
New York			✓	
Georgia			✓	
South Carolina			✓	
Massachusetts		✓ 1 and 2		
New Hampshire		✓ 1 and 2		
Vermont		✓ 1 and 2		

1=religion-specific assurance(s) in Constitution
2=religion-specific assurance(s) in Declaration of Rights

The specificity becomes necessary only because the Constitution ratification process in 1787 and 1788 produced arguments against an amendatory bill of rights predicated upon the absence of specific "Declarations" in some states. Although technically correct, that argument obscured the whole story.

(1). Virginia's 1776 Declaration of Rights and 1786 Act for Establishing Religious Freedom

Although insufficient standing alone to curtail the authority of the establishment in Virginia,[173] Article 16 in Virginia's 1776 Declaration of Rights in conjunction with Virginia's 1786 Act Establishing Religious Freedom proved sufficiently broad to provide a "no-compelled-worship" assurance, a "no-compelled-financial-support" assurance, and an "equal-rights-and-privileges" assurance:

16. That Religion, or the duty which we owe to our Creator, and the manner of discharging it, can be directed only by reason and conviction, *not by force or violence;* and, therefore, all men are equally entitled to the free exercise of religion, according to the dictates of conscience; and that it is the mutual duty of all to practise Christian forbearance, love, and charity, towards each other.[174]

II. Be it enacted by the General Assembly, That *no man shall be compelled to frequent or support any religious worship, place, or ministry whatsoever, nor shall be enforced, restrained, molested, or burthened in his body or goods,* nor shall otherwise suffer on account of his religious opinions or belief; but that all men shall be free to profess, and by argument to maintain, their opinion in matters of religion, and that *the same shall in no wise diminish, enlarge, or affect their civil capacities.*[175]

(2). New Jersey's 1776 Constitution

New Jersey's 1776 Constitution[176] supplied a "no-compelled-worship" assurance, a "no-compelled-funding" assurance, a "no-establishment" assurance, and an "equal-rights-and-privileges" assurance:

That no person shall ever, within this Colony, be *deprived of the inestimable privilege* of worshipping [*sic*] Almighty God in a manner agreeable to the dictates of his own conscience; nor, under any pretence [*sic*] whatever, be *compelled to attend* any place of worship, contrary to his own faith and judgment; nor shall any person, within this Colony, ever be *obliged to pay tithes, taxes, or any other rates,* for the purpose of building or repairing any other church or churches, place or places of worship, or for the maintenance of any minister or ministry, contrary to what he believes to be right. . . .[177]

⇒•◇•⇐

That there shall be *no establishment* of any one religious sect in this Province, *in preference to another;* and that no Protestant inhabitant of this Colony *shall be denied the enjoyment of any civil right,* merely on account of his religious principles; but that all persons, professing a belief in the faith of any Protestant sect . . . shall *fully and freely enjoy every privilege and immunity,* enjoyed by others their [*sic*] fellow subjects.[178]

(3). Delaware's 1776 Constitution and Separate Declaration of Rights

Delaware's 1776 Constitution and related 1776 Declaration of Rights together supplied a "no-establishment" assurance, a "no-compelled-worship" assurance, and an "equal-rights-and-privileges" assurance:

There shall be *no establishment* of any one religious sect in the State, *in preference to another[.] . . ."*[179]

⇒•◇•⇐

That all men have a natural and unalienable right to worship Almighty God according to the dictates of their own consciences and understandings; that no man ought or of right can be *compelled to attend any religious worship or maintain any ministry* contrary tó or against his own free will and consent, and that no authority can or ought to be vested in, or assumed by any power whatever that shall in any case interfere with, or in any manner controul [*sic*] the right of conscience in the free exercise of religious worship."[180]

That all persons professing the Christian religion ought forever to enjoy *equal rights and privileges* in this State . . . [.][181]

(4). Pennsylvania's 1776 Constitution (Incorporating a Declaration of Rights)

Pennsylvania's 1776 Constitution[182] supplied a "no-compelled-worship" assurance, a "no-compelled-financial-support" assurance, and an "equal-rights-and-privileges" assurance:

. . . And that no man ought or of right can be *compelled to attend any religious worship, or erect or support any place of worship, or maintain any ministry,* contrary to, or against, his own free will and consent; Nor can any man, who acknowledges the being of a God, *be justly deprived or abridged of any civil right* as a citizen, on account of his religious sentiments or peculiar mode of religious worship[.] . . .[183]

. . . And all *religious societies* or bodies of men heretofore united or incorporated for the advancement of religion or learning, . . . shall be encouraged and *protected in the enjoyment of the privileges, immunities and estates* which they were accustomed to enjoy, or could of right have enjoyed, under the laws and former constitution of this state.[184]

(5). Maryland's 1776 Declaration of Rights

Maryland's 1776 Declaration of Rights[185]—distinct from a separately adopted 1776 Constitution[186]—supplied an "equal-rights-and-privileges" assurance and a limited "no-compelled-financial-support" assurance, but, atypically among the various states, it included authorization for a non-preferential "general and equal tax" for "the Christian religion":

. . . [A]ll persons, professing the Christian religion, are *equally entitled to protection* in their religious liberty; wherefore no person ought by any law to be molested in his person or estate, or on account of his religious persuasion or profession, or for his religious practice; . . . [N]or ought any person to be *compelled to request or*

> *maintain, or contribute, unless on contract, to maintain any particular place of worship,* or any particular ministry; yet the Legislature may, in their discretion, *lay a general and equal tax,* for the support of the Christian religion; leaving to each individual the power of appointing the payment over of the money, collected from him, to the support of any particular place of worship or minister, or for the benefit of the poor of his own denomination, or the poor in general of any particular county[.] . . ."[187]

(6). North Carolina's 1776 Constitution (Incorporating a Declaration of Rights)

North Carolina's 1776 Constitution[188] supplied a "no-establishment" assurance, a "no-compelled-worship" assurance, a "no-compelled-financial-support" assurance, and what may fairly be labeled an "equal-rights-and-privileges" assurance:

> That there shall be *no establishment* of any one religious church or denomination in this State *in preference to any other;* neither shall any person, on any pretence [*sic*] whatsoever, be *compelled to attend any place of worship* contrary to his own faith or judgment, nor be *obliged to pay, for the purchase of any glebe*[189]*, or the building of any house of worship, or for the maintenance of any minister or ministry,* contrary to what he believes right; but all persons shall be at *liberty to exercise their own mode* of worship[.] . . .[190]

(7). New York's 1777 Constitution

New York's 1777 Constitution[191] supplied a "no-preference" (or what might be characterized as a quasi-"equal rights") assurance and, similar to the five states which had constitutions with "no-establishment" provisions,[192] supplied a *dis*establishment provision:

> . . . That all such parts of the said common law [of England], and all such of the said statutes and acts aforesaid, or parts thereof, as may be construed to *establish or maintain any particular denomination of Christians or their ministers,* . . . over the colony of New York and its inhabitants, or are repugnant to this constitution, be, and they hereby are, *abrogated and rejected. . . . [.]*[193]

> . . . [T]his convention doth further . . . ordain, determine, and declare, that the free exercise and enjoyment of religious profession and worship, *without discrimination or preference,* shall forever hereafter be allowed, within this State, to all mankind[.] . . .[194]

(8). Georgia's 1777 and 1789 Constitutions

Both Georgia's 1777 Constitution and 1789 Constitution supplied "no-compelled-financial-support" assurances[195]:

> *1777 Constitution:* All persons whatever shall have the free exercise of their religion; . . . and shall not, *unless by consent,* support any teacher or teachers except those of their same profession.[196]

> *1789 Constitution:* All persons shall have the free exercise of religion, *without being obliged to contribute* to the support of any religious profession but their own.[197]

(9). South Carolina's 1778 Constitution

South Carolina's 1778 Constitution[198] supplied a "no-compelled-financial-support" assurance and an "equal-rights-and-privileges" assurance, but, unlike the other states, it included an "establishment" provision:

> That all persons and religious societies who acknowledge that there is one God, . . . and that God is publicly to be worshiped, *shall be freely tolerated.* The Christian Protestant religion shall be deemed, and is hereby constituted and declared to be, the *established* religion of this State. That all denominations of Christian Protestants in this State . . . *shall enjoy equal religious and civil privileges.* . . .

> No person shall, by law, be *obliged to pay* towards the maintenance and support of a religious worship that he does not freely join in, or has not voluntarily engaged to support. . . .[199]

(10). Massachusetts's 1780 Constitution (Incorporating a Declaration of Rights)

Massachusetts's 1780 Constitution[200] supplied an "equal-rights-and-privileges" assurance and a "no-establishment" assurance but, atypically among the various states, it included a "compelled-financial-support" authorization for the legislature (albeit non-preferential as to Protestants):

> It is the right as well as the duty of all men in society, publicly and at stated seasons, to worship the Supreme Being, the great Creator and Preserver of the universe. And *no subject shall be hurt, molested, or restrained, in his person, liberty, or estate,* for worshipping [*sic*] God in the manner and season most agreeable to the dictates of his own

conscience, or for his religious profession or sentiments . . . [.][201]

⇒◆⇐

. . . [T]he people of this commonwealth have a right to invest their legislature with power to authorize and require, and the *legislature shall,* from time to time, authorize and require the several towns, parishes, and other bodies politic, or religious societies, to *make suitable provision, at their own expense, for the institution of the public worship of God, and for the support and maintenance of public Protestant teachers. . .[.][202]*

⇒◆⇐

And every denomination of Christians . . . shall be equally under the protection of the law; and *no subordination* of any one sect or denomination shall ever be *established* by law."[203]

(11). New Hampshire's 1784 Constitution (Incorporating a Declaration of Rights)

New Hampshire's 1784 Constitution[204] supplied a "no-establishment" assurance, but, atypically among the various states, it included a "compelled-financial-support" authorization for the legislature (albeit non-preferential for Protestants):

. . . [T]he people of this state have a right to impower [*sic*], and *do hereby fully impower [sic] the legislature to authorize* from time to time, the several towns, parishes, bodies-corporate, or religious societies within this state, *to make adequate provision at their own expence [sic], for the support and maintenance of public Protestant teachers* of piety, religion, and morality;

Provided notwithstanding, . . . no portion of any *one particular religious sect or denomination,* shall ever be *compelled to pay* towards the support [of] the teacher of teachers of *another persuasion, sect or denomination.*

And every denomination of christian [*sic*] . . . shall be equally under the protection of the law; and *no subordination* of any one sect or denomination to another, shall ever be *established* by law."[205]

(12). Vermont's 1777 and 1786 Constitutions (Incorporating Declarations of Rights)[206]

Both Vermont's 1777 Constitution[207] and 1786 Constitution[208] supplied "no-compelled-worship" assurances, "no-compelled-financial-support" assurances, and "equal-rights-and-privileges" assurances:

1777 Constitution: . . . [T]hat no man ought, or of right can be *compelled to attend* any religious worship, or *erect, or support* any place of worship, *or maintain* any minister, contrary to the dictates of his conscience; nor can any man who professes the Protestant religion be justly *deprived or abridged of any civil right,* as a citizen, on account of his religious sentiment, or peculiar mode of religious worship[.] . . . [209]

1786 Constitution: . . . [T]hat no man ought, or of right can be *compelled to attend* any religious worship, or *erect, or support* any place of worship, *or maintain* any minister, contrary to the dictates of his conscience; nor can any man be justly *deprived or abridged of any civil right* as a citizen, on account of his religious sentiments, or peculiar mode of religious worship[.] . . . [210]

(13). Summary of Religion-Specific Provisions in State Constitutions as of 1789

"Equal-rights-and-privileges" (*viz.,* non-discrimination): Eleven state constitutions (or separate declarations of rights) implemented ecclesiastical-specific "equal rights and privileges" assurances (*viz.,* non-discrimination guarantees): those of Virginia, New Jersey, Delaware, Pennsylvania, Maryland, North Carolina, New York, South Carolina, Massachusetts, New Hampshire, and Vermont.[211] (Technically, North Carolina had not yet become a state by the time the First Congress convened in 1789, as explained in the following chapter.)

"No-compelled-financial-support": Nine state constitutions (or separate declarations of rights) implemented "no-compelled-financial-support" assurances: those of Virginia, New Jersey, Delaware, Pennsylvania, Maryland, North Carolina, Georgia, South Carolina, and Vermont.[212] (The Massachusetts and New Hampshire constitutions authorized their respective legislatures to enable towns and parishes to provide non-preferential financial support for "public Protestant teachers," but they forbade any *preferential* financial support.[213])

"No establishment": Six state constitutions (or separate declarations of rights) implemented specific "no-establishment" assurances (*viz.,* no "preferred" religion, church, denomination, faith, sect, creed, or religious society): those of New Jersey, Delaware, North Carolina, New York, Massachusetts, and New Hampshire.[214] The New Jersey, Delaware, and North Carolina constitutions actually contained the phrase "no establishment"; the New York constitution dis-"established" religion;

both the Massachusetts and New Hampshire constitutions declared that no preference shall be "established" or tolerated.

"No-compelled-worship": Six state constitutions (or separate declarations of rights) implemented "no-compelled-worship" assurances: those of Virginia, New Jersey, Delaware, Pennsylvania, North Carolina, and Vermont.[215]

Constitutional authorization for a non-preferential legislative tax or legislatively-directed financial support: Three state constitutions (or separate declarations of rights) provided authorizations for the state legislatures to enact a *non*-preferential tax for the support of religion in general, or to require *non*-preferential financial support to religious institutions of one's choosing: those of Maryland, Massachusetts, and New Hampshire.[216]

"Established" religion: Unlike all other state constitutions, the South Carolina constitution contained a specific reference to a state-established "religion": the "Christian Protestant religion."[217]

The following table summarizes the ecclesiastical-specific provisions in the various state constitutions as of 1789, when Congress convened to consider, among other business, the proposed constitutional amendment that became the Establishment Clause:

"equal-rights–and-privileges"	no compelled financial support	no "establishment"	no compelled worship	non-preferential tax authorized
Virginia	Virginia		Virginia	
New Jersey	New Jersey	New Jersey[218]	New Jersey	
Delaware	Delaware	Delaware[219]	Delaware	
Pennsylvania	Pennsylvania		Pennsylvania	
Maryland	Maryland			Maryland[220]
North Carolina	North Carolina	North Carolina[221]	North Carolina	
New York		New York[222]		
	Georgia			
South Carolina	South Carolina			
Massachusetts		Massachusetts[223]		Massachusetts[224]
New Hampshire		New Hampshire[225]		New Hampshire[226]
Vermont	Vermont		Vermont	

With the exception of Georgia (with only one category of constitutional assurance), all of the states with ecclesiastical-specific constitutional assurances had adopted provisions that targeted two or more of the characteristics of an "establishment":

- the merger of legislative and ecclesiastical authority;
- the deprivation of various civil rights—or "civil incapacitations"—as punishment for establishment opponents;
- the preferential reward of various honors and privileges (or "emoluments") to establishment supporters;
- the compelled allegiance to (and attendance of) the establishment; and
- the compelled financial support of the establishment[227] via governmental taxes.

Thus, the states' implementation of constitutional assurances from 1776 (Virginia) to 1784 (New Hampshire) that posed direct challenges to the establishment furnished a highly pertinent historical context for the work of the First Congress in 1789.

4

The States' Demands for a "Bill of Rights" as Part of the Constitution

Having secured anti-establishment assurances within their own constitutions or bills of rights, the states—or, more specifically, half of them—pressed for a similar assurance within the newly written Constitution that would forbid the federal government from effectively implementing a "national" establishment. The states ultimately arrived at that goal, although the route proved tortuous and riddled with political potholes endemic of the times.

History also records how a reluctant but brilliant Virginian—James Madison—found himself at the helm, often alone, throughout the journey that led to the Establishment Clause as well as all of the other provisions included within the Constitution's Bill of Rights (*viz.*, the first ten amendments). Without this individual manning the laboring oar for three of the most tempestuous years in our nation's history (1787, 1788, and 1789) we would very likely not have achieved anything like the Bill of Rights.

A. The Debate over Timing and the "Massachusetts Compromise"

On September 12, 1787, five days before the Philadelphia Constitutional Convention adjourned, a lone Convention delegate—George Mason of Virginia—proposed the addition of a specific "bill of rights" as part of the Constitution, something that would mimic at the federal level the various declarations of rights that the states had separately adopted in their own constitutions.[1] Mason, who (with some help from James Madison) had spearheaded Virginia's influential Virginia Declaration of Rights,[2] insisted that "[i]t would give great quiet to the people; and with the aid of the State declarations, a bill might be prepared in a few hours."[3] But the Convention unanimously rejected the idea of appointing a committee for that purpose so late in the process.[4] "Fatigue was certainly a factor."[5] An infuriated Mason actually refused to sign the Constitution because it lacked a separate bill of rights.[6]

Mason's concerns proved prophetic; "[t]he decision not to include a list of individual rights was a misjudgment on the part of supporters of the Constitution that would have dire consequences,"[7] and represented "the one serious miscalculation the framers made."[8] During the post-Convention ratification debates in the states throughout 1787 and 1788, the necessity of a constitutional bill of rights of the kind urged by Mason proved contentious. Proponents of a prompt ratification of the Constitution "as is" (*viz.,* those who urged no delay despite the absence of a bill of rights) advanced two arguments. *First,* because the Constitution delegated to Congress no power to do those things that a bill of rights might prohibit, no bill of rights would be necessary. *Second,* because any amendatory bill of rights might protect against congressional powers that the Constitution did not specifically mention, it could impliedly support the notion that the newly formed federal government possessed more powers than the Constitution expressly conferred on Congress.[9] For instance, Alexander Hamilton argued in the *Federalist Papers*[10] that

> . . . [B]ills of rights . . . are not only unnecessary in the proposed Constitution, but would even be dangerous. They would contain various exceptions to powers not granted; and, on this very account, would afford a colorable pretext to claim more than were granted. For why declare that things shall not be done which there is no power to do?"[11]

Ironically, Madison himself proved lukewarm to the notion that a bill of rights proved necessary, although his reticence may have been motivated by a disinclination to criticize something for which he bore primary responsibility in the first place:

> My own opinion has always been in favor of a bill of rights; provided it be so framed as not to imply powers not meant to be included in the enumeration. At the same time I have never thought the omission a material defect, nor been anxious to supply it even by subsequent amendment, for any other reason than that it is anxiously desired by others. I have favored it because I supposed it might be of use, and if properly executed could not be of disservice. . . .[12]

———✦———

I freely own that I have never seen in the Constitution as it now stands those serious dangers which have alarmed many respectable Citizens. Accordingly whilst it remained unratified, and it was necessary to unite the States in some one plan, I opposed all previous alterations as calculated to throw the States into dangerous contentions, and to furnish the secret enemies of the Union with an opportunity of promoting its dissolution.[13]

Madison also disparaged the necessity for an amendatory bill of rights in some of his *Federalist* essays, albeit indirectly;[14] having seen firsthand how the Virginia legislature worked, Madison had long held the cynical view that any "bill of rights" could scarcely forestall an activist legislature that purported to implement the will of the majority—and, for instance, install the Church of England as Virginia's "official" church.[15] And during the pivotal Virginia Ratifying Convention debates in June 1788, Madison also sought to calm the anxieties of disestablishment proponents—who advocated for some disestablishment assurance of some sort in any bill of rights—by arguing, with some logic, that the "multiplicity" of religious "sects" that had begun to flourish would itself serve to thwart any establishment potential:

> The honorable member has introduced the subject of religion. Religion is not guarded; there is no bill of rights declaring that religion should be secure. . . . Happily for the states, they enjoy the utmost freedom of religion. This freedom arises from that multiplicity of sects which pervades in America, and which is the best and only security for religious liberty in any society; for where there is such a variety of sects, there cannot be a majority of any one sect to oppress and persecute the rest. Fortunately for this commonwealth, a majority of the people are decidedly against any exclusive establishment. . . . [T]he United States abound in such a variety of sects, that it is a strong security against religious persecution; and it is sufficient to authorize a conclusion, that no one sect will ever be able to outnumber or depress the rest.[16]

Furthermore, argued Madison, a bill of rights might well be ineffective against a true establishment that effectively represented the government:

> Would the bill of rights, in this state, exempt the people from paying for the support of one particular sect, if such sect were exclusively established by law? If there were a majority of one sect, a bill of rights would be a poor protection for liberty.[17]

From almost the moment the Constitution had exited the 1787

Convention until the First Congress convened in early 1789, Madison defended his view that a deferral of the bill of rights debate during the 1787 Convention had been necessary in order to ensure a swift ratification process unencumbered by an extraneous debate concerning proposed amendments.[18] But "[t]he absence of a bill of rights in the original Constitution would soon become its most conspicuous flaw, and one that supporters would be unable to successfully defend."[19] Ratification opponents remained less trusting of the new federal government and considered the absence of a bill of rights a major political issue, insisting that no ratification of the Constitution occur without one. Patrick Henry, for instance (and Madison's longtime Virginia political and establishment nemesis), urged that Virginia refuse ratification unless and until the Constitution included a specific bill of rights.[20] And if Virginia refused to ratify the Constitution, most of the states that had not yet voted would likely refuse as well.[21]

Occupying a middle ground, some supporters of a swift and unencumbered Constitution ratification process (such as Paris resident Thomas Jefferson, whom Madison kept apprised of events) also advocated the necessity of constitutional amendments (including a bill of rights) for various reasons. Although he had been in France since 1784 as the United States' envoy, after the Constitutional Convention adjourned in late 1787 Jefferson advised Madison of his concerns about the Constitution's non-specificity concerning a "bill of rights," lamenting

> . . . I will now add what I do not like. First the omission of a bill of rights providing clearly & without the aid of sophisms for freedom of religion, freedom of the press, protection against standing armies, restriction against monopolies, the eternal & unremitting force of the habeas corpus laws, and trials by jury in all matters of fact triable by the laws of the land & not by the law of nations. To say . . . that a bill of rights was not necessary because all is reserved in the case of the general government which is not given, while in the particular ones all is given which is not reserved, might do for the audience to whom it was addressed, but is surely a *gratis dictum,* opposed by strong inferences from the body of the instrument[.] . . . Let me add that a bill of rights is what the people are entitled to against every government on earth, general or particular, & what no just government should refuse, or rest on inferences. . . .[22]

Jefferson thus proposed a ratification strategy that he hoped would placate both sides of the debate. He urged, within the constraints of the nine-vote ratification requirement of Article VII of the Constitution,[23] that nine states swiftly ratify the Constitution "as is" in order to implement it and get the new government installed (consisting of a Congress composed of those nine states[24]), but that the remaining states withhold ratification until the Constitution could be amended to include a bill of rights, effectively conditioning a unanimous ratification on congressional amendments.[25] That strategy would allow for the implementation of the Constitution without a delaying debate about the necessity for an amendatory bill of rights, but, with only a bare minimum ratification vote, would prod the newly formed government to augment the Constitution with a separate bill of rights in order to achieve a much desired—and politically necessary—unanimity of ratification votes. Jefferson made his views known in a number of different letters to various recipients:

. . . [T]he new Constitution will undoubtedly be received by a sufficiency of the States to set it going.[26]

—————≫•◊•≪—————

I am glad to hear that our new constitution is pretty sure of being accepted by states enough to secure the good it contains, & to meet such opposition in some others as to give us hopes it will be accommodated to them by the amendment of its most glaring faults, particularly the want of a declaration of rights.[27]

—————≫•◊•≪—————

Were I in America, I would advocate it warmly till nine [states] should have adopted, and then as warmly take the other side to convince the remaining four that they ought not to come into it till the declaration of rights is annexed to it. By this means we should secure all the good of it, and procure so respectable an opposition as would induce the accepting states to offer a bill of rights.[28]

—————≫•◊•≪—————

I wish with all my soul, that the nine first [state ratifying] Conventions may accept the new Constitution, because this will secure to us the good it contains, which I think great and important. But I equally wish, that the four latest conventions, whichever they be, may refuse to accede to it, till a declaration of rights be annexed. This would probably command the offer of such a declaration[.] . . .[29]

—————≫•◊•≪—————

In this way there will have been opposition enough to do good, and not enough to do harm. [30]

(Jefferson had a change of heart a couple of months later, but word did not arrive from Paris in time for Madison to learn of it before the Virginia Ratifying Convention in June 1788.[31])

Fellow Virginian (and Constitutional Convention president[32]) George Washington, on the other hand, disliked linking the completion of the Constitution's ratification process to promises of post-ratification amendments.[33] Indeed, Jefferson's idea posed serious problems. For one thing, if the bare minimum nine states ratified the Constitution the new government would only consist of those nine states—and, at the time (early 1788), none of the most pivotal and influential states had completed their ratification conventions; only Delaware, New Jersey, Pennsylvania, Georgia, and Connecticut had thus far ratified the Constitution, although Massachusetts did so in the midst of Jefferson's various letters quoted above. But without states like Virginia and New York, any new government would be less capable of actually achieving an amendatory constitutional bill of rights.

> . . . [I]f Virginia and New York—states with almost a third of the nation's population and vital in both political and economic terms— were to reject its defining document, the new nation would have little chance of success.[34]

The lack of unity among the states would be disastrous from any perspective. "Madison knew that it would not be enough for the Constitution to be approved by the minimum nine states."[35]

The quick ratifications of Delaware (December 7, 1787), New Jersey (December 12, 1787), Pennsylvania (December 18, 1787), Georgia (December 31, 1787), and Connecticut (January 9, 1787) masked another long-simmering problem: some states railed against the reality that the Continental Congress—to whom the 1787 Philadelphia Convention had submitted the proposed Constitution upon adjournment[36]—had submitted the Constitution to them for ratification on an "up-or-down" vote; that is, the states could only approve the Constitution or reject it, but they could not ratify only parts of it or condition any ratification upon amendments.[37] Article VII of the Constitution provided no obvious solution, as it simply declared that "[t]he ratification of the conventions of nine states, shall be sufficient for the establishment of this Constitution between the states so ratifying the same."[38] Ratification proponents envisioned all kinds of problems if the states undertook to modify the Constitution or hold its ratification hostage to some particular desire.[39]

Ultimately, a fourth ratification strategy proved successful in securing the ratification votes of the last few states—the most crucial and influential states: the combination of an unconditional ratification vote joined with proposed or recommended constitutional amendments. As the powerful anti-ratification factions in pivotal states such as Virginia, Massachusetts, New York, and North Carolina fought to prevent ratification of any Constitution that lacked a bill of rights (in effect holding the Constitution hostage),[40] the Massachusetts Ratifying Convention arrived at a solution known as the "Massachusetts Compromise"[41]: the remaining states that desired an amendatory bill of rights would be free to submit to the First Congress whatever proposed amendments they desired, but would do so as part of a favorable ratification vote.[42] The Massachusetts Ratifying Convention inserted the following language in their ratification submittal that implemented that strategy:

> And the Convention do [sic], in the name and in behalf of the people of this commonwealth, enjoin it upon their representatives in Congress, at all times, until the alterations and provisions aforesaid have been considered, agreeably to the 5th article of the said Constitution, to exert all their influence, and use all reasonable and legal methods, to obtain a ratification of the said alterations and provisions, in such manner as is provided in said article.[43]

Of the Massachusetts solution, Madison wrote to George Washington a week after Massachusetts's ratification that "the amendments are a blemish, but are in the least Offensive form."[44] In his reply, Washington characterized the Massachusetts solution more favorably, declaring that "the decision . . . is a severe stroke to the opponents of the proposed Constitution in this State [Virginia]."[45]

Even Jefferson changed his mind upon learning of the Massachusetts solution, writing that "the plan of Massachusetts is far preferable, and will, I hope, be followed by those who are yet to decide,"[46] and that

> [a]t first, I wished that when nine States should have accepted the constitution, so as to insure [sic] us what is good in it, the other four might hold off till the want of the bill of rights at least might be supplied. But I am now convinced that the plan of Massachusetts is the best, that is, to accept, and to amend afterwards.[47]

Other states followed suit; the "Massachusetts Compromise" ultimately helped secure the ratification votes of South Carolina, New Hampshire, Virginia, and New York, each of which took the opportunity to propose a host of constitutional amendments with their ratification votes. The significance of that solution can scarcely be overstated; Virginia ratified the Constitution largely, if not solely, because of the opportunity afforded by the Massachusetts tactic, and New York then voted to ratify because Virginia had done so.[48]

But North Carolina (expressly) and Rhode Island (impliedly) decided to hold their ratification votes hostage to constitutional amendments, each voting to ratify the Constitution only after the First Congress adopted a host of amendments to send to the states in September 1789 (as discussed in detail in Chapter 5). North Carolina conducted its first ratifying convention in July and August 1788,[49] and on August 1, 1788, that first convention passed the following resolution that effectively conditioned North Carolina's ratification on the First Congress's adoption of an amendatory bill of rights:

> Resolved, that a *declaration of rights,* asserting and securing from encroachment the great principles of civil and religious liberty, and the unalienable rights of the people, together with amendments to the most ambiguous and exceptionable parts of the said Constitution of government, *ought to be laid before Congress,* and the convention of the states that shall or may be called for the purpose of amending the said Constitution, for their consideration, *previous to the ratification of the Constitution* aforesaid on the part of the state of North Carolina.[50]

North Carolina ultimately ratified the Constitution on November 21, 1789.[51]

For reasons left to speculation, Rhode Island, in an act of "political futility,"[52] delayed the submittal of *both* its ratification vote *and* proposed amendments until May 29, 1790,[53] by which time eight states had already ratified Congress's first set of proposed constitutional amendments.[54]

But by withholding their ratification votes, North Carolina and Rhode Island forfeited any opportunity to actually participate in the First Congress and work toward that goal, as Article VII of the Constitution limited the new government to those states that had ratified the Constitution, providing that the Constitution would be "established . . . between the states so ratifying the same."[55] As a result, senators[56] and representatives[57] from North Carolina and Rhode Island did not participate in the new government until the Second and Third Sessions, respectively, of the First Congress. Ultimately, the belated North Carolina and Rhode Island votes proved inconsequential, although they did afford the ratification process the unanimity that many desired.

The ratification of the Constitution occurred as follows:

- *first:* Delaware ratified the Constitution on December 7, 1787, but included no proposed amendments with its vote.[58]
- *second:* Pennsylvania ratified the Constitution on December 12, 1787, but included no proposed amendments with its vote.[59]
- *third:* New Jersey ratified the Constitution on December 18, 1787, but included no proposed amendments with its vote.[60]
- *fourth:* Georgia ratified the Constitution on December 31, 1787 (and apparently on January 2, 1788, as well), but included no proposed amendments with its vote.[61]
- *fifth:* Connecticut ratified the Constitution on January 9, 1788, but included no proposed amendments with its vote.[62]
- *sixth:* Massachusetts ratified the Constitution on February 6, 1788, and included a host of proposed amendments with its vote.[63]
- *seventh:* Maryland ratified the Constitution on April 26, 1788, but included no proposed amendments with its vote.[64]
- *eighth:* South Carolina ratified the Constitution on May 23, 1788, and included a host of proposed amendments with its vote.[65]
- *ninth:* New Hampshire ratified the Constitution on June 21, 1788, and included a host of proposed amendments with its vote.[66]

[With New Hampshire's ninth vote, the Constitution achieved ratification. On July 2, 1788, the Continental Congress reported that with New Hampshire's vote, as the requisite ninth ratification, it referred the various ratifications to a committee "to examine the same and report an Act of Congress for putting the said constitution into operation . . . [.]"[67]]

- *tenth:* Virginia ratified the Constitution on June 25, 1788, and included a host of proposed amendments with its vote, including a separate declaration of rights.[68]
- *eleventh:* New York ratified the Constitution on July 26, 1788, and included a host of proposed amendments with its vote, including a separate declaration of rights.[69]

[Only those eleven states participated in the inaugural session of Congress.]

- *twelfth:* although North Carolina delayed its ratification of the Constitution until a second ratifying convention vote on November 21, 1789, its first ratifying convention submitted a host of proposed amendments, including a declaration of rights.[70]
- *thirteenth:* Rhode Island ratified the Constitution on May 29, 1790, and needlessly included a host of proposed amendments with its vote, including a separate declaration of rights.[71]

On September 13, 1788, the Continental Congress declared the Constitution officially ratified.[72]

B. The States' Proposed Religion-Specific Constitutional Amendments

Of the five states that submitted proposed constitutional amendments to the First Congress (Massachusetts, South Carolina, New Hampshire, Virginia, and New York), three proposed specific amendments (or declarations of rights) that addressed the relationship between government and religion: New Hampshire, Virginia, and New York.

New Hampshire: New Hampshire's ratification convention worded its proposed religion-specific amendment so broadly as to deprive it of apparent meaning:

> Congress shall make no laws *touching* religion.[73]

From an objective perspective, those words bear an inherently uncertain meaning, and no historical record offers any explanation. (When New Hampshire representative Samuel Livermore proposed that same verbiage during the First Congress's consideration of proposed constitutional amendments (as detailed in the next chapter),[74] James Madison described it as "so broad as to be vague."[75])

Virginia: Virginia's ratification convention proposed the following religion-specific amendment:

> That religion, or the duty which we owe to our Creator, and the manner of discharging it, can be directed only by reason and conviction, not by force or violence; and therefore all men have an equal, natural, and unalienable right to the free exercise of religion, according to the dictates of conscience, and that *no particular religious sect or society ought to be favored or established, by law, in preference to others.*[76]

With the exception of the last clause, Virginia's proposed amendment replicated the famous Article 16 in Virginia's 1776 Declaration of Rights, which provided:

> 16. That Religion, or the duty which we owe to our Creator, and the manner of discharging it, can be directed only by reason and conviction, not by force or violence; and, therefore, all men are equally entitled to the free exercise of religion, according to the dictates of conscience; and that it is the mutual duty of all to practise [*sic*] Christian forbearance, love, and charity, towards each other.[77]

New York: New York's ratification convention proposed a religion-specific amendment that mimicked the Virginia proposal:

> That the people have an equal, natural, and unalienable right freely and peaceably to exercise their religion, according to the dictates of conscience; and that *no religious sect or society ought to be favored or established by law in preference to others.*[78]

(Although the North Carolina ratification convention copied the text of the Virginia proposal *verbatim,*[79] North Carolina did not participate in the First Congress.)

Thus, two of the three states that proposed religion-based constitutional amendments for the First Congress to consider—the pivotal and influential states of Virginia and New York—selected the following phrasing:

> *No [particular] religious sect or society ought to be favored or established by law in preference to others.*[80]

Those words supply a number of readily identifiable, establishment-specific elements whose unique context yields a singular purpose, function, and meaning.

"[R]eligious sect or society." The words "religious sect or society" exemplified the historical reality that, within the context of establishment concerns, the states had never quibbled about any presumed semantic or philosophical differences among the terms "religion," "church," "denomination," "faith," "sect," "creed," and "religious society." The dominant institutional culprits—which, among the states, had long been the Anglicans (or the Church of England) in the southern and middle states and the Congregationalists (or the Puritans) in the northern states—could be readily identified as discrete entities regardless of how anyone might choose to characterize them. And "sect or society" worked as well as any.

"[F]avored or established by law." The phrase "favored or established by law" implemented the classic, long-understood meaning of "establishment," and specifically incorporated the element of "law"; unless recognized (or "established") by *law* (*viz.,* governmental edict or action), an establishment could scarcely exist. Indeed, the establishment's promotion *as a matter of law* proved indispensable.

"[I]n preference to others." The phrase "in preference to others" confirmed the historical concern about the potential dominance of a *single,* dominant ecclesiastical institution, and the related

potential for discrimination, partiality, or prejudice based upon that dominance. Stated differently, any *non*-preferential relationship between government and ecclesiastical institutions had scarcely troubled the states.

C. Madison's Change of Heart: Pre-Congress Support for a Constitutional Bill of Rights

From France, Thomas Jefferson wrote James Madison in July 1788, after New Hampshire's ninth ratification vote resulted in the Constitution's ratification, urging Madison to now press the inaugural Congress for an amendatory bill of rights to be added to the Constitution:

> I sincerely rejoice at the acceptance of our new constitution by nine states. It is a good canvas, on which some strokes only want retouching. What these are, I think are *sufficiently manifested by the general voice from North to South, which calls for a bill of rights.* . . . I hope therefore a bill of rights will be formed to guard the people against the federal government, as they are already guarded against their state governments in most instances.[81]

In October 1788, Madison responded to Jefferson, and he included for Jefferson's perusal the various amendments that the states had proposed with their ratification votes:

> The little pamphlet herewith inclosed [*sic*] will give you a collective view of the alterations which have been proposed for the new Constitution. . . . As far as these may consist of a constitutional declaration of the most essential rights, it is probable they will be added; though there are many who think such addition unnecessary, and not a few who think it misplaced in such a Constitution. . . .[82]

Madison could scarcely play much of a role in the First Congress's adoption of an amendatory bill of rights unless he actually participated in that Congress. But, following his defeat at the Virginia ratifying convention, Patrick Henry decided to punish Madison politically, and Madison's efforts to serve in the First Congress suffered accordingly.[83]

Virginians desperately wanted Madison to serve in the First Congress, preferably the Senate where he might have greater influence than in the much larger House of Representatives.[84] Madison much preferred the House, viewing the Senate as too elite.[85] But he succumbed to pressure from George Washington and others to campaign for the Senate if the state needed him.[86] And it did; only Madison and two others—both anti-Federalists—ran for Senate. Unfortunately, the anti-Federalist-dominated Virginia legislature voted for its new senators, and they elected two of their own.[87] Madison finished third in the voting, snubbed by partisan politics in the one arena that Virginia Federalists did not control.[88]

However, the selection of representatives remained, and Madison, at the urging of all of Federalist Virginia, campaigned for election to the House and ultimately prevailed in a bitter fight against Patrick Henry's anti-Federalist supporters.[89] Throughout the House campaign, Madison's opponents attacked him relentlessly on both the ratification issue and his earlier view that the Constitution required no bill of rights. Finally, compelled by politics to dissociate himself from those who opposed any constitutional amendments at all, and also falsely accused as being insensitive to the necessity of religion-specific (*viz.,* anti-establishment) assurances in the new Constitution,[90] Madison ultimately embraced wholeheartedly the necessity of constitutional amendments—particularly in the area of religious assurances.[91] Thus, he publicly acknowledged that the absence of a constitutional bill of rights ought to be cured by the First Congress with some priority. Indeed, "the most important issue in the campaign for Congress was the Constitution's lack of a bill of rights."[92]

Madison contacted influential Virginia Baptist leaders in January 1789 to seek their support, and he took the opportunity to proclaim his support for "the most satisfactory provisions for all essential rights, particularly the rights of Conscience in the fullest latitude":

> Being informed that reports prevail not only that I am opposed to any amendments whatever to the new federal Constitution; but that I have ceased to be a friend to the rights of Conscience; . . . I am led to trouble you with this communication . . . [.] As a private Citizen it could not be my wish that erroneous opinions should be entertained, with respect to either of those points, *particularly, with respect to religious liberty.* But having been induced to offer my services to this district as its representative in the federal Legislature, considerations of a public nature make it proper that, with respect to both, my principles and views should be rightly understood.
>
> I freely own that I have never seen in the Constitution as it now stands those serious dangers which have alarmed many respectable Citizens. Accordingly whilst it remained unratified, and it was necessary

to unite the States in some one plan, I opposed all previous alterations as calculated to throw the States into dangerous contentions,
and to furnish the secret enemies of the Union with an opportunity
of promoting its dissolution. *Circumstances are now changed:* The
Constitution is established on the ratifications of eleven States and a
very great majority of the people of America; and *amendments, if pur-
sued with a proper moderation and in a proper mode, will be not only safe, but
may serve the double purpose of satisfying the minds of well meaning opponents, and of providing additional guards in favour [sic] of liberty.* Under
this change of circumstances, it is my sincere opinion that the
Constitution ought to be revised, and that the first Congress meeting
under it, ought to prepare and recommend to the States for ratification, the most satisfactory provisions for all essential rights, particularly the rights of Conscience in the fullest latitude, the freedom of the
press, trials by jury, security against general warrants &c. . . .[93]

That letter to the Virginia Baptists proved momentous for
Madison's campaign. From that point forward, Madison campaigned for election to the House of Representatives by publically
urging a constitutional provision for religious liberty.[94]

As part of his campaign, Madison penned additional letters to
political allies that explained his commitment to a constitutional bill
of rights (including an anti-establishment assurance), and campaign
supporters saw to it that his letters received a wide publication in a
host of state newspapers.[95] For instance, Madison wrote to his friend
and political ally, Thomas Randolph, explaining his views and
encouraging Randolph to publicize the letter:

   . . . I have thought it proper to give written communications of my
   real opinions, to several of my acquaintances in your [sic], and the
   other Counties. The report, which, I have reason to believe is most
   injurious, charges me with being a strenuous advocate for the perfec-
   tion of the Constitution as it stands, and an inflexible opponent to the
   change of a single letter. The truth, on the contrary, is that I have ever
   thought it might be improved in several points, although I never
   could see the dangers which alarmed many[.] . . .

   It is accordingly, my sincere opinion, and wish, that in order to
   effect [revisions], the Congress, which is to meet in March, should
   undertake the salutary work.[96]

A day later, Madison wrote George Washington:

   It has been very industriously inculcated that I am dogmatically
   attached to the Constitution in every clause, syllable & letter, and

therefore not a single amendment will be promoted by my vote . . . .
[.] This is the report most likely to affect the election, and most difficult to combat with success . . . [.][97]

Two weeks later, Madison penned a commentary that he had published in a local newspaper:

> The offer of my services to the district, rests on the following
> grounds: That although I always conceived the constitution might be
> improved, yet I never could see in it, as it stands, the dangers which
> have alarmed many respectable citizens. . . . That the [Constitution
> has now been ratified] leaves me free to espouse such amendments as
> will, in the most satisfactory manner, guard essential rights, and will
> render certain vexatious abuses of power impossible[.] . . .

> With regard to the mode of obtaining amendments, I have not
> withheld my opinion that they ought to be recommended by the First
> Congress, rather than be pursued by way of a General Convention.[98]

In effect, Madison "offered what amounted to a campaign pledge
that if he was elected, he would sponsor a bill of rights in the First
Congress and work diligently toward its passage."[99] Indeed, Madison
had put his credibility and integrity on the line. And, as Chapter 5
details, he followed through; indeed, "were it not for Madison, a bill
of rights might never have been added to the Constitution."[100]

Madison won his election to the House of Representatives. As the
First Congress prepared to convene in the spring of 1789, Jefferson
wrote Madison yet again on the same subject and implored Madison
to exert the latter's best efforts to implement the various amendments that the states had proposed:

> The Declaration of rights is like all other human blessings alloyed
> with some inconveniences, and not accomplishing fully its object. But
> the good in this instance vastly overweighs [sic] the evil. I cannot
> refrain from making short answers to the objections which your letter
> states to have been raised. . . .

> . . . A positive declaration of some essential rights could not be
> obtained in the requisite latitude. Answer. Half a loaf is better than no
> bread. If we cannot secure all our rights, let us secure what we can. . . .

> . . . I am much pleased with the prospect that a declaration of rights
> will be added: and hope it will be done in that way which will not endan-
> ger the whole frame of the government, or any essential part of it.[101]

By that point, Madison scarcely needed further prompting from

Jefferson or anyone else, as his election to the First Congress's House of Representatives had been secured on the basis of his advocacy for a bill of rights.

Madison also formulated a sound rationale by which he could introduce the subject of amendments to the First Congress: he perceived the uncertain implications of the Constitution's "necessary and proper" clause ("The Congress shall have Power . . . [t]o make all Laws which shall be *necessary and proper* for carrying into Execution the foregoing Powers . . .[.]"[102]), and he advised the First Congress of his concerns in that regard in June 1789, very early in the First Congress's proceedings, discussed in full in Chapter 5.

Those who earlier viewed any constitutional declaration of rights as superfluous because of Congress's limited constitutional authority had overlooked the reality that the "necessary and proper" clause seemed to furnish authorization for congressional action that the Constitution might not specify elsewhere—an authorization that Madison, for one, viewed as a dangerous "sweeping power."[103] And Madison did not stand alone in that view; in one of his numerous *Federalist* essays, Alexander Hamilton impliedly recognized the far-reaching potential of such relatively loose verbiage in the "necessary and proper" clause but also explained why, in his view, the same legislative authority would exist even if the Constitution made no mention of it.[104]

But Madison also recognized the political necessity of calming the states'-rights apologists' fears of a supreme (and preemptive) "national" government that might tread upon whatever sovereignty the states retained; otherwise the work of the inaugural Congress could well become mired in that enduring debate. After all, the implications of a "national" government voiced by some during the 1787 Constitutional Convention led the Convention to excise the word "national" from the Constitution's description of the government during debate on June 20, 1787.[105] To this day, the Constitution omits the word "national."

Against that background, the inaugural Congress contended not only with the business of governing a new nation, but effectuating the desires of some of the more politically powerful states to undertake amendments to a document whose very existence had been contentious from the outset. And, not unlike his inimitable leadership throughout the 1787 Constitutional Convention, James Madison assumed the helm of the First Congress's House of Representatives for what he surely knew would be blustery sailing from the outset.

5

The First Congress's Consideration of a Bill of Rights: May to September 1789

After the eleven states ratified the Constitution in 1787 and 1788, the nation's inaugural Congress convened in March 1789 to begin consideration of a host of proposed constitutional amendments that five of the eleven states had demanded as part of their ratification votes. Out of those proposals came the First Amendment's Establishment Clause. The full record of those 1789 congressional proceedings proves indispensable not merely from the strictly historical perspective of assuring the objectivity of that being reported, but as the only means by which the author's development of the Establishment Clause can be witnessed within the unique context in which the author—Congress—wrote it.

What do we know of the work of the 1789 First Congress—the author of the Establishment Clause and the rest of the historic Bill of Rights?

> It has been the misfortune of history that a personal knowledge and an impartial judgment of things rarely meet in the historian. The best history of our Country, therefore, must be the fruit of contributions bequeathed by contemporary actors and witnesses to successors who will make an unbiased use of them. And if the abundance and authenticity of the materials which still exist in the private as well as public repositories among us should descend to hands capable of doing justice to them, the American History may be expected to contain more truth, and lessons certainly not less valuable, than those of any Country of age.[1]

So wrote James Madison in 1823, after having reflected upon the historic accomplishments he had witnessed half a century earlier in the late 1700s, and commenting upon the value of enduring chronicles that faithfully reported those accomplishments. For purposes of the Establishment Clause specifically, the following historical materials objectively chronicle the various events of the First Session of the First Congress in 1789.

The House Journal. The House Journal represents the journal maintained by the House of Representatives in accordance with the mandate in Article I of the Constitution that "[e]ach House shall keep a Journal of its Proceedings[.]"[2] On May 28, 1789, the House approved a committee report that authorized its clerk to arrange for private publication of its Journal.[3] Although the House neglected to arrange for any contemporaneous publication of its Journal for House members during the inaugural Congress, the House Journal from Congress's inaugural session in 1789 remains intact nonetheless.[4] The official House of Representatives Journal from the First Session of the inaugural Congress has been reproduced in two publications cited throughout this chapter: III *Documentary History . . . First Federal Congress* and 1 *House Journal*.

The Senate Journal. The Senate Journal represents the House's counterpart, maintained by the Senate in accordance with the mandate in Article I of the Constitution. On May 19, 1789, the Senate accepted a committee recommendation that the Senate publish a journal of "legislative" proceedings.[5] In June 1789 the Senate contracted to have its Journal printed and published privately for the benefit of senators for each session of the First Congress.[6] The official Senate Journal from the First Session of the inaugural Congress, originally published in 1789 by Thomas Greenleaf,[7] has been reproduced in two publications cited throughout this chapter: I *Documentary History . . . First Federal Congress* and 1 *Senate Journal*.

The Senate Executive Journal. The Senate Executive Journal represents a separate journal distinct from the Senate Journal discussed in the preceding paragraph. For a reason or reasons peculiar to the times, on May 19, 1789, the Senate accepted a committee recommendation that it publish only a journal of "legislative" proceedings, but that "the proceedings of the Senate, when they act in their *executive capacity*, shall be entered and kept in separate and distinct books."[8] Thus, on May 25, 1789, the Senate began maintaining dual journals[9] and it kept its "executive journal" private for four decades; not until April 4, 1828, did it authorize publication of all then-existing executive journals.[10] The official Senate Executive Journal from the First Session of the inaugural Congress has been reproduced in two publications cited throughout this chapter: II *Documentary History . . . First Federal Congress* and 1 *Senate Executive Journal*.

Legislative History of the Bill of Rights. "The documentary histories of all legislation introduced [with respect to the constitutional amendments that Congress adopted in 1789] have been reconstructed" using the official Senate and House Journals as well as the Senate and House records in the National Archives, and have been augmented with "independent accounts" and "several first hand accounts."[11] That legislative history of the first set of proposed constitutional amendments, which utilizes "the official documents relating to the legislative work of the First Congress,"[12] has been reproduced in the publication cited throughout this chapter as IV *Documentary History . . . First Federal Congress.*

Contemporary Daily Reports of Congress's Proceedings. Daily excerpts from then-contemporary publications of the debates in the inaugural session of the House of Representatives have been reproduced in four publications cited throughout this chapter: 1 *Annals of Congress,* X *Documentary History . . . First Federal Congress,* XI *Documentary History . . . First Federal Congress,* and the *Complete Bill of Rights.*

The first volume of the *Annals of Congress*—the pertinent volume for purposes of the Establishment Clause—contains both Senate proceedings[13] and House of Representatives proceedings[14] during the First Congress, First Session, from March 1789 through September 1789. (In reality, the Annals' report of the Senate proceedings could only replicate the Senate Journal, as the Senate allowed no observers at all during the First Session.)

Volumes X and XI in the series *Documentary History . . . First Federal Congress,* as well as the separate publication, the *Complete Bill of Rights,* reproduce reports of the April-May and June-September 1789 House of Representatives proceedings originally published in: (1) the *Congressional Register,* a private contemporary publication, (2) the *Gazette of the United States,* also a private contemporary publication, (3) the New York *Daily Advertiser,* a contemporary New York newspaper, and (4) *The New-York Daily Gazette,* also a contemporary New York newspaper, all of which reported (to varying extents) the House of Representatives proceedings during the inaugural session of the First Congress in 1789.

Not until the Second Session of the Third Congress that began on November 3, 1794, did the Senate open its sessions to the public; before then it conducted both its legislative and executive sessions behind closed doors.[15] Late in the First Session of the Third Congress, the Senate approved a resolution to open the Senate galleries to the public, beginning "after the end of the present session of Congress."[16] And not until 1802 did the Senate authorize stenographers to sit on the Senate floor to record the proceedings.[17]

Unlike the Senate, the House of Representatives opted at the outset to open its debates to the public, thus affording a host of unofficial reporters and journalists access to its proceedings. Newspapers and other publications understood the newsworthiness and revenue potential associated with such a historical event.[18] Thus, the published reporting initially appeared in the form of various newspaper accounts and a couple of specialized commercial publications launched solely for the purpose of selling congressional reporting.[19]

The multiplicity of sources referenced in the following pages serves an essential purpose. Although a single source may or may not accurately portray historical events, multiple independent sources that report the same subject matter confirm the independence, accuracy, thoroughness, and objectivity of the historical chronicle that follows. Thus, the reality that, in this case, multiple independent sources coalesce to confirm the occurrence of various historical events buttresses the conclusion that such events occurred in the manner as reported. (To the extent that sources differ on various events, the following narrative reports any differences. All differences prove minor.)

A. House of Representatives Proceedings: May 1789 to August 1789

Although the House of Representatives first convened on March 4, 1789,[20] no quorum existed until April 1, 1789,[21] as members arrived throughout the spring and summer as travel schedules in those days allowed.[22]

(1). May 4, 1789

Four days after [President] Washington's inauguration, Madison began in Congress to fulfill his promise, made repeatedly since February 1788, to add a bill of rights to the Constitution.[23]

On May 4, 1789, scarcely two months after the inaugural Congress convened in March 1789, Representative James Madison addressed the House and reported that "[o]n the 4th Monday [May 25, 1789] the consideration of the fifth article of the Constitution will be submitted to the [H]ouse, or motion to go into committee of the whole."[24] By reference to the "fifth article of the Constitution," Madison meant the Constitution's amendment process described in Article V:

> The Congress, *whenever two-thirds of both houses shall deem it necessary,* shall propose amendments to this Constitution, or, on the application of the legislatures of two-thirds of the several states, shall call a convention for proposing amendments, which, in either case, shall be valid to all intents and purposes, as part of this Constitution, when ratified by the Legislatures of three-fourths of the several states, or by conventions in three-fourths thereof, as the one or the other mode of ratification may be proposed by the Congress[.] . . .[25]

With his announcement, Madison not only reaffirmed his publicized resolve to implement an array of constitutional amendments thought necessary by Virginia and other states, but he effectively announced his ambition to shepherd the process through Congress.

(2). May 25, 1789

On May 25, 1789, Madison informed the House that he would postpone the motion that he had announced on May 4, 1789, for a "fortnight" (*viz.,* two weeks), or until June 8, 1789.[26]

(3). June 8, 1789

On June 8, 1789,[27] Madison "rose [in the House of Representatives] and reminded the House that this was the day that he had heretofore named [on May 25] for bringing forward amendments to the Constitution . . . ,"[28] at which time he moved that the House, as a "Committee of the whole on the state of the Union,"[29] debate various proposed amendments to the Constitution.

Madison reminded the House that, although eleven of the thirteen states had ratified the Constitution, those votes had been secured in large part by assurances that the First Congress would forthwith debate an amendatory bill of rights.[30]

After a prickly debate about the timing of Madison's proposals within the context of the vitally important matters that the First Congress needed to address and the propriety of amendments to a document whose ink had barely dried,[31] Madison withdrew his motion that the whole House consider any amendments (as a concession to the press of House business). But Madison scarcely relented; he moved, instead, "that a select committee be appointed" to review his proposed amendments and report to the whole

Congress.[32] A "select committee" comprised of a single representative from each state would be better equipped to consider the proposed amendments far more expeditiously, and could do so without occupying the entire House.

Madison's persistence (and stature) prevailed; Madison supplied an extended and compelling argument in favor of tackling the business of constitutional amendments forthwith, if only with a "select" committee. He reminded the House that five of the eleven states that had thus far ratified the Constitution by the time the First Congress convened—Massachusetts, South Carolina, New Hampshire, Virginia, and New York[33]—did so with the assurance that the First Congress would address their demands for a separate bill of rights in the Constitution.[34] Indeed, throughout that First Congress Madison never lost sight of the importance of following through on what, at least for him, amounted to a pledge to the various states; even after Congress eventually had begun debate on proposed constitutional amendments Madison continued to press his view that congressional approval of proposed constitutional amendments proved critical to the states' continued support of the Constitution itself:

> . . . In many States the Constn. [*sic*] was adopted under a tacit compact in favr. [*sic*] of some subsequent provisions on this head. In Virga. [*sic*] it would have been certainly rejected, had no assurances been given by its advocates that such provisions would be pursued. As an honest man I feel my self bound by this consideration. . . . In Virga. [*sic*] a majority of the Legislature last elected is bitterly opposed to the Govt. [*sic*] and will be joined, if no amends. [*sic*] be proposed, by great nos. [*sic*] of the other side who will complain of being deceived. Some amendts. [*sic*] are necssy [*sic*] for N. Carola. [*sic*] I am so informed by the best authorities in that State. . . .[35]

Moreover, Madison argued to his fellow representatives that day that if Congress considered the various proposed amendments North Carolina and Rhode Island—neither of which had yet ratified the Constitution—might be persuaded to submit ratification votes and thus render the ratification unanimous.

During the debate that day, Representative Gerry echoed Madison's observation that some pivotal states—and not necessarily only those that proposed constitutional amendments—had voted to ratify the Constitution predicated upon an assurance that a bill of rights would quickly be added (or at least considered) by the First Congress:

The ratification of the constitution in several States would never have taken place, had they not been assured that the objections would have been duly attended to by Congress. And I believe many members of these conventions would never have voted for it, if they had not been persuaded that Congress would notice them with that candor and attention which their importance requires.[36]

Gerry, from Massachusetts, likely spoke of the significance of the "Massachusetts Compromise" and its impact on the various states that had ratified after Massachusetts.[37]

In the middle of his remarks urging Congress to consider the various proposed amendments, Madison deftly segued into a reading of the various amendments themselves—or at least the versions that he had assembled.[38] He followed with a point-by-point rebuttal of the various arguments that might be made against the amendments, thus preempting the debate and cleverly depriving any opponents of an initial opportunity to urge counter arguments themselves.[39]

Madison read perhaps fifteen to twenty separate amendments on June 8, 1789, depending upon how one counts them.[40] As he read them to the House that day from his speech notes,[41] he grouped the various proposed amendments from "First"[42] to "Ninthly,"[43] although his groupings each incorporated a variety of individual amendments; for instance, within the group that Madison labeled "Fourthly" appear not only the six subjects that ultimately formed the First Amendment but subjects that eventually became the Second through Sixth Amendments as well.[44]

Madison also reminded his fellow representatives that the Constitution in fact conveyed to Congress extensive (and nebulous) authority in the form of the broadly worded "necessary and proper" clause in Article I, Section 8,[45] that might well enable Congress to legislate on subjects for which the Constitution otherwise does not expressly provide. Although both he and Hamilton had sought to minimize the states' apprehensions concerning the apparent breadth of the "necessary and proper" clause in their *Federalist Papers* commentaries,[46] Madison now cited the as-yet-unknown extent of the congressional authority as an additional reason to pursue the various proposed constitutional amendments as early as practicable.[47]

Among the proposed amendments that Madison read to the House of Representatives that day appeared the following religion-specific proposal:

Fourthly. That in article 1st, section 9 [of the recently ratified Constitution], between clauses 3 and 4, be inserted these clauses, to wit:

"The civil rights of none shall be abridged on account of religious belief or worship, *nor shall any national religion be established,* nor shall the full and equal rights of conscience be in any manner, or on any pretext, infringed."[48]

(Both then and now, Clauses (or paragraphs) 3 and 4 in Article I, Section 9, of the Constitution read:

No bill of attainder or ex post facto law shall be passed.

No capitation, or other direct, tax shall be laid, unless in proportion to the census or enumeration herein before directed to be taken.[49])

Considering the reality that the various states already had anti-establishment provisions in their own constitutions (or bills of rights),[50] the seven-word phrase "nor shall any *national* religion be established" evinced Madison's meaning and purpose succinctly and precisely, without semantic ambiguity or definitional fuzziness. Thus, the phrase "national religion" in Madison's proposal bore no uncertainty (although, as explained in a moment, the word "national" bore a contentious connotation). Similarly, the word "established" within the context of religion in the states throughout the 1600s and 1700s bore a plain enough meaning, *viz.,* a *single,* dominant ecclesiastical institution (or "church," "religion," "denomination," "faith," "sect," "creed," or "religious society") that derived its financial support directly from the government and which represented an indistinguishable union with government.

Those aspects of Madison's proposal for what eventually became the Establishment Clause have always borne historical certainty, and, as Madison later wrote, "[k]nown words express known ideas . . . [.]"[51] Madison's biographer reports—and a host of Madison's writings confirm[52]—that Madison consistently viewed *preferential* public governmental aid to a single, favored, dominant ecclesiastical institution as the chief establishment evil.[53] Madison's celebrated speech to the 1788 Virginia Ratifying Convention has left no doubt on that point:

. . . Would the bill of rights, in this state, exempt the people from paying for the support of *one particular sect, if such sect were exclusively established by law?* If there were a *majority of one sect,* a bill of rights would be a poor protection for liberty. Happily for the states, they enjoy the utmost freedom of religion. This freedom arises from that *multiplicity of sects,* which pervades America, and which is the best and only security for religious liberty in any society. For where there is such a *variety of sects,* there cannot be a *majority of any one sect* to oppress and persecute the rest. Fortunately for this commonwealth, a majority of the people are decidedly against any *exclusive establishment*—I believe it to be so in the other states. . . . . A particular state might concur in *one religious project.* But the United States abound in such a *variety* of sects, that it is a strong security against religious persecution, and it is sufficient to authorise [*sic*] a conclusion, that *no one sect will ever be able to outnumber or depress the rest.*[54]

The emphasized words in those remarks express Madison's concerns with a precision and clarity sufficient to leave it plain enough that Madison opposed governmental *preferences* among ecclesiastical institutions—by whatever label. Indeed, a *preference* proved essential to the notion of any "establishment."[55]

Madison offered no explanation why he proposed to insert the various unrelated amendments that he had grouped with "Fourthly" at that particular location, nor did he explain why he proposed to actually modify the text of the existing Constitution instead of placing the various amendments in a supplemental document.

Madison also never identified to the First Congress the specific sources of his proposed amendments. The June 9, 1789, edition of the *New-York Daily Gazette* (reporting the House of Representatives proceedings of June 8, 1789), reported that "[o]n motion of Mr. Gerry, it was ordered that the amendments, *recommended by five of the adopting states,* be laid on the Clerk's table . . . [.]"[56] And the legislative records of the House proceedings that day include copies of all the various proposed constitutional amendments submitted with the ratification votes of five states: Massachusetts, South Carolina, New Hampshire, Virginia, and New York.[57] That assemblage inferentially identifies the sources for all of Madison's proposed constitutional amendments as:

• amendments proposed by the Massachusetts Ratifying Convention on February 6, 1788;

• amendments proposed by the South Carolina Ratifying Convention on May 23, 1788;

• amendments proposed by the New Hampshire Ratifying Convention on June 21, 1788;

• amendments proposed by the Virginia Ratifying Convention on June 27, 1788; and,

• amendments proposed by the New York Ratifying Convention on July 26, 1788.[58]

Of those five ratifying states, only New Hampshire, Virginia, and New York submitted religion-specific amendment proposals.

The documentary record suggests that, at least with respect to the actual wording that became the Establishment Clause, Madison crafted his own version by merging his long-standing anti-establishment sentiments with the proposed declaration of rights that Virginia's ratifying convention submitted along with its ratification vote in June 1788 (". . . [N]o particular religious sect or society ought to be favored or established, by law, in preference to others."[59]). New York replicated Virginia's wording.[60]

Madison's biographer reports that, for purposes of all of the various amendments that Madison proposed to Congress on June 8, 1789, Madison reviewed the host of constitutional amendments proposed by the ratifying conventions of Massachusetts, South Carolina, New Hampshire, Virginia, New York, and North Carolina, as well as the amendments proposed by the minority ratification votes in Pennsylvania and Maryland.[61] But that same biographer also reports that, when it came to putting pen to paper for purposes of the amendment that ultimately became the Establishment Clause, Madison drew that particular proposal "almost entirely" from that proposed by the Virginia Ratifying Convention in 1788.[62]

Although debate raged against the House's consideration of amendments at that point, Madison's advocacy of the necessity for a constitutional bill of rights prevailed on June 8, 1789. Madison renewed his motion for the appointment of a select committee at the conclusion of his remarks that day:

> . . . I shall content myself, for the present, with moving "that a committee be appointed to consider of [*sic*] and report such amendments as ought to be proposed by Congress to the Legislatures of the States, to become, if ratified by three-fourths thereof, part of the constitution of the United States."[63]

After further debate, Representative Laurence[64] successfully moved to have the full House consider the proposed amendments instead of a select committee,[65] and the House referred consideration of Madison's proposed amendments to a Committee of the Whole.[66]

(4). July 21, 1789

The House then ignored Madison's proposed amendments from June 8 to late July, at which point Madison lost his patience with the House's inaction. The House of Representatives' delay from June 8, 1789, to July 21, 1789, remains unexplained, but may likely have resulted from a combination of congressional distractions and reordered priorities; one scholar explains Madison's predicament as well as any:

> By the time the First Congress mustered a quorum in April 1789, it was not evident that action on amendments was imperative. Most Federalists had grown indifferent to the question, nor were former Anti-Federalists not sitting in Congress any more insistent, largely because they knew that the substantive changes they desired in the Constitution lay beyond their reach. Nearly all Madison's colleagues in Congress thought the entire subject could be deferred until the new government was safely operating, by which point the desire for a bill of rights might well have evaporated.[67]

Madison, however, remained above that, and remained focused, a reflection of his character and commitment. After all, he had personally assured a lot of Virginians that his election to Congress would bear fruit in the form of constitutional amendments, and he had likely perceived that his fellow congressmen would gladly allow the responsibility for following through to fall on the one person most responsible for crafting the Constitution in the first place.

Thus, Madison "insisted that Congress had to act sooner, not later,"[68] and on July 21, 1789, he moved "to go into a Committee of the Whole" to debate the various amendments.[69]

Representative Ames promptly moved that the House instead refer the amendments to a select committee in order to "facilitate business"[70]—effectively resurrecting the same procedural motion that Madison had urged—albeit unsuccessfully—on June 8. Ames's motion provoked another extended debate about amendment methodology that reflected the difficulties that Madison could expect in his quest to implement an amendatory bill of rights:

• some representatives agreed that a select committee would prove more expeditious[71];

• other representatives maintained that the entire House should consider the various amendments[72];

• one representative thought the matter to be a waste of time altogether, questioning whether it might be "probable that three-fourths of the eleven States [that ratified the Constitution][73] will agree to amendments offered on mere speculative points, when the constitution has had no kind of trial whatever"[74];

• one representative sought to debate the separate question whether the amendments proposed by Madison ought to be the only amendments that the House might consider[75]; and,

• one representative wanted to defer the entire matter to "a time of greater leisure than the present, from the business of organizing the Government."[76]

Ultimately, the House voted to discharge the Committee of the Whole to which it had referred the matter on June 8, 1789,[77] and it referred Madison's proposed amendments to a select committee (as so moved by Representative Ames) that consisted of one representative from each state.[78] The Speaker of the House appointed Madison to the select committee as Virginia's delegate.[79]

(5). July 28, 1789

On July 28, 1789, the House of Representatives' select committee appointed on July 21, 1789, to consider Madison's proposed constitutional amendments submitted its report to the full House.[80] The committee report delineated a total of nineteen proposed amendments—some changes to existing constitutional text and some entirely new provisions. With respect to Madison's proposed fourth amendment (*viz.*, the text that ultimately became the Establishment Clause), the report recommended:

> [4] ART. 1, SEC. 9—Between PAR. 2 and 3 insert, "No religion shall be established by law, nor shall the equal rights of conscience be infringed."[81]

The select committee revised Madison's proposed location of the amendment, moving its insertion point from between paragraphs (or clauses) three and four in Article I, Section 9, to between paragraphs (or clauses) two and three—an insignificant revision.[82] However, the committee also modified Madison's proposed wording by (1) eliminating the modifier "national" and (2) eliminating the first clause. In the following excerpt, brackets with strikeout ("[-]") signify the House select committee's deletions from Madison's proposal while *italic* text represents text added by the select committee:

> [~~The civil rights of none shall be abridged on account of religious belief or worship,~~] *No* [~~nor shall any national~~] religion *shall* be established by law, nor shall the [~~full and~~] equal rights of conscience be [~~in any manner, or on any pretext,~~] infringed.

Realistically, the first clause in Madison's proposed wording bore an uncertain meaning or scope at the outset; neither the word "rights," nor the term "civil rights," nor the word "abridged," nor the phrase "on account of" bore any self-apparent meaning and likely would have sparked time-consuming debate. Thus the select committee's removal of that clause in light of the retention of the substance of the other two clauses would not appear material. Nor would the select committee's removal of the phrases "full and" and "in any manner, or on any pretext" in the third clause of Madison's original verbiage seem material, as those words added little.

Nor, finally, would the select committee's deletion of the word "national" necessarily bear any materiality; the proposed amendment could only apply to congressional authority in any event. As such, the term "national" represented something of a superfluosity that could be jettisoned, particularly to soothe the nerves of those representatives for whom it bore political overtones.

Some, however, might point to the committee's unexplained elimination of the term "national" as reflective of an assumed committee intention to alter the thrust of Madison's original wording. But those who would do so overlook two historical realities: *First,* Madison himself served on the select committee, and, as the remainder of this chapter leaves plain, he ultimately got what he wanted with respect to the First Amendment's religion clauses. *Second,* the committee's reason for the deletion likely lay elsewhere.

Unfortunately, when on June 8, 1789, Madison broached the subject of an "establishment"-specific constitutional amendment to the House of Representatives and invoked the term "national," the Anti-Federalists now elected to the inaugural Congress—or, perhaps more accurately by 1789, the states' rights advocates—experienced a renewal of their fears that the Constitution and its new kind of government threatened to usurp the sovereignty and independence of the various state governments. Madison's biographer confirmed that "[t]he word 'national' was anathema to Antifederalists, who associated it with consolidation of state and federal governments."[83] Indeed, the 1787 Constitutional Convention had barely finished debating the significance of the word "national" in the Constitution itself:

• On May 29, 1787, Virginia's Randolph introduced, as part of the "Virginia Plan" (actually, Madison's plan[84]) a fifteen-part resolution concerning "the establishment of a *national* government" in which the word "national" appeared nineteen times in relationship to a new government.[85]

• On May 30, 1787, the Convention agreed to the following resolution:

> Resolved that it is the opinion of this Committee that a *national* government ought to be established consisting of a supreme Legislative [*sic;* "Legislature"], Judiciary, and Executive.[86]

• On June 19, 1787, the Convention approved a modified nineteen-resolution version of Randolph's initial resolutions, in which the word "national" appeared twenty-six times in relationship to a new government.[87]

• On June 20, 1787, however, the Convention surrendered to the concerns of the states' rights advocates and voted to strike the word "national" from any description of the new constitutional government.[88]

> The large-state men, having accomplished their main purpose, were now willing to make some concessions for the sake of harmony. For example, the objectionable word "national" was stricken out of the first resolution by a unanimous vote, and it was "as of course" dropped out of each of the subsequent resolutions in turn.[89]

The reference to "as of course" comes from Madison's description of the rest of the June 20, 1787, proceedings.[90] One of Madison's biographers writes that "[t]he Wilson-Madison forces agreed to delete the word 'national' from the first clause, to placate the states' rights men, a point Madison conceded because he was ready to accept a novel 'composite' of national and federal principles."[91]

To this day, the word "national" appears nowhere in the Constitution.

Thus, some in the inaugural Congress recoiled at the word "national" in Madison's proposed amendment, just as they lambasted it just two years earlier during the Constitutional Convention in Philadelphia.

(6). August 3, 1789

On August 3, 1789, the House of Representatives postponed consideration of the select committee's report until the following week.[92]

(7). August 13, 1789

On August 13, 1789, the House of Representatives debated Representative Lee's motion that the full House address the select committee's report concerning Madison's proposed amendments.[93] Some representatives urged that the House agree to the report "without hesitation,"[94] while some thought the timing inappropriate given the unfinished business that the First Congress had yet to complete.[95] Ultimately, Lee's motion carried, and the "House resolved itself into a Committee of the whole" to address the select committee's report.[96]

Ironically, at that point the House of Representatives found itself entangled with an imprecision in the Constitution; it discovered that the Constitution's amendment process failed to prescribe a method to assimilate amendments within the Constitution, *viz.,* whether amendments ought to be physically inserted within the text of the Constitution that the 1787 Convention approved and signed (and which the states had ratified as such), or whether any amendments must reside in a supplemental document in order to preserve the sanctity of the 1787 document. Article V of the Constitution declares that any amendment "shall be valid to all intents and purposes, as part of this Constitution, when ratified . . . ,"[97] but remains silent as to the method by which any amendment might be made a part of the Constitution.

Representative Stone reflected the sentiments of others when he warned that interlineations made directly into the Constitution would leave the appearance that the thirty-nine signatories to the Constitution[98] had approved the various amendments.[99] And Representative Sherman similarly pleaded that

> [w]e ought not interweave our propositions into the work itself, because it will be destructive of the whole fabric.[100]

Upon Representative Sherman's motion that any constitutional amendments occur in the form of a separate supplement,[101] the House opted instead to insert amendments directly in the Constitution's existing text.[102] (On August 19, 1789, the House would reverse itself on that subject.)

Having apparently exhausted itself with that contentious debate (which consumed almost the entire day[103]), the House adjourned for the day without addressing the substance of the various proposed constitutional amendments.[104]

(8). August 14, 1789

On August 14, 1789, the full House resumed consideration of the select committee's report on the proposed amendments.[105]

After an entire day of discussion on the first three of the proposed amendments, the House adjourned before it addressed Madison's "fourth" amendment (*viz.,* the text that eventually became the Establishment Clause).[106]

(9). August 15, 1789

On August 15, 1789, the full House resumed consideration of the select committee's report on the proposed amendments.[107] Madison's "fourth" proposed amendment appeared at the head of the list that day:

> The fourth proposition being under consideration, as follows:
>
> "Article 1, Section 9. Between paragraphs two and three insert 'no religion shall be established by law . . . [.]'"[108]

Because of its significance within the context of the historical foundations of the Establishment Clause, the August 15 debate has been reproduced here in its entirety (as reported in the *Annals of Congress* and confirmed by corroborative sources):

> MR. SYLVESTER[*sic;* "Silvester"][109] had some doubts of the propriety of the mode of expression used in this paragraph. He apprehended that it was liable to a construction different from what had been made by the committee. He feared it might be thought to have a tendency to abolish religion altogether.[110]

[The nature of Representative Silvester's "apprehension" remains unexplained, but, given the nature of his "fear," it may have been rooted in the use of a verb—"established"—instead of the one distinctive noun—"establishment"—that more readily characterized the goal of the proposed amendment. Silvester may have been concerned that no "religion" could even be *recognized* "by law" for any purpose.]

Mr. Vining suggested the propriety of transposing the two members [*viz.*, clauses] of the sentence.[111]

Mr. Gerry said it would read better if it was [changed to read] that ["]no *religious doctrine* shall be established by law.["][112]

[Representative Gerry hailed from Massachusetts,[113] where the Congregationalists remained an entrenched establishment.[114] His proposed wording, which described merely one aspect of an establishment, would have undermined Madison's purpose to thwart the possibility of any establishment at the *institutional* level.]

Mr. Sherman thought the amendment altogether unnecessary, inasmuch as Congress had no authority whatever delegated to them by the constitution to make religious establishments; he would, therefore, move to have it struck out.[115]

[Although correct as to the Constitution's express delegation of specific powers, Representative Sherman overlooked the possibility that, as Madison explained to the House of Representatives on June 8, 1789, the Constitution conveyed to Congress extensive authority in the form of the broadly worded "necessary and proper" Clause in Article I, Section 8, of the Constitution ("The Congress shall have Power . . . [t]o make all Laws which shall be *necessary and proper* for carrying into Execution the foregoing Powers . . .[.]")[116] that might well enable Congress to legislate on subjects that the Constitution did not specifically identify.]

Mr. Carroll [said] As the rights of conscience are, in their nature, of peculiar delicacy, and will little bear the gentlest touch of governmental hand; and as many sects have concurred in that they are not well secured under the present constitution, he said he was much in favor of adopting the words. He thought it would tend more towards conciliating the minds of the people to the Government than almost any other amendment he had heard proposed. He would not contend with gentlemen about the phraseology, his object was to secure the wishes of the honest part of the community.[117]

Mr. Madison said, he apprehended the meaning of the words to be, that *Congress should not establish a religion, and enforce the legal observation of it by law, nor compel men to worship God in any manner contrary to their conscience.* Whether the words are necessary or not, he did not mean to say, but they had been required by some of the State Conventions, who seemed to entertain an opinion that under the clause of the constitution, which *gave power to Congress to make all laws necessary and proper to carry into execution the constitution, and the laws made under it,* enabled them to make laws of such a nature as might infringe the rights of conscience, and *establish a national religion;* to prevent these effects he presumed the amendment was intended, and he thought it as well expressed as the nature of the language would admit.[118]

[Madison, responding to Representative Sherman's opinion that the Constitution endowed Congress with no authority over religion in any event, again reminded the House of the significance of the broadly worded "necessary and proper" Clause in Article I, Section 8, of the Constitution.]

MR. HUNTINGTON said that he feared, with the gentlemen first up on this subject [*viz.*, Representative Silvester], that the words might be taken in such latitude as to be extremely hurtful to the cause of religion. *He understood the amendment to mean what had been expressed by the gentleman from Virginia* [*viz.*, Representative Madison]; but others might find it convenient to put another construction upon it. The ministers of their congregations to the Eastward were maintained by the contributions of those who belonged to their society; the expense of building meeting-houses was contributed in the same manner. These things were regulated by by-laws. If an action was brought before a Federal Court on any of these cases, the person who had neglected to perform his engagements could not be compelled to do it; for a support of ministers, or building of places of worship might be construed into a religious establishment.

By the charter of Rhode Island, no religion could be established by law; he could give a history of the effects of such a regulation; indeed the people were now enjoying the blessed fruits of it. He hoped, therefore, the amendment would be made in such a way as to secure the rights of conscience, and a free exercise of the rights of religion, but not to patronize those who professed no religion at all.[119]

[Madison's biographer explains that "[a] Connecticut member [a reference to Representative Huntington] was afraid this [*viz.*, the proposed wording] would close the federal courts to suits to collect contributions pledged to church societies[.]"[120]]

MR. MADISON thought, *if the word [*"*]national[*"*] was inserted before [*"*]religion,[*"*] it would satisfy the minds of honorable gentlemen.*[121] He believed that the *people feared one sect might obtain a pre-eminence, or two combine together,* and establish a religion to which they would compel others to conform. He thought *if the word [*"*]national[*"*] was introduced,* *it would point the amendment directly to the object it was intended to prevent.*[122]

MR. LIVERMORE was not satisfied with that amendment; but he did not wish them to dwell long on the subject. He thought it would be better if it was altered, and made to read in this manner,[123] that ["]Congress shall make no laws touching religion, or infringing the rights of conscience.["][124]

[Representative Livermore hailed from New Hampshire, and, not coincidentally, New Hampshire's constitution ratification vote in June 1788 included the following proposed constitutional amendment on this very subject—a proposal uniquely worded by New Hampshire alone: "Congress shall make no laws touching religion."[125] The term "touching" would seem to pose boundless interpretive difficulties, and New Hampshire alone preferred that amorphous term. Indeed, Madison's biographer reports that Madison had viewed Livermore's proposal as "so broad as to be vague."[126] The *Daily Advertiser*'s report of the August 15, 1789, proceedings recites that Representative Livermore "observed that tho' the sense of both provisions was the same [*viz.,* the select committee's wording and Livermore's wording], yet the former might seem to wear an ill face and was subject to misconstruction."[127] That report does not, however, elaborate on that characterization.]

MR. GERRY *did not like the term* ["]*national*["]*,* proposed by the gentleman from Virginia, and he hoped it would not be adopted by the House. It *brought to his mind some observations that had taken place in the conventions at the time they were considering the present constitution.* It had been insisted upon by those who were called antifederalists, that this form of Government consolidated the Union; the honorable gentleman's motion[128] shows that he considers it in the same light. Those who were called antifederalists at that time complained that they had injustice done them by the title, because they were in favor of a Federal Government, and the others were in favor of a national one; the federalists were for ratifying the constitution as it stood, and the others not until amendments were made. . . .[129]

[With those words, Gerry—a Massachusetts delegate to the 1787 Constitutional Convention[130] and one of only three delegates who expressly refused to sign the Constitution[131]—resurrected the divisiveness prompted by the word "national" that had caused the 1787 Constitutional Convention to remove any reference to it in the Constitution itself, as explained earlier.]

Mr. Madison withdrew his motion,[132] but observed that the words "no national religion shall be established by law," did not imply that the Government was a national one[133]; the question was then taken on Mr. Livermore's motion, and passed in the affirmative, thirty-one for, and twenty against it.[134]

Upon its approval of Representative Livermore's "motion," the House modified Madison's "fourth" proposed amendment to read:

> Congress shall make no laws touching religion, or infringing the rights of conscience.[135]

(10). August 17, 1789

Although the House of Representatives conducted further hearings on the select committee's report on the proposed amendments on August 17, 1789,[136] no further discussion of Madison's proposed "fourth" amendment (*viz.*, the religion clauses) occurred until August 20.

(11). August 18, 1789

Although the House of Representatives conducted further hearings on the select committee's report on the proposed amendments on August 18, 1789,[137] no further discussion of Madison's proposed "fourth" amendment (*viz.*, the religion clauses) occurred until August 20, 1789.

However, during the August 18 proceedings the House considered two motions (from Representatives Gerry and Tucker)[138] that would have expanded the proposed constitutional amendments well beyond those contained in the select committee's report and would have added to the existing list. *First,* Representative Gerry moved that the House add seventeen additional amendments to the select committee's report, the substance of which had not been mentioned let alone considered by the House select committee thus far. *Second,* Representative Tucker moved that the House consider all amendments proposed by the five states[139] whose individual proposals the House select committee did *not* consider. Those motions failed.[140]

(12). August 19, 1789

Although the House of Representatives conducted further hearings on the select committee's report on August 19, 1789,[141] no further discussion of Madison's proposed "fourth" amendment (*viz.,* the religion clauses) occurred until August 20, 1789.

However, a historically significant event occurred that day: the House reversed its vote of August 13, 1789, concerning the manner by which amendments ought to be added to the Constitution.

On August 13, 1789, the House had rejected Representative Sherman's motion that any amendments occur in the form of a separate supplement, accepting instead the contention that any amendments ought to be interlineated directly into the Constitution.[142] On this day, the House reconsidered the matter on yet another motion by Representative Sherman,[143] and reversed itself.[144] Too many representatives thought it unacceptable, not to mention impracticable, to physically alter the original Constitution that had been signed and ratified as such.[145]

(13). August 20, 1789

On August 20, 1789, the House of Representatives resumed hearings on the select committee's report on the proposed amendments,[146] and Madison's "fourth" proposed amendment received a brief consideration. With no reported discussion, Representative Ames moved to modify the wording that the House had approved on August 15, 1789, to read:

> Congress shall make no law *establishing religion,* or to prevent the free exercise thereof, or to infringe the rights of conscience.[147]

The House approved Ames's motion without debate.[148]

In the following excerpt, brackets with strikeout ("[-]") signify deletions from the August 15 version while *italic* text represents text added to the August 20 version via Representative Ames's motion:

> Congress shall make no law[s] [~~touching~~] *establishing* religion, *or to prevent the free exercise thereof,* or *to infringe* [~~infringing~~] the rights of conscience.

With this modification, the House implemented three significant changes. *First,* the phrase "free exercise" appeared for the first time—a phrase that still endures in the Free Exercise Clause in the First Amendment ("Congress shall make no law . . . prohibiting the free exercise [of religion]").[149] *Second,* the House incorporated the religion-pertinent term "establishing," a variant of the well-understood term "establishment" that it had abruptly eliminated from the select committee's version on August 15, 1789. *Third,* the House mercifully jettisoned the uncertain and troublesome term "touching."

The reversion to an amendment that specifically utilized a variant of "establish" had been engineered by Representative Madison, who had so disliked the vague New Hampshire-based wording ("touching") that the House had approved five days earlier, and who viewed the term "touching" as inherently problematic. According to Madison's biographer, although the version approved on August 20, 1789, had been introduced by Representative Ames, "[t]here can be little doubt that this [particular version] was written by Madison."[150]

(14). August 21, 1789

The House of Representatives scheduled further hearings on the select committee's report on the proposed amendments on August 21, 1789,[151] and on that day the House approved seventeen proposed "articles" of constitutional amendments—paring the select committee's original list of nineteen proposals.[152]

The list that the House approved on August 21 included the following proposed amendment (identified as the third "article" in the list):

> Congress shall make no law *establishing religion,* or prohibiting the free exercise thereof, nor shall the rights of conscience be infringed.[153]

One might not notice the slight modification from the version that the House had approved only the day before; in the following excerpt, brackets with strikeout ("[-]") signify deletions from the August 20 version while *italic* text represents text added to the August 20 version:

> Congress shall make no law establishing religion, or [~~to prevent~~] *prohibiting* the free exercise thereof, [~~or to infringe~~] *nor shall* the rights of conscience *be infringed.*

Neither the official House Journal, nor the *House Journal,* nor those sources that relied upon contemporary news reporting sources (*viz.,* the *Annals of Congress,* XI *Documentary History . . . First Federal Congress,* and *Complete Bill of Rights*) explain the minor change from the wording that the House had approved just a day earlier[154]; the change simply appears in the wording of the various amendments that the House approved with the requisite two-thirds vote on August 21, 1789.[155] In any event, the text changes would seem inconsequential in substance.

(15). August 22, 1789

The House of Representatives conducted further hearings on the proposed constitutional amendments on August 22, 1789.[156]

After rejecting a spate of last-minute additions to the list of amendments approved the previous day,[157] the House finished its consideration of the various proposed amendments and assigned three representatives—Benson, Sherman, and Sedgwick—the task of arranging the various amendments for transmittal to the Senate.[158]

(16). August 24, 1789

On August 24, 1789, the House of Representatives finalized its report on the arrangement of the proposed amendments[159] and forwarded the proposed amendments to the Senate.[160] The House accompanied its transmittal to the Senate with a proposed resolution of submittal to the various states.[161]

The text that ultimately became the First Amendment's Establishment Clause and Free Exercise Clause appeared as "Art. III." in the House list:

Article the Third

Congress shall make no law establishing religion, or prohibiting the free exercise thereof, nor shall the rights of conscience be infringed.[162]

B. Senate Proceedings: August 1789 and September 1789

The Senate conducted all of its proceedings behind closed doors until the second session of the third Congress in November 1794, when the Senate approved a resolution to open the Senate galleries to the public beginning "after the end of the present session of Congress."[163] Thus, the record of the first Senate's consideration of the proposed constitutional amendments remains less developed than the record of the House of Representatives proceedings.[164] Even though Pennsylvania senator Maclay maintained a personal diary of various Senate proceedings from April 24, 1789, to March 3, 1791, the senator's family declined to allow publication of the diary until the very late 1800s—1890 to be precise.[165] Due to Maclay's illness at the time the Senate began debates concerning the amendments,[166] Maclay's diary mentions the proposed constitutional amendments only once, reporting that on August 25, 1789, the

Senate received the proposed amendments from the House of Representatives.[167]

Nonetheless, the first volume of the *Annals of Congress* contains a report of the Senate debates during the First Session in the same format as its report of the House of Representatives debates during that time, albeit much less extensive (*viz.*, 81 pages for the Senate versus 865 pages for the House).[168] Apparently, the *Annals'* report of the First Congress's Senate proceedings merely replicates the contents of the *Senate Journal's* first volume—which had already been published in 1820[169]—as well as portions of the *Senate Executive Journal*; the First Session's Senate proceedings in the *Senate Journal* span 90 pages,[170] while the First Session's Senate proceedings in the first volume of the *Annals of Congress* span a roughly comparable 81 pages.[171]

<hr/>

On an altogether separate subject, because the House of Representatives arranged the proposed constitutional amendments so that the religion clauses appeared as the third in a series of proposals (or "Articles" of amendment), from this point forward in the chronology all references to the "proposed third amendment"—or the "third Article of amendment," or simply the "third Article"—shall mean the House of Representatives' proposed constitutional amendment identified in the House list as "Article the Third"—*viz.*, the religion clauses. This clarification becomes necessary because of the cumbersome and confusing manner in which the Senate identified its own amendments to the list of Articles that it received from the House of Representatives.

The Senate substantially revised the list of proposed constitutional amendments it received from the House, and it numbered each of its own amendments separately from the Articles to which the Senate amendments corresponded. The Senate recorded twenty-six separate amendments to the House of Representatives' list of Articles,[172] yielding a lengthy list of, in effect, "amendments to the amendments." As a result, an unadorned reference to the "third amendment" from the Senate's perspective would not reference the religion clauses—*viz.*, the third Article of amendment in the House's list—but, instead, would reference the *first* Article of amendment, which the Senate's third amendment modified.[173] Actually, the Senate's "fifth amendment" involved the religion clauses.[174]

In addition to the reference clarification just mentioned, from this point forward in this chronology all references to any of the

Senate's twenty-six separate modifications of the House of Representatives' proposed list of constitutional amendments shall occur by using the terms "modification" or "modifications" in lieu of the terms "amendment" or "amendments" (except when actually quoting from Senate records).

(1). August 25, 1789

On August 25, 1789, the Senate received the House of Representatives' transmittal of the list of seventeen proposed Articles of amendment.[175] The Senate quickly rejected a preliminary motion to postpone consideration of the proposed Articles to the next session of Congress,[176] and it scheduled a hearing for September 2, 1789, to debate the proposed amendments.[177]

(2). September 2, 1789

On September 2, 1789, the Senate debated a host of proposed modifications to the House version of the proposed Articles of amendment.[178] None of the Senate's proposed modifications involved the House's third proposed Article of amendment (*viz.*, "Congress shall make no law establishing religion . . . [.]").

(3). September 3, 1789

On September 3, 1789, the Senate continued debate on proposed modifications of the House's list of constitutional amendments.[179]

In a flurry of motions, the Senate debated seven proposed modifications to the House's proposed third amendment (or third Article) before deciding on its preferred wording—wording that embraced the House's version but without the final clause. Had the Senate debates been recorded, the proceedings of September 3, 1789, might well supply some interesting reading.

First Senate Vote. The Senate first rejected a motion to strike the words "religion or prohibiting the free exercise thereof" and to replace them instead with the phrase "one religious sect or society in preference to others."[180] One can only speculate as to the reasoning that underlay that proposed modification. The Senate rejected that motion on the first vote.

Second Senate Vote. However, upon an unexplained motion for reconsideration, the Senate promptly reversed course and passed the very motion that it had just rejected.[181]

Thus, at that point the text of the House of Representatives' proposed third amendment (or third Article) read:

> Congress shall make no law establishing one religious sect or society in preference to others, nor shall the rights of conscience be infringed.[182]

The reason for that change in wording remains unexplained, as does its meaning (if indeed different in some respect from the House version).

Third Senate Vote. Next, the Senate rejected a motion that the proposed third amendment (or third Article) be stricken altogether.[183]

Fourth Senate Vote. Next, the Senate rejected a motion that would have slightly modified the just-changed wording in the proposed third amendment (or third Article) to read "Congress shall not make any law infringing the rights of conscience, or establishing any religious sect or society."[184] That proposed alteration would seemingly have been inconsequential; except for the proposed deletion of the phrase "in preference to others" and the proposed substitution of "any" for "no" (both of which represent proposed changes of no real consequence within the context of "establishment"), that text version would merely have replicated the version the Senate had just approved.[185] (Although this new proposed wording omitted the reference to "preference," the reference to "establishing" necessarily supplied that element as one of the derisive aspects of any establishment.)

Fifth Senate Vote. Next, the Senate rejected a motion that would have modified the just-changed wording of the proposed third amendment (or third Article) to read "Congress shall make no law establishing any particular denomination of religion in preference to another, or prohibiting the free exercise thereof, nor shall the rights of conscience be infringed."[186] Again, a change in wording from "one religious sect or society" to "any particular denomination of religion" merely swapped interchangeable terminology and thus replicated the version the Senate had just approved.

Sixth Senate Vote. Next, the Senate rejected a motion to accept the wording "as it came from the House of Representatives."[187]

Seventh Senate Vote. Finally, the Senate took one last vote that, oddly enough, negated the series of votes just described; it passed a motion to accept the wording of the House version but with the removal of the clause that read "nor shall the rights of conscience be infringed."[188]

Thus, the Senate approved the following wording for the proposed third amendment (or third Article) by the end of business on September 3, 1789:

> Congress shall make no law establishing religion, or prohibiting the free exercise thereof.[189]

The difference between the version the Senate approved on September 3, 1789, and the version that it received from the House on August 25, 1789, can be seen in the following, with brackets and strikeout ("[-]") representing deletions from the House version:

> Congress shall make no law establishing religion, or prohibiting the free exercise thereof[, ~~nor shall the rights of conscience be infringed~~].

(4). September 4, 1789

On September 4, 1789, the Senate resumed deliberations on the House of Representatives' list of proposed amendments, and it voted on a number of proposed modifications of the House versions.[190] But no votes addressed the House's third Article (the religion clauses); the Senate resumed debate on the House's proposed amendments beginning with the fourth Article proposed by the House and proceeded through the eleventh Article.[191]

Thus, the order in which the Senate considered the various proposed Articles of amendment on September 4, 1789, suggests that it had completed its debate concerning the religion clauses (*viz.*, the proposed third amendment) on September 3, 1789.

(5). September 7, 1789

On September 7, 1789, the Senate resumed deliberations on the House of Representatives' list of proposed amendments, and it also considered a number of proposed modifications of the House versions as well as proposals for additional amendments beyond those that the House proposed.[192]

But no votes that day addressed the House's proposed third amendment (the religion clauses); the Senate resumed debate on the House's proposed amendments beginning with the twelfth

Article proposed by the House of Representatives and proceeded through the seventeenth Article.[193]

(6). September 8, 1789

On September 8, 1789, the Senate resumed deliberations on the House of Representatives' list of proposed amendments, confining its votes to proposed modifications of the amendments in the House list. None of the proposed modifications passed.[194]

(7). September 9, 1789

On September 9, 1789, the Senate resumed deliberations on the House of Representatives' list of proposed amendments, confining its votes to a host of proposed modifications to the amendments on the House list.[195] But, in addition, the Senate not only voted to modify its prior approval of the proposed third amendment (*viz.,* the religion clauses) but to combine the third and fourth proposed amendments into the third.

First, the Senate voted to change the text of the religion clauses that it had approved on September 3, 1789, to read as follows:

> Congress shall make no law establishing articles of faith or a mode of worship, or prohibiting the free exercise of religion.[196]

Second, the Senate voted to append the then-existing fourth proposed amendment to the third, so that the new third amendment (or third Article) would provide, as augmented:

> Congress shall make no law establishing articles of faith or a mode of worship, or prohibiting the free exercise of religion, or abridging the freedom of speech, or the press, or the rights of the people peaceably to assemble, and petition to the government for the redress of grievances.[197]

The difference between the version of the religion clauses that the Senate approved on September 3, 1789, and the version changed on September 9, 1789, can be seen as follows, with brackets and strike-out ("[-]") representing deletions from the September 3 version and *italic* text representing new text added on September 9:

> Congress shall make no law establishing [~~religion~~] *articles of faith or a mode of worship,* or prohibiting the free exercise [~~thereof~~] *of religion.*

That particular Senate modification infuriated Madison when he learned of it; it sabotaged the point of a disestablishment provision by flippantly targeting mere religious elements or aspects of an establishment, rather than the establishment itself. Madison fought for two assurances contained in any bill of rights: *first,* no "establishment" (*viz.,* no single, dominant governmentally ordained or governmentally preferred ecclesiastical institution,) and *second,* a "total exclusion of government [financial] aid to religion" (*viz.,* the establishment institution).[198] A mere reference to some subordinate aspect of establishment, such as "articles" of faith or "mode" of worship, remained unacceptable to Madison.[199] And the Senate's revision on September 9 frustrated both of Madison's goals.

Madison well knew that the Senate's September 9 retreat on the establishment issue had been backed by the Senate's New England and Virginia "establishment" advocates; "New England supporters of established churches were leagued with Senator Lee of Virginia, a partisan of the 1784 [legislative tax] assessment scheme."[200] Madison viewed the Senate's limitation to "creed and ritual" as so conspicuously narrow that it that would do nothing to thwart government financial support to an establishment or establishment-supported schools—scarcely a "disestablishment" in Madison's view.[201]

At the end of the day on September 9, 1789, the Senate returned to the House of Representatives a list of twenty-six proposed modifications to the various constitutional amendments in the House's list.[202] As returned to the House, the religion clauses appeared as the fifth and sixth modifications on the Senate's list:

[5]To erase from the 3d. Article the word *"Religion"* & insert— *"articles of faith or a mode or worship."*

[6]And to erase from the same article the words *"thereof, nor shall the rights of Conscience be infringed"* & insert— *"of Religion; or abridging the freedom of speech, or of the press or [of] the right of the people peaceably to assemble, & to petition to the government for a redress of grievances."*[203]

C. House of Representatives and Senate Proceedings: September 10, 1789, to September 28, 1789

(1). September 10, 1789
(House of Representatives)

On September 10, 1789, the House of Representatives received the Senate's proposed modifications, but it deferred consideration of the Senate's work product to September 19, 1789.[204]

(2). September 19, 1789
(House of Representatives)

On September 19, 1789, the House of Representatives only briefly considered the Senate's modifications of the proposed amendments, postponing further debate until September 21, 1789.[205]

(3). September 21, 1789
(House of Representatives and Senate)

On September 21, 1789, three pertinent events transpired in both chambers of Congress.

First, of the twenty-six modifications that the Senate returned to the House of Representatives on September 9, 1789, the House accepted ten and rejected sixteen—the latter group including the Senate's version of the proposed third amendment (or third Article).[206] The House so advised the Senate that same day.[207]

Second, upon being advised of the House's disagreement with a number of its modifications of the proposed amendments, the Senate immediately relented with respect to its version of the proposed third amendment (*viz.,* the religion clauses) and advised the House that it had "recede[d]" from the version that it had approved on September 9, 1789. But the Senate disagreed with the House as to all others:

> Resolved, That the Senate do recede from their [*sic*] *third* amendment, and do insist on all the others.[208]

Given the reality that, as mentioned a few pages earlier, the Senate labeled its own modifications as "amendments," the reference to "third amendment" might seem ambiguous. But the historical records leave no doubt but that, from the Senate's perspective, the Senate's "third amendment" (or third Article) at that point consisted of the religion clauses (as augmented by the Senate on September 9, 1789, to include references to "speech," "press," etc.). When the House of Representatives sent the proposed amendments to the Senate on August 24, 1789, the religion clauses appeared in the proposed third amendment (or "Article the Third"), and when the Senate returned its version of the proposed

Articles of amendment to the House on September 9, 1789, the religion clauses still appeared as the proposed third amendment (or "Article the Third").[209]

Third, the House then requested, and the Senate concurred, that a House-Senate conference committee resolve lingering differences concerning the remaining twenty-five Senate modifications.[210] The House of Representatives appointed Representatives Madison, Sherman, and Vining to represent it on the Conference Committee,[211] while the Senate appointed Senators Ellsworth, Carroll, and Paterson to represent its interests.[212]

One might suppose that, because the Senate "recede[d]"[213] from its version of the proposed third Article of amendment (the religion clauses), the Conference Committee would have no need to address that particular topic. But it seems that, in congressional parlance, to "recede" from a particular proposal did not necessarily *concede* that same proposal, meaning that the Senate merely declined to insist on its particular version of the proposed third amendment (or third Article) but otherwise did not acquiesce in the House of Representatives' version. Thus, the final versions of the proposed third amendment (or third Article) remained undecided at that point, and therefore among the matters to be resolved by the Conference Committee.

(4). September 23, 1789
(House of Representatives)

On September 23, 1789, Representative Madison advised the House of Representatives that the Conference Committee appointed on September 21 had completed its report on the proposed Articles of amendment.[214] The House postponed consideration of that report until the following day.[215] (The Senate records fail to reflect whether the full Senate received the Conference Committee report on September 23 or 24.)

(5). September 24, 1789
(House of Representatives and Senate)

On September 24, 1789, both the House of Representatives and the Senate separately addressed the Conference Committee's report on the proposed Articles of amendment.[216] The sense of the various reporting sources suggests that, by the beginning of business in each chamber on September 24, 1789, the Senate had relented to the House's demands concerning the third and eighth proposed amendments (or third and eighth Articles), while the House had relented to the Senate modifications of the remaining Articles.[217]

The text of the Conference Committee Report of September 24, 1789, reads, in pertinent part for purposes of the text that eventually became the Establishment Clause (*viz.*, the third Article):

> The Committees of the two Houses appointd [*sic*] to confer on thier [*sic*] different votes on the Amendments proposed by the Senate to the [House] Resolution proposing Amendments to the Constitution, and disagreed to by the House of Representatives, have had a conference, and have agreed that it will be proper for the House of Representatives to agree to the said Amendments proposed by the Senate, with an Amendment to their [*viz.*, the Senate's] fifth Amendment, so that the third Article shall read as follows: "Congress shall make no law *respecting an establishment of Religion . . . [.]*[218]

The reference to "*their* fifth amendment" in that Conference Committee Report necessarily corresponds to the various *Senate* modifications of the House proposals[219]; the list of Senate amendments includes, as the Senate's "fifth" amendment (or modification), a proposal to alter the text of the religion clauses.[220]

In conference, Madison had insisted that the Committee reject the Senate version of the third proposed Article of amendment (*viz.*, the religion clauses) and that it bear the following wording instead:

> "ART. 3. Congress shall make no law respecting an establishment of religion, or prohibiting the free exercise thereof . . . [.]"[221]

Madison prevailed; the Conference Committee's wording of the religion clauses substantially resurrected the wording that the House of Representatives had approved on August 24, 1789, as well as the wording that the Senate had approved on September 3, 1789, replacing only the word "establishing" with the substitutive phrase "respecting an establishment of"—a functional equivalency that merely replaced a reference to the *act* of implementing an establishment with a reference to the institution itself.

Madison's biographer credits Madison with exercising the latter's influence in the Conference Committee to obtain the desired result,[222] and one prominent historian reports that Madison played the "key role" in the Conference Committee's product.[223] Madison's influence had always been conspicuous and respected; "[Madison] owed his preeminence in the first House of Representatives to his disciplined and logical mind, his sound judgment, and his deep knowledge and understanding of the public issues of the day."[224] And the fact that, even before the First Congress convened, President-elect George Washington had "made clear his intention to have Madison at his right hand to aid discreetly, as he had opportunity, in Madison's election to the House of Representatives"[225] boosted Madison's stature immensely.

One of Madison's fellow Representatives in that First Congress—Fisher Ames—reported that, early on in that inaugural Congress, ". . . by common consent the 'first man' in the House was J[ames] M[adison]."[226] And Thomas Jefferson once wrote this eloquent tribute to Madison's persona and stature:

> . . . [H]e [*viz.,* Madison] acquired a habit of self-possession, which placed at ready command the rich resources of his luminous and discriminating mind, and of his extensive information, and rendered him the first of every assembly afterwards, of which he became a member. [227]

After it considered the Conference Committee's report, the House of Representatives "recede[d]" from its disagreement with the Senate on all of the various Senate modifications except two: the third and eighth of the proposed Articles of amendment.[228] (The House also urged a one-word change in the first of the proposed Articles of amendment, seemingly to correct a scrivener's error.[229]) The House thus yielded to twenty-four of the twenty-six Senate modifications, but remained resolute that the third proposed Article of amendment (the religion clauses) be revised from the Senate version so that it conformed to the wording in the Conference Committee's Report, *viz.:*

> Congress shall make no law respecting an establishment of religion, or prohibiting the free exercise thereof . . . [.][230]

That same day, the House of Representatives voted thirty-seven to fourteen—three votes more than the requisite two-thirds required by Article V of the Constitution[231]—to finalize its stance concerning the various proposed Articles of amendment.[232] The House instructed its clerk to notify the Senate accordingly.[233]

The Senate received notice of the House of Representatives' vote that same day; it received a report from the House which confirmed the latter's acquiescence in the Conference Committee's Report of September 24, 1789, and correlatively advised the Senate that the House had (1) "receded" from its disagreement as to all but two Senate modifications, and (2) urged a one-word change to another amendment.[234] The Senate thus learned that the House insisted that the proposed "Article the Third"—which by now included four other guarantees in addition to the two religion clauses[235]—begin with the words

"Congress shall make no law respecting an establishment of religion . . . [.]"[236]

The Senate postponed further consideration of the proposed Articles of amendment until the following day (September 25, 1789).[237]

Meanwhile, the House of Representatives separately resolved on September 24, 1789,

That the President of the United States be requested to transmit to the executives of the several states which have ratified the Constitution, copies of the amendments proposed by Congress to be added thereto; and like copies to the executives of the states of Rhode Island and North Carolina.[238]

(6). September 25, 1789
(Senate)

On September 25, 1789, the Senate concurred in the House of Representatives' modifications of the previous day[239] and so notified the House.[240] At this point, all congressional consideration of the proposed constitutional amendments ended.

The Senate also received the House's September 24, 1789, resolution to transmit the various Articles of amendment to the states.[241]

(7). September 26, 1789
(Senate)

On September 26, 1789, the Senate concurred in the House's proposed resolution to transmit the various Articles of amendment to the states.[242]

(8). September 28, 1789
(House of Representatives)

On September 28, 1789, the House of Representatives learned that the Senate had concurred in the resolution to have the President send the proposed amendments to the various states.[243]

D. Soon Thereafter

President Washington thereafter forwarded a joint congressional resolution to the various states, accompanied by a list of twelve proposed constitutional amendments styled as "Articles of Amendment."[244] The text of what has long since become the Establishment Clause appeared as the first ten words in proposed "Article III" in the list of twelve proposed amendments:

> Art. III. *Congress shall make no law respecting an establishment of religion,* or prohibiting the free exercise thereof; or abridging the freedom of speech, or of the press; or the right of the people peaceably to assemble, and to petition the Government for a redress of grievances.[245]

Before the 75 percent ratification threshold prescribed by the Constitution[246] had been achieved (*viz.,* ratifications by ten of the thirteen states that existed when the First Congress adjourned its first session in September 1789), Vermont became the fourteenth state on March 4, 1791.[247] At that point the requisite approval threshold increased to eleven state votes (*viz.,* 75 percent of fourteen).

When on December 15, 1791, Virginia voted to ratify eleven of the proposed amendments,[248] eleven of the then-existing fourteen state legislatures—at least 75 percent of the then-existing states per Article V of the Constitution—had ratified ten of the twelve proposed Articles of amendment:

- New Jersey   November 20, 1789   all except Article II[249]
- Maryland   December 19, 1989   all Articles[250]
- North Carolina   December 22, 1789   all Articles[251]
- South Carolina   January 19, 1790   all Articles[252]
- New Hampshire   January 25, 1790   all except Article II[253]
- Delaware   January 28, 1790   all except Article I[254]
- New York   February 24, 1790   all except Article II[255]
- Pennsylvania   March 10, 1790   all except Articles I and II[256]

- Rhode Island June 7, 1790 all except Article II[257]
- Vermont November 3, 1791 all except Article II[258]
- Virginia December 15, 1791 all Articles[259]

11 of 14 states=79%[260]

Although Congress had granted Kentucky statehood in early 1791 before Virginia's eleventh ratification vote,[261] the statehood act ordained an effective date of June 1, 1792.[262] Thus, the necessary 75 percent ratification threshold had already been achieved (via Virginia's December 15, 1791, vote) six months prior to the effective date of Kentucky's statehood. Although sources also report that Kentucky failed to return a ratification vote,[263] whether it did or not became immaterial when Virginia's vote served to ratify ten of the twelve proposed amendments.

With Virginia's ratification vote, the requisite three-fourths of the states had ratified proposed Articles of amendment three through twelve. Thus, those amendments became part of the Constitution at that point. However, the states had failed to ratify the first two of the twelve proposed Articles of amendment, a historical fortuity that promptly transformed "Article III" into the "First Amendment" (and which similarly transformed Articles IV through XII into the Second through Tenth Amendments, respectively). Proposed Article I had received only nine ratification votes when Virginia's vote resulted in a completed ratification of ten of the twelve amendments, and proposed Article II had by that time received only five ratification votes.

(The amendment proposed as Article I by the First Congress has yet to achieve the requisite votes from three-fourths of the states. However, the amendment proposed as Article II by the First Congress finally became the Constitution's twenty-seventh amendment effective May 7, 1992, two hundred years later, when Michigan and New Jersey simultaneously supplied the thirty-eighth vote and thirty-ninth vote necessary to achieve the requisite 75 percent ratification vote threshold.[264])

This detailed chronology of the 1789 congressional proceedings yields not the slightest suggestion that the author of the First Amendment's Establishment Clause wrote it for any reason except to implement at the federal (or "national") level of government the same kind of anti-establishment assurance(s) that the states themselves had already written into their own constitutions (or declarations of rights). It prohibited the congressional implementation of a classic national "establishment," but prohibited nothing more.

E. Why the Term "National" Disappeared
from Madison's Original Proposal

If one compared only the wording of Madison's original proposal with the wording of the Establishment Clause as ultimately approved by Congress and ratified by the states, it would be tempting to cite the disappearance of the term "national" as a congressional rebuff of Madison's goal of disabling Congress from implementing a "national" establishment (but nothing more). Those who would arrive at that conclusion purport to infer from those facts alone that the Establishment Clause must, therefore, mean something else entirely.[265] But those who would urge that conclusion all too conveniently ignore everything in the historical record that furnishes an indispensable context. And the context in which words arise simply cannot be jettisoned that readily; indeed, the rejection of context strains credibility.

If, on the one hand, nothing about the congressional proceedings between June 4, 1789, and September 25, 1789 (when Congress concluded its work and sent the proposed amendments to President Washington[266]), yielded facts sufficient to explain the reason why the term "national" disappeared, then certainly one would be entitled to infer that Congress, for some reason, indeed rebuffed Madison in that regard. But if, on the other hand, historical reality supplies facts sufficient not only to explain that disappearance but also to connect the disappearance to a reason wholly unrelated to establishment considerations, then the truth resides in the latter facts. And one can ignore facts only at one's peril.

> Historical reality proves formidable. Most embrace it as the unalterable truth. But to some it discredits contrary predispositions. Nevertheless, in the face of all the machinations that humanity concocts to deflect the intransigence of reality, the underlying truth never changes.[267]

Fortunately, history furnishes the underlying truth about the disappearance of the word "national."

On June 4, 1789, Madison proposed the following amendment in the House of Representatives:

> The civil rights of none shall be abridged on account of religious belief or worship, *nor shall any national religion be established,* nor shall the full and equal rights of conscience be in any manner, or on any pretext, infringed.[268]

The July 28, 1789, select committee report, however, contained no mention of the term "national," and the historical record furnishes no explanation.[269]

During the August 15, 1789, debates, Madison—who had served on the select committee[270]—supplied an explanation pertinent to the question posed in the caption of this final topic:

> MR. MADISON said, he apprehended the meaning of the words to be, that *Congress* should not establish a religion, and enforce the legal observation of it by law, nor compel men to worship God in any manner contrary to their conscience. . . . [T]hey had been required by some of the State Conventions, who seemed to entertain an opinion that . . . Congress . . . might infringe the rights of conscience, and *establish a national religion;* to prevent these effects he presumed the amendment was intended, and he thought it as well expressed as the nature of the language would admit.[271]

As you read those words, a single meaning emerges—a reason why Madison wrote what he wrote in the first place.

Representative Huntington understood Madison's goal:

> MR. HUNTINGTON said that he feared, with the gentlemen first up on this subject [*viz.*, Representative Silvester], that the words might be taken in such latitude as to be extremely hurtful to the cause of religion. *He understood the amendment to mean what had been expressed by the gentleman from Virginia* [*viz.*, Representative Madison]; but others might find it convenient to put another construction upon it. . . .[272]

(As explained in the August 15 debates, Huntington had a particular reason for his "fear.")

After some further remarks by other representatives, Madison reiterated the "national"-oriented impact of his proposed anti-establishment amendment:

> MR. MADISON thought, *if the word [*"*]national[*"*] was inserted before [*"*]religion[*"*]*, it would satisfy the minds of honorable gentlemen. . . . He thought *if the word [*"*]national[*"*] was introduced*, it would point the amendment directly to the object it was intended to prevent.[273]

No one disputed Madison's anti-national-establishment understanding (either on August 15 or at any other time), although Representative Gerry disliked the term "national" for a reason having nothing to do with establishment issues:

> MR. GERRY *did not like the term [*"*]national[*"*]*, proposed by the

gentleman from Virginia, and he hoped it would not be adopted by the House. It *brought to his mind some observations that had taken place in the conventions at the time they were considering the present constitution.* It had been insisted upon by those who were called antifederalists, that this form of Government consolidated the Union; the honorable gentleman's motion shows that he considers it in the same light. Those who were called antifederalists at that time complained that they had injustice done them by the title, because they were in favor of a Federal Government, and the others were in favor of a national one; the federalists were for ratifying the constitution as it stood, and the others not until amendments were made. . . .[274]

Representative Gerry's candid remarks on August 15, 1789, leave no rational doubt but that Gerry had in mind the contentious debates during the 1787 Constitutional Convention over Randolph's various proposed resolutions—the so-called Virginia Plan—that included the word "national." Gerry had been a Convention delegate, so he would know.[275] So, what happened during the 1787 Convention?

(1). Constitutional Convention Proceedings of May 29, 1787

On May 29, 1787, Randolph of Virginia introduced, as part of the "Virginia Plan" (actually, Madison's plan[276]) a resolution concerning "the establishment of a national government" in which the word "national" appears nineteen times:

1. Resolved that the articles of Confederation ought to be so corrected & enlarged as to accomplish the objects proposed by their institution; namely, "common defence [*sic*], security of liberty and general welfare."

2. Res[olve]d, therefore that the rights of suffrage in the *national* Legislature ought to be proportioned to the Quotas of contribution, or to the number of free inhabitants, as the one or the other rule may seem best in different cases.

3. Res[olve]d, that the *national* Legislature ought to consist of two branches.

4. Res[olve]d, that the members of the first branch of the *national* Legislature ought to be elected by the people of the several States every _____ for the term of _____; to be of the age of _____ years at least, to receive liberal stipends by which they may be compensated for the devotion of their time to public service; to be ineligible to any office established by a particular State, or under the authority of the

United States, except those beculiarly [*sic;* "peculiarly"] belonging to
the functions of the first branch, during the term of service, and for
the space of _____ after its expiration; to be incapable of re-election
for the space of _____ after the expiration of their term of service,
and to be subject to recall.

5. Resol[ve]d, that the members of the second branch of the
national Legislature ought to be elected by those of the first, out of
a proper number of persons nominated by the individual
Legislatures, to be of the age of _____ years at least; to hold their
offices for a term sufficient to ensure their independency, to receive
liberal stipends, by which they may be compensated for the devotion
of their time to public service; and to be ineligible to any office
established by a particular State, or under the authority of the
United States, except those peculiarly belonging to the functions of
the second branch, during the term of service, and for the space of
_____ after the expiration thereof.

6. Resolved, that each branch ought to possess the right of originating Acts; that the *national* Legislature ought to be impowered [*sic*] to
enjoy the Legislative Rights vested in Congress by the Confederation
& moreover to legislate in all cases to which the separate States are
incompetent, or in which the harmony of the United States may be
interrupted by the exercise of individual Legislation; to negative [*sic*]
all laws passed by the several States, contravening in the opinion of
the *national* Legislature the articles of Union; and to call forth the
force of the Union agst. [*sic*] any member of the Union failing to fulfill its duty under the articles thereof.

7. Res[olve]d, that a *national* Executive be instituted; to be chosen
by the *national* Legislature for the term of _____ years, to receive
punctually at stated times, a fixed compensation for the services rendered, in which no increase or diminution shall be made so as to
affect the Magistracy, existing at the time of increase or diminution,
and to be ineligible a second time; and that besides a general authority to execute the *national* laws, it ought to enjoy the Executive rights
vested in Congress by the Confederation.

8. Res[olve]d, that the Executive and a convenient number of the
national Judiciary, ought to compose a council of revision with authority to examine every act of the *national* Legislature before it shall operate, & every act of a particular Legislature before a Negative thereon
shall be final; and that the dissent of the said Council shall amount to
a rejection, unless the Act of the *national* Legislature be again passed,
or that of a particular Legislature be again negatived by _____ of the
members of each branch.

9. Res[olve]d, that a *national* Judiciary be established to consist of

one or more supreme tribunals, and of inferior tribunals to be chosen by the *national* Legislature, to hold their offices during good behaviour [*sic*]; and to receive punctually at stated times fixed compensation for their services, in which no increase or diminution shall be made so as to affect the persons actually in office at the time of such increase or diminution. [T]hat the jurisdiction of the inferior tribunals shall be to hear & determine in the first instance, and of the supreme tribunal to hear and determine in the dernier resort, all piracies & felonies on the high seas, captures from an enemy; cases in which foreigners or citizens of other States applying to such jurisdictions may be interested, or which respect the collection of the *national* revenue; impeachments of any *national* officers, and questions which may involve the *national* peace and harmony.

10. Resolv[e]d, that provision ought to be made for the admission of States lawfully arising within the limits of the United States, whether from a voluntary junction of Government & Territory or otherwise, with the consent of a number of voices in the *national* legislature less than the whole.

11. Res[olve]d, that a Republican Government & the territory of each State, except in the instance of a voluntary junction of Government & territory, ought to be guaranteed by the United States to each State[.]

12. Res[olve]d, that provision ought to be made for the continuance of Congress and their authorities and privileges, until a given day after the reform of the articles of Union shall be adopted, and for the completion of all their engagements.

13. Res[olve]d, that provision ought to be made for the amendment of the Articles of Union whensoever it shall seem necessary, and that the assent of the *national* Legislature ought not to be required thereto.

14. Res[olve]d, that the Legislative[,] Executive & Judiciary powers within the several States ought to be bound by oath to support the articles of Union[.]

15. Res[olve]d, that the amendments which shall be offered to the Confederation, by the Convention ought at a proper time, or times, after the approbation of Congress to be submitted to an assembly or assemblies of Representatives, recommended by the several Legislatures to be expressly chosen by the people, to consider & decide thereon.[277]

All but three of Randolph's proposed resolutions—numbers 1,

11, and 14—contained the word "National." In the following three weeks, the Convention would approve each of Randolph's proposals that contained the word "national."

(2). Constitutional Convention Proceedings of May 30, 1787

On May 30, 1787, the Convention's committee of the whole House—referenced from this point forward as simply the "Convention," unless specified otherwise—postponed consideration of Randolph's first proposed resolution in order to consider three new resolutions, the third of which read:

> Resolved that a *national* government ought to be established consisting of a Supreme Legislative [*sic*], Judiciary and Executive.[278]

By the end of the day, the Convention agreed to the following resolution:

> Resolved that it is the opinion of this Committee that a *national* government ought to be established consisting of a supreme Legislative [*sic; Legislature*], Judiciary, and Executive.[279]

Madison described the debate on that resolution as focused "less however on its general merits than on the force and extent of the particular terms *national* & *supreme.*"[280] Madison reported simply that Morris "explained the distinction between a *federal* and *national, supreme,* Govt,"[281] and he reported no other mention of the term "national" that day concerning the resolution at issue.[282]

(3). Constitutional Convention Proceedings of May 31, 1787

On May 31, 1787, the Convention agreed to Randolph's third proposed resolution:

> Resolved that the *national* legislature ought to consist of two branches.[283]

It further agreed to the following clause from Randolph's fourth proposed resolution:

> Resolved that the members of the first branch of the *national* legislature ought to be elected by the people of the several states[.][284]

The Convention then postponed consideration of the remainder of Randolph's fourth proposed resolution for that day.[285]

Next, the Convention *rejected* Randolph's fifth proposed resolution (*viz.:* "Resolved that the members of the second branch of the *national* legislature ought to be elected by those of the first[.]").[286] But it approved all but the final clause of Randolph's sixth proposed resolution (postponing consideration of that final clause):

> Resolved that each branch ought to possess the right of originating Acts; that the *national* Legislature ought to be impowered [*sic*] to enjoy the Legislative Rights vested in Congress by the Confederation & moreover to legislate in all cases to which the separate States are incompetent, or in which the harmony of the United States may be interrupted by the exercise of individual Legislation; to negative [*sic*] all laws passed by the several States, contravening in the opinion of the *national* Legislature the articles of Union[.][287]

(4). Constitutional Convention Proceedings of June 1, 1787

On June 1, 1787, the Convention approved the first clause of Randolph's seventh proposed resolution:

> Resolved that a *national* executive be instituted[.][288]

And it approved the following text to be added immediately after the preceding resolution:

> . . . with such power to carry into execution the *national* laws, to appoint to office in cases not otherwise provided for . . .[289]

(5). Constitutional Convention Proceedings of June 4, 1787

On June 4, 1787, the Convention postponed consideration of Randolph's eighth proposed resolution, agreeing instead to the following:

> Resolved that the *national* executive shall have a right to negative [*sic*] any legislative act which shall not be afterwards passed unless by two[-]thirds of each branch of the *national* legislature.[290]

It also approved the first clause of Randolph's ninth proposed resolution, as amended with additional language:

> Resolved that a *national* judiciary be established to consist of one supreme tribunal, and of one or more inferior tribunals[.][291]

(6). Constitutional Convention Proceedings of June 5, 1787

On June 5, 1787, the Convention deleted the phrases "one or more" and "and of inferior tribunals" from the first clause of Randolph's ninth proposed resolution as approved on June 4,[292] and added additional language as well as a blank to be filled in later, to then read:

> Resolved that a *national* judiciary be established to consist of one supreme tribunal, to be chosen by, _____, [and] that the *national* legislature be empowered to appoint inferior tribunals[.][293]

The Convention then postponed consideration of that part of Randolph's ninth proposed resolution that contained the term "national" in the last two clauses,[294] and approved Randolph's tenth proposed resolution:

> Resolved that provision ought to be made for the admission of States lawfully arising within the limits of the United States, whether from a voluntary junction of Government & Territory or otherwise, with the consent of a number of voices in the *national* legislature less than the whole.[295]

It also postponed consideration of Randolph's thirteenth proposed resolution, the only remaining resolution that contained the term "national."[296]

(7). Constitutional Convention Proceedings of June 7, 1787

On June 7, 1787, the Convention approved a substitute for Randolph's fifth proposed resolution (which the Convention had rejected on May 31):

> Resolved that the members of the second branch of the *national* Legislature ought to be chosen by the individual Legislatures.[297]

(8). Constitutional Convention Proceedings of June 11, 1787

On June 11, 1787, the Convention approved the following resolution, apparently as a substitute for the second of Randolph's proposals:

> Resolved that the right of suffrage in the first branch of the *national* Legislature ought not to be according to the rule established in the

articles of confederation[,] but according to some equitable ratio of representation [etc.].[298]

The Convention then approved the following related resolution:

Resolved that the right of suffrage in the second branch of the *national* Legislature ought to be according to the rule established for the first.[299]

It then postponed consideration of Randolph's thirteenth proposed resolution (the only remaining resolution that contained the term "national"),[300] and approved Randolph's fourteenth proposal.[301]

(9). Constitutional Convention Proceedings of June 12, 1787

On June 12, 1787, the Convention approved Randolph's fifteenth—and final—proposed resolution.[302]

(10). Constitutional Convention Proceedings of June 19, 1787

After another week of debates and further modifications to various proposals, on June 19, 1787, the Convention approved the following modified version of Randolph's initial resolutions, in which the word "national" appears twenty-six times:

"1. *Resolved,* That it is the opinion of this committee [of the whole House] that a *national* government ought to be established, consisting of a supreme legislative [*sic*], judiciary, and executive.

"2. *Resolved,* That the *national* legislature ought to consist of two branches.

"3. *Resolved,* That the members of the first branch of the *national* legislature ought to be elected by the people of the several states, for the term of three years; to receive fixed stipends, by which they may be compensated for the devotion of their time to public service, to be paid out of the *national* treasury; to be ineligible to any office established by a particular state, or under the authority of the United States, (except those peculiarly belonging to the functions of the first branch), during the term of service, and under the *national* government, for the space of one year after its expiration.

"4. *Resolved,* That the members of the second branch of the *national* legislature ought to be chosen by the individual legislatures; to be of the age of thirty years, at least; to hold their offices for a term sufficient to ensure their independency—namely, seven years; to receive fixed stipends, by which they may be compensated for the devotion of their time to public service, to be paid out of the *national* treasury; to be ineligible to any office established by a particular state, or under the authority of the United States (except those peculiarly belonging to the functions of the second branch), during the term of service, and under the *national* government, for the space of one year after its expiration.

"5. *Resolved,* That each branch ought to possess the right of originating acts.

"6. *Resolved,* That the *national* legislature ought to be empowered to enjoy the legislative rights vested in Congress by the Confederation; and, moreover, to legislate in all cases to which the separate states are incompetent, or in which the harmony of the United States may be interrupted by the exercise of individual legislation; to negative all laws passed by the several states contravening, in the opinion of the *national* legislature, the articles of union, or any treaties subsisting under the authority of the Union.

"7. *Resolved,* That the right of suffrage in the first branch of the *national* legislature ought not to be according to the rule established in the Articles of Confederation, but according to some equitable ratio of representation; namely, in proportion to the whole number of white and other free citizens, and inhabitants of every age, sex, and condition, including those bound to servitude for a term of years, and three[-]fifths of all other persons not comprehended in the foregoing description, except Indians, not paying taxes, in each state.

"8. *Resolved,* That the right of suffrage in the second branch of the *national* legislature ought to be according to the rule established for the first.

"9. *Resolved,* That a *national* executive be instituted, to consist of a single person; to be chosen by the *national* legislature, for the term of seven years; with power to carry into execution the *national* laws; to appoint to offices in cases not otherwise provided for; to be ineligible a second time; and to be removable on impeachment and conviction of malpractice, or neglect of duty; to receive a fixed stipend, by which he may be compensated for the devotion of his time to public service, to be paid out of the *national* treasury.

"10. *Resolved,* That the *national* executive shall have a right to negative any legislative act, which shall not be afterwards passed unless by two[-]third parts of each branch of the *national* legislature.

"11. *Resolved,* That a *national* judiciary be established, to consist of one supreme tribunal; the judges of which [are] to be appointed by the second branch of the *national* legislature; to hold their offices during good behavior; to receive punctually, at stated times, a fixed compensation for their services, in which no increase or diminution shall be made, so as to affect the persons actually in office at the time of such increase or diminution.

"12. *Resolved,* That the *national* legislature be empowered to appoint inferior tribunals.

"13. *Resolved,* That the jurisdiction of the *national* judiciary shall extend to cases which respect the collection of the *national* revenue, impeachment of any *national* officers, and questions which involve the *national* peace and harmony.

"14. *Resolved,* That provision ought to be made for admission of states, lawfully arising within the limits of the United States, whether from a voluntary junction of government and territory, or otherwise, with the consent of a number of voices in the *national* legislature less than the whole.

"15. *Resolved,* That provision ought to be made for the continuance of Congress and their authorities, until a given day after the reform of the articles of union shall be adopted, and for the completion of all their engagements.

"16. *Resolved,* That a republican constitution, and its existing laws, ought to be guarantied [*sic*] to each state by the United States.

"17. *Resolved,* That provision ought to be made for the amendment of the articles of union, whensoever it shall seem necessary.

"18. *Resolved,* That the legislative, executive, and judiciary powers, within the several states, ought to be bound, by oath, to support the articles of union.

"19. *Resolved,* That the amendments which shall be offered to the Confederation by the Convention, ought, at a proper time or times after the approbation of Congress, to be submitted to an assembly, or assemblies of representatives, recommended by the several legislatures to be expressly chosen by the people to consider and decide thereon."[303]

(11). Constitutional Convention Proceedings of June 20, 1787

On June 20, 1787, the full Convention—with Madison and other supporters of the "Virginia Plan" acceding—surrendered to the concerns of the states' rights advocates and voted unanimously to amend the first resolution approved by the Committee on May 30 and June 19, to remove the word "national" and insert the term "United States" instead.[304] Ellsworth, who moved the deletion, remarked that the term "national" appeared to imply that the Articles of Confederation no longer existed, when the Articles furnished the authority for the very proceedings.[305] (Randolph chided Ellsworth for not giving the real reason.[306])

In the following excerpt, brackets with strikeout ("[-]") signify deletions from the resolution approved on May 30 and June 19, while *italic* text represents text added by the Convention on June 20:

> Resolved that [~~a national~~] the government *of the United States* ought to [~~be established consisting~~] *consist* of a Supreme Legislative [*sic*], Judiciary and Executive.

Neither the Convention Journal nor Madison's own notes records the slightest quibble concerning the removal of the word "national" at that point. Madison reported simply that Ellsworth's motion "was acquiesced in"[307] and both Madison and Yates (another notekeeper) reported that the vote occurred "nem. con," an abbreviation for "nemine contradicente" or "without dissent."[308]

Two months after the Convention ended, Maryland delegate Luther Martin—a devoted states' rights proponent and anti-"national" delegate[309]—explained to the Maryland legislature the reason for the disappearance of the word "national":

> . . . Nay, so far were the friends of the system from pretending that they meant it, or considered it as a federal system, that on the question being proposed, "that a union of the States, merely federal, ought to be the sole object of the exercise of the powers vested in the convention," it was negatived [*sic*] by a majority of the members, and it was resolved "that a national government ought to be formed." Afterwards *the word "national" was struck out by them, because they thought the word might tend to alarm . . . [.]*

> Viewing it as a national, not a federal government, as calculated and designed not to protect and preserve, but to abolish and annihilate the State governments, it was opposed . . . [.][310]

Martin's view that a "national" government would obliterate state sovereignty scarcely proved unique during the 1787 Convention.

(Ironically, Martin did not even arrive at the 1787 Convention until June 9, 1787, well after the Convention had already approved most of Randolph's proposed resolutions that contained the word "national."[311] And Madison later reported that Martin and others "left the Convention long before it compleated [*sic*] its work[,] & appear to have reported in angry terms, what they had observed with jaundiced eyes."[312])

Madison's primary biographer described the June 20 replacement of "national" as more form than substance:

> At this jockeying stage, the words "a national government" in the first Virginia resolve was changed to "the government of the United States." This was done, Madison explained to jubilant State Righters who discovered it in 1819,[313] not to change the meaning, but merely to get rid of a term which might be liable to mistake or misrepresentation.[314]

Indeed, in one of his *Federalist* essays Madison had explained that

> . . . [t]he act, therefore, establishing the Constitution will not be a *national* but a *federal* act.

> That it will be a federal and not a national act, as these terms are understood by the objectors—the act of the people, as forming so many independent States, not as forming one aggregate nation—is obvious . . . [.] . . . In this relation, then, the new Constitution will, if established, be a *federal* and not a *national* constitution.[315]

Another of Madison's biographers similarly wrote that

> [t]he Wilson-Madison forces agreed to delete the word "national" from the first clause, to placate the states' rights men, a point Madison conceded because he was ready to accept a novel "composite" of national and federal principles.[316]

Professor Farrand, editor of the celebrated Farrand's *Records,* wrote in explanation that Madison (and others) simply allowed the term "national" to disappear after it became plain enough that the Constitutional Convention had, by June 20, 1787, already approved a new constitutional government sufficiently favorable that the term "national" could simply be negotiated away in favor of the replacement term "United States":

> The large-state men, having accomplished their main purpose, were now willing to make some concessions for the sake of harmony. For example, the objectionable word "national" was stricken out of

the first resolution by a unanimous vote, and it was "as of course" dropped out of each of the subsequent resolutions in turn.[317]

(The reference to "as of course" comes from Madison's description of the rest of the proceedings.[318])

Madison himself later wrote that no one ought suppose "that the term <u>national</u> as applied to the contemplated Government, in the early stage of the Convention, particularly in the propositions of Mr. Randolph, was equivalent to <u>unlimited</u> or consolidated."[319] Rather, wrote Madison, "[t]he term was used, not in contradistinction to a limited, but to a <u>federal</u> government."[320] He explained that "[t]he change [from "national" to "United States"] may be accounted for by a desire to avoid a misconception of the former, the latter being preferred as a familiar caption. That the change could have no effect on the real character of the Govt. [*sic*] was & is obvious[.]"[321]

In other letters, Madison clarified a misunderstanding to a professor of government who had supplied Madison with a copy of certain "lectures":

> What alone I mean to notice is a passage in which you have been misled by the authorities before you, & by a misunderstanding of the term "National" used in the early proceedings of the Convention of 1787. Both Mr. Yates and Mr. Martin brought to the Convention predispositions agt. [*sic*] its object . . . [.] With respect to the term "National" as contradistinguished from the term "federal," it was not meant to express the <u>extent</u> of power, but the <u>mode</u> of its operation, which was to be not like the power of the old Confederation operating on the States . . . [.] The term "National" was used in the original propositions offered on the part of the Virga. [*sic*] Deputies, not one of whom attached to it any other meaning than that here explained. . . .[322]

=>•◇•<=

> . . . [T]he term <u>National</u>, as contradistinguished from <u>Federal</u>, was not meant to express more than that the powers to be vested in the new Govt. [*sic*] were to operate as in a Natl. [*sic*] Govt. [*sic*] directly on the people, & not as in the Old Confedcy. [*sic*] on the States only.[323]

Two years after the 1787 Convention, Madison similarly acquiesced just as quietly during the First Congress's proceedings, after the select committee removed the word "national" from the text of what eventually became the Establishment Clause. He realized in the summer of 1789, as likely he (and others) did during the summer of 1787, that the inclusion of the term "national" proved desirable yet unnecessary, inasmuch as his proposed amendment could only apply to Congress in any event. And Madison further realized that any benefit of its inclusion scarcely measured up against the disadvantage that would arise from inclusion of such a divisive word so soon after the acrimonious ratification conventions in the states in 1787 and 1788. Indeed, Gerry's remarks on August 15, 1789, during the First Congress's debate confirmed Madison's perceptions.

Thus, history reveals the true context in which the term "national" disappeared from the Constitution in 1787, and why, for the same reason(s), it similarly disappeared from Madison's proposed constitutional amendment in 1789. Those who would arrive at some different conclusion remain unassisted by any historical context to the contrary.

6

The Meaning of "Meaning":
Words Mean Today, and Tomorrow,
What They Meant When Written

Someone once wrote that

[w]ords are to be understood in their ordinary and common acceptation[.][1]

That someone happened to be the United States Supreme Court—the author as well of this terse, three-sentence view of constitutional reality:

The Constitution is a written instrument. As such[,] its meaning does not alter. That which it meant when adopted, it means now.[2]

Although some disagree with that view of the Constitution, they do so because of the inherent nature of a "constitution," and not because of any disagreement with the notion that "meaning" of written words remains fixed. But, for purposes of the Establishment Clause, that generalized debate proves merely distractive, as the text of the Establishment Clause remains remarkably free from doubt for those who know its history.

With the conclusion of the preceding chapter, the history of the development of the words "respecting an establishment of religion" has been unfolded in its entirety. And that history, and the context that it supplies, affords no uncertainty concerning the meaning of those words when Congress authored the Establishment Clause in September 1789. "An establishment" meant . . .

• A *single,* dominant ecclesiastical institution (or, in the vernacular of the times, religion, church, denomination, faith, sect, creed, or religious society) that . . .

• enjoyed a government-*preferred,* government-*sanctioned,* government-*financed,* and government-*protected* status within a state, . . .

• and which represented an indistinguishable union with government and the preferred (or "established") ecclesiastical institution.

123

As one constitutional scholar puts it,

> [a]n uncontested and incontestable fact that stands out from the
> [E]stablishment [C]lause is that the United States cannot constitu-
> tionally enact any law *preferring* one church over others in any man-
> ner whatever.[3]

Yet despite the clarity of meaning that history affords, debates
tend to proliferate about the "meaning" of "the Constitution" as if
"the Constitution" comprised merely a concept, or as if it consisted
merely of lofty, imprecise phrases. Those debates endure for any
number of reasons:

• a tendency to apply a label to that which cannot so readily be
labeled;

• a tendency to conflate the Constitution's disparate provisions—
including the various amendments—into some solitary indeterminate concept;

• an inability to differentiate among the non-interchangeable
words "meaning," "intent," and "understanding";

• a tendency to view the Constitution as if "meaning" lacked qual-
ities of constancy and invariability;

• a tendency to view the Constitution as if the architects of language who purposefully and selectively assemble specific words to
express specific thoughts and meanings necessarily anticipate that
those thoughts and meanings might evolve and fluctuate according
to the whims of all manner of readers.

But each of those tendencies corrupts and obliterates "meaning."

Those who urge an "evolutionary" view of the "Constitution"—an
iconoclastic notion dependent upon evolving contemporary values
or subjective perspectives—advance their thesis solely in terms of
the *concept* of a "constitution," bypassing the reality that the
Constitution employs words that, for the most part, bear specific
meanings. Early twentieth-century Supreme Court justice Oliver
Wendell Holmes, a brilliant yet vainglorious legal mind who regularly deemed himself better able to discern the meaning of a statute or
constitutional provision than the latter's author,[4] appears to have
popularized that view of the Constitution. Indeed, former Supreme
Court chief justice William Rehnquist attributed the origin of the
oft-heard phrase "living constitution" to a 1920 Holmes opinion.[5]
(Holmes also claimed to have discerned an extraordinary law-based
"penumbra"—that is, a special shadow of sorts—and he wielded that

inherently imprecise term to characterize aspects of the law that he felt implicit but nonetheless absent.[6] To Holmes, it seemed, a "penumbra" lurked somewhere between the actual words in a law.)

Granted, some constitutional text leaves something to be desired in terms of clarity, and perhaps for some untold political reason the 1787 Constitutional Convention sought precisely that. "But likely the Convention delegates sought clarity."[7] That general debate, however, need not be resolved here; not only do the various constitutional amendments authored by the 1789 Congress represent something altogether different from the grand document produced by the 1787 Constitutional Convention, but the historical records testify to the certainty of meaning for the ten words in the Establishment Clause.

Two elemental truths simplify any debate.

First, words have "meaning" only within a specific, singular, idiosyncratic context; they have no meaning otherwise—no meaning divorced from the framework within which their author(s) assembled them. Correlatively, words relinquish "meaning" when deprived of context, and no rational argument could be made to the contrary. The world of homonyms supplies the proof; those who doubt the importance of context should try rendering a single correct definition for true homonyms like "affect," "bear," "call," "dash," "excise," "fast," "fathom," "glare," "graft," "hit," "inclination," "jam," "jerk," "keeper," "kind," "lap," "mark," "needle," "notice," "order," "pack," "seal," and "tense"—or, for that matter, "establishment"—without the benefit of an underlying context.

Those who believe that context is overrated should consider this fact: In 1855, Abraham Lincoln wrote that he preferred to live in Russia, but if anyone reported as much without the underlying context, that report would be inexcusably misleading; what Lincoln actually wrote yields an entirely different perspective:

> As a nation, we began by declaring that "all men are created equal." We now practically read it "all men are created equal, except Negroes." When [a certain political group] get control, it will read "all men are created equal, except Negroes and foreigners and Catholics." When it comes to this, I shall prefer emigrating to some country where they make no pretense of loving liberty—to Russia, for instance, where despotism can be taken pure and without the base alloy of hypocrisy[8]

Second, words written within a discrete context in 1789 continue to bear the meaning that they bore when written. Although the *thought, concept,* or *impression* expressed by a particular word may (or may not) change within a lifetime or later, once an author wields a *particular* word at a *particular* time to convey a *particular* thought, concept, or impression, the then-existing meaning of that word necessarily becomes, and thus remains, fixed. As if to underscore the reality of that elemental notion, even the detractors of fixed "meaning" expect their voluminous essays on the subject to benefit from the truth inherent in the previous sentence. Any *subsequent* view, perspective, belief, or understanding necessarily remains merely an *interpretation,* but certainly not a new or different "meaning."

James Madison once worded these thoughts more tersely still:

> [T]he legitimate meaning of the instrument must be derived from the text itself[.][9]

Unfortunately, some who occupy—or have occupied—seats on the Supreme Court have been purposefully disdainful of that truth.[10]

Those who find it difficult to accept the above truths persist with discussions that wield problematic terms like "original intent." But "intent" does not necessarily yield "meaning," although they may well coincide. In fact, the term "original intent" itself makes no sense; not only does the superfluous modifier "original" serve no articulable purpose (as it implies the existence of some other type of "intent") but the term "intent" itself misleads; an author's "intent" may or may not comport with the words actually written, and may be unexpressed or expressed unclearly. The *words* control, not writers' "intent;" the meaning of their words derives from the words alone, as assembled within a specific context, and not from any enigmatic "intent" divined from some other source at some other time. Words presumably *convey* "intent." And if one neglects or fails altogether to express one's "intentions" within the confines of the words that one employs, then "intent" remains inconsequential.

Terms like "original meaning" fare no better, as the modifier "original" suggests the existence of some other kind of "meaning" that develops at some later point in time. Only when an author crafts an inherently equivocal product does the search for "meaning" move beyond the words themselves. At that point, although the words still bear intrinsic meaning, the *correct* meaning becomes apparent only from context and, if available and reliable, the author's contemporaneous declaration(s) of meaning. (James Madison said precisely the same thing less than two years after the

First Congress authored the Establishment Clause.[11]) And, finally, if an author's product remains hopelessly indefinite, then its "meaning" becomes nothing more than speculation.

Thus, words within a unique context bear a unique "meaning"—*the* meaning—ascribed by the author when written. Authors mean what they write when they write it, and they write with neither the intention, nor the supposition, nor the apprehension that the meaning of their words might change over time. It may well be true that the meanings of *language in general* may change with time, but, once committed to writing, meaning does not—indeed, cannot—fluctuate.

The 1789 Congress furnished sufficient documentary history of the creation of the text that became the Establishment Clause that the Clause's purpose, function, and meaning can be known with an objective certainty. The Establishment Clause further benefits from the reality that Congress wrote it for a specific reason and tailored it to have a singular purpose and function, and the historical records confirm as much with an objective simplicity.

The historical record reveals that at no point during any of the various debates in the House of Representatives[12] concerning the text that became the Establishment Clause did anyone question the meaning or import of the phrase "respecting an establishment of religion." Unlike commentators who, hundreds of years after the fact, foment academic quibbles over imagined differences among terms like "religion," "church," "denomination," "faith," "sect," "creed," and "religious society," neither Madison nor anyone else in the First Congress perceived any distinctions between or among those terms within the context of the "establishment"; to the contrary, speakers and writers wielded these terms interchangeably throughout the 1600s and 1700s.

Then-contemporary legal scholars well understood the plain meaning of the text of the Establishment Clause. Although not dispositive of the meaning of the phrase "an establishment of religion," the published views of such contemporaries certainly outweigh the views of those centuries removed. Two of the most prominent nineteenth-century commentators on the Constitution—longtime Supreme Court justice Joseph Story[13] and nineteenth-century constitution law expert Professor Thomas Cooley[14]—agreed that, although the Establishment Clause certainly barred Congress from implementing a preferred, dominant *national* ecclesiastical institution with the exclusive patronage of the federal government, it most certainly did *not* proscribe complete governmental disassociation with all things "religious" in nature.

For instance, Justice Story, who knew the Establishment Clause's context, purpose, function, and meaning as well as any of his late eighteenth-century and early nineteenth-century contemporaries, wrote:

> Now, there will probably be found few persons in this, or any other, Christian country, who would deliberately contend, that it was unreasonable, or unjust[,] to foster and encourage the Christian religion generally, as a matter of sound policy, as well as of revealed truth. In fact, every American colony, from its foundation down to the revolution, with the exception of Rhode Island (if, indeed, that state be an exception) did *openly, by the whole course of its laws and institutions, support and sustain, in some form, the Christian religion; and almost invariably gave a peculiar sanction to some form of its fundamental doctrines. . . .* Indeed, in a republic, there would seem to be a peculiar propriety in viewing the Christian religion as the great basis on which it must rest for its support and permanence.[15]

⇒◇⇐

> Probably at the time of the adoption of . . . the [Establishment Clause], the general if not the universal sentiment in American was that *Christianity ought to receive encouragement from the State so far as was not incompatible* with the private rights of conscience and the freedom of religious worship. An attempt to level all religions, and to make it a matter of state policy to hold all in utter indifference, would have created universal disapprobation, if not universal indignation.[16]

⇒◇⇐

> The *real object of the [First] amendment* was, not to countenance, much less to advance Mahometanism [*sic*], or Judaism, or infidelity, by prostrating Christianity; but to *exclude all rivalry* among Christian sects, and *to prevent any national ecclesiastical establishment,* which should give to an hierarchy the exclusive patronage of the national government.[17]

⇒◇⇐

> In some of the states, [E]piscopalians constituted the predominant sect; in others, [P]resbyterians; in others, [C]ongregationalists; in others, [Q]uakers; and in others again, there was a close numerical rivalry among contending sects. It was impossible, that there should not arise perpetual strife and perpetual jealousy on the subject of ecclesiastical ascendancy, if the national government were left free to create a religious establishment. . . . *Thus, the whole power over the subject of religion is left exclusively to the state governments, to be acted upon according to their own sense of justice, and the state constitutions[.]*[18]

Justice Story's observations scarcely stand as the perspective of a lone commentator; one need only recall that, in the words of the Supreme Court itself written more than a century closer to the creation of the Establishment Clause than the current Court, " [T]his is a Christian nation."[19]

Professor Cooley wrote similarly:

> *It was never intended by the Constitution that the government should be prohibited from recognizing religion,* or that religious worship should never be provided for in cases where a proper recognition of Divine Providence in the working of government might seem to require it, and where it might be done without drawing any invidious distinctions between different religious beliefs, organizations, or sects. *The Christian religion was always recognized in the administration of the common law; and so far as that law continues to be the law of the land, the fundamental principles of that religion must continue to be recognized in the same cases and to the same extent as formerly.* The propriety of making provisions for the appointment of chaplains for the two houses of Congress, and for the army and navy, has been sometimes questioned; but the general sentiment of the country has approved it, and the States make corresponding provision for legislative bodies and state institutions.[20]

Justice Story, whose celebrated 1833 *Commentaries on the Constitution of the United States* remained the preeminent treatise on that subject until the late 1800s and endures today as one of the most-cited treatises, wrote similarly in his landmark opinion in *Terrett v. Taylor,*[21] the Supreme Court's first opinion to explore a church/state relationship and disestablishment considerations arising from the disestablishment of the Church of England in Virginia. *Terrett* posed the question whether the Virginia legislature possessed the requisite authority to repeal a late eighteenth-century law which ensured that all lands then held by the formerly established Church of England remained Church property. In 1801, as the final step in the disestablishment of the Church of England in Virginia, the state legislature repealed that earlier law as, in its opinion, inconsistent with Virginia's 1776 Declaration of Rights[22] and Virginia's 1786 Act Establishing Religious Freedom.[23]

The Supreme Court declared Virginia's 1801 repeal void, concluding that it interfered with the vested property rights of the Church of England (or the Anglicans [Episcopalians]), notwithstanding the reality that the earlier law had singularly benefited the Church. In so doing, the Court necessarily concluded that a *non*-preferential law that served no "establishment" considerations whatsoever did not run afoul of the Virginia religious-freedom enactments; as Justice Story explained, no establishment concerns presented themselves in the absence of any governmental *preference,* governmental *coercion,* or governmental *financial support* of a *single,* dominant ecclesiastical institution:

> It is conceded on all sides that, at the revolution, the Episcopal church no longer retained its character as an exclusive religious establishment. And there can be no doubt that it was competent to the people and to the legislature to deprive it of its superiority over other religious sects, and to withhold from it any support by public taxation. But, although it may be true that "religion can be directed only by reason and conviction, not by force or violence," and that "all men are equally entitled to the free exercise of religion according to the dictates-of-conscience," as the bill of rights of Virginia declares,[24] yet *it is difficult to perceive how it follows as a consequence that the legislature may not enact laws more effectually to enable all sects to accomplish the great objects of religion by giving them corporate rights for the management of their property, and the regulation of their temporal as well as spiritual concerns.* Consistent with the constitution of Virginia the legislature could not create or continue a religious establishment which should have *exclusive rights and prerogatives,* or *compel the citizens to worship* under a stipulated form or discipline, or to *pay taxes to those whose creed they could not conscientiously believe.* . . . While, therefore, *the legislature might exempt the citizens from a compulsive attendance and payment of taxes in support of any particular sect, it is not perceived that either public or constitutional principles required the abolition of all religious corporations.*[25]

Unfortunately, the Supreme Court's subsequent expositions on the Establishment Clause, explained in detail in Chapters 14 and 15, have inexplicably ignored Story's insight and commentaries—a particularly odd circumstance given the reality that Story served on the Court. Indeed, the Court never mentioned Story's commentaries until 1984,[26] by which time the Court had written twenty-nine opinions in which it discussed the Establishment Clause.[27] And even then, the Court referenced but a single sentence from the excerpts quoted just above; it only quoted Story's observation that

> "The real object of the [First] Amendment was . . . to prevent any national ecclesiastical establishment, which should give to an hierarchy the exclusive patronage of the national government."[28]

One can only ask how many times must someone like James Madison or Justice Story confirm the well-known historical context, purpose, function, and meaning—and correlative limits—of the term "establishment"? Those prominent individuals who witnessed the birth of the Establishment Clause have long left it as plain as plain might ever be that the Establishment Clause served *not* to prevent *general* governmental encouragement of "religion" or "religious activities," but only to prevent Congress from recognizing any *single* government-*preferred*, government-*sanctioned*, government-*financed* ecclesiastical institution by the newly formed national government.

Some might argue that the members of the First Congress who crafted the Establishment Clause could never have envisioned that, hundreds of years later, their elegant wordsmithing might yet retain the meaning that its authors accorded it by the words that they selected. But, in order to accept that notion, one must believe not only that words written in 1789 (or any time in the past) could not be expected to retain their meaning over time, but must further believe that authors actually contemplate as much. To describe that belief as irrational would be to shroud its absurdity in understatement. Ironically, advocates of that notion necessarily embrace the hypocritical stance that the meaning of *their writings* on that very subject will not change over time.

The 1789 Congress had no idea how long the Constitution—or the First Amendment—might endure; thus it could scarcely have written the Establishment Clause with the implicit assumption that cultural or societal changes might alter the meaning of the words "Congress shall make no law respecting an establishment of religion" simply because of the passage of time. Indeed, that notion represents the very antithesis of that which the First Congress desired.[29]

Furthermore, the fact that the 1787 Constitutional Convention implemented a specific, and exclusive, amendment process in Article V of the Constitution obliterates the notion that it could have envisioned that changes in meaning might occur simply by the passage of time; Article V provided in 1787, and still provides:

> The Congress, whenever two[-]thirds of both Houses shall deem it necessary, shall propose Amendments to this Constitution, or, on the Application of the Legislatures of two[-]thirds of the several States, *shall call a Convention for proposing Amendments*, which, in either Case, shall be valid to all Intents and Purposes, as Part of this Constitution, when ratified by the Legislatures of three[-]fourths of the several States, or by Conventions in three[-]fourths thereof, as the one or the other Mode of Ratification may be proposed by the Congress[.] . . .[30]

Constitution or no Constitution, an author would scarcely provide a unique amendment process for a specific document unless the author desired that any alterations of meaning or content could only occur via that process. Indeed, the United States Supreme Court first embraced that reality in its 1793 decision in *Chisholm v. Georgia*[31]:

> If the Constitution is found inconvenient in practice in this or any other particular, it is well that a regular mode is pointed out for amendment.[32]

James Madison, the architect and chief protagonist of the First Amendment's religion clauses, left little doubt concerning his agreement with the realities of the last few paragraphs:

> . . . I entirely concur in the propriety of resorting to the sense in which the Constitution was accepted and ratified by the nation. In that sense alone it is the legitimate Constitution. And if that be not the guide in expounding it, there can be no security for a consistent and stable, more than for a faithful[,] exercise of its powers. If the meaning of the text be sought in the changeable meaning of the words composing it, it is evident that the shape and attributes of the Government must partake of the changes to which the words and phrases of all living languages are constantly subject. *What a metamorphosis would be produced in the code of law if all its ancient phraseology were to be taken in the modern sense.*[33]

Madison also lamented of a condition that, unfortunately, remains unabated:

> . . . [T]hat the language of our Constitution is already undergoing interpretations unknown to its founders, will, I believe, appear to all unbiased enquirers [*sic*] into the history of its origin and adoption. . . .[34]

⇒◆⇐

> It may often happen, as experience proves, that erroneous constructions, not anticipated, may not be sufficiently guarded against in the language used; and it's due to the distinguished individuals who have misconceived that intention of those proceedings to suppose that the meaning of the legislature, though well comprehended at the time, may not now be obvious to those unacquainted with the contemporary indications and impressions.[35]

In other words, some folks lamentably disregard contextual meaning in order to advocate some varying or evolutionary "meaning."

In a criticism of United States Supreme Court chief justice John

Marshall's tendency to pontificate upon matters wholly unnecessary to the cases before the Court,[36] Thomas Jefferson echoed Madison's views of "meaning" as dependent upon words used in a specific, historical context:

> . . . On every question of construction, carry ourselves back to the time when the constitution was adopted, recollect the spirit manifested in the debates, and instead of trying what meaning may be squeezed out of the text, or invented against it, conform to the probable one in which it was passed. . . .[37]

Unfortunately, during the House of Representatives' proceedings in the summer of 1789 no one slipped James Madison a note reminding him to add the following three-sentence prologue to the various constitutional amendments that Congress passed that summer and sent to the states for ratification:

> As Congress approves of these various amendments, it means what it says in the text of the amendments, and it writes with neither the intention nor the apprehension that the meaning of that text will change over time. The meaning of the various amendments shall derive from the ordinary meaning of the words themselves, a meaning inextricably linked to the historical context from which they have emerged. And, as if we need say it, the meaning of the various amendments shall not derive from commentary that post-dates Congress's approval of the same.

Then again, Madison could scarcely have envisioned that future generations could wreak havoc with constitutional text.

⸺⯈◆⯇⸺

All of that having been said, no discussion of constitutional "meaning" would be complete—or faithful to all that history affords—without some mention of a peculiar historical circumstance unique to the Constitution itself. Some might insist that it upsets everything just said, but most recognize it as a quirk of any ratification process. The circumstance involves the effect of one of the ratification processes prescribed by the Constitution,[38] and the way James Madison viewed the significance of that process *vis-à-vis* "meaning."

Madison augmented his advocacy of constitutional "meaning" as derived from the words themselves with the politically motivated notion[39] that, because the Constitution bore no substance unless and until ratified, the "understanding" of the ratifiers—the states—must be considered as well.[40] However, that Madisonion gloss on "meaning" originated with the political reality that the ratifiers themselves rendered the Constitution's text *operative,* and thus, to Madison's thinking, accorded it an enduring "meaning." Indeed, constitutional text bears no *operative* "meaning" until ratification occurs. But, although the various ratifying states no doubt entertained some *understanding* of constitutional text, in reality the ratifiers themselves actually added nothing to the *meaning* of the words that they ratified.

During a 1796 debate about the Constitution's treaty provisions, Madison explained his "meaning-comes-from-ratification" viewpoint:

> But, after all, whatever veneration might be entertained for the body of men who formed our Constitution, the sense of that body could never be regarded as the oracular guide in expounding the Constitution. As the instrument came from them it was nothing more than the draft of a plan, nothing but a dead letter, until life and validity were breathed into it by the voice of the people, speaking through the several State Conventions. If we were to look, therefore, for the meaning of the instrument beyond the face of the instrument, we must look for it, not in the General Convention, which proposed, but in the State Conventions, which accepted and ratified the Constitution.[41]

Of course, in 1787 and 1788 the various state ratifying conventions merely accepted or rejected the Constitution "as is"; they neither added to, nor subtracted from, its text (although they did propose amendments). But Madison's remarks originated with a different consideration altogether; for years after the 1787 Convention's creation of the Constitution, Madison and others feared the possibility of political backlash if the Convention delegates could not convince skeptics that the *states* had actually "created" the Constitution, and not simply the thirty-nine individuals who signed it.[42] (Today that dilemma might well be termed "media spin.")

And, like Madison, when others suggest that one needs to explore the unknown "understandings" of "ratifiers" in order to determine "meaning," they have in mind Madison's notion that the states themselves gave the Constitution "meaning" by breathing life into it:

> The Constitution became supreme law not because it was proposed by the Federal Convention of 1787, but because it was ratified by the state conventions of 1787–88. *By this criterion,* the *intentions of the framers were legally irrelevant* to its interpretation, but the *understandings of the ratifiers* could provide a legitimate basis for attempting to fix the original meaning of the Constitution.[43]

Certainly the unknown *"intentions* of the framers"—*viz.*, either the 1787 Constitutional Convention with respect to the Constitution or the 1789 Congress with respect to the Bill of Rights—would be "legally irrelevant," because, as explained earlier, *words* convey "intent" and thus render "intent" superfluous. But the notion that the *ratifiers'*—*viz.*, the *states'*—"understandings" assumes any importance remains problematic, for at least three reasons:

• *First,* no historical record furnishes anything that truly merits the label "understandings of the ratifiers" with respect to either the Constitution or the Bill of Rights.

• *Second,* the "ratifiers" could neither add to nor subtract from the text of the document to be ratified, *viz.*, either the Constitution as presented to them by the 1787 Constitutional Convention or the Establishment Clause as presented to them by the First Congress (via President Washington); they either accepted the meaning of the words as already authored, or they rejected it. But the "ratifiers" most certainly expressed no "understandings" about "meaning" that might be gleaned from a vote to ratify.

• *Third,* by the time the First Congress finished its authorship of the Establishment Clause in September 1789, the words "Congress shall make no law respecting an establishment of religion" *already* bore "meaning"; indeed, Congress sought the states' approval of that meaning. If anything, in that circumstance the "ratifiers" made their views known *before* Congress ever wrote the Establishment Clause.

But for the fact that Madison himself abided by this ratification-specific view of "meaning," the last few paragraphs would likely bear scant pertinence to any discussion of constitutional "meaning."

7

The Author's Own Understanding: Congress's Contemporaneous Acts in 1789

Although the purpose, function, and meaning of the words that comprise the Establishment Clause have long been apparent from the words themselves as used within the historical context of the 1789 congressional proceedings, contemporaneous (or near-contemporaneous) compositions by the same author that embrace the same subject matter can, and in this case do, furnish independent verifications of that meaning. Even James Madison recognized that "[c]ontemporary and concurrent expositions are a reasonable evidence of the meaning of the parties."[1] And, not insignificantly, the United States Supreme Court has said as much—more than once.

Chisholm v. Georgia (1793)[2]: Barely two years after the ink had dried on the Constitution, the First Congress enacted the Judiciary Act of 1789[3]—legislation that established the cornerstone of what has become the federal judiciary system, and the first bill ever introduced in Congress; the Senate began debate of the Judiciary Act on June 12, 1789, just two months after it first attained a quorum on April 6, 1789.[4]

Although Article III of the Constitution establishes the "judicial power" of the Supreme Court and all other federal courts, that power has never been considered "self-executing" in the sense that it needs no legislation in order to implement it; to the contrary, the Constitution endowed Congress with the authority to enact laws that implemented the constitutional powers of the federal courts—and the Supreme Court itself so ruled early on.[5] And the 1789 Judiciary Act served as the essential legislative implementation of the Constitution's judicial authority.

Among other things, the 1789 Judiciary Act implemented that part of Article III of the Constitution which authorizes the Supreme Court to decide certain type of "cases" and "controversies."[6] The dispute in *Chisholm* posed the question of whether the 1789 Judiciary Act—

which, oddly, received but the briefest of references in the Supreme Court's decision[7]—exceeded the authority in Article III by authorizing the federal courts to resolve litigation brought by a citizen against a state. A Georgia citizen sued the state of Georgia directly in the Supreme Court, and the state insisted that Article III of the Constitution did not subject states to Supreme Court jurisdiction in that manner. If Georgia's argument proved correct, then the 1789 Congress had enacted an unconstitutional law.

Although the 1789 Congress and the 1787 Constitutional Convention technically represent distinct institutional authors, in reality many members of the First Congress had also been delegates at the 1787 Constitutional Convention. Indeed, the author of the 1789 Judiciary Act—Senator Ellsworth[8]—had been an influential participant in the 1787 Convention.

Of the ten senators appointed by the inaugural Senate to a committee "to bring in a bill for organizing the Judiciary of the United States" (Ellsworth, Bassett, Carroll, Few, Izard, Lee, Maclay, Paterson, Strong, and Wingate[9]), five—Ellsworth, Bassett, Few, Paterson, and Strong—had served as delegates to the 1787 Constitutional Convention.[10] Moreover, of the Senate's twenty-two senators in 1789 (two from each of the ratifying states except North Carolina and Rhode Island[11]) ten had been delegates to the 1787 Convention.[12] In the House of Representatives (which also voted on the Senate's proposed Judiciary Act), eight of the fifty-nine representatives during the First Session of the First Congress in 1789[13] had been delegates to the 1787 Convention.[14]

The Supreme Court concluded, correctly,[15] that the 1789 Judiciary Act did not run afoul of the Constitution, but, instead, proved consistent with it. Although the *Chisholm* decision did not say so in so many words, it would be silly to ignore the reality that the Court in fact viewed the 1798 Judiciary Act as a contemporaneous composition by much of the same group that had just authored the Constitution. In fact, the Court said just that in two subsequent decisions (below).

Ames v. Kansas (1884)[16]: In *Ames,* the Court again confronted a dispute concerning the Supreme Court's jurisdiction conferred by Article III, Section 2, of the Constitution (as now affected by the Eleventh Amendment). Concluding that related jurisdictional provisions in Congress's 1789 Judiciary Act—which still controlled ninety-five years later—served to clarify the Constitution in that respect, the Court remarked that

[i]t thus appears that the first congress, in which were many who had been leading and influential members of the convention, and who were familiar with the discussions that preceded the adoption of the constitution by the states, and with the objections urged against it, wrote the 1789 Judiciary Act to reflect the meaning of Article III, Section 2, of the Constitution.[17]

As such, the 1789 Congress rendered a near-contemporaneous construction of the Constitution via the 1789 legislation—a construction that warranted deferential respect given the reality that the First Congress consisted of many Constitutional Convention delegates.[18]

The *Ames* opinion resolved the dispute not simply by relying upon the apparent meaning of the words of Article III, Section 2, of the Constitution, but also "[i]n view of the practical construction put on this provision of the constitution by congress at the very moment of the organization of the government[.]"[19] Thus, as it did in *Chisholm*, the Court (again) viewed the 1798 Judiciary Act as a near-contemporaneous composition relating to a constitutional power, thus furnishing an independent verification of meaning.

Wisconsin v. Pelican Insurance Co. (1888)[20]: In *Pelican Insurance Co.*, the Supreme Court again declared that a particular provision of the 1789 Judiciary Act that defined an aspect of the Supreme Court's jurisdiction constituted "contemporaneous and weighty evidence of [the] true meaning" of Article III, Section 2 (by then amended by the Eleventh Amendment).[21]

Myers v. United States (1926)[22]: In *Myers*, in a lengthy 1926 opinion that examined the extent of the president's constitutional appointment and removal powers, the Supreme Court declared that the relationship between the outcome of the 1787 Constitutional Convention and related legislation enacted by the First Congress just two years later—in that case, the 1789 law that established the Executive Department[23]—could scarcely be exaggerated:

> What, then, are the elements that enter into our decision of this case? We have, first, a construction of the Constitution made by a Congress [*viz.*, the 1789 Congress] which was to provide by legislation for the organization of the government in accord with the Constitution which had just then been adopted, and in which there were, as Representatives and Senators, a considerable number of those who had been members of the convention that framed the Constitution and presented it for ratification. It was the Congress that launched the government. It was the Congress that rounded out the

Constitution itself by the proposing of the first 10 amendments . . . [.]
It was a Congress whose constitutional decisions have always been
regarded, as they should be regarded, as of the greatest weight in the
interpretation of that fundamental instrument. . . . This court has
repeatedly laid down the principle that *a contemporaneous legislative expo-*
sition of the Constitution, when the founders of our government and framers of
our Constitution were actively participating in public affairs, acquiesced in for
a long term of years, fixes the construction to be given its provisions.[24]

Congress has similarly furnished a host of contemporaneous
actions that independently substantiate the purpose, function, and
meaning of the Establishment Clause.

A. Congress's 1789 Appointment of Taxpayer-Funded Chaplains

In session for only about a month, on April 25, 1789, the inaugural
Senate appointed a chaplain as one of its first official acts,[25] and on
May 1, 1789, the inaugural House of Representatives did likewise.[26]

A month prior to the adjournment of that inaugural congressional session, on August 10, 1789, the House passed a bill that included
taxpayer-funded compensation for the congressional chaplains.[27]
The Senate approved that bill on August 31, 1789,[28] and, after the
Senate agreed to certain House amendments, both houses sent the
chaplain compensation measure to President Washington on
September 14, 1789, for signature.[29] President Washington signed it
on September 22, 1789[30]—three days before Congress approved the
text of the Establishment Clause.

Those legislative acts by the institutional author of the
Establishment Clause belie the notion, advanced two centuries later
by secular "separation" advocates, that the Establishment Clause
compels the government to completely disassociate itself from
generic "religious" subject matter or "religious activities." Not only
do both houses of Congress continue to have paid chaplains,[31] but
both the Senate and the House of Representatives also open their
daily sessions with prayer in accordance with their respective rules.[32]

In its 1983 decision in *Marsh v. Chambers*,[33] the Supreme Court
resolved the question of whether the Nebraska Legislature's practice
of opening each legislative day with a nondenominational (*viz.*, non-
preferential) prayer by a chaplain paid by the State ran afoul of the
Establishment Clause. Given the historical reality that in that same

legislative session the author of the Establishment Clause also provided for taxpayer-funded congressional chaplains, the answer to the question would seem all too apparent. Answering that question with a resounding "no," the Court acknowledged the reality that

> [t]he opening of sessions of legislative and other deliberative public bodies with prayer is deeply embedded in the history and tradition of this country,[34]

and declared, correctly, that

> [f]rom colonial times through the founding of the Republic and ever since, the practice of legislative prayer has coexisted with the principles of disestablishment and religious freedom.[35]

More importantly, though, the Court abided by the historical reality that, as detailed above, the same Congress that wrote the Establishment Clause also authorized congressional chaplains to open each daily session of Congress with prayer—a tradition actually carried over from the pre-constitutional Continental Congresses.[36] Thus, the Court acknowledged the obvious and the incontestable: the institutional author of the Establishment Clause perceived no incongruity between the meaning of that Clause and the practice of nondenominational prayers in the nation's legislative assemblies:

> Clearly the men who wrote the First Amendment Religion Clauses did not view paid legislative chaplains and opening prayers as a violation of that Amendment, for the practice of opening sessions with prayer has continued without interruption ever since that early session of Congress. . . .

> Standing alone, historical patterns cannot justify contemporary violations of constitutional guarantees, but there is far more here than simply historical patterns. In this context, historical evidence sheds light not only on what the draftsmen intended the Establishment Clause to mean, but also on how they thought that Clause applied to the practice authorized by the First Congress—their actions reveal their intent. An Act

>> "passed by the first Congress assembled under the Constitution, many of whose members had taken part in framing that instrument, . . . is contemporaneous and weighty evidence of its true meaning."[37]

The Court's opinion in *Marsh* also supplied what might well be considered the most understated characterization of the historical reality that the text of the Establishment Clause never served to purge "religion" in general (or "religious activities") from government; after observing that, just days before the First Congress approved the Establishment Clause it had enacted legislation that authorized compensation for the chaplains of the Senate and the House of Representatives,[38] the Court declared that:

> [i]t can hardly be thought that[,] in the same week Members of the First Congress voted to appoint and to pay a chaplain for each House and also voted to approve the draft of the First Amendment for submission to the states, they intended the Establishment Clause of the Amendment to forbid what they had just declared acceptable.[39]

Indeed. The *Marsh* opinion also comments that, "interestingly" (the Court's term), on the very day that Congress delivered the initial set of proposed constitutional amendments to President Washington to forward to the states, it adopted its initial Thanksgiving Proclamation in which Congress again specifically referenced prayer.[40]

B. Congress's 1789 Judiciary Act

On September 24, 1789, Congress created the federal court system via the 1789 Judiciary Act.[41] As relevant here, that Act prescribed the following oaths:

> SEC. 7 . . . [T]he Supreme Court, and the district courts[,] shall have the power to appoint clerks for their respective courts, . . . and each of the said clerks shall, before he enters upon the execution of his office, take the following oath or affirmation, to wit: "I, A.B., being appointed clerk of _____, do solemnly swear or affirm, . . . that I will faithfully and impartially discharge and perform all the duties of my office, according to the best of my abilities and understanding. *So help me God.*" Which words, ["]so help me God,["] shall be omitted in all cases where an affirmation is admitted instead of an oath. . . .
>
> SEC. 8 . . . [T]he justices of the Supreme Court, and the district judges, before they proceed to execute the duties, shall take the following oath or affirmation, to wit: "I, A.B., do solemnly swear or affirm, . . . that I will faithfully and impartially discharge and perform all the duties incumbent on me as _____, according to the best of my abilities and understanding, agreeably to the constitution and laws of the United States. *So help me God.*"[42]

The references to "[s]o help me God" in that law—authored by Congress one day before it approved the Establishment Clause— prove consistent with the purpose, function, and meaning of the Establishment Clause within the historical context in which the 1789 Congress wrote it, *viz.*, the disablement of the federal government from implementing any single, preferred national ecclesiastical institution with the exclusive patronage of the federal government—nothing more.

And federal law continues to reference "God" in the oath of office for federal court judges.[43]

C. Congress's 1789 Renewal of the Northwest Territory Ordinance

Few folks likely recall either the 1787 "Northwest Ordinance" or its renewal by the 1789 Congress. But that congressional enactment expressly acknowledged not only that "religion, morality, and knowledge" remain essential to "good government," but that "schools and the means of education" prove indispensable to the attainment of "religion, morality, and knowledge."

On September 18, 1786, the Second Continental Congress appointed a committee to prepare a plan for the temporary government of the "Western Territory," *viz.*, new districts or territories northwest of the Ohio River,[44] and on September 19, 1786, the committee delivered its proposed plan.[45] The Continental Congress *Journals* describe the affected territory as "such districts or new States as shall be laid out by the United States upon the principles of the acts of cession from individual States and admitted into the confederacy [Union]."[46] The Continental Congress debated the proposal on eight occasions from September 1786 to July 1787 without any reported opposition.[47]

As of July 11, 1787, the text of the proposed Ordinance for the Government of the Territory of the United States North West of the River Ohio[48] provided, in pertinent part:

> *Article the Third.* Institutions for the *promotion of religion and morality, schools and the means of education* shall forever be encouraged . . . [.][49]

As finally passed two days later,[50] the first sentence in the third Article of what has become known as the "Northwest Ordinance" had been ever so slightly revised to make its purpose and meaning more clear:

> *Article the Third. Religion,* morality, and knowledge, being *necessary to good government* and the happiness of mankind, schools and the means of education shall forever be encouraged. . . .[51]

Those words bear but one grammatical meaning as written: "[r]eligion, morality, and knowledge" prove integral ("necessary") to "good government and the happiness of mankind." In turn, "schools and the means of education" prove integral to the teaching of "[r]eligion, morality, and knowledge." The historical record mentions no opposition to the pointed references to the necessity of "religion, morality, and knowledge" as essential to *both* government *and* education.

The 1787 Northwest Ordinance also included the requirement that all constitutions and governments adopted by any new state admitted to the Union in accordance with the Ordinance must conform "to the principles" contained therein:

> *Article the Fifth.* . . . [W]henever any of the said States shall have sixty thousand free Inhabitants therein, such State shall be admitted by its Delegates into the Congress of the United States, on an equal footing with the original States in all respects whatever, and shall be at liberty to form a permanent Constitution and State Government, provided the Constitution and Government so to be formed shall be republican and *in conformity to the principles contained in these articles.* . . [.][52]

Two years later, on July 16, 17, and 20, 1789, the House of Representatives of the First Congress considered a proposed bill to renew the Northwest Ordinance in full,[53] finally passing the bill on July 21, 1789, and sending it to the Senate.[54] The House records report no proposal to alter the existing text of the Ordinance's third Article (quoted just above).

The Senate considered the proposed bill on July 21, July 31, and August 3, 1789,[55] and finally passed it, with amendments on August 4, 1789.[56] The Senate records likewise report no proposal to alter the existing text of the Ordinance's third article.

On August 5, 1789, the House received word that the Senate had passed the bill to renew the Northwest Ordinance, with certain amendments.[57] The House accepted the Senate amendments the same day, informed the Senate accordingly,[58] and prepared a final version of the law on August 6, 1789.[59] Neither the House records nor the Senate records report any proposal to alter the existing text of the Ordinance's third article.

On August 7, 1789, the House and Senate jointly delivered the bill to President Washington for signature,[60] and the president signed it the same day.[61] Like its pre-Constitution predecessor, the renewed Northwest Ordinance declared in the first sentence in Article III:

> Art. III. *Religion,* morality, and knowledge, being *necessary to good government* and the happiness of mankind, schools and the means of education shall forever be encouraged. . . .[62]

These words continue to bear but one grammatical meaning as written: "[r]eligion, morality, and knowledge" prove integral ("necessary") to "good government and the happiness of mankind." In turn, "schools and the means of education" prove integral to the teaching of "[r]eligion, morality, and knowledge."

And, also like its predecessor, the renewed Northwest Ordinance ordained that all constitutions and governments adopted by any new state admitted to the Union in accordance with the Ordinance must conform "to the principles" contained therein:

> *Article the Fifth.* . . . [W]henever any of the said States shall have sixty thousand free Inhabitants therein, such State shall be admitted by its Delegates into the Congress of the United States, on an equal footing with the original States in all respects whatever, and shall be at liberty to form a permanent Constitution and State Government, provided the Constitution and Government so to be formed shall be republican and *in conformity to the principles contained in these articles.* . . [.][63]

For reasons yet to be explained, the Supreme Court seems quite unaware of the significance of the Northwest Ordinance's Third Article. Indeed, the Ordinance remained unmentioned at all in the Court's first seven Establishment Clause decisions from 1947 to 1961.[64] Not until 1962 did any of the nine justices reference it within the context of the Establishment Clause,[65] and even then the reference occurred only in a concurring opinion of one of the individual justices rather than the Court's own opinion; in his concurring opinion, Justice Douglas remarked that "[r]eligion was once deemed to be a function of the public school system," citing the Northwest Ordinance.[66]

The Northwest Ordinance received no further mention in any of the Court's next twenty-two Establishment Clause decisions until 1985,[67] and even then the reference occurred only in the chief justice's dissenting opinion.[68] Another ten years elapsed— and the Court rendered yet an additional fifteen Establishment

Clause decisions—before the Northwest Ordinance received further mention,[69] and, again, the reference occurred only in an individual justice's concurring opinion.[70]

Thus, in its Establishment Clause decisions the Court seems to presume that the Northwest Ordinance lost its vitality at some unknown point—either that, or it purposefully disregards it after having been alerted to its significance no later than 1985, if not earlier in 1962. But any such presumption would be unwarranted; the Fifth Article in the Northwest Ordinance requires all new states to conform their respective governments and constitutions to the Ordinance's various provisions as a condition of admittance to the nation, and even the Supreme Court has declared that aspect of the Ordinance as controlling.

For instance, in a mid-nineteenth-century decision, the Supreme Court discussed the significance of the Northwest Ordinance *vis-à-vis* Louisiana's admission to the United States:

> By the act of April 8, 1812, Louisiana was admitted according to the mode prescribed by the act of 1811 [*viz.,* the law that authorized admittance as a state]; Congress declared it should be on the conditions and terms contained in the 3d section of that act; which should be considered, deemed and taken, as fundamental conditions and terms upon which the state was incorporated in the union. *All Congress intended, was to declare in advance, to the people of the territory, the fundamental principles their constitution should contain;* this was every way proper under the circumstances: the instrument having been duly formed, and presented, *it was for the national legislature to judge whether it contained the proper principles, and to accept it if it did or reject it if it did not.*[71]

And in an early twentieth-century opinion the Court similarly wrote:

> . . . Congress may require, under penalty of denying admission, that the organic law of a new state at the time of admission shall be such as to meet its approval.[72]

Although any state may certainly alter its constitution *after* admission to the United States, the Northwest Ordinance nevertheless endures as a congressional enactment, and it plainly declares that all constitutions and governments adopted by any new state admitted to the Union in accordance with the Ordinance must conform "to the principles" contained therein.[73] That declaration can scarcely be considered an inconsequential mandate.

Thus, under federal law adopted by the same Congress that

authored the Establishment Clause, "[r]eligion, morality, and knowledge" prove integral to "good government and the happiness of mankind," and, in turn, "schools and the means of education" prove integral to the teaching of "[r]eligion, morality, and knowledge." Those declarations would necessarily conflict with the Establishment Clause *if,* as some presume, the Establishment Clause does more than merely proscribe a "national establishment."

D. Congress's 1789 Resolution
for a Thanksgiving Proclamation

On September 25, 1789, the day after it voted final approval to the text of the Establishment Clause, the House of Representatives passed the following "thanksgiving" resolution:

> *Resolved,* That a joint committee of both Houses be directed to wait upon the President of the United States, to request that he would recommend to the people of the United States a day of *public thanksgiving and prayer,* to be observed by acknowledging, with grateful hearts, the many signal favors of *Almighty God,* especially by affording them an opportunity peaceably to establish a Constitution of government for their safety and happiness.[74]

The Senate concurred in that resolution the following day.[75] Congress's Thanksgiving Resolution "passed by a great majority."[76] A summary of Representative Sherman's contemporaneous remarks reads:

> MR. SHERMAN justified the practice of thanksgiving, on any signal event, not only as a laudable one in itself, but as warranted by a number of precedents in holy writ: for instance, the solemn thanksgivings and rejoicing which took place in the time of Solomon, after the building of the temple, was a case in point. This example, he thought, worthy of Christian imitation on the present occasion[.] . . .[77]

President Washington delivered just such a Thanksgiving Proclamation on October 3, 1789:

> Whereas it is the duty of all nations to acknowledge the providence of Almighty God, to obey His will, to be grateful for His benefits, and humbly to implore His protection and favor; and
> Whereas both Houses of Congress have, by their joint committee, requested me "to recommend to the people of the United States a

day of public thanksgiving and prayer, to be observed by acknowledging with grateful hearts the many and signal favors of Almighty God, especially by affording them an opportunity peaceably to establish a form of government for their safety and happiness";

Now, therefore, I do recommend and assign Thursday, the 26th day of November next, to be devoted by the people of these States to the service of that great and glorious Being who is the beneficent author of all the good that was, that is, or that will be; that we may then all unite in rendering unto Him our sincere and humble thanks for His kind care and protection of the people of this country previous to their becoming a nation; for the signal and manifold mercies and the favorable interpositions of His providence in the course and conclusion of the late war; for the great degree of tranquillity, union, and plenty which we have since enjoyed; for the peaceable and rational manner in which we have been enabled to establish constitutions of government for our safety and happiness, and particularly the national one now lately instituted; for the civil and religious liberty with which we are blessed, and the means we have of acquiring and diffusing useful knowledge; and, in general, for all the great and various favors which He has been pleased to confer upon us.

And also that we may then unite in most humbly offering our prayers and supplications to the great Lord and Ruler of Nations, and beseech Him to pardon our national and other transgressions; to enable us all, whether in public or private stations, to perform our several and relative duties properly and punctually; to render our National Government a blessing to all the people by constantly being a Government of wise, just, and constitutional laws, discreetly and faithfully executed and obeyed; to protect and guide all sovereigns and nations (especially such as have shown kindness to us), and to bless them with good governments, peace, and concord; to promote the knowledge and practice of true religion and virtue, and the increase of science among them and us; and, generally, to grant unto all mankind such a degree of temporal prosperity as He alone knows to be best.[78]

That contemporaneous 1789 Thanksgiving Proclamation, authored by the same institutional author of the Establishment Clause, proves consistent with the purpose, function, and meaning of the Establishment Clause within the historical context in which Congress wrote it, *viz.*, the disablement of the federal government from implementing any single preferred national ecclesiastical institution with the exclusive patronage of the federal government—but nothing more.

Thus, both the 1789 Congressional Thanksgiving resolution and President Washington's resulting proclamation prove antithetical to the notion that Congress implemented the Establishment Clause to "separate" government from "religion" altogether. To arrive at a contrary conclusion one must necessarily presume an absurdity, *viz.,* that the institutional author of the Thanksgiving resolution contemplated that the words of the Establishment Clause had been designed to prohibit the government from uttering such a resolution.

8

The Author's Own Understanding:
Congress's Subsequent Acts

Normally, an "after-the-fact" congressional opinion concerning the meaning of an earlier congressional work product assumes little significance because an *opinion* of "meaning" never substitutes for "meaning"—so says the Supreme Court.[1] The same may be said of any author's subsequent opinions; what an author says today about the meaning of words written yesterday cannot alter the meaning of the words written yesterday.

But the author can well confirm (or reaffirm) the meaning of words written yesterday. Thus, subsequent actions by the institutional author of a constitutional amendment might well be examined to determine whether those subsequent actions have at least been consistent with—and thus tend to substantiate—the meaning of the Establishment Clause when Congress wrote it in 1789.

Four post-Establishment Clause congressional enactments—*viz.:* (1) the inscription on all United States coins and currency; (2) the Pledge of Allegiance; (3) the United States' National Motto; and (4) the National Day of Prayer—each bear witness to Congress's consistent post-Establishment Clause understanding that the Establishment Clause targets only a *single, dominant, preferred ecclesiastical institution,* but does *not* otherwise prohibit the government's non-preferential references to, or associations with, "religion" or "religious activities" in general.

A. Inscription on All United States Coins
and Currency: "In God We Trust"

In 1864, Congress authorized the director of the National Mint to determine appropriate "mottoes" for United States coins.[2] A year later, Congress authorized the director of the National Mint "to cause the motto 'In God we trust' to be placed upon such coins hereafter to be issued as shall admit of such legend [i.e., inscription] thereon."[3] Congress expanded that authorization for additional coinage in 1873.[4]

In 1908, Congress *required* the inclusion of the phrase "In God We Trust" on all United States coins on which it had previously appeared.[5] And in 1955, Congress required the inscription of the words "In God We Trust" on all United States currency as well.[6]

The phrase "In God We Trust" scarcely implements a single, dominant ecclesiastical institution that enjoys a government-preferred, government-sanctioned, government-financed, and government-protected status. As such, it bears not the slightest relationship to an "establishment" within the meaning of the Establishment Clause when Congress wrote that Clause in 1789.

(As of this writing, a challenge to the constitutionality of the words "In God We Trust" remains pending in the federal courts.[7])

B. The Pledge of Allegiance and Reaffirmation: "One Nation under God"

Congress enacted the Pledge of Allegiance in 1942,[8] and it added the words "one Nation under God" in 1954[9]:

> I pledge allegiance to the Flag of the United States of America, and to the Republic for which it stands, one Nation under God, indivisible, with liberty and justice for all.[10]

The House of Representatives report that accompanied the 1954 legislation observes that, "[f]rom the time of our earliest history our peoples and our institutions have reflected the traditional concept that our Nation was founded on a fundamental belief in God."[11]

Again, the phrase "one Nation under God" scarcely implements a single, dominant ecclesiastical institution that enjoys a government-preferred, government-sanctioned, government-financed, and government-protected status. As such, it bears not the slightest relationship to an "establishment" within the meaning of the Establishment Clause when Congress wrote that Clause in 1789.

In June 2002 the United States Ninth Circuit Court of Appeals declared a portion of the Pledge of Allegiance unconstitutional because, according to the Court, the words "under God" ran afoul of the Establishment Clause.[12] The controversy originated with a California state law that required all public schools to recite the Pledge of Allegiance at the beginning of each school day. The Pledge proved offensive to an atheist father, although not because of any personal impact, but, instead, because, in the mouth-dropping words of the Ninth Circuit Court of Appeals,

> his daughter is injured when she is compelled to *"watch and listen"* as her state-employed teacher in her state-run school leads her class-mates in a ritual proclaiming that there is a God, and that our's [*sic*] is "one nation under God."[13]

The Court of Appeals believed that the Pledge conflicted with the Establishment Clause because, as directed by federal law, the Pledge includes the words "under God." The Court of Appeals also read the Supreme Court's Establishment Clause decisions to disallow any com-mingling of "government"—which encompasses all public institu-tions—and "religion" or "religious activities" (whatever those terms might encompass).[14] But how or why the words "under God" serve to implement a single ecclesiastical institution remains unexplained.

Fortunately, the Supreme Court accepted review of that Pledge case, and it confirmed what many had already believed to be a piv-otal procedural flaw; it turns out that, not only did the "offended" daughter not even live with her father, but that *neither* the daughter *nor* her mother—who had legal custody of the daughter—had ever been offended by the Pledge. Thus, the Supreme Court concluded that the father had improperly sought to litigate his personal biases through the conduit of someone else when, in fact, he had suffered no injury whatsoever.[15] (As of this writing, a continued challenge to the constitutionality of the words "under God" in the Pledge of Allegiance remains pending in the federal courts.[16])

Just five months after the Ninth Circuit Court of Appeals ruling (but prior to the Supreme Court's ultimate reversal), an outraged Congress reaffirmed the existing text of the Pledge in a combined vote of 500–5.[17] As part of its November 2002 reaffirmation, Congress rendered the following legislative findings:

> Congress finds the following:
>
> (1) On November 11, 1620, prior to embarking for the shores of America, the Pilgrims signed the Mayflower Compact that declared: "Having undertaken, *for the Glory of God and the advancement of the Christian Faith* and honor of our King and country, a voyage to plant the first colony in the northern parts of Virginia."
>
> (2) On July 4, 1776, America's Founding Fathers, after appealing to the "Laws of Nature, and of *Nature's God*" to justify their separation from Great Britain, then declared: "We hold these Truths to be self-evident, that all Men are created equal, that they are endowed by

their *Creator* with certain unalienable Rights, that among these are Life, Liberty, and the Pursuit of Happiness."

(3) In 1781, Thomas Jefferson, the author of the Declaration of Independence and later the Nation's third President, in his work titled "Notes on the State of Virginia" wrote: *"God who gave us life gave us liberty.* And can the liberties of a nation be thought secure when we have removed their only firm basis, a conviction in the minds of the people that *these liberties are of the Gift of God.* That they are not to be violated but with His wrath? Indeed, I tremble for my country when I reflect that God is just; that his justice cannot sleep forever."

(4) On May 14, 1787, George Washington, as President of the Constitutional Convention, rose to admonish and exhort the delegates and declared: "If to please the people we offer what we ourselves disapprove, how can we afterward defend our work? Let us raise a standard to which the wise and the honest can repair; *the event is in the hand of God!*"

(5) On July 21, 1789, on the same day that it approved the Establishment Clause concerning religion,[18] the First Congress of the United States also passed the Northwest Ordinance, providing for a territorial government for lands northwest of the Ohio River, which declared: *"Religion,* morality, and knowledge, *being necessary to good government* and the happiness of mankind, schools and the means of education shall forever be encouraged."

(6) On September 25, 1789, the First Congress unanimously approved a resolution calling on President George Washington to proclaim a National Day of Thanksgiving for the people of the United States by declaring, "a day of public thanksgiving and prayer, to be observed by acknowledging, with grateful hearts, the many signal favors of *Almighty God,* especially by affording them an opportunity peaceably to establish a constitution of government for their safety and happiness."

(7) On November 19, 1863, President Abraham Lincoln delivered his Gettysburg Address on the site of the battle and declared: "It is rather for us to be here dedicated to the great task remaining before us—that from these honored dead we take increased devotion to that cause for which they gave the last full measure of devotion—that we here highly resolve that these dead shall not have died in vain—that *this Nation, under God,* shall have a new birth of freedom—and that Government of the people, by the people, for the people, shall not perish from the earth."

(8) On April 28, 1952, in the decision of the Supreme Court of the United States in *Zorach v. Clauson,* 343 U.S. 306 (1952), in which school children were allowed to be excused from public schools for

religious observances and education, Justice William O. Douglas, in writing for the Court stated:

> *"The First Amendment, however, does not say that in every and all respects there shall be a separation of Church and State."* Rather, it studiously defines the manner, the specific ways, in which there shall be no concern or union or dependency one on the other. That is the common sense of the matter. Otherwise the State and religion would be aliens to each other—hostile, suspicious, and even unfriendly. Churches could not be required to pay even property taxes. Municipalities would not be permitted to render police or fire protection to religious groups. Policemen who helped parishioners into their places of worship would violate the Constitution. Prayers in our legislative halls; the appeals to the Almighty in the messages of the Chief Executive; the proclamations making Thanksgiving Day a holiday; "so help me God" in our courtroom oaths— these and all other references to the Almighty that run through our laws, our public rituals, our ceremonies would be flouting the First Amendment. A fastidious atheist or agnostic could even object to the supplication with which the Court opens each session: "God save the United States and this Honorable Court."

(9) On June 15, 1954,[19] Congress passed and President Eisenhower signed into law a statute that was clearly consistent with the text and intent of the Constitution of the United States, that amended the Pledge of Allegiance to read: "I pledge allegiance to the Flag of the United States of America and to the Republic for which it stands, one Nation under God, indivisible, with liberty and justice for all."

(10) On July 20, 1956,[20] Congress proclaimed that the national motto of the United States is "In God We Trust," and that motto is inscribed above the main door of the Senate, behind the Chair of the Speaker of the House of Representatives, and on the currency of the United States.

(11) On June 17, 1963, in the decision of the Supreme Court of the United States in *Abington School District v. Schempp*, 374 U.S. 203 (1963), in which compulsory school prayer was held unconstitutional, Justices Goldberg and Harlan, concurring in the decision, stated:

> "But untutored devotion to the concept of neutrality can lead to invocation or approval of results which partake not simply of that noninterference and noninvolvement with the religious which the Constitution commands, but of a brooding and pervasive devotion to the secular and a passive, or even active, hostility to the religious. Such results

are not only not compelled by the Constitution, but, it seems to me, are prohibited by it. Neither government nor this Court can or should ignore the significance of the fact that a vast portion of our people believe in and worship God and that many of our legal, political, and personal values derive historically from religious teachings. Government must inevitably take cognizance of the existence of religion and, indeed, under certain circumstances the First Amendment may require that it do so."

(12) On March 5, 1984, in the decision of the Supreme Court of the United States in *Lynch v. Donnelly*, 465 U.S. 668 (1984), in which a city government's display of a nativity scene was held to be constitutional, Chief Justice Burger, writing for the Court, stated:

"There is an unbroken history of official acknowledgment by all three branches of government of the role of religion in American life from at least 1789. . . . [E]xamples of reference to our religious heritage are found in the statutorily prescribed national motto "In God We Trust" (36 U.S.C. § 186) [now 36 U.S.C. § 302], which Congress and the President mandated for our currency, *see* (31 U.S.C. § 5112(d)(1) (1982 ed.)), and in the language "One Nation under God" as part of the Pledge of Allegiance to the American flag. That pledge is recited by many thousands of public school children—and adults—every year. . . . Art galleries supported by public revenues display religious paintings of the 15th and 16th centuries, predominantly inspired by one religious faith. The National Gallery in Washington, maintained with Government support, for example, has long exhibited masterpieces with religious messages, notably the Last Supper, and paintings depicting the Birth of Christ, the Crucifixion, and the Resurrection, among many others with explicit Christian themes and messages. The very chamber in which oral arguments on this case were heard is decorated with a notable and permanent—not seasonal—symbol of religion: Moses with the Ten Commandments. Congress has long provided chapels in the Capitol for religious worship and meditation."

(13) On June 4, 1985, in the decision of the Supreme Court of the United States in *Wallace v. Jaffree*, 472 U.S. 38 (1985), in which a mandatory moment of silence to be used for meditation or voluntary prayer was held unconstitutional, Justice O'Connor, concurring in the judgment and addressing the contention that the Court's holding would render the Pledge of Allegiance unconstitutional because

Congress amended it in 1954 to add the words "under God," stated

> "In my view, the words 'under God' in the Pledge, as codified at 36 U.S.C. § 172 [now 4 U.S.C. § 4], serve as an acknowledgment of religion with 'the legitimate secular purposes of solemnizing public occasions, [and] expressing confidence in the future.'"

(14) On November 20, 1992, the United States Court of Appeals for the 7th Circuit, in *Sherman v. Community Consolidated School District 21*, 980 F.2d 437 (7th Cir. 1992), held that a school district's policy for voluntary recitation of the Pledge of Allegiance including the words "under God" was constitutional.

(15) The 9th Circuit Court of Appeals erroneously held, in *Newdow v. U.S. Congress* (9th Cir. June 26, 2002),[21] that the Pledge of Allegiance's use of the express religious reference "under God" violates the First Amendment to the Constitution, and that, therefore, a school district's policy and practice of teacher-led voluntary recitations of the Pledge of Allegiance is unconstitutional.

(16) The erroneous rationale of the 9th Circuit Court of Appeals in *Newdow* would lead to the absurd result that the Constitution's use of the express religious reference "Year of our Lord" in Article VII violates the First Amendment to the Constitution, and that, therefore, a school district's policy and practice of teacher-led voluntary recitations of the Constitution itself would be unconstitutional.[22]

The author of the Establishment Clause has spoken. (The weight that the courts accord such express congressional findings remains a murky question.)

C. The United States' National Motto: "In God We Trust"

In 1956, Congress ordained that the phrase "In God We Trust," which had appeared on the nation's coins for almost a century, "shall henceforth be the United States' national motto."[23] As part of Congress's reaffirmation of the Pledge of Allegiance in 2002 (previous topic), it purposefully reaffirmed the motto.[24]

Again, the phrase "In God We Trust" scarcely implements a single, dominant ecclesiastical institution that enjoys a government-preferred, government-sanctioned, government-financed, and government-protected status. As such, it bears not the slightest relationship to an "establishment" within the meaning of the Establishment Clause when Congress wrote that Clause in 1789.

(As of this writing, a challenge to the constitutionality of the words "In God We Trust" remains pending in the federal courts.[25])

D. "The Star-Spangled Banner" as National Anthem —with "In God Is Our Trust"

In 1931 Congress adopted the "The Star-Spangled Banner" as our nation's National Anthem.[26] Penned by lawyer Francis Scott Key on a ship in Chesapeake Bay at dawn on September 14, 1814, after an all-night British naval assault on Fort McHenry at the close of the War of 1812,[27] the fourth and final verse contains the phrase "may the heav'n-rescued land [p]raise the Pow'r that hath made and preserv'd us a nation," and also coins the phrase "In God is our trust":

> O thus be it ever when free-men shall stand
> Between their lov'd home and the war's desolation;
> Blest with vict'ry and peace, may the heav'n-rescued land
> Praise the Pow'r that hath made and preserv'd us a nation!
> Then conquer we must, when our cause it is just,
> And this be our motto: "In God is our trust!"
> And the star-spangled banner in triumph shall wave
> O'er the land of the free and the home of the brave!

It seems that no one has yet challenged the National Anthem's reference to the words "In God is our trust" as violative of the Establishment Clause.

E. National Day of Prayer

In 1952, Congress prescribed a "National Day of Prayer"[28] and it reaffirmed that legislation in 1998:

> The President shall issue each year a proclamation designating the first Thursday in May as a National Day of Prayer on which the people of the United States may turn to God in prayer and meditation at churches, in groups, and as individuals. [29]

Again, such congressional directive scarcely implements a single, dominant ecclesiastical institution that enjoys a government-preferred, government-sanctioned, government-financed, and government-protected status. As such, it bears not the slightest relationship to an "establishment" within the meaning of the Establishment Clause when Congress wrote that Clause in 1789.

A Meaning Consistent with the States' Own Constitutions and Laws in 1789

Although not determinative of the meaning of the ten words in the Establishment Clause, the various disestablishment provisions in the states' constitutions and laws as of 1789 nevertheless furnish a highly relevant perspective. As examined in detail earlier,[1] when the First Congress convened in the spring of 1789 the states had already adopted various establishment-related provisions in their own state constitutions or laws:

"equal-rights–and-privileges"	no compelled financial support	no "establishment"	no compelled worship	non-preferential tax authorized
Virginia	Virginia		Virginia	
New Jersey	New Jersey	New Jersey[2]	New Jersey	
Delaware	Delaware	Delaware[3]	Delaware	
Pennsylvania	Pennsylvania		Pennsylvania	
Maryland	Maryland			Maryland
North Carolina	North Carolina	North Carolina[4]	North Carolina	
New York		New York[5]		
	Georgia			
South Carolina	South Carolina			
Massachusetts		Massachusetts[6]		Massachusetts
New Hampshire		New Hampshire[7]		New Hampshire
Vermont	Vermont		Vermont	

In addition, as explained in Chapters 4 and 10, three of the states that ratified the Constitution submitted proposed establishment-related constitutional amendments for the First Congress to consider.[8]

No historical record hints that the states had the slightest inclination to press the inaugural Congress to alter the collective assurances against a dominant, preferred ecclesiastical establishment in the then-existing state constitutions. To the contrary, when the First Congress acted on Madison's proposal to install a similar assurance in the newly ratified Constitution, it wrote, debated, and approved a measure that mimicked the existing protections in the various state constitutions—implementing at the federal level the very assurance that the individual states had already implemented among themselves.

A Meaning Consistent with Amendments Proposed by the Ratifying States

Although not determinative of the meaning of the ten words in the Establishment Clause, the various constitutional amendments proposed by the ratifying states as part of the states' ratification votes in 1787 and 1788 nevertheless furnish a highly relevant corroborative perspective. The text of these proposed amendments drew upon the various assurances that the states themselves had implemented within their own constitutions,[1] and that conformity attests to the reality that the wording of the Establishment Clause served to supply at the federal level a comparable assurance. Indeed, Madison crafted the proposed constitutional amendments from the proposed amendments furnished by the states with their ratification votes.[2]

Of the five ratifying states that adopted proposed amendments for the First Congress to consider (Massachusetts, South Carolina, New Hampshire, Virginia, and New York[3]), three proposed amendments that addressed the relationship between government and religion—or, more precisely, the establishment: New Hampshire, Virginia, and New York.

- *New Hampshire:* "Congress shall make no laws *touching* religion."
- *Virginia:* "That . . . all men have an equal, natural, and unalienable right to the free exercise of religion, according to the dictates of conscience, and that *no particular religious sect or society ought to be favored or established, by law, in preference to others."*
- *New York:* "That the people have an equal, natural, and unalienable right freely and peaceably to exercise their religion, according to the dictates of conscience; and that *no religious sect or society ought to be favored or established by law in preference to others."*

The New Hampshire proposal—which the 1789 Congress rejected[4]—proved so nebulous that it lacked any discernible meaning.

But the Virginia and New York proposals invoked the non-preferential, equality-of-treatment goal of the anti-establishment advocates, and specifically prohibited any single, dominant ecclesiastical institutional "establish[ment]" (*viz.*, that no particular "religious sect or society ought to be *favored or established, by law, in preference* to others"). The likelihood that the First Congress accorded the ten words in the Establishment Clause a different meaning than the anti-preference amendments proposed by Virginia and New York proves sufficiently remote that it can be declared improbable. Indeed, the historical record furnishes not a syllable to the contrary.

11

A Meaning Consistent with Madison's Passions

Although not determinative of the meaning of the ten words in the Establishment Clause, the well-publicized, exhaustively chronicled "establishment" views of the one individual most responsible for the Bill of Rights—1789 Congressman James Madison—certainly ought to be assessed in order to determine the extent to which those views align with the meaning of the Establishment Clause when Congress finalized it in the fall of 1789. Indeed, no discussion on that subject would be otherwise complete.

In mid-eighteenth-century Virginia, Madison had long witnessed the negative effects of an entrenched establishment in Virginia: the merger of legislative and ecclesiastical authority; the deprivation of various civil rights—or "civil incapacitations"—as punishment for establishment opponents; the preferential reward of various honors and privileges (or "emoluments") to establishment supporters; the compelled allegiance to (and attendance of) the establishment institution; and the compelled financial support of the establishment via governmental taxes.

Indeed, Madison rejected Virginia's own William and Mary as his college choice precisely for that reason. Because he loathed the reality that the Church of England remained the established church in his home state of Virginia,[1] Madison refused to attend the College of William and Mary as he believed the latter to be "run by incompetent Anglicans"[2] and he "was out of sympathy with the established church."[3] Madison opted instead to attend Princeton University in 1769[4] (the College of New Jersey at the time[5]), an anti-establishment environment.[6]

After graduating from Princeton in 1771[7] as "a paragon of a well-educated scholar,"[8] Madison began to voice his beliefs and questioned whether established churches could ever be viewed as necessary to government. He corresponded with Princeton classmate William Bradford on that very subject; in a December 1773 letter to Bradford, Madison asked:

> Is an Ecclesiastical Establishment absolutely necessary to civil society in a supream [*sic*] Government? & how far is it hurtful to a dependent state?[9]

In two subsequent letters to Bradford in early 1774, Madison specifically lambasted the Virginia establishment that he experienced upon his return home from Princeton:

> If the Church of England had been the established and general Religion in all the Northern Colonies as it has been among us here, and [if] uninterrupted tranquility had prevailed throughout the continent, it is clear to me that slavery and subjection might and would have been gradually insinuated among us. Union of Religious Sentiments begets a surprizing [*sic*] confidence, and Ecclesiastical Establishments tend to great ignorance and Corruption, all of which facilitate the Execution of Mischievous Projects.[10]

⇒•◇•⇐

> Our Assembly is to meet the first of May, When It is expected something will be done in behalf of the Dissenters. Petitions I hear are already forming among the Persecuted Baptists and I fancy it is in the thoughts of the Presbyterians also to intercede for greater liberty in matters of Religion. . . . The Sentiments of our people of Fortune & fashion on this subject are vastly different from what you have been used to. That liberal catholic and equitable way of thinking as to the rights of Conscience, which is one of the Characteristics of a free people, and so strongly marks the People of your province, is but little known among the Zealous adherents to our Hierarchy. . . . [T]he Clergy are a numerous and powerful body, have great influence at home by reason of their connection with & dependence on the Bishops and Crown, and will naturally employ all their art & Interest to depress their rising Adversaries; for such they must consider dissenters who rob them of the good will of the people and may in time endanger their livings & security.[11]

Madison's efforts in Virginia in the 1770s and 1780s to curtail the establishment excesses have been detailed earlier,[12] and his anti-establishment struggles continued unabated at the national level as well.[13] In remarks to the House of Representatives during debate on the text that ultimately became the First Amendment's Establishment Clause, Madison furnished a view for the purpose and effect of that proposed amendment with which no one disagreed (although some Establishment adherents in the House and Senate certainly wanted to derail it[14]):

> MR. MADISON said, he apprehended the meaning of the words to be, that *Congress should not establish a religion, and enforce the legal observation of it by law,* nor compel men to worship God in any manner contrary to their conscience. Whether the words are necessary or not, he did not mean to say, but they had been required by some of the State Conventions, who seemed to entertain an opinion that under the clause of the constitution, which gave power to Congress to make all laws necessary and proper to carry into execution the constitution, and the laws made under it, enabled them to make laws of such a nature as might infringe the rights of conscience, and *establish a national religion; to prevent these effects he presumed the amendment was intended, and he thought it as well expressed as the nature of the language would admit.*[15]

The historical records of the 1789 congressional proceedings afford but one rational conclusion concerning Madison's impact on the proposed amendment that became the Establishment Clause: Madison offered it to implement at the national level the same type of anti-establishment assurances that the states had already adopted in their own constitutions. The end result conformed perfectly to his long-held passions and his determination to forever disable the newly formed federal government from implementing any single, dominant ecclesiastical institution that enjoyed a government-*preferred*, government-*sanctioned*, government-*financed*, and government-*protected* status, and which represented an indistinguishable union with government.

Madison's stature during that inaugural Congress in 1789 assured that the wording of the Establishment Clause would conform to Madison's long-held and well-known desires and goals; Madison not only successfully ousted the poorly worded New Hampshire version of the Establishment Clause,[16] he also persuaded the joint Conference Committee to reject the Senate's weakened proposal[17] and adopt instead the wording of the Establishment Clause that endures today.[18] (And, during the congressional proceedings in the summer of 1789, had Madison not reluctantly yielded to some citizens' aversion to the word "national,"[19] the Establishment Clause would very likely read today as he worded it on June 8, 1789 ["nor shall any national religion be established"[20]].)

An exceptional performance during the 1787 Constitutional

Convention in Philadelphia had rendered Madison almost larger than life even before the First Congress convened in 1789. History has long accorded Madison the title of "the father of the Constitution,"[21] a title described variously as "richly deserved"[22] and "deeply deserved."[23] Indeed, Madison proved to be by far the most knowledgeable delegate at the 1787 Convention; "[n]o one was better prepared."[24]

> What allowed him to perform the crucial role he assigned himself in the movement for reform was not only the originality of his ideas but also their comprehensiveness. In the year preceding the Federal Convention, his political intelligence proved profoundly integrative, both in his deeper range of issues the delegates would confront and in his assessment of the political obstacles and opportunities they would encounter.[25]

Madison readily distinguished himself as highly conversant in issues of government and exceptionally knowledgeable about the histories of failed "confederations" in Europe, thanks to dozens of volumes of treatises and other books that Jefferson sent him from Paris during Jefferson's ambassadorship from 1784 to 1789; Jefferson's generosity enabled his fellow Virginian to master theories of constitutional government unlike any of his contemporaries.[26] Jefferson supplied Madison with roughly two hundred books from Paris[27] (or roughly "two trunkloads"[28]), a treasure trove that enabled Madison—already an "extraordinarily studious statesman"[29] —to "engage in what has been described as 'probably the most fruitful piece of scholarly research ever carried out by an American.'"[30] And that compliment may well be an understatement.

> Even his political foes admitted that on nearly every question before any legislative body in which sat he [viz., Madison] was likely to be the best-informed member.[31]

Thomas Jefferson praised Madison as no other:

> . . . [H]e [viz., Madison] acquired a habit of self-possession, which placed at ready command the rich resources of his luminous and discriminating mind, and of his extensive information, and rendered him the first of every assembly afterwards, of which he became a member.[32]

Thus, to no one's real surprise "the amendments [Congress] eventually submitted to the states in September 1789 followed closely the proposals he introduced in June."[33] Madison's biographer reports that "[t]he guaranty that became part of the Constitution [as the First Amendment's religion clauses] could be ascribed to Madison on the basis of the legislative history, even if its wording did not clearly identify him as the author."[34]

One of Madison's fellow representatives in the First Congress—Fisher Ames—reported that early on in that inaugural Congress ". . . by common consent the 'first man' in the House was J[ames] M[adison]."[35]

> [Madison] owed his preeminence in the first House of Representatives to his disciplined and logical mind, his sound judgment, and his deep knowledge and understanding of the public issues of the day.[36]

Madison quite simply proved to be a man without whom the Constitution and Bill of Rights would likely not exist.[37] "For were it not for Madison, a bill of rights might never have been added to the Constitution."[38]

> Madison was not merely one participant among many or even primus inter pares ["first among equals"]; he was the key actor whose purposes deserve scrutiny for that reason alone.[39]

History affords no disagreement with that observation.

Following the inaugural 1789 Congress, Virginia reelected Madison to three more two-year terms in the House of Representatives, ending in 1797. He later served as President Jefferson's secretary of state from 1801 to 1809,[40] and served as the nation's fourth president from 1809 to 1817.[41]

Late in life Madison still consistently viewed the "establishment" as a preferential governmental association with, and an affirmation of, a single, dominant ecclesiastical institution endowed with governmental financial support:

> In most of the Govts. [*sic*] of the old world, the *legal establishment of a particular religion* and without or with very little toleration of others makes a part of the Political and Civil organization and there are few of the most enlightened judges who will maintain that the system has been favorable either to Religion or to Govt. Until Holland ventured on the experiment of combining a liberal toleration with *the establishment of a particular creed*, it was taken for granted, that an *exclusive & intolerant establishment* was essential, and notwithstanding the light thrown on the subject by the experiment, the prevailing opinion in Europe, England not excepted, has been that Religion could not be

preserved without the support of Govt. nor Govt. be supported with[ou]t an *established* religion that *there must be at least an alliance of some sort between them.*

It remained for North America to bring the great & interesting subject to a fair, and finally to a decisive test.

In the Colonial State of the Country, there were four examples, R[hode] I[sland][,] N[ew] J[ersey][,] Penn[sylvania][,] and Delaware, & the greater part of N[ew] Y[ork] where there were no *religious Establishments;* the *support of Religion being left to the voluntary associations & contributions* of individuals; and certainly the religious condition of those Colonies, will well bear a comparison with that where *establishments* existed.[42]

Unlike most of his contemporaries, Madison's larger-than-life persona as constitutional architect endures centuries later. In 2000 Congress created the James Madison Commemoration Commission, and it rendered the following legislative findings that exemplify the extent of Madison's influence in the early years of the United States:

Sec. 2. Congressional Findings.

Congress finds that—

(1) March 16, 2001, marks the 250th anniversary of the birth of James Madison;

(2) as a delegate to the Continental Congress, and to the Annapolis Convention of 1786, James Madison foresaw the need for a more effective national government and was a persuasive advocate for such a government at the Philadelphia Constitutional Convention of 1787;

(3) James Madison worked tirelessly and successfully at the Constitutional Convention to mold a national charter, the United States Constitution, that combined both energy and restraint, empowering the legislature, the executive, and the judiciary, within a framework of limited government, separated powers, and a system of federalism;

(4) James Madison was an eloquent proponent of the first 10 amendments to the Constitution, the Bill of Rights;

(5) James Madison faithfully served his country as a Representative in Congress from 1789 to 1797, as Secretary of State from 1801 to 1809, and as President of the United States from 1809 to 1817;

(6) as President, James Madison showed courage and resolute will in leading the United States to victory over Great Britain in the War of 1812;

(7) James Madison's political writings, as exemplified by his Notes on the Federal Convention and his contributions to The Federalist Papers, are among the most distinguished of American state papers;

(8) by his learning, his devotion to ordered liberty, and by the force of his intellect, James Madison made an indispensable contribution to the American tradition of democratic constitutional republicanism embodied in the Constitution of the United States, and is justifiably acclaimed as father of the Constitution;

(9) it is appropriate to remember, honor, and renew the legacy of James Madison for the American people and, indeed for all mankind; and

(10) as the Nation approaches March 16, 2001, marking the anniversary of the birth of James Madison, it is appropriate to establish a commission for the commemoration of that anniversary.[43]

Again, although not determinative of the meaning of the ten words in the Establishment Clause (indisputably Madison's own product), nevertheless the theme and contents of Madison's letters, Madison's Memorial and Remonstrance, Madison's Act for Establishing Religious Freedom, Madison's various speeches excerpted throughout the preceding chapters, and Madison's compelling presence throughout the 1789 congressional proceedings furnish historical perspectives from which the purpose, function, and meaning of the Establishment Clause may be independently assessed with a fair degree of certainty.

Simply put, to presume that the purpose, function, and meaning of the text of the Establishment Clause might somehow differ from Madison's well-documented passions in the context of ecclesiastical institutions and "religion" would be to presume the irrational.

Irony of Ironies: The Supreme Court Extends the Establishment Clause's Disablement to the States

Those who wonder by this point—or have been asking since the beginning—what bearing the Congress-specific Establishment Clause could possibly have on such distinctly local headline-makers as prayer or creationism in public schools, nativity scenes in city halls, Christmas holidays, and so on, should know that the United States Supreme Court simply enlarged the text of the Establishment Clause via judicial fiat.

A. The First Amendment, as Written by Congress

The phrase "Congress shall make no law"—the first five words of the Bill of Rights—would seem sufficiently unambiguous that the author's target bears no uncertainty: the author itself, Congress. Longtime early-nineteenth-century Supreme Court justice Joseph Story, a contemporary of Madison and a prodigious constitutional law scholar well-acquainted with the 1789 congressional efforts from the outset, likewise viewed the Establishment Clause's prohibition simply as the disablement of the federal government to act upon the subject, but nothing more:

> The real object of the amendment was . . . to prevent any *national* ecclesiastical establishment, which should give to an hierarchy the exclusive patronage of the *national* government.[1]

Even the Supreme Court itself remained unconfused by the Establishment Clause's specific limitation to Congress—at least until the early twentieth century. In its 1833 decision in *Barron v. Baltimore*,[2] the Court declared precisely what Madison and Congress had known in 1789, and it rebuffed the argument that the ten amendments in the Bill of Rights burdened the states as well as the federal government:

The constitution was ordained and established by the people of the United States for themselves, for their own government, *and not for the government of the individual states.* Each state established a constitution for itself, and, in that constitution, provided such limitations and restrictions on the powers of its particular government as its judgment dictated.[3]

━━━━▰◆▰━━━━

These amendments contain no expression indicating an intention to apply them to the state governments. This court cannot so apply them.[4]

Twelve years later in *Permoli v. Municipality No. 1 of the City of New Orleans,*[5] the Court spurned the more specific argument that the First Amendment's religion clauses burdened the states:

The Constitution makes no provision for protecting the citizens of the respective states in their religious liberties; *this is left to the state constitutions and laws* nor is there any inhibition imposed by the Constitution of the United States in this respect on the states.[6]

Thus, "[f]or protection of their rights against invasion by *state* governments, the people relied primarily upon *state* constitutions."[7]

Somehow, the Fourteenth Amendment changed all of that in 1866—without any mention of the Establishment Clause.

B. The First Amendment, as Rewritten by the Supreme Court

In 1866, Congress wrote (and by July 1868 the states had finished ratifying) the celebrated Fourteenth Amendment, designed primarily to annul the Supreme Court's infamous 1857 *Dred Scott* decision.

In *Dred Scott v. Sandford,*[8] the Court ruled that a former slave— Scott—could not maintain an action in federal court against one Sandford because he did not qualify as a "citizen" of the United States within the meaning of Article III of the Constitution, which authorizes the federal courts to decide, among other types of cases, litigation "between citizens of different states." Scott maintained that he held Missouri citizenship, while Sandford held New York citizenship. Sandford, however, argued that a former slave like Scott could not be a "citizen" and thus could not bring any action in federal court.

In response, Scott demonstrated that he had attained citizenship while living in a non-slave territory outside the state of Missouri and had thus been freed from all disabilities that otherwise burdened slaves in that era—in other words, he had acquired the same rights as "free" citizens in non-slave states. In that respect, Article IV, Section 2, of the Constitution provides that

> The Citizens of each State shall be entitled to all Privileges and Immunities of Citizens in the several States.[9]

However, the Supreme Court concluded that an individual state lacked the inherent authority to accord citizenship status sufficient to render Scott a "citizen" of the United States. The decision prompted Congress to prepare the Constitution's Fourteenth Amendment in 1866, which effectively overruled *Dred Scott.*

Section 1 of the Fourteenth Amendment supplies three historic clauses directed specifically to the states—or, more realistically at the time, to some of them:

> . . . [1] No State shall make or enforce any law which shall abridge the *privileges or immunities* of citizens of the United States; [2] nor shall any State deprive any person of life, liberty, or property, *without due process of law;* [3] nor [shall any State] deny to any person within its jurisdiction the *equal protection* of the laws.[10]

Those three clauses have long been known as the Fourteenth Amendment's[11] "privileges or immunities" clause, "due process" clause, and "equal protection" clause, respectively. Although the meaning and scope of those clauses have been debated for a century and a half, suffice it to say that those words in and of themselves scarcely altered the reality that the Constitution's Establishment Clause—indeed, the entire First Amendment—burdened only *Congress,* and not the states.

Armed with a new constitutional tool crafted from noble aspirations but afflicted with a less-than-plain meaning, enterprising litigants did not wait long to wield the Fourteenth Amendment's three clauses in attempts to bypass (or obliterate) disagreeable state laws. Within just a few years after the ratification of the Fourteenth Amendment, some began to urge that the Fourteenth Amendment's amorphous "privileges or immunities" clause functioned to burden the states as if the ten amendments in the Bill of Rights applied to the states directly. But in the late 1800s the Supreme Court rejected that tactic (even though, ironically, it may well be that the Fourteenth Amendment's "privileges or immunities" clause actually had no other purpose), and that situation has remained unchanged since at least the nineteenth century.[12]

However, twentieth-century litigants convinced a much different Supreme Court to embrace the *ipse-dixit* proposition[13] that the abstract reference to "liberty" in the Fourteenth Amendment's "due process" clause ("nor shall any State deprive any person of . . . liberty . . . without due process of law") assures citizens of certain fundamental, albeit non-specific, rights *vis-à-vis* the states, and that some of those fundamental rights happen to exist in the Constitution's first ten amendments. Language in earlier Supreme Court opinions appeared to support that notion, to some uncertain extent.

Not only did two of the Court's early Fourteenth Amendment opinions[14] allude to some indeterminate species of transcendent citizen-based "rights" that might be protected in some imprecise manner by that Amendment, but later decisions confirmed those earlier remarks. For instance, in 1908 the Court commented that

> [t]he 14th Amendment withdrew from the states powers theretofore enjoyed by them *to an extent not yet fully ascertained,* or rather, to speak more accurately, limited those powers and restrained their exercise.[15]

These kinds of remarks—which confirm the existence of the indescribable—prove reminiscent of one of the most magnificent observations ever uttered by a Supreme Court justice; in a legendary concurring opinion in a mid-1960s case in which the Court struggled with the extent to which the First Amendment's "free speech" guarantee allowed states to regulate "hard-core pornography,"[16] Justice Stewart confessed that

> I have reached the conclusion . . . that under the First and Fourteenth Amendments criminal laws in this area are constitutionally limited to hard-core pornography. I shall not today attempt further to define the kinds of material I understand to be embraced within that shorthand description; and perhaps I could never succeed in intelligibly doing so. *But I know it when I see it.*[17]

Ultimately, in a baffling 1937 decision[18] the Supreme Court rendered two seemingly contradictory proclamations concerning the Fourteenth Amendment's "due process" clause:

- *First,* it *rejected* the notion that whatever would be a violation of the Bill of Rights if done by the federal government *necessarily* translates to a violation of the Fourteenth Amendment if done by a state.[19]

- *Second,* it simultaneously *endorsed* the unhistorical notion that, in its words, "the due process clause of the Fourteenth Amendment *may* make it unlawful for a state to abridge" *certain* (unspecified) rights found in the Bill of Rights if the Court concluded that some aspect of the Bill of Rights represented a right *implicit in the concept of ordered liberty"*[20] —whatever that meant.

The first of these two declarations makes sense. But the Court simply made up the second declaration—not, unfortunately, an uncommon occurrence. One writer aptly characterizes that 1937 decision as nothing less than an "invention of the Supreme Court" that thumbed the Court's nose at historical reality.[21] The reasoning by which the Court arrived at its conclusion remains unexplained—at least in terms of the legislative history of the Fourteenth Amendment.

The Supreme Court thereafter began to earmark various aspects of the Bill of Rights that, in its opinion, qualified as rights "implicit in the concept of ordered liberty," to use the Court's own phraseology. "Originally a set of largely structural guarantees applying only against the federal government, the Bill has become a bulwark of rights against *all* government conduct."[22]

Thus, in a 1940 decision[23] that involved both the "free exercise" and "speech" components of the First Amendment,[24] the Supreme Court declared that "[t]he fundamental concept of liberty embodied in [the Fourteenth] Amendment embraces the liberties guaranteed by the *First Amendment.*"[25] As authority for that proposition, the Court cited a lone decision that it had rendered a year earlier that involved only the "speech" and "press" components of the First Amendment, not the Free Exercise Clause.[26] In any event, one-half of the First Amendment's two religion clauses then burdened the states, regardless of whether or not a state's own constitution might provide differently.

The other shoe—the Establishment Clause—dropped in the Court's 1947 decision in *Everson v. Board of Education,*[27] in which the Supreme Court no longer differentiated among any of the First Amendment assurances and declared, again on its own say-so, that "[t]he First Amendment [has been rendered] applicable to the states by the Fourteenth [Amendment]"—the *entire* First Amendment.[28] The Court cited as precedent a single 1943 decision that involved *neither* of the First Amendment's religion clauses.[29]

At that point, the Court had swept the various First Amendment assurances into one undifferentiated bunch based solely on its own opinion of what constituted, in its words, a "fundamental concept of liberty"[30] protected by the Fourteenth Amendment. The 1789 Congress's desire that the states remain free to do what they desired in the area of religion had been eviscerated entirely, with nary a syllable in recognition of the irony that an extension of the Establishment Clause to the states achieved precisely the *opposite* result implemented by the 1789 Congress.

Scholars have long butted heads over the question of whether the 1866 Congress worded the Fourteenth Amendment to effectively incorporate some, or all, of the Bill of Rights. The legislative records of the 1866 congressional proceedings cast doubt on any conclusion that the Fourteenth Amendment functions in that manner,[31] but those who advocate otherwise rely upon esoteric grammatical clues from a variety of sources (although not necessarily the 1866 congressional proceedings).[32] Even the individual justices on the Supreme Court have battled vociferously over the issue. One need only compare the celebrated concurring and dissenting opinions of Justice Frankfurter and Justice Black, respectively, in the 1947 decision in *Adamson v. California*[33] to appreciate the reality that no one truly knows whether, or to what extent, the Fourteenth Amendment serves to render portions of the first ten amendments applicable to the various states. But, then again, if five justices on the Supreme Court agree on a certain point, it matters not what anyone else thinks.

In any event, the Supreme Court has now declared multiple times that the First Amendment's Establishment Clause burdens the states via the "liberty" component of the Fourteenth Amendment's "due process" clause. And, unfortunately, at least since 1803,[34] whatever the Supreme Court says about the Constitution remains final—even if absurd.

13

Jefferson's Metaphorical "Wall of Separation": A Wall of Colloquial Concoction

The preceding chapters have thus far examined a host of historical realities:

- the well-known meaning of the term "establishment" within the context of religious affairs, and the linkage of that term to a specific, dominant, government-favored ecclesiastical institution;
- the goal of the various dis-"establishment" influences at work in the states during the mid-eighteenth century;
- the various religion-specific constitutional amendments that the states proposed to the inaugural Congress; and
- the chronological development of the ten words that comprise the Establishment Clause, as authored by the First Congress.

And yet, there remains for exploration what many consider the single most influential issue in the history of religious affairs in this nation: the notorious "wall of separation" between "church and state," a fortuity of almost mythical proportions that never meant what a poorly informed United States Supreme Court once said it does.

Historical reality proves formidable. Most embrace it as the unalterable truth, warts and all. To others, though, it discredits contrary predispositions and thus proves unendurable; they ignore it, rationalize it, manipulate it, "correct" it, or disdain it altogether. But, in the face of all the machinations that humanity concocts to deflect the intransigence of historical reality, the underlying truth never changes. And so it goes with the "wall."

One former Supreme Court justice lambasted the law's tendency toward indiscriminate uses of metaphors, describing a particularly vague and vexing court-invented catchphrase in use for decades as

an excellent illustration of the extent to which uncritical use of words bedevils the law. A phrase begins life as a literary expression;

its felicity leads to its lazy repetition; and repetition soon establishes it as a legal formula, undiscriminatingly used to express different and sometimes contradictory ideas.[1]

A more apt critique of the problem would be hard to find.

Most Americans would be dumbfounded to learn that the now-immortalized "wall of separation" said to exist somewhere between "church" and "state" *nowhere appears* in the Constitution. And they certainly ought to be distressed by the reality that the source of the figurative "wall" had no involvement with the formation of either the Constitution or the Bill of Rights. Nevertheless, that famous colloquialism likely "represents the sum total of what many people know about the subject."[2] And, as Chapter 14 explains in detail,[3] the extent of the public's education in that respect derives entirely from a misinformed Supreme Court that jettisoned the reality of history in favor of fictional characterizations of the meaning of the first ten words in the Bill of Rights.

The phrase "wall of separation" first entered the vernacular on January 1, 1802, more than twelve years *after* Congress finalized the Establishment Clause in September 1789. And the person who coined it—then-president Thomas Jefferson—had played no role in the genesis of the Establishment Clause (or the Constitution, for that matter), as he had not even been in the country; Jefferson sailed for France in July 1784 to succeed Benjamin Franklin as the nation's representative and did not return to the United States until November 1789[4]—two months after President Washington had already transmitted the first set of proposed constitutional amendments to the states for ratification. In other words, Jefferson had as much involvement with Congress's authorship of the Establishment Clause as an ordinary citizen.

Jefferson's relationship to the 1789 congressional proceedings proved so tenuous that none of Jefferson's various biographies mentions any events associated with those proceedings beyond Jefferson's infrequent intercontinental letters to James Madison and others during that time—none of which explored the proposal that eventually became the Establishment Clause. From the adjournment of the Constitutional Convention on September 17, 1787, to the adjournment of the First Congress at the end of September 1789, Jefferson sent Madison letters dated September 17, 1787,[5] October 8, 1787,[6] December 20, 1787,[7] February 6, 1788,[8] March 8, 1788,[9] May 1, 1788,[10] May 3, 1788,[11] May 28, 1788,[12] July 31, 1788,[13] August 4,

1788,[14] November 18, 1788,[15] January 12, 1789,[16] March 15, 1789,[17] May 11, 1789,[18] June 18, 1789,[19] July 22, 1789,[20] July 29, 1789,[21] August 28, 1789,[22] September 6, 1789,[23] and September 17, 1789.[24] None of these letters referenced the concept embodied in the Establishment Clause. Indeed, in that portion of Jefferson's "Autobiography" that discusses various events from May 1789 to November 1789, Jefferson mentions nothing concerning the First Congress and the Bill of Rights.[25]

Nor did any of Madison's own letters to Jefferson during that same time period explore the subject; from the adjournment of the Constitutional Convention on September 17, 1787, to the adjournment of the First Congress at the end of September 1789, Madison sent Jefferson letters dated September 6, 1787,[26] October 24, 1787,[27] December 9, 1787,[28] December 20, 1787,[29] February 19, 1788,[30] February 20, 1788,[31] April 22, 1788,[32] July 24, 1788,[33] August 10, 1788,[34] August 23, 1788,[35] September 21, 1788,[36] October 8, 1788,[37] October 17, 1788,[38] December 8, 1788,[39] December 12, 1788,[40] March 29, 1789,[41] May 9, 1789,[42] May 23, 1789,[43] May 27, 1789,[44] June 13, 1789,[45] June 30, 1789,[46] and August 2, 1789.[47] None of these letters referenced the concept embodied in the Establishment Clause.

Nonetheless, more than a decade after the fact Jefferson felt nudged by the political realities of the times to publish a personal opinion about the Establishment Clause—albeit for a reason having little to do with the Establishment Clause itself.

A. The Danbury Baptists' Letter to Jefferson

In an October 7, 1801, letter to then-president Jefferson, the Danbury (Connecticut) Baptists expressed concerns that the Congregationalist-dominated establishment/government in Connecticut[48] might successfully stifle dissenting sects—theirs in particular. The letter carried the Danbury Baptists' plea for Jefferson's assistance, or at least the lending of Jefferson's presidential stature, to thwart establishment-driven, government-sanctioned discrimination against religious minorities.

The letter's significance to Jefferson requires a peek back to the 1800 presidential contest—a bitter fight between the Federalists and Jefferson's new Republicans, and between then-president John Adams and candidate Jefferson. The Congregationalists in New England—Federalists—disliked Jefferson intensely,[49] and northern-state Federalists and establishment supporters had attacked

Jefferson relentlessly on religious issues during the 1800 presidential campaign.[50]

> In a real sense, if not a technical one, the Congregationalist clergy, magistrates, and more prosperous citizens of New England constituted an Establishment. Members and defenders of this found ready reason to oppose [Jefferson] . . . [.][51]

During the 1800 presidential campaign, "Jefferson's political foes had frequently denounced him in press and pulpit as an atheist."[52] "Indeed, it may be claimed that the personal attacks on the chief Republican were the most in any presidential campaign on record."[53] Thus, when the Danbury Baptists delivered their letter to Jefferson they well knew that "the Congregational clergy, magistrates, and more prosperous citizens of New England constituted an Establishment" that Jefferson despised.[54]

Adding fuel to still-smoldering issues of the 1800 election, Jefferson's omission of any Thanksgiving or other devotional proclamations during the Jefferson presidency rankled some detractors as signifying a distaste for religion.[55] But, in reality, Jefferson simply believed that the president's function under the Constitution did not allow for such proclamations; in his view, because "Congress was inhibited by the Constitution from acts respecting religion, and [because] the executive was authorized only to execute their acts, he had refrained from prescribing 'even occasional performances of devotion.'"[56]

Jefferson later said as much in his own words; in defense of his practice to shun presidential proclamations of "thanksgiving and prayer," Jefferson explained that the office of presidency remains

> interdicted by the Constitution from intermeddling with religious institutions, their doctrines, discipline, or exercises. . . . Certainly, no power to prescribe any religious exercise, or to assume authority in religious discipline, has been delegated to the General Government. *It must then rest with the States, as far as it can be in any human authority.*[57]

Thus, within that historical context the Danbury Baptists wrote to Jefferson:

> Sir,
>
> . . . Our sentiments are uniformly on the side of religious liberty—that religion is at all times and places a matter between God and individuals—that no man ought to suffer in name, person, or

effects on account of his religious opinions—that the legitimate power of civil government extends no further than to punish the man who works ill to his neighbors; But, sir, our constitution of government is not specific. Our ancient charter together with the law made coincident therewith, were adopted as the basis of our government, at the time of our revolution[58]; and such had been our laws and usages, and such still are; that religion is considered as the first object of legislation; and therefore *what religious privileges we enjoy (as a minor part of the state) we enjoy as favors granted, and not as inalienable rights; and these favors we receive at the expense of such degrading acknowledgements [sic] as are inconsistent with the rights of freemen.* It is not to be wondered at therefore; if those who seek after power and gain under the pretense of government and religion should reproach their fellow men—should reproach their order magistrate, as a enemy of religion, law, and good order, because he will not, dare not, assume the prerogatives of Jehovah and make laws to govern the kingdom of Christ.

Sir, we are sensible that the president of the United States is not the national legislator, and also sensible that the national government cannot destroy the laws of each state; but our hopes are strong that the sentiments of our beloved president, which have had such genial effect already, like the radiant beams of the sun, will shine and prevail through all these states and all the world, till hierarchy and tyranny be destroyed from the earth. . . .

Signed in behalf of the association,

Nehemiah Dodge, Ephraim Robbins, Stephen S. Nelson.[59]

The Danbury Baptists purposefully played directly to Jefferson's passions—both religious and political. And they succeeded.

B. Jefferson's Celebrated Reply

Jefferson penned a reply dated January 1, 1802. In the second paragraph of a three-paragraph response, Jefferson alluded to the Establishment Clause as a symbol of that which might benefit the Baptists *if,* like other states, the then-existing Connecticut "Constitutional Ordinance" included a comparable assurance. (As written, the Establishment Clause did not apply to the states. And the Danbury Baptists' letter bemoaned the absence of a *state* constitution only; it made no mention of the Establishment Clause.)

In his letter, Jefferson conceived the metaphorical concept of a "wall of separation" as a shorthand characterization of what he believed to be the Establishment Clause's goal, *viz.,* the disestablishment of a *single,* government-*preferred,* government-*sanctioned,* and government-*financed* ecclesiastical institution that represented an indistinguishable union with the national government—in other words, a "state [or "national"] church," or a "church-state" (or "church-nation" unity):

> The affectionate sentiments of esteem and approbation which you are so good as to express towards me, on behalf of the Danbury Baptist association, give me the highest satisfaction. My duties dictate a faithful & zealous pursuit of the interests of my constituents, & in proportion as they are persuaded of my fidelity to those duties, the discharge of them becomes more and more pleasing.

> Believing with you that religion is a matter which lies solely between Man & his God, that he owes account to none other for his faith or his worship, *that the legitimate[60] powers of government reach actions only, & not opinions,* I contemplate with sovereign reverence that act of the whole American people [*viz,* referring to the First Amendment's religion clauses] which declared that their legislature should "make no law respecting an establishment of religion, or prohibiting the free exercise thereof," *thus building a wall of separation between Church & State.* Adhering to this expression of the supreme will of the nation in behalf of the rights of conscience, I shall see with sincere satisfaction the progress of those sentiments which tend to restore to man all his natural rights, convinced he has no natural right in opposition to his social duties.

> I reciprocate your kind prayers for the protection & blessing of the common father and creator of man, and tender you for yourselves & your religious association, assurances of my respect & esteem.

> Th: Jefferson
> Jan. 1. 1802.[61]

The emphasized text represents the pivotal passages in Jefferson's letter; the first and third paragraphs, as well as most of the second paragraph, offer little of substance.

The reality that Jefferson wielded the phrase "wall of separation between church and state" as directed solely to an establishment "state church" or "church/state" can be seen in his earlier advice-seeking letter to Attorney General Levi Lincoln that same day (discussed just below), in which Jefferson referenced his intention to address "a con-demnation of the *alliance* between Church and State."[62] Jefferson's use of the term "alliance" suggests something stronger than the notion that government ought to shun any relationship with "religion" in general—such as, for example, the nation's twenty-first-century befud-dlement with prayer or creationism in public schools, nativity scenes on government properties, and Christmas holidays.

Unfortunately, most readers unthinkingly presume an out-of-con-text literalness to Jefferson's metaphor that applies with infinite reach, as if "church" and "state" could never intersect in any arena—and as if they comprehended Jefferson's meaning of inherently imprecise verbiage. Indeed, as a politician Jefferson may well have designed his letter to be less than clear. But, as with everything, words have meaning only within a specific context, and few Americans have the slightest notion of the historical context within which Jefferson penned his comment.

A number of underlying considerations bear on the meaning of Jefferson's historic phraseology.

C. Context, Context, Context

(1). Jefferson's Primary Purpose: Political Abstruseness

Jefferson well knew that any written response would be both ill-received in Connecticut and quickly publicized.[63] ". . . [T]here was much in the Jeffersonian philosophy that might have been expected to disquiet authoritarians, absolutists, and dogmatists of any sort."[64] And, of course, the Connecticut Congregationalists qualified as pre-cisely that type of individuals.

Thus, before he finalized his famous response letter, Jefferson wrote to Attorney General Levi Lincoln asking him to review a draft so that Lincoln, who hailed from Connecticut and knew the local ecclesiastical/political climate,[65] might assess its political impact. (Jefferson also sought the advice of Postmaster General Gideon Granger concerning the likely political fallout from the proposed response to the Danbury Baptists.[66] Granger, who, like Attorney General Lincoln, hailed from Connecticut, recommended no changes at all to Jefferson's draft.[67])

In his letter to Lincoln, Jefferson revealed that he wanted to craft his response to the Danbury Baptists to serve as a general political comment, and beneficial for, in Jefferson's words, "sowing useful truths & principles among the people, which might germinate and become rooted among their political tenets":

> Averse to receive addresses, yet unable to prevent them, I have generally endeavored to turn them to some account, by making them the occasion, by way of answer, of sowing useful truths & principles among the people, which might germinate and become rooted among their political tenets. The Baptist address, now enclosed, admits of a condemnation of the alliance between Church and State, under the authority of the Constitution. *It furnishes an occasion, too, which I have long wished to find, of saying why I do not proclaim fastings & thanksgivings, as my predecessors did.*
>
> The address, to be sure, does not point at this, & it's [*sic*] introduction is awkward. *But I foresee no opportunity of doing it* [*viz.,* providing an explanation of Jefferson's disinclination to proclaim "fastings & thanksgivings"] *more pertinently.* I know it will give great offence to the New England clergy; but the advocate of religious freedom is to expect neither peace nor forgiveness from them. Will you be so good as to examine the answer, and suggest any alterations which might prevent an ill effect, or promote a good one among the people? You understand the temper of those in the North, and can weaken it, therefore, to their stomachs: it is at present seasoned to the Southern taste only. I would ask the favor of you to return it, with the address, in the course of the day or evening. Health & affection.[68]

Jefferson's first draft of his response letter and the final version as actually sent warrant comparison so that Jefferson's initial purpose can be seen—*viz.,* explaining his presidential aversion to public declarations of "thanksgiving" as, in his view, beyond the scope of a limited constitutional executive authority:

Jefferson's Draft Letter
(with deleted text in strikeout, and with revised text in italics)

Gentlemen

The affectionate sentiments of esteem & approbation which you are so good as to express towards me, on behalf of the Danbury Baptist association, give me the highest satisfaction. [M]y duties dictate a faithful & zealous pursuit of the interests of my constituents, and, in proportion as they are persuaded of my fidelity to those duties, the discharge of them becomes more & more pleasing.

Believing with you that religion is a matter which lies solely between man & his god, that he owes account to none other for his faith or his worship, that the legitimate powers of government reach actions only and not opinions, I contemplate with sovereign reverence that act of the whole American people which declared that their legislature should "make no law respecting an establishment of religion, or prohibiting the free exercise thereof;" thus building a wall of [eternal] separation between Church & State. [Congress thus inhibited from acts respecting religion, and the Executive authorised only to execute their acts, I have refrained from prescribing even those occasional performances of devotion, practiced indeed by the Executive of another nation as the legal head of its church, but subject here, as religious exercises only to the voluntary regulations and discipline of each respective sect,]

[After that text, Jefferson first wrote: *"confining myself therefore to the duties of my station, which are merely temporal, be assured that your religious rights shall never be infringed by any act of mine and that."* He crossed out those words and then wrote: *"concurring with,"* which he then crossed out and substituted this phrase: *"Adhering to this great act of national legislation in behalf of the rights of conscience."* He then crossed out that phrase and wrote: *"Adhering to this expression of the supreme will of the nation in behalf of the rights of conscience I shall see with friendly dispositions the progress of those sentiments which tend to restore to man all his natural rights, convinced that he has no natural rights in opposition to his social duties."*]

I reciprocate your kind prayers for the protection & blessing of the common father and creator of man, and tender you for yourselves & [the Danbury Baptist] *your religious* association assurances of my high respect & esteem."[69]

Jefferson's Final Version as Sent to the Danbury Baptists

Gentlemen

The affectionate sentiments of esteem and approbation which you are so good as to express towards me, on behalf of the Danbury Baptist association, give me the highest satisfaction. My duties dictate a faithful & zealous pursuit of the interests of my constituents, & in proportion as they are persuaded of my fidelity to those duties, the discharge of them becomes more and more pleasing.

Believing with you that religion is a matter which lies solely between Man & his God, that he owes account to none other for his faith or his worship, that the legitimate powers of government reach actions only, & not opinions, I contemplate with sovereign reverence that act of the whole American people which declared that their legislature should "make no law respecting an establishment of religion, or prohibiting the free exercise thereof," thus building a wall of separation between Church & State. Adhering to this expression of the supreme will of the nation in behalf of the rights of conscience, I shall see with sincere satisfaction the progress of those sentiments which tend to restore to man all his natural rights, convinced he has no natural right in opposition to his social duties.

I reciprocate your kind prayers for the protection & blessing of the common father and creator of man, and tender you for yourselves & your religious association, assurances of my respect & esteem.[70]

In the late 1990s, the FBI employed late twentieth-century technology to restore Jefferson's original editorial changes on the first draft so that Jefferson's inked-out deletions could be read for the first time.[71] The Library of Congress's explanation of the text of the original (unedited) draft of Jefferson's January 1, 1802, "wall of separation" letter to the Danbury Baptists explains the significance of Jefferson's changes:

A WALL OF SEPARATION

Thomas Jefferson's reply of January 1, 1802, to an address of congratulations from the Danbury (Connecticut) Baptist Association contains a phrase familiar in today's political and judicial circles: "a wall of separation between church and state." Many in the United States, including the courts, have used this phrase to interpret the Founders' intentions regarding the relationship between government and religion, as set down by the First Amendment to the Constitution: "Congress shall make no law respecting an establishment of religion . . ." However, the meaning of this clause has been the subject of passionate dispute for the past fifty years.

Presented here are both the handwritten, edited draft of the letter and an adjusted facsimile showing the original unedited draft. The draft of the letter reveals that, far from dashing it off as a "short note of courtesy," as some have called it, Jefferson labored over its composition. Jefferson consulted Postmaster General Gideon Granger of Connecticut and Attorney General Levi Lincoln of Massachusetts while drafting the letter. That Jefferson consulted two New England politicians about his messages indicated that he regarded his reply to the Danbury Baptists as a political letter, not as a dispassionate theoretical pronouncement on the relations between government and religion.[72]

⇒◆⇐

The celebrated phrase, "a wall of separation between church and state," was contained in Thomas Jefferson's letter to the Danbury Baptists. American courts have used the phrase to interpret the Founders' intentions regarding the relationship between government and religion. The words, "wall of separation," appear just above the section of the letter that Jefferson circled for deletion. In the deleted section Jefferson explained why he refused to proclaim national days of fasting and thanksgiving, as his predecessors, George Washington and John Adams, had done. In the left margin, next to the deleted section, Jefferson noted that he excised the section to avoid offending "our republican friends in the eastern states" who cherished days of fasting and thanksgiving.

The Library of Congress is grateful to the Federal Bureau of Investigation Laboratory for recovering the lines obliterated from the Danbury Baptist letter by Thomas Jefferson. He originally wrote "a wall of eternal separation between church and state," later deleting the word "eternal." He also deleted the phrase "the duties of my station, which are merely temporal." Jefferson must have been unhappy with the uncompromising tone of both of these phrases, especially in view of the implications of his decision, two days later, to begin attending church services in the House of Representatives.[73]

Within that unique historical context, Jefferson had no intention of penning what the United States Supreme Court has precipitously—and improperly—hailed as "an authoritative declaration of the scope and effect" of the Establishment Clause.[74] Jefferson's letter served as nothing of the kind.

Rather, all the analysis in the world cannot overcome the reality that, given the letter's political undertones and the lingering memories of the nasty 1800 election during which Jefferson's faith had been questioned and Jefferson had been accused of a host of evils, Jefferson's phraseology had very probably been designed to mock the Connecticut establishment yet, at the same time, yield an inherent abstruseness that would preclude any definitive declaration.

For instance, Jefferson used the terms "church" and "state" to describe the entities on either side of his proverbial "wall," yet the Establishment Clause employs neither of those terms. Nor do any such terms appear in the historical records of the 1789 Congress's consideration of the Establishment Clause. In other words, Jefferson designed his proposed response to function as a quintessential political commentary meant to both indulge its recipient and befuddle others.

One of Jefferson's chief biographers confirms that Jefferson's letter sought nothing more than "to encourage the dissenting minority in Connecticut and to rebuke the politico-religious rulers of that Commonwealth"[75] with the same energy that Jefferson had decades earlier devoted to ridding Virginia of the established Church of England.[76] Jefferson had long loathed the establishment influence that the Church of England had maintained for decades in his home state of Virginia from the late 1600s and well into the 1700s, and as he entered Virginia politics in the 1770s the "[d]estruction of the power of the Anglican clergymen . . . became a private crusade occupying enormous reserves of his energy."[77]

In other words, Jefferson's famous letter

> was a *political statement* written to reassure Jefferson's Baptist constituents in New England of his continuing commitment to their religious rights and to strike back at the Federal-Congregationalist establishment in Connecticut . . . [.][78]

and it represented

> "a *political letter,* not . . . a dispassionate theoretical pronouncement on the relations between government and religion."[79]

Professor Dreisbach's terse characterization of the whole affair says it best: "In short, 'it was meant to be a political manifesto, nothing more.'"[80]

According to renowned constitutional scholar Edward Corwin, "the late dean of American constitutional scholars,"[81] Jefferson's lore-laden Danbury Baptists letter

> was not improbably motivated by an impish desire to heave a brick at the Congregationalist-Federalist hierarchy of Connecticut . . . [.][82]

Professor Corwin would be the one to know. Longtime Princeton professor of jurisprudence and presidential advisor on constitutional law, Edward Corwin has authored a host of books on the Constitution,[83] and Professor Dreisbach's description of Corwin as the "dean of American constitutional scholars"[84] proves to be well warranted.[85]

At least Jefferson's prescience concerning the probability of publication for political purposes quickly proved correct; at least eight unfriendly New England newspapers published Jefferson's reply from January 18, 1802, to February 15, 1802.[86] Then, likely because of its short-lived political value, Jefferson's Danbury Baptist letter disappeared for half a century until its inclusion in the 1853 publication of Jefferson's writings.[87]

(2). Jefferson Could Only Have Meant a *National* "Church"

As the Establishment Clause by its express terms applied exclusively to Congress (at least until the Supreme Court first declared otherwise in 1947),[88] Jefferson's reference to "a wall of separation between Church and State" and the inferential connection to the First Amendment could only have referred to a *national* ("state") entity, *viz.*, a "national (government) church" or a "church-nation" ecclesiastical institution of the kind that had long endured in England with the Church of England. Because the individual states had implemented their own anti-establishment assurances, he could not have contemplated anything else.

Although some states had adopted new constitutions between 1789[89] and 1802, as of January 1, 1802, the individual states maintained their own independent views about any relationship between government and ecclesiastical institutions. By the time Jefferson wrote his celebrated letter to the Danbury Baptists . . .

• Massachusetts's 1780 constitution[90] had endured unchanged, thus leaving unaffected its constitution's legislative authorization for "compelled-financial-support" for the funding of Protestant teachers.[91]

• Pennsylvania had adopted a new constitution in 1790, and had crafted a religion-specific provision to suit its needs.[92] The 1790 constitution incorporated a modified version of Article II in the Declaration of Rights component of Pennsylvania's 1776 constitution:

> That all men have a natural and indefeasible right to worship Almighty God according to the dictates of their own consciences; that no man can of right be compelled to attend, erect, or support any place of worship, or to maintain any ministry, against his consent; that no human authority can, in any case whatever, control or interfere with the rights of conscience; and that no preference shall ever be given, by law, to any religious establishments or modes of worship.[93]

Pennsylvania's 1790 constitution endured until 1838.[94]

• South Carolina had adopted a new constitution in 1790, and had crafted a religion-specific provision to suit its needs.[95] The 1790 constitution eliminated the provision in the 1778 constitution—Art. XXXVIII[96]—that "established" the Protestant religion in the state:

> The free exercise and enjoyment of religious profession and worship, without discrimination or preference, shall forever hereafter be allowed within this State to all mankind[.] . . .[97]

South Carolina's 1790 constitution endured until 1865.[98]

• Delaware had adopted a new constitution in 1792, and had crafted a religion-specific provision to suit its needs.[99] The 1792 constitution incorporated within a single paragraph the interrelated provisions contained in Article 29 of the 1776 constitution and §§ 2 and 3 of the separate 1776 Declaration of Rights[100]:

> Although it is the duty of all men frequently to assemble together for the public worship of the Author of the universe, and piety and morality, on which the prosperity of communities depends, are thereby promoted; yet no man shall or ought to be compelled to attend any religious worship, to contribute to the erection or support of any place of worship, or to the maintenance of any ministry, against his own free will and consent; . . . nor shall a preference be given by law to any religious societies, denominations, or modes of worship.[101]

Delaware's 1792 constitution endured until 1831.[102]

• New Hampshire had adopted a new constitution in 1792, and had crafted a religion-specific provision to suit its needs—including the reinstitution of a legislative authorization for "compelled-financial-support" for the funding of religious teachers.[103] Atypical among the various states, Article VI in the Declaration of Rights component of New Hampshire's 1784 constitution included a "compelled-financial-support" authorization for the legislature.[104] The replacement 1792 constitution provided:

> As morality and piety, rightly grounded on evangelical principles, will give the best and greatest security to government, and will lay in the hearts of men the strongest obligations to due subjection; and as a knowledge of these is most likely to be propagated through a society by the institution of the public worship of the Deity, and of *public instruction in morality and religion;* therefore, to promote these important purposes, *the people of this State have a right to empower, and do hereby fully empower, the legislature to authorize, from time to time, the several towns, parishes, bodies corporate, or religious societies within this State, to make adequate provisions, at their own expense, for the support and maintenance of public protestant teachers of piety, religion, and morality.*"[105]

New Hampshire's 1792 constitution endured until 1902.[106]

• Vermont had adopted a new constitution in 1793, and had crafted a religion-specific provision to suit its needs.[107] Chapter I, Article 3, of Vermont's 1793 constitution[108] reproduced verbatim the religion-pertinent text in Chapter I, Article 3, of the 1786 constitution.[109] Vermont's 1793 constitution still endures.

• Georgia had adopted a new constitution in 1798, and had crafted a religion-specific provision to suit its needs.[110] The 1798 constitution replaced the religion-pertinent provision in Article IV, § 5, of the 1789 constitution[111] with the following:

> No person within this State shall, upon any pretence [sic], be deprived of the inestimable privilege of worshipping [sic] God in a manner agreeable to his own conscience, nor be compelled to attend any place of worship contrary to his own faith and judgment; nor shall he ever be obliged to pay tiths [sic], taxes, or any other rate, for the building or repairing [of] any place of worship, or for the maintenance of any minister or ministry, contrary to what he believes to be right or hath voluntarily engaged to do. No one religious society shall ever be established in this State, in preference to another[.] . . .[112]

Georgia's 1798 constitution endured until 1865.[113]

• New York did not adopt a new constitution until 1821,[114] thus leaving intact the religion-specific provisions in its 1777 constitution[115] as suited its needs.

• Virginia did not adopt a new constitution until 1829,[116] thus leaving intact the religion-specific provisions in its 1776 Constitution and Declaration of Rights as suited its needs.[117]

• New Jersey did not adopt a new constitution until 1844,[118] thus leaving intact the religion-specific provisions in its 1776 constitution[119] as suited its needs.

• Maryland did not adopt a new constitution until 1851,[120] thus leaving intact the religion-specific provisions in its 1776 constitution[121] as suited its needs.

• North Carolina did not adopt a new constitution until 1868,[122] thus leaving intact the religion-specific provisions in its 1776 constitution[123] as suited its needs.

Within that states-went-their-own-way historical context, Jefferson's allegory could not have borne the expansive nationalistic meaning later attributed to it by the Supreme Court in 1947 (as Chapter 14 explains[124]).

(3). Jefferson Built His "Wall" between "Actions" and "Opinions"

Jefferson's remark in his famous letter that "the legitimate powers of government reach *actions* only and *not opinions*"[125] expressly differentiates only between "conduct" and "opinion." And that distinction furnishes the context for what follows in the letter. Thus, the reader can well infer—and grammatical context demands the inference—that the "wall" mentioned in the letter's next clause related to *that distinction alone.*

Professor Dreisbach's explanation of Jefferson's distinction can scarcely be improved:

> One interpretation of the "wall" that links the letter's opening substantive clauses ("that religion is a matter which lies solely between Man & his God, that he owes account to none other for his faith or his worship, that the legitimate powers of government reach actions only, & not opinions") with the famous metaphoric clause suggests that Jefferson located his "wall" between religious opinion (the realm of the church) and conduct subversive of peace and public order (the realm of the civil state). Whereas mere *religious opinion* was beyond the reach of civil magistrates, the civil state could legitimately regulate *religious conduct* that threatened good order. . . .[126]

In other words, the grammatical context of Jefferson's "wall" suggests that, to the extent that it "separates" anything, it disables the "state" from interfering with the "church" in the arena of "opinions," but not with respect to "actions." Whatever "wall" Jefferson had in mind in his letter to the Danbury Baptists received mention solely within the context of a constitutional amendment that *functioned solely to limit governmental authority,* but nothing more. In other words, the First Amendment bears but a single function: the limitation of the *government,* no one else. And words have meaning only within a specific context.

Indeed, as explained in detail in Chapter 14,[127] only for that reason did the letter's most famous promoter—the United States Supreme Court—mention Jefferson's letter in the first place.

> This may have been the Supreme Court's view of the "wall" in *Reynolds v. United States* (1878),[128] a case concerned with legislation that prohibited the Mormon practice of polygamy. The *Reynolds* Court was clearly focused on whether the Constitution granted Congress

authority to prohibit *conduct* motivated by religious belief but deemed subversive of good order.[129]

(Professor Dreisbach concludes his summary of the "opinion" versus "conduct" distinction with the overly cautious concern that "[o]ne cannot be certain that either Jefferson or the *Reynolds* Court thought this was precisely what the 'wall' separated."[130] Although one may not be "certain," the fact remains that, within the context of Jefferson's letter, the lionized "wall" could "separate" little else.)

Thus, a "wall" within Jefferson's context would, then, necessarily connote a "wall" impacting *government* alone—or, as Jefferson phrased it, the "state," meaning *not* "the states" of the Union but the international term for a national government.

To add to the significance of the Danbury Baptist letter's pointed differentiation between "opinions" and "actions," Jefferson had written previously—twenty-one years earlier—about precisely the same distinction, when he wrote in his 1781 *Notes on the State of Virginia*[131] that, with respect to religious freedom, "[t]he legitimate powers of government extend to such acts only as are injurious to others."[132] Indeed, the phrasing matches remarkably:

> 1781 *Notes:* "the *legitimate powers* of government extend to such *acts* only as are injurious to others."

> 1802 letter: "the *legitimate powers* of government reach *actions* only and not opinions."

Note that Jefferson replicated the key phrase "legitimate powers" in his 1802 letter to the Danbury Baptists, which, as Professor Dreisbach discusses, has long been mistranscribed in collections of Jefferson's letters.[133]

(4).Jefferson Did Not Confine His Letter Only to the "Establishment Clause"

The fact that Jefferson's letter mentions *both* of the First Amendment's religion clauses also furnishes an interpretive context for the conclusion that Jefferson's "wall" does *not* relate specifically or exclusively to the Establishment Clause—a reality that the Supreme Court and others have badly misjudged. Jefferson wrote:

> I contemplate with sovereign reverence that act of the whole American people which declared that their legislature should *"make no*

law respecting an establishment of religion or prohibiting the free exercise thereof," thus building a wall of separation between Church and State.[134]

Jefferson linked the metaphorical "wall of separation" to *both* the Establishment Clause *and* the Free Exercise Clause. Yet, for reasons attributed solely to the Supreme Court's 1947 decision in *Everson v. Board of Education,* discussed in Chapter 14,[135] the courts have always associated Jefferson's figurative "wall" with the Establishment Clause alone; with but three inconsequential exceptions (in which symbolic references to Jefferson's "wall" occur in another context), as of this writing the Supreme Court's invocations of Jefferson's 1802 letter to the Danbury Baptists have occurred exclusively within decisions that involve the Establishment Clause.[136] Jefferson, though, did not differentiate—as the letter leaves plain beyond question.

(5). "Separation" as Meaning What, Exactly?

Although Jefferson had written about the religious establishment in the mid-1700s, he had never before wielded the term "separation," or, for that matter, the phrase "wall of separation," or any equivalent verbiage, within that context.

When, for example, Jefferson drafted a resolution in November 1776 to disestablish the Church of England in Virginia,[137] the resolution, while specifically referencing the "establishment," furnished no reference to "separation"—synonymous or otherwise—and conveyed only the expected anti-*preference* theme. Jefferson's biographers confirm that Jefferson never opposed the *non*-preferential treatment of religion,[138] and, in fact, embraced the *non*-preferential treatment of ecclesiastical institutions.[139] Jefferson opposed only governmental *preference* and governmental *compulsion* related to a specific ecclesiastical institution—the quintessential "establishment."

Jefferson's earlier work in Virginia during the 1770s attests to the Jeffersonian view of the "establishment." Jefferson, who, like Madison (although not necessarily *with* Madison), had long railed against the established church in Virginia,[140] included the following proposed text in Article IV, "Rights, Private and Public" of his June 1776, Draft Constitution for Virginia (his third and final draft):

> All persons shall have full and free liberty of religious opinion; *nor shall any be compelled to frequent or maintain any religious institution.*[141]

Jefferson's proposal challenged the established church's reliance upon compelled attendance ("frequent") and compelled financial support ("maintain")—two of the most derisive, if not *the* most derisive, attributes of the establishment. Unfortunately, the Virginia legislature "all but ignored" Jefferson's draft[142]; the constitution that Virginia approved in 1776 furnished only a framework for government.[143]

Jefferson also penned a Draft of Bill Exempting Dissenters from Contributing to the Support of the Church, dated November 30, 1776, which provided (in pertinent part):

> Whereas it is represented by many of the Inhabitants of this Country who dissent from the Church of England *as by Law established* that they consider the *Assessments and Contributions which they have been hitherto obliged to make* towards the support and Maintenance of the said Church and its Ministry as grievous and oppressive, and an Infringement of their religious Freedom.
>
> For Remedy whereof . . . , Be it Enacted by the General Assembly . . . that
>
> [A]ll Dissenters of whatever Denomination from the said Church shall from and after the passing this Act be totally free and *exempt from all Levies Taxes and Impositions whatever towards supporting and maintaining the said Church as it now is or may hereafter be established and its Ministers.* . . .
>
> And whereas great Varieties of Opinions have arisen touching *the Propriety of a general Assessment or whether every religious society should be left to voluntary Contributions* for the support and maintenance of the several Ministers and Teachers of the Gospel who are of different Persuasions and Denominations, and this Difference of Sentiments cannot now be well accommodated, so that it is thought most prudent to defer this matter to the Discussion and final Determination of a future assembly when the Opinions of the Country in General may be better known.
>
> To the End therefore that so important a Subject may in no Sort be prejudged, Be it Enacted by the Authority aforesaid that nothing in this Act contained shall be construed to affect or influence the said Question of a *general Assessment* or voluntary Contribution in any respect whatever.
>
> Provided always that in the mean time *the Members of the Established Church shall not in any Parish be subject to the payment of a greater tax for the support of the said Church & its Minister than they would have been,* had the Dissenters not been exempted from paying their accustomed proportion, any Law to the contrary notwithstanding. . . .[144]

The Virginia legislature enacted Jefferson's "exemption" proposal.[145]

(6). Both the Danbury Baptists' Letter and Jefferson's Celebrated Reply Viewed the "Church" as an *Institution,* Not a Concept

The Supreme Court in its 1947 *Everson* decision (see Chapter 14) and a host of other people since have simply assumed, without any articulable rationale for doing so, that Jefferson's allegorical "church" referenced *religion* in general, as opposed to the more probable reference to a *physical institution* of the kind always associated with an "establishment." Indeed, an association of the term "church" to anything *but* a single, dominant ecclesiastical institution within the context of the Establishment Clause simply makes no sense whatsoever.

The Danbury Baptists had written Jefferson in the first place to complain about the establishment evils of Connecticut's Congregationalists, *precisely* the kind of dominant ecclesiastical institution that the Establishment Clause prohibits on a national level. They did *not*, by comparison, complain to Jefferson of mere "religion" or "religious" affairs. Thus, any supposition that Jefferson's reference to "church" could have alluded to something else would be unwarranted by reality.

D. The Offhand Musings of the Uninvolved Never Yield "Meaning"

Finally, even beyond the historical context of Jefferson's 1802 letter to the Danbury Baptists, the fact remains that not only did Jefferson play no role in the development of the Establishment Clause (or, for that matter, the Constitution itself), but his unauthoritative, subjective perceptions expressed many years after the fact could not possibly ascribe "meaning" to words written by someone else entirely years earlier within a historical context in which Jefferson did not participate. And that reality by no means confines itself to Jefferson. Might the offhand musings of the uninvolved ascribe "meaning" to someone else's words written years earlier? Never.

It would seem that those who pretend that Jefferson's 1802 letter could be "authoritative" in any respect do so only because of one of two possibilities: (1) they presume too much from Jefferson's comparatively brief association with Madison in the Virginia legislature decades earlier, or (2) they remain ignorant of history.

Many presume—incorrectly (and this includes the Supreme Court[146])—that Jefferson's figurative "wall" conformed to Madison's views based upon the widely held misperception that Jefferson and

Madison worked sufficiently close on religious issues that one could necessarily speak for the other. History, however, says otherwise; not only did Jefferson and Madison not even meet until the late 1770s, but they never worked together in any context until Jefferson's Virginia governorship that began in 1779. The first of dozens of letters exchanged between the two did not occur until 1780.[147] Jefferson then left the country in 1784, not to return until November 1789—two months after Congress had finalized the Bill of Rights and President Washington had forwarded the proposed amendments to the states for ratification.[148]

Jefferson, eight years older than Madison,[149] first attended the College of William and Mary in 1760 at the age of seventeen and graduated two years later,[150] at which point he began studying law.[151] From 1769 to 1773, Jefferson served in the Virginia legislature,[152] and in 1775 he joined the Virginia delegation to the Second Continental Congress[153] and returned again in 1776.[154] He began a three-year term in the Virginia House of Delegates in the latter part of 1776,[155] during which time he and George Mason (author of Virginia's 1776 Declaration of Rights[156]) found themselves in alignment on contemporary concerns.[157] Jefferson, an elegant writer whose "reputation had gone before him,"[158] garnered the reputation as the states' first champion of religious freedom,[159] owing not merely to Virginia's political and economic dominance among the states but also to, among other writings, his groundbreaking (albeit unsuccessful) June 1779, Bill for Establishing Religious Freedom.[160] The Virginia legislature selected Jefferson as the state's governor in 1779,[161] after which he met Madison for the first time[162]; Jefferson "had not known [Madison] well" before the former's governorship in 1779.[163] In July 1784 Jefferson left for Paris to replace Benjamin Franklin as the nation's ambassador to France,[164] and he learned, upon his return in November 1789 that he had been appointed as President Washington's secretary of state (and confirmed by the Senate) even before arriving.[165]

Madison, eight years younger than Jefferson[166] (a "considerable" age difference in Madison's view[167]), entered Princeton University in 1769[168] and graduated in 1771 after only three years,[169] and "[f]or the rest of his life Madison had a reputation as a scholar."[170] His first foray into public office came in 1774 when his home county elected him to the County Committee.[171] Madison attended Virginia's Revolutionary Convention in 1776 as a county delegate,[172] and the Convention promptly appointed him to the committee tasked with drafting a groundbreaking declaration of rights and a state constitution[173]—Virginia's first. At the time, Madison and Jefferson had only met briefly[174] ("I was a stranger to Mr. Jefferson [till] the year 1776"[175]), and did not begin a serious working relationship of any magnitude until 1779, after Jefferson began his first term as governor of Virginia.[176] Madison served in the first Virginia legislature in 1776–77[177] and in 1777 the legislature elected him to the Governor's Council,[178] an honor for a comparatively inexperienced legislator.

> He was elected without knowledge and with no personal backing whatever in the ordinary political sense. . . . His former colleagues in the house . . . wanted him within reach because of his willingness and skill in the preparation of public papers.[179]

In 1779, the Virginia voters elected Madison to the Virginia delegation to the Continental Congress, a position he held until 1783.[180] In late 1783, Madison returned to Virginia as a member of Virginia's legislature (the House of Delegates), in which he served until 1786,[181] at which point he briefly returned to the Virginia delegation to the Continental Congress until 1787.[182] In 1787, Madison represented Virginia at the Constitutional Convention.[183] In 1788, he served in both the Virginia Ratifying Convention and the Continental Congress.[184] In 1789, Virginia elected Madison to the House of Representatives for the inaugural Congress in 1789,[185] and reelected him for three more terms in the House, ending in 1797. He served as President Jefferson's secretary of state from 1801 to 1809,[186] and as the nation's fourth president from 1809 to 1817.[187]

A summarized year-by-year comparison for the twenty-year period from 1769 to 1789 reveals little overlap in Jefferson's and Madison's respective political careers (the bold-faced text identifies the overlap years):

YEAR	JEFFERSON	MADISON
1769	Served in the Virginia legislature	Attended Princeton University
1770	Served in the Virginia legislature	Attended Princeton University
1771	Served in the Virginia legislature	Graduated from Princeton University
1772	Served in the Virginia legislature	Returned to Virginia; studied law and became involved in local politics
1773	Served in the Virginia legislature	
1774	Served in the Virginia legislature	Served on local County Committee

YEAR	JEFFERSON	MADISON
1775	Served in the Virginia delegation to the Continental Congress	
1776	Served in the Virginia delegation to the Continental Congress Drafted Declaration of Independence **Served in the Virginia legislature** **First met Madison**	Attended the Virginia Revolutionary Convention; appointed to committee to draft state Declaration of Rights and state constitution **Served in the Virginia legislature** **First met Jefferson**
1777	**Served in the Virginia legislature**	**Served on the Governor's Council and in the Virginia legislature**
1778	**Served in the Virginia legislature**	Served on the Governor's Council and **in the Virginia legislature**
1779	**Served in the Virginia legislature** Drafted Bill for Establishing Religious Freedom Elected Virginia governor **First worked with Madison**	**Served on the Governor's Council and in the Virginia legislature** **First worked with Jefferson** (after Jefferson was elected governor) Served in the Virginia delegation to the Continental Congress
1780	Reelected Virginia governor	Served in the Virginia delegation to the Continental Congress
1781	Virginia governor until term expired in June	Served in the Virginia delegation to the Continental Congress
1782		Served in the Virginia delegation to the Continental Congress
1783	**Served in the Virginia delegation to the Continental Congress**	**Served in the Virginia delegation to the Continental Congress**
1784	Left for France in July to replace Benjamin Franklin as United States representative	Served in the Virginia legislature

YEAR	JEFFERSON	MADISON
1785	Served as United States representative in France	Served in the Virginia legislature Drafted Memorial and Remonstrance against Religious Assessments Drafted Act for Establishing Religious Freedom
1786	Served as United States representative in France	Served in the Virginia legislature Served in the Virginia delegation to the Continental Congress
1787	Served as United States representative in France	Virginia delegate to Constitutional Convention
1788	Served as United States representative in France	Delegate to the Virginia ratifying convention Served in the Virginia delegation to the Continental Congress
1789	Served as United States representative in France Returned to Virginia in November	Elected to the House of Representatives for the First Congress Drafted text originally proposed for the Establishment Clause (sent to the states for ratification in September)

In that twenty-year period ending with Congress's approval of the initial set of proposed constitutional amendments in the fall of 1789, the Jefferson and Madison political careers overlapped only briefly: during the four-year period that both served in the Virginia legislature from 1776 to 1779, and when both served in the Virginia delegation to the Continental Congress in 1783. What later became a lifelong friendship and working relationship did not actually begin until 1779 after Jefferson had been elected governor and Madison served on the Governor's Council; prior to 1779 they had merely been acquaintances in the Virginia legislature.

Thus, history fails to confirm the supposition held by many—and, unfortunately, nurtured by many—that Jefferson spoke for Madison on religious issues (and *vice versa*) and that Jefferson's metaphoric "wall" conformed to Madison's views of the Establishment Clause. (Amazingly, the historical record furnishes no evidence that Jefferson sought Madison's input with respect to the Danbury Baptists letter.)

14

The Supreme Court Flunks First Amendment History and Sends Religion, God, and Christmas Underground

If the Supreme Court declared one plus one to now equal three, would that make it so?[1]

The historical realities explained in the previous chapters leave no rational uncertainties concerning the purpose for, and the corresponding meaning of, the words "an establishment of religion" in the First Amendment's Establishment Clause. Like it or not, historical realities represent objective truths. Truth may well be ignored, misused, confused, or rejected, but it never changes.

But the Establishment Clause constitutes law as well. And since 1803 our nation has embraced a peculiarity unknown to both colonial America and England and has accorded a single institution the inherent and conclusive authority to advise as to constitutional law: the courts.[2] And therein lies an enduring enigma: does historical reality bind the courts, or can "law" transcend historical reality?

For courts, "truth" has always been a vexing and elusive notion, as they have traditionally viewed "truth" as something unearthed by the judicial process, as something declared into existence on a particular occasion under particular circumstances. Thus, the courts often view "truth" as "facts" determined by a particular judge or jury, even though a different judge or jury might well arrive at different "facts." But, in reality, courts do not exist to declare "truth."

Nonetheless, the courts as an institution jealously preserve the fiction that they have the final word on "truth" and "reality." And fiction it has always been.

Modern civics textbooks portray America's Supreme Court as the ultimate interpreter of America's supreme law, first among the branches in the art of constitutional interpretation. The Constitution itself presents a more balanced picture, listing the judicial branch third, pronouncing the justices "supreme" over other judges but not over other branches . . . [.][3]

Moreover, the courts as an institution remain enamored of the notion that having the last word necessarily makes them "right." In the words of one former Supreme Court justice (his personal opinion), "We are not final because we are infallible, but we are infallible only because we are final."[4]

Thus, courts typically make the worst historians because they have a tendency to look no further back than their last review of the issue at hand—which they presumptively view as "right." With infrequent exceptions, they simply accept the correctness of the prior result involving comparable issues, although to a large extent the principle of *stare decisis* nurtures that tendency. The Latin term *stare decisis* means, literally, "to abide by, or adhere to, decided cases."[5] Generally, the judge-made principle of *stare decisis* exhorts a court to continue to apply a rule of law in the same manner as that court applied it in prior cases.

However, as former Supreme Court chief justice Rehnquist best expressed it, *stare decisis* "may bind courts as to matters of law, but it cannot bind them as to matters of history."[6] Nevertheless, errors perpetuate themselves, sometimes to the point that the notion of correcting them after a long period of time proves simply unimaginable—to the courts, that is. A little over a week after the 1787 Constitutional Convention finalized the proposed Constitution, an editorial urged that a certain population-based provision ought not be allowed to fester uncorrected for an ever-increasing nation:

> Errors sanctified by long usage are not easily relinquished. Their age attaches the people, and renders a reform difficult.[7]

For the United States Supreme Court, that understated observation exemplifies the problem with a constitutional branch of government policed only by itself.

The Supreme Court's disconcerting inability to reach farther back in time than the Court's prior opinion on a subject occasionally spawns some farcical remarks, such as this 1984 boast about the Court's treatment of the Establishment Clause:

> The Court's interpretation of the Establishment Clause has comported with what history reveals was the contemporaneous understanding of its guarantees.[8]

As this chapter leaves sufficiently plain, that self-flattery may conservatively be characterized as nonsense; no matter what the Supreme Court may say, its decidedly unhistorical view of the Establishment Clause has *never* "comported" with historical reality or the "contemporaneous understanding" of anyone, let alone the 1789 congressional author of the Establishment Clause.

Against the factual background painstakingly detailed in the previous chapters, one might well believe that no one, or no single entity, could rewrite historical reality in any enduring fashion. But, given its unique role within our nation's constitutional structure, and also given its largely self-declared status as the final arbiter of the meaning of the Constitution (and thus the "more equal" of the three constitutional branches), the United States Supreme Court can do—and, unfortunately, has done—precisely that.

This chapter examines two of the Supreme Court's decisions in which the Court inexplicably flunked First Amendment history and declared the Establishment Clause to mean something that the 1789 Congress would scarcely recognize. Quite simply, the Court rewrote historical reality. But before moving on to that discussion, one needs to understand the peculiar circumstances in which the United States Supreme Court achieved—or, more accurately, accorded itself—such celebrity in the first place.

A. Some Essential Background: How the Supreme Court Rendered Itself the Only Voice of Constitutional Meaning

Why does our nation unquestioningly look to the Supreme Court as the ultimate authority for the meaning of the Constitution and its various amendments? After all, nothing in the Constitution empowers the Court alone to "interpret" or declare the "meaning" of any aspect of the Constitution. Indeed, as written the Constitution impliedly authorizes each of the three constitutional branches—legislative, executive, and judiciary—to render independent opinions in that regard.[9]

As former Supreme Court chief justice William Rehnquist wrote, "One need understand only a few of its cases to understand the Supreme Court's role in our nation's history."[10] The means by which the Supreme Court ascended to the top of the three otherwise-equal constitutional branches of government purely on its own say-so happens to be one of those cases, a bewildering legal and political escapade at the turn of the nineteenth century that featured outgoing Federalist president John Adams, incoming Republican president Thomas Jefferson, incoming Republican secretary of state James Madison, legendary Supreme Court chief justice (and Adams political ally) John Marshall, and a disgruntled low-level political appointee whose indignation lit the fuse. (Those who believe that the Supreme Court never plays politics may want to stop reading at this point.)

(1). President Adams's "Midnight" Judges

The case originated in the politics of the times, with political parties—the long-dominant Federalists and the newly empowered Jeffersonian Republicans—fighting over judicial appointments during a tempestuous change of presidential administrations.

Jefferson had just won the bitterly contested 1800 presidential election, and stood to take office in the first week of March 1801. Not coincidentally, on February 13, 1801, a lame-duck Federalist-dominated Congress enacted a revamped Judiciary Act[11] that, among other things, divided the federal court system into new districts within the various states and thus created the opportunity for the president to appoint a host of new lifetime-tenured federal judges.

Two weeks later, on February 27, 1801 (a scant five days before a change in the administrations), the same Congress passed a similar law for the newly formed District of Columbia that, among other things, authorized the president to appoint as many new justices of the peace in the District as he might "think expedient."[12] Either outgoing president John Adams could appoint a host of Federalist judges and justices of the peace to fill those new positions in his final days of office, or he could allow incoming president Thomas Jefferson to install Republican judges. The choice proved simple enough.

Thus, from February 18 to February 28, 1801, Adams deluged the Senate with twenty-eight nominations for new federal judges, all of which the Senate confirmed by March 3, 1801.[13] Additionally, on March 2, 1801, with barely two days left in his presidency, Adams sent the Senate forty-two nominations for new justices of the peace for the District of Columbia[14]—a number that one constitutional scholar labels "preposterous."[15] The name "William Marberry" [sic; actually Marbury] appeared in that latter list. The Senate promptly confirmed all forty-two justices of the peace the next day,[16] and Congress just as promptly adjourned—

one day prior to President Jefferson's planned inauguration.[17]

The moment the Senate approved his judicial nominations, Adams signed presidential commissions for all of the newly created positions—and, as expected, peeved Jefferson accordingly. In Jefferson's own words,

> The last day of his political power, the last hours, and even beyond the midnight, were employed in filling all offices, and especially permanent ones, with the bitterest [F]ederalists, and providing for me the alternative, either to execute the government by my enemies . . . or to incur the odium of such numerous removals from office, as might bear me down.[18]

Adams's last-minute judgeships have long been known as the "midnight" appointments, owing to Jefferson's characterization of the affair.[19]

In a separate move that turned out to have monumental consequences for justice-of-the-peace-to-be Marbury (and the nation), just a month earlier Adams had nominated John Marshall, his recently appointed secretary of state[20] and political ally, as chief justice of the United States Supreme Court after Oliver Ellsworth left the Court in mid-December, 1800;[21] Adams advised the Senate of Marshall's nomination on January 20, 1801,[22] and the Senate approved and confirmed Marshall's nomination a week later.[23] Marshall took the oath of office as chief justice on February 4, 1801. He also retained his position as secretary of state for another month.

In a remarkable twist of events that makes the story well worth telling in detail, Marshall, who also still served as Adams's secretary of state until March 4, 1801, somehow neglected to deliver the judicial commissions that Adams had signed.[24] When Jefferson assumed occupancy of the presidential quarters on March 4, he found the signed-but-undelivered judicial commissions lying on a desk in the secretary of state's office; in Jefferson's words:

> Among the midnight appointments of Mr. Adams, were commissions to some federal justices of the peace for Alexandria. These were signed and sealed by him, but not delivered. I found them on the. table of the department of State, on my entrance into the office, and I forbade their delivery.[25]

Thus, Jefferson's incoming secretary of state, James Madison, dutifully refused to deliver the signed judicial commissions—and gleefully thwarted Adams's "midnight appointments." Or so he thought.

(Actually, Jefferson eventually issued most of Adams's undelivered commissions.[26] But not the one that mattered.)

(2). The Disgruntled Mr. Marbury

One of the displeased Federalist appointees—Marbury, one of Adams's forty-two justices of the peace, an appointment that Marshall's own biographer deemed "trifling"[27]—did what today would seem extraordinarily odd: he proceeded directly to the Supreme Court and asked it to issue a "writ of mandamus," Latin for "we command"[28] and essentially an order directing Secretary of State Madison to recognize the validity of the signed-but-undelivered commissions.

Marbury maintained that Congress's 1789 Judiciary Act authorized the Supreme Court to do so. And nothing would have pleased Supreme Court chief justice John Marshall—Federalist, Adams supporter, Jefferson antagonist—more than the ability to order the Jefferson administration to do something as small as that which Marbury wanted.

The case name, *Marbury v. Madison,*[29] has long remained a decision that every first-year law student reads early on. "Nowadays, *Marbury* is customarily the first case assigned in a law-school course on the Constitution,"[30] although *Marbury* most certainly involved more than merely a legal dispute.

(3). Up Next: One of the Nation's Earliest Laws and a Lesson in Context

As mentioned above, in a move that would certainly be viewed today as odd if not pointless altogether, Marbury had gone directly to the Supreme Court in the first instance. Although in general the Supreme Court has always functioned more as a court of last resort and only rarely as a court of first resort, Marbury read the 1789 Judiciary Act to authorize the particular writ (or court order) that he sought. Although the grammatical arrangement of the provisions in a pivotal section of the Judiciary Act rendered Marbury's reading less than certain, that proved not to be the deciding issue.

Among other things, the 1789 Judiciary Act described three distinct areas of Supreme Court "jurisdiction": "original," "exclusive," and "appellate."[31] "Original" jurisdiction connotes a court's authority to resolve matters in the first instance, without the necessity that a litigant proceed in some other court first. "Exclusive" jurisdiction signifies that only one court, and no other court, possesses the authority to resolve certain matters. And "appellate" jurisdiction means that a court has the authority to review a lower court's decision. Marbury presumed that the Supreme Court had "original" jurisdiction of his case.

Within its jurisdictional provisions, a single clause in the 1789 Act seemed to authorize the Supreme Court to issue the kind of writ (or order) that Marbury sought; the specific language read:

> . . . The Supreme Court . . . shall have power to issue . . . writs of *mandamus* . . . to any courts appointed, or persons holding office, under the authority of the United States.[32]

All would likely agree that those words seem to authorize the Court to give Marbury his writ. But that clause appeared within a context that proved otherwise; it not only followed the act's description of the Court's *"appellate"* jurisdiction, it also appeared within the same sentence, separated only by a semicolon. Thus, the all-important context placed Marbury's reading of the Judiciary Act in doubt; Marbury had not invoked the Supreme Court's "appellate" jurisdiction.

But that problem made the case far too simple for Chief Justice Marshall.

(4). The Constitution Always Controls—But Only If Pertinent

If the Court lacked the authority under the 1789 Judiciary Act to do what Marbury wanted, the end result would be simple and straightforward: Marbury would lose. And, for reasons explained just below, that possibility much displeased Chief Justice John Marshall; Marshall—Adams's friend and ally and also Marbury's ally simply by political association—desperately sought something more punitive for the new Jefferson administration. So Marshall looked elsewhere for a resolution. Politics? Most certainly.

Neither Marbury nor Madison—or anyone else—had considered the Constitution's limits on judicial authority; after all, nothing about Marbury's case hinted of any constitutional issue—at first. Of course, the Constitution, as the "supreme" law, always controls.[33] But it only controls as a last resort. And Marbury's case presented no constitutional issues if, as seemed the case, Marbury had simply misread a simple statute. But in the twists and turns of the

Constitution, Chief Justice John Marshall found something lurking.

Article III of the Constitution authorizes the Supreme Court to decide only certain types of litigation—nine categories of "cases" and "controversies"[34]—and it separately prescribes two distinct types of Supreme Court jurisdiction, that is, the actual authority to decide matters. Under the Constitution . . .

• the Supreme Court has *"original"* jurisdiction in "all cases affecting ambassadors, other public ministers and consuls," and "those in which a state shall be a party";

• the Court otherwise has *"appellate"* jurisdiction "in all the other cases before mentioned" in the first paragraph of Article III, Section 2 (*viz.*, the nine categories of "cases" or "controversies").[35]

Recall that Marbury had invoked the Supreme Court's "original" jurisdiction under the 1789 Judiciary Act by proceeding directly to the Supreme Court in the first instance. But, *from a constitutional perspective* Marbury's request did not—*could* not—invoke the Supreme Court's "original" jurisdiction, as it did not involve an "ambassador," a "public minister," a "consul," or a "state." So, again from a constitutional perspective the Court could only give Marbury the writ he wanted if the Court could do so as part of its *"appellate"* jurisdiction. Thus, *both* the 1789 Judiciary Act *and* the Constitution seemed to doom Marbury.

Not so fast, thought Marshall. If on the other hand, the lone clause in the 1789 Act upon which Marbury relied could be read *outside* of its actual context, then Marbury might win. But, in that case, the Judiciary Act would conflict with the Constitution—which would mean that, although the Supreme Court would really like to give Marbury what he wanted (and slap the Jefferson administration as well), the Constitution forbade it from doing so.

(5). The 1789 Judiciary Act: A Legendary Work Written by No Ordinary Congress

But did the 1789 Judiciary Act truly conflict with the 1787 Constitution? How could that be possible?

Although Article III of the Constitution establishes the "judicial power" of the Supreme Court (and all other federal courts), that barebones power has never been considered "self-executing" in the sense that it needs no legislation in order to implement it; to the contrary, the Constitution specifically endows Congress with the authority to enact laws that implement the constitutional powers of the federal courts—and the Supreme Court itself so ruled early on.[36] Accordingly, Congress wrote the 1789 Judiciary Act to implement Article III of the Constitution. And that act had to conform to the Constitution.

The legislation at the heart of the dispute—the 1789 Judiciary Act—could scarcely be considered just an ordinary congressional product, just one of dozens or even hundreds of law enacted each congressional session. To the contrary, the 1789 Judiciary Act bore an almost legendary significance, larger than life; barely two years after the ink had dried on the Constitution, the First Congress, meeting in its inaugural session, passed the act to establish the cornerstone (if not the entire foundation) of what has become our nation's federal court system. The first bill ever introduced in Congress (Senate Bill 1),[37] the passage of the 1789 Judiciary Act followed extensive debates throughout the summer in both the House and the Senate.

Although the 1789 Congress and the 1787 Constitutional Convention technically represent distinct institutional authors, in reality many members of the First Congress had also been delegates at the 1787 Constitutional Convention. Indeed, the author of the 1789 Judiciary Act—Senator Ellsworth[38]—had been an influential participant in the 1787 Convention. And, ironically, he also preceded John Marshall as chief justice of the United States Supreme Court—the person singularly responsible for Marbury's predicament in the first place. Thus, then-senator Ellsworth not only attended the 1787 Convention but also wrote the 1789 law that his successor on the Supreme Court would now examine in the *Marbury* case.

Of the ten senators appointed by the inaugural 1789 Senate to a committee "to bring in a bill for organizing the Judiciary of the United States" (Ellsworth, Bassett, Carroll, Few, Izard, Lee, Maclay, Paterson, Strong, and Wingate[39]), five of those senators—(Ellsworth, Bassett, Few, Paterson, and Strong) had served as delegates to the 1787 Constitutional Convention.[40] Moreover, of the Senate's twenty-two senators in 1789 (two from each of the ratifying states[41]) ten had been delegates to the 1787 Convention.[42] And in the House of Representatives (which also voted on the Senate's proposed Judiciary Act), eight of the fifty-nine representatives during the First Session of the First Congress in 1789[43] had been delegates to the

1787 Convention.[44] Thus, the 1789 Congress could scarcely have been uninformed about the implications of Article III of the Constitution.

Now, Marbury's challenge to the Jefferson administration might well put in question the constitutionality of one of the most pivotal aspects of the 1789 Judiciary Act: the Supreme Court's jurisdiction.

(6). Justice Marshall's Grand Plan

Marshall had a long memory, and he had never agreed with Jefferson's (and Madison's) disestablishment efforts in Virginia in the 1770s.[45] Furthermore, Marshall, a longtime Federalist,[46] had been a political opponent of the Jeffersonian Republicans for years.[47] By the dawn of the nineteenth century, Marshall had earned a reputation as a leading Federalist[48] and thus a natural political enemy of Jefferson. One of Marshall's biographers writes that, after it became clear enough that Jefferson would prevail in the 1800 election, "Marshall's hostility toward Jefferson was such that he could not visualize the man as President. . . . They were political enemies."[49]

As chief justice, Marshall exercised the chief's prerogative and assigned the case to himself. Given Marshall's pivotal connection with the whole Marbury episode, one might well wonder why Marshall even participated in the matter, let alone wrote the Court's opinion. But Marshall had already grasped the reality that, as chief justice of the United States Supreme Court, he could pretty much do as he wanted. And Marshall had an ulterior motive: to cast the newly elected Jefferson administration as arrogant and a danger to the fledgling republic. More crudely, he sought to "lecture the President of the United States and the Secretary of State on what the law was"[50]—the law according to John Marshall. Suffice it to say that "[m]uch more was at stake than William Marbury's commission."[51]

As the person who would decide more than simply Marbury's fate, Marshall confronted a thorny thicket of political considerations. The law aside, Marshall feared that, if the Court *granted* Marbury's request and ordered Madison to deliver the judicial commission, Madison (and Jefferson) would simply ignore the Court's ruling—not merely a political disaster[52] but a scenario that the separation of governmental powers in the Constitution does not plainly prohibit.

Thomas Jefferson, James Madison and the other Republicans who then controlled both the executive and legislative branches of the federal government, were understandably concerned that the judiciary might seize this opportunity to establish its authority to direct high officers of the executive branch how to discharge their official responsibilities. If the federal courts could order James Madison, the secretary of state, appointed by the President, to deliver a commission to a justice of the peace, what would they next be ordering a cabinet officer to do?[53]

On the other hand, if the Court *rejected* Marbury's request on the merits it would incur the wrath of Federalists everywhere as a milquetoast abdication to Jefferson and the Republican administration. So, to Marshall's thinking the Court obviously could not do either—from a political perspective. (From a *legal* perspective, the Court would have had an easy time of it.)

As former Supreme Court chief justice William Rehnquist put it (with an understatement that yields little hint of the monumental consequences),

> It was in this atmosphere of bitter, divisive hostility between the two principal parties that a Supreme Court consisting entirely of Federalist appointees was called upon to judge the claim of another Federalist appointee, William Marbury, against a Republican Secretary of State, James Madison.[54]

Within this conundrum, Marshall the politician calculated the perfect solution; he concocted a means to chastise the Jefferson administration for withholding Marbury's commission while at the same time avoiding a confrontation with the new president by simultaneously ruling that the Court lacked the authority to grant Marbury his requested writ in the first place. In other words, "The Court would decide the case if it could, but it cannot." Ingenious. And, as a bonus, Marshall would seize his self-created opportunity to declare the Supreme Court to be, in effect, the "first among equals" with respect to the other two constitutional branches of government: Congress and the president. As chief justice of the nation's premier court, and also as an ardent Federalist determined to exercise whatever authority he had to benefit his political beliefs, Marshall viewed the Supreme Court as an ideal vehicle by which to decide and define all kinds of issues of national import likely to confront the new nation in decades to come.

(7). The *Marbury* Decision

Back to *Marbury*. Purposefully putting first things last in order to afford himself the opportunity to chastise the Jefferson administration,[55] Marshall ultimately ruled—at the very end of a lengthy dissertation[56]—that: (1) the 1789 Judiciary Act authorized the Court to issue the writ that Marbury wanted, but (2) the Supreme Court lacked the *constitutional* authority to do so, meaning that the *Judiciary Act itself* conflicted with the Constitution.[57] Marshall simply made up that claim; he deliberately misread the Judiciary Act in order to set up a false constitutional issue.

> Why did the First Congress try to expand the Supreme Court's original jurisdiction, contrary to Article III's letter and spirit? *The short answer is that Congress in fact did no such thing.* The statutory sentence that the *Marbury* Court flamboyantly refused to enforce did not say what the Court accused it of saying.[58]

The result in *Marbury* seemed as preposterous then as it does now. According to Marshall, the revered 1789 Congress had somehow stumbled, however improbably. Only John Marshall would have dared to declare the 1789 Judiciary Act as less than sacrosanct. But his dislike for the Jeffersonian Republicans made it easy. At the same time, Marshall impliedly absolved Marbury, a lowly presidential appointee but more importantly a Federalist, of any error in his reading of the 1789 Judiciary Act. (But Marbury never did receive his commission.[59])

Marshall's determination that the Court lacked the authority to give Marbury any relief ought to have ended the matter at the outset, not at the end of an otherwise pointless lecture on executive obligations—as even the Court itself later acknowledged[60]; if a court lacks the jurisdiction to hear a matter in the first place, then it certainly lacks the authority to discuss substantive aspects of the case— a case it cannot decide. But Marshall deliberately reversed the logical order of questions that Marbury's own lawyer had argued. In the Court's words,

> The questions argued by the counsel for [Marbury] were, 1. Whether the supreme court can award the writ of mandamus in any case. 2. Whether it will lie to a secretary of state, in any case whatever. 3. Whether in the present case the court may award a mandamus to James Madison, secretary of state.[61]

From a lawyer's (and court's) perspective, Marbury's lawyer correctly understood the usual order of issues. And the answer to Marbury's first question—"no"—would have decided the case.

But Marshall, instead of beginning and ending with the declaration that the Court lacked jurisdiction and that Marbury's complaint must be dismissed, first explained in great detail why, in his view, Secretary of State Madison had wrongfully refused to deliver the commissions and had, in effect, flouted the law.[62] Marshall thus took a purposeful slap at the Jefferson administration, and all saw it as the "first purpose of [Marshall's] decision."[63] As this latter aspect of the Court's decision—"a seemingly gratuitous question"[64]—proved quite unnecessary to the ultimate ruling, Jefferson believed that Marshall had inserted it in the opinion purposefully, to chastise Jefferson's administration. As one of Marshall's biographers wrote, "Because of the political backgrounds of the Chief Justice and the President, little that they did could be considered outside the political context."[65]

The opinion in *Marbury* aggravated Jefferson to no end; in Jefferson's words,

> This practice of Judge Marshall, of traveling out of his case to prescribe what the law would be in a moot case not before the court, is irregular and very censurable. . . . The court determined at once, that being an original process, they had no cognizance of it; and therefore the question before them was ended. But the Chief Justice went on to lay down what the law would be, had they jurisdiction of the case . . . [.] . . . Yet this case of Marbury and Madison is continually cited by bench and bar, as if it were settled law, without any animadversion [*sic*] on its being merely an *obiter* dissertation of the Chief Justice. [66]

As proof of Marshall's contrivance that the Court lacked the constitutional authority to issue the writ of mandamus that Marbury wanted, Marshall's own opinion in *Marbury* reveals that, in fact, the Court had indeed *already* dealt with a request to issue a writ of mandamus in an unnamed case involving certain 1793 legislation—meaning that the Court had *already* presumed that it possessed the requisite authority to do so. Marshall's opinion in *Marbury* provides:

> It must be well recollected that in 1792 an act passed, directing the secretary at war to place on the pension list such disabled officers and soldiers as should be reported to him by the circuit courts . . . .[.]
>
> . . . [T]he question whether those persons . . . were entitled . . . to

be placed on the pension list, was a legal question, properly determinable in the courts, although the act of placing such persons on the list was to be performed by the head of a department.

That this question might be properly settled, Congress passed an act in February 1793, making it the duty of the secretary of war, in conjunction with the attorney general, to take such measures as might be necessary to obtain an adjudication of the supreme court of the United States on the validity of any such rights . . . [.]

After the passage of this act, a mandamus was moved for, to be directed to the secretary at war . . . [.]

When the subject was brought before the court [viz., the Supreme Court*] the decision was, not, that a mandamus would not lie to the head of a department,* directing him to perform an act, enjoined by law, . . . but that a mandamus ought not to issue *in that case . . . [.]*[67]

That prior instance preceded Marshall's tenure on the Court, but remained precedent nonetheless—and Marshall *knew* about it. Although Marshall offered enough detail in his *Marbury* opinion that the legislation he described can be known with certainty,[68] and although he also explained that the Court declined to issue the writ only because it believed it unnecessary in that case, he omitted any explanation of why the Court had not raised in that case the constitutional question that it raised in *Marbury* on its own initiative.

(8). *Marbury's* Legacy

Marshall's opinion in *Marbury v. Madison* retains such notoriety that one constitutional scholar views *Marbury* as "one of the worst opinions ever delivered by the Supreme Court,"[69] yet labels it "probably the most glorified and certainly the most celebrated opinion in American history."[70] It remains the first instance in which the Court deemed an Act of Congress unconstitutional, and not until more than fifty years later did the Court do so again.[71]

Most accounts of the significance of *Marbury v. Madison* tend to merge two distinctly different questions—one rather simple and one rather not: *First,* does a congressional enactment that contravenes the Constitution retain any validity? *Second,* which of the three constitutional branches of government—the Congress, the president, or the judiciary—possesses the authority to resolve the first question? Marshall's opinion in *Marbury* simply presumes the answer to the second question, yet that second question proved to be by far the more important.

The Court's decision in *Marbury* implemented for the first time at the Supreme Court level the concept long known since as the power of "judicial review," that is, the inherent authority of the Supreme Court (or other federal courts) to declare whether the words in a statute (or an act of the executive branch) contradict the words in the Constitution. Although everyone seemed to suppose that neither the executive nor Congress (nor, for that matter, the judiciary) could undertake actions that conflicted with the Constitution, no one had yet agreed as to which of the three constitutional branches, if any, could render such a declaration—or whether perhaps each branch could do so, unimpeded by the others. Suffice it to say that the Constitution says nothing about the authority of one branch of government to preempt the others.

Chief Justice Marshall, however, had long been an advocate of such unfettered judicial authority, as had some of his fellow Supreme Court justices, and he could now wield it at the highest level. Fifteen years prior to *Marbury* Marshall had argued for the same concept of "judicial review" during a speech in support of the Constitution to the Virginia Ratifying Convention in June 1788.[72] And in a case eight years before *Marbury* Justice Iredell expressed his personal belief[73] that the Supreme Court could render such a declaration:

> If any act of Congress, or of the Legislature of a state, violates those constitutional provisions, it is unquestionably void; though, I admit, that as the authority to declare it void is of a delicate and awful nature, the Court will never resort to that authority, but in a clear and urgent case.[74]

In his individual opinion in that same case Justice Chase expressed less certainty, posing the rhetorical question "[w]ithout giving an opinion, at this time, whether this Court has jurisdiction to decide that any law made by Congress, contrary to the Constitution of the United States, is void."[75] However, in an opinion two years later Justice Chase expressed his belief that the Court could likely do so:

> It is, indeed, a general opinion, it is expressly admitted by all this bar, and some of the Judges have, individually, in the Circuits, decided, that the Supreme Court can declare an act of congress to be unconstitutional, and, therefore, invalid; but there is no adjudication of the Supreme Court itself upon the point.[76]

Marshall had written his opinion in *Marbury* not only to chastise the Jefferson administration but also to deliver a discourse that he wanted to be viewed as a political essay aimed to avert national anarchy, as a decision that preserved the rule of law for the nation—and thereby boosted Marshall's (and the Court's) status.

> [Marshall's opinion] often has been read as a political diatribe against the leader of the opposition party; and such a motive may well have existed. Those same paragraphs can be read as the act of a petty man seeking to embarrass a foe against whom he has had objections and complaints for years; and this too may have been true. But [the opinion] can also be read as a demand that all men obey the law, even the President of the United States and the Secretary of State, that all men understand that the law is not capricious, that it may not be bent to suit one person's biases or political fortunes. . . .[77]

Of course, the "law" according to Marshall in *Marbury* had not been that clear in the first place; it has always seemed less than obvious that an undelivered judgeship commission would necessarily be valid. Marshall wrote as he did in order to embellish the Supreme Court's status with respect to both the executive and legislative branches of the federal government, and effectively render the Supreme Court the ultimate adjudicator of constitutional matters.

Because of the grandiose scope of Marshall's opinion, the result in *Marbury v. Madison* expanded well beyond the seemingly straightforward declaration that the courts had the inherent right to determine whether a statute conflicted with the Constitution. The result assumed a larger-than-life persona, such that the Supreme Court had ensconced itself as the final arbiter of the meaning and import of the Constitution in all circumstances—in practical effect, instituting itself as the "last word" among the three constitutional branches as to the Constitution's meaning. (Remember that the dispute in *Marbury* did not necessarily require the Court to interpret the Constitution.)

Marshall's decision in *Marbury* effectively established the Supreme Court as a partner in government such that its say-so could either sustain or deny the *legislative* function accorded Congress in the Constitution as well as the *executive* function accorded the president in the Constitution.[78] But in reality, the Supreme Court achieved more than merely equality; within the construct of the three governmental branches implemented by the Constitution (*viz.*, the legislative, the executive, and the judiciary, in that order), the Supreme Court had, in practical effect, established itself as "more equal" than the others—an ironic outcome considering the reality that in 1787 Alexander Hamilton (and, presumably, James Madison and others) considered the Supreme Court to be the "least dangerous" and "weakest" branch:

> Whoever attentively considers the different departments of power must perceive that, in a government in which they are separated from each other, the *judiciary*, from the nature of its functions, will always be the *least dangerous* to the political rights of the Constitution . . . [.] The judiciary . . . *may truly be said to have neither force nor will but merely judgment;* and must ultimately depend upon the aid of the executive arm even for the efficacy of its judgments.

> This simple view of the matter suggests several important consequences. It proves incontestably that *the judiciary is beyond comparison the weakest of the three departments of power;* that it can never attack with success either of the other two[.] . . .[79]

Thus far, neither Congress nor the president have ever pretended to possess the authority to ignore a Supreme Court ruling, no matter how ridiculous it might be—although President Lincoln once came close; after the Supreme Court delivered its infamous *Dred Scott* decision in 1857[80]—in which the Court ruled that a former slave could not maintain an action in federal court because he did not qualify as a "citizen" of the United States, and thus prompted Congress to prepare the Constitution's Fourteenth Amendment—Lincoln's first inaugural address in 1861 seemed to ponder the matter as he lamented the reality that judicial decisions can impact more than merely the immediate parties:

> I do not forget the position assumed by some, that constitutional questions are to be decided by the Supreme Court; nor do I deny that such decisions must be binding, in any case, upon the parties to a suit, as to the object of that suit, while they are also entitled to very high respect and consideration in all parallel cases by all other departments of the government. . . . At the same time, that candid citizen must confess that if the policy of the government upon vital questions affecting the whole people, is to be irrevocably fixed by decisions of the Supreme Court, the instant they are made, . . . the people will have ceased to be their own rulers, having, to that extent, practically resigned their government into the hands of that eminent tribunal.[81]

Later, President Andrew Jackson reportedly taunted the Supreme Court to enforce a pair of decisions in the 1830s. In two related cases the Court—via Chief Justice Marshall—frustrated Georgia's attempts to strip the Cherokee Indians of their lands in the state.[82] After learning of the Court's second decision, President Jackson—a Southerner who had announced his support of Georgia's efforts and who condemned the Supreme Court's decisions—reportedly said, "John Marshall has made his decision; now let him enforce it!"[83] Jackson's taunt, however, may be more lore than actuality.[84]

President Nixon once pondered thumbing a presidential nose at the Court after it ordered him to comply with a subpoena to produce certain Oval Office recordings in 1973.[85] The Court ruled unanimously against President Nixon, and the president resigned seventeen days later.[86] (Apparently, the continued efficacy of the Supreme Court's self-endowed preeminence depends solely upon the absence of any challenge to it.)

One chronicler of John Marshall's career characterized the Supreme Court's view of its ascendant constitutional role in the "Marshall era" as born of "a philosophy of institutional self-justification,"[87] and derided the Court's *Marbury* opinion as a product of Marshall's judicial ego:

> What can be said with confidence is that in *Marbury v. Madison* Marshall seems to have been motivated by one compelling purpose. His aim was to furnish the Court and the country with a rationale for subjecting the whole domain of governmental activity to overall control by the judiciary.[88]

Years later, Jefferson himself lambasted the Supreme Court's post-*Marbury* role within the constitutional scheme:

> The constitution, on this hypothesis [*viz.*, that the Supreme Court's declarations about the Constitution reign supreme among the three constitutional branches], is a mere thing of wax in the hands of the judiciary, which they may twist and shape into any form they please.[89]

Late in life, James Madison separately wrote that, although at the time of the 1787 Constitutional Convention he envisioned that Article III of the Constitution accorded the Supreme Court preeminence with respect to constitutional disputes between the *federal* and *state* governments, he said nothing about the Supreme Court's authority over Congress or the Executive branches. But Madison did express his consternation that the Court had in recent years—again, during the Marshall era—"manifested a propensity to enlarge the general authority in derogation of the local, and to amplify its own jurisdiction, which has justly incurred the public censure," and suggested that a constitutional amendment might be in order to rectify the Court's extravagant view of judicial preeminence:

> We arrive at the agitated question whether the Judicial Authority of the U. S. be the constitutional resort for determining the line between the federal & State jurisdictions. Believing as I do that the General Convention regarded a provision within the Constitution for deciding in a peaceable & regular mode all cases arising in the course of its operation, as essential to an adequate System of Govt. [*sic*] that it intended the Authority vested in the Judicial Department as a final resort in relation to the States, . . . and that this intention is expressed by the articles declaring that the federal Constitution & laws shall be the supreme law of the land, and that the Judicial Power of the U. S. shall extend to all cases arising under them. Believing moreover that this was the prevailing view of the subject when the Constitution was adopted & put into execution . . . [.]
>
> I am not unaware that the Judiciary career has not corresponded with what was anticipated. At one period the Judges perverted the Bench of Justice into a rostrum for partizan [*sic*] harangues. And latterly the Court, by some of its decisions, still more by extrajudicial reasonings & dicta, has manifested a propensity to enlarge the general authority in derogation of the local, and to amplify its own jurisdiction, which has justly incurred the public censure. But the abuse of a trust does not disprove its existence. And if no remedy of the abuse be practicable under the forms of the Constitution, *I should prefer a resort to the Nation for an amendment of the Tribunal itself*, to continual appeals from its controverted decisions to that Ultimate Arbiter.[90]

Given the courts' self-imposed supremacy and the belief that only the courts can correct themselves, one finds that, within an institutionalized decision-making framework that emphasizes conformity for its own sake, judicial mistakes perpetuate themselves beyond the confines of rational explanation. Yet, as former Supreme Court chief justice William Rehnquist once proclaimed, "[N]o amount of repetition of historical errors in judicial opinions can make the errors true."[91]

With that understanding in place, the following discussion recounts the missteps by which the Supreme Court, in its self-anointed role as the ultimate authority on the Constitution, almost nonchalantly, if not purposefully, ignored historical reality and declared an utterly fictional meaning for the First Amendment's Establishment Clause that endures to this day.

B. *Reynolds v. United States*

Former Supreme Court justice Oliver Wendell Holmes once observed that "a page of history is worth a volume of logic,"[92] an apt expression since repeated in a host of Establishment Clause decisions both by the Court and by various Supreme Court justices in individual opinions in those decisions.[93] Of course, the "history" of which Holmes wrote must be true for it to be "worth" anything.

In its 1878 opinion in *Reynolds v. United States,*[94] the Supreme Court visited Jefferson's figurative "wall of separation" for the first time[95]—and wreaked havoc in a number of ways. The Court's "page of history" about Jefferson's long-forgotten 1802 letter to the Danbury Baptists, which had only been published relatively recently in 1853 as part of an early publication of Jefferson's letters,[96] bore scant resemblance to truth and historical reality.

The Utah Territorial court convicted Reynolds of violating a federal bigamy prohibition. Reynolds maintained that the First Amendment's Free Exercise Clause ("Congress shall make no law . . . prohibiting the free exercise [of religion]") exonerated him:

> On the trial, . . . the accused proved that at the time of his alleged second marriage he was, and for many years before had been, a member of the Church of Jesus Christ of Latter-Day Saints, commonly called the Mormon Church, and a believer in its doctrines; that it was an accepted doctrine of that church "that it was the duty of male members of said church, circumstances permitting, to practise [*sic*] polygamy; . . . that this duty was enjoined by different books which the members of said church believed to be of divine origin . . . ; that the failing or refusing to practise [*sic*] polygamy by such male members of said church, when circumstances would admit, would be punished . . . [.]" He also proved "that he had received permission from the recognized authorities in said church to enter into polygamous marriage; . . . and that such marriage ceremony was performed under and pursuant to the doctrines of said church."

Upon this proof he asked the court to instruct the jury that if they found from the evidence that he was married as charged—if he was married—in pursuance of and in conformity with what he believed at the time to be a religious duty, that the verdict must be "not guilty." This request was refused . . . [.][97]

The Court's opinion leaves it free from doubt that the Free Exercise Clause, and it alone, lay at the heart of the matter:

> . . . [T]he question is raised, *whether religious belief can be accepted as a justification of an overt act made criminal by the law of the land.* The inquiry is not as to the power of Congress to prescribe criminal laws for the Territories, but as to the guilt of one who knowingly violates a law which has been properly enacted, if he entertains a religious belief that the law is wrong.

> Congress cannot pass a law for the government of the Territories which shall prohibit the *free exercise of religion.* The first amendment to the Constitution expressly forbids such legislation. . . . The question to be determined is, whether the law now under consideration comes within this prohibition.[98]

(1). Why the Supreme Court Found Jefferson's "Wall" Pertinent at All—and the Reason Had Nothing to Do with the Establishment Clause

The key constitutional question in Reynolds's defense became whether the "free exercise" of religion assured by the First Amendment extends to *conduct* as well as *beliefs.* And Jefferson's 1802 letter did, in fact, refer to just such a distinction.

Thus, a host of writers have concluded, logically enough, that, because the case required the Court to address a "belief" versus "conduct" difference in the scope of the Free Exercise Clause, the Court wanted to quote a portion of Jefferson's letter which seemed pertinent to the defendant's claim that the Free Exercise Clause protected *conduct.*[99] After all, Jefferson's 1802 letter to the Danbury Baptists did remark—albeit not for the first time in Jefferson's writings—that "the legitimate[100] powers of the government reach *actions only, and not opinions,*"[101] an observation which, within the context of the Supreme Court's opinion in *Reynolds,* would seem pertinent, although albeit certainly not Jefferson's major premise in the letter.

But, for reasons which some attribute to a desire to supply a thorough context for Jefferson's "actions" versus "opinions" commentary, the opinion quoted far more from Jefferson's letter than would otherwise be necessary to isolate Jefferson's famous five-word phrase. The *Reynolds* opinion quotes the following text from Jefferson's 1802 "wall" letter:

> "Believing with you that religion is a matter which lies solely between man and his God; that he owes account to none other for his faith or his worship; that *the legitimate powers of government reach actions only and not opinions,* I contemplate with sovereign reverence that act of the whole American people [*viz.,* referring to the First Amendment] which declared that their legislature should 'make no law respecting an establishment of religion or prohibiting the free exercise thereof,' thus building a wall of separation between Church and State.'"[102]

Only the emphasized eleven-word passage in that excerpt could be viewed as pertinent to Reynolds's "free exercise" defense. But the opinion not only quoted far more than necessary from Jefferson's letter, it neglected to specify what portion of the quoted text the Court believed pertinent, leaving readers to mistakenly presume that the Court viewed *all* of the quoted text as pertinent. Thus, some theorize that the reference to Jefferson's figurative "wall" in the *Reynolds* opinion amounted to a fortuity of mid-nineteenth-century editing. As one commentator frames it,

> [Chief Justice Waite, the author of the *Reynolds* opinion] wanted to use another phrase in Jefferson's letter to support his decision[,] but he could not edit the letter to leave out the wall. The remark of Jefferson on which the Chief Justice relied was that powers of government could reach only the *action* of men, not their *opinions.*[103]

The context of the Court's opinion in *Reynolds* confirms that theory; in the sentence that follows the Court's excerpt from Jefferson's letter, the opinion declares that Jefferson's letter reflects an understanding that

> Congress was deprived of all legislative power over mere *opinion,* but was left free to reach *actions* which were in violation of social duties or subversive of good order, [104]

hinting that the Court perceived Jefferson's letter as relevant to that specific proposition.

Indeed, Jefferson had differentiated between "opinion" and "conduct" before, a reality that seems to have been overlooked. Jefferson had written of precisely the same distinction decades earlier, when he wrote in "Query XVII" (Religion) in his famous 1781 *Notes on the State of Virginia*[105] that, with respect to religious freedom, "[t]he legitimate powers of government extend to such *acts only* as are injurious to others."[106]

Jefferson's phrasing in each instance match remarkably:

> 1781 *Notes:* "the *legitimate powers* of government extend to such *acts* only as are injurious to others."
>
> 1802 letter: "the *legitimate powers* of government reach *actions* only and not opinions."

Thus, it appears that the *Reynolds* Court indeed understood that Jefferson's letter supported such a differentiation—although why the Court opted to cite the remarks of someone who had nothing to do with the First Amendment remains unexplained.

But, unfortunately, the Court's opinion fails to make it plain that the Court referenced Jefferson's 1802 letter solely for purposes of including Jefferson's differentiation between "opinion" and "conduct," and not for any other reason. That lamentable imprecision in the opinion tainted another Supreme Court opinion seven decades later, discussed later in this chapter.

(2). Jefferson Had No Involvement Whatsoever with the First Amendment

The *Reynolds* opinion also overstates Jefferson's involvement with the First Amendment—another monumental error that exacerbated the Court's overly broad reliance on Jefferson's letter in the first place. The Court's opinion quotes from Jefferson's 1802 letter and then proclaims in the next sentence in its opinion that

> [c]oming as this does from an *acknowledged leader* of the advocates of the measure, it may be accepted *almost as an authoritative declaration* of the scope and effect of the amendment thus secured [*viz.*, referencing the First Amendment and its religion clauses].[107]

History labels as incontrovertibly false the Supreme Court's remark about Jefferson's role as an "acknowledged leader" of "the measure," *viz.*, the First Amendment. Jefferson had no involvement with Congress's adoption of the First Amendment in 1789, living as he did in France from mid-1784 to late 1789. Indeed, Jefferson's relationship to the constitutional amendments adopted by Congress in 1789 proves so tenuous that none of Jefferson's various biographies mentions any events associated with the First Congress amendments beyond Jefferson's infrequent intercontinental exchanges of letters with Madison (and others) from the time the First Congress convened in March 1789 until it adjourned in September 1789—and neither Jefferson's letters to Madison[108] nor Madison's letters to Jefferson during those months[109] explored the proposal that eventually became the First Amendment's Establishment Clause.

Madison wrote Jefferson only three letters between June 8, 1789 (when Madison first introduced the subject of amendments to the House of Representatives), and September 25, 1789 (when the First Congress finalized the Bill of Rights),[110] and he wrote Jefferson no letters at all during Congress's debates in August 1789 and September 1789.

In a May 27, 1789, letter to Jefferson, Madison advised that he intended to propose some constitutional amendments as well as a proposed Bill of Rights,[111] yet Jefferson never inquired as to the details or furnished any particular input. And in his June 30, 1789, letter to Jefferson (by which time Madison had already introduced the various amendments in the First Congress), Madison wrote:

> Inclosed [*sic*] is a copy of sundry amendments to the Constitution lately proposed in the House of Representatives. Every thing of a controvertible nature that might endanger the concurrence of two-thirds of each House and three-fourths of the States was studiously avoided.[112]

Still, Jefferson expressed no interest in the meaning of the words that Madison proposed for what became the Establishment Clause; Jefferson entrusted the religious freedom aspect of any post-Constitution bill of rights to Madison, confident that Madison would do what he viewed as necessary, as Jefferson's interests lay elsewhere at the time.[113]

Finally, in an August 2, 1789, letter Madison supplied Jefferson with a copy of the House Select Committee Report of July 28, 1789, and still Jefferson did not inquire about the details or pose any questions about the text of the Establishment Clause.[114]

And although Jefferson wrote Madison six letters between June 8, 1789, and September 25, 1789 (the date that the Senate concurred in the House of Representatives' approval of the proposed amendments), he omitted any mention of the religion clauses that became part of the First Amendment.

Thus, the Supreme Court's remark in *Reynolds* that Jefferson ought to be considered "an acknowledged leader of the advocates of the measure,"[115] and the Court's uninformed belief that Jefferson's 1802 letter to the Danbury Baptists "may be accepted almost as an authoritative declaration" in some respect,[116] simply belie historical reality. Unfortunately, these fictions uttered by an institution that deems itself the ultimate constitutional authority etched Jefferson's colloquial allegory into history with a permanence that defies rational explanation.

(3). Jefferson Likewise Had No Involvement with Patrick Henry's Famous 1784 "Establishment" Tax Proposal

The *Reynolds* opinion also glamorizes Jefferson in yet another fictional capacity. After it accurately summarizes some of the conditions in the states in the 1600s and early 1700s that spawned the disestablishment movement that culminated years later,[117] the *Reynolds* opinion remarks—inaccurately:

> This [*viz.*, Patrick Henry's proposed 1784 Virginia establishment tax[118]] brought out a determined opposition. Amongst others, Mr. Madison prepared a "Memorial and Remonstrance," which was widely circulated and signed, and in which he demonstrated "that religion, or the duty we owe the Creator," was not within the cognizance of civil government. . . . At the next session the proposed bill [offered by Patrick Henry] was not only defeated, but another, "for establishing religious freedom," drafted by Mr. Jefferson, was passed. . . .[119]

First of all, the reason those remarks bear any pertinence to the issue to be decided in *Reynolds*—which had nothing to do with any establishment considerations—remains unexplained. And second, most of those remarks prove to be fictional:

• The phrase "amongst others" proves inaccurate because *only* James Madison prepared and circulated any written opposition.

• Thomas Jefferson never offered any legislation during the "next session" following Henry's proposed tax, because he had been in France since July 1784—more than a year before the "next session" that began in the fall of 1785.

• Only Madison offered any legislation remotely related to "religious freedom" during the 1785 Virginia legislative session.[120]

Sadly enough, the Supreme Court does not stand alone in that errant view of history. One writer oddly accords credit to Thomas Jefferson for opposing Patrick Henry's proposed tax, declaring that "Jefferson opposed the bill . . . ," wielding quotes from portions of

Jefferson's *Notes on the State of Virginia* that in fact bear no relationship to any such assertion.[121] Jefferson would have been hard-pressed to have opposed Henry's proposal—within his *Notes* or otherwise. First of all, Jefferson composed his *Notes on the State of Virginia* in 1781, three years *before* Henry even introduced his proposed tax in December 1784.[122] An introduction at the beginning of Jefferson's *Notes* contains the following:

> The following Notes were written in Virginia in the year 1781, and somewhat corrected and enlarged in the winter of 1782 . . . [.][123]

And second, Jefferson had been out of the country since July 1784—four months *before* Henry even introduced his proposed tax—and did not return until November 1789. Indeed, Jefferson wrote Madison *from Paris* in early 1786, thanking Madison for the latter's opposition to Henry's proposal ("I thank you for the communication of the remonstrance against the assessment.").[124]

All of Jefferson's legislative efforts in the Virginia legislature in the area of religious freedom occurred *prior* to 1785:

• In June 1776, Jefferson penned his never-implemented Draft Constitution for Virginia, which included a "free exercise" provision and a "disestablishment" provision in Article IV, "Rights, Private and Public."[125]

• In November 1776, Jefferson prepared a Draft of Bill Exempting Dissenters from Contributing to the Support of the Church.[126]

• And in June 1779, Jefferson drafted a proposed Bill for Establishing Religious Freedom, and introduced it to the Virginia legislature the next day.[127]

Incredibly, in one of its late-twentieth-century Establishment Clause decisions the Supreme Court repeated these same historical inaccuracies about Jefferson; in 1962 it wrote:

> In 1785–1786, those opposed to the established Church, led by James Madison and Thomas Jefferson, who, though themselves not members of any of these dissenting religious groups, opposed all religious establishments by law on grounds of principle, obtained the enactment of the famous "Virginia Bill for Religious Liberty" by which all religious groups were placed on an equal footing so far as the State was concerned.[128]

How Jefferson might have accomplished as much from France remains unexplained by the Court.

Ultimately, the *Reynolds* opinion set the stage for one of the Supreme Court's most factually detached opinions of all time, discussed in Part C of this chapter.

(4). The Personal Opinions of the Uninvolved Contribute Nothing to "Meaning"

Finally, the *Reynolds* opinion fails to explain why the Court understood Jefferson's personal belief(s) to be of any significance within the context of the case. As the Court itself has observed in later opinions, expressions of personal opinion carry no significance for purposes of discerning the meaning of text written by someone else years earlier.[129]

Thus, Jefferson's subjective, *ad hoc* reference to some figurative "wall" more than a decade after the fact ought to be accorded no more authoritative weight than the views of any ordinary citizen.

C. *Everson v. Board of Education*

In 1947, the Supreme Court rendered its blockbuster opinion in *Everson v. Board of Education,*[130] in which the Court supplied a host of fictional pronouncements in its initial look at the meaning of the Establishment Clause. Those fictions have spawned an ever-lengthening series of Supreme Court decisions involving the Establishment Clause in which each successive decision further skews, if not disregards altogether, the historical reality explained in detail in the preceding chapters. And the Court's 1878 decision in *Reynolds* played a pivotal role in *Everson.*

If you wonder why . . .

• public schools and local governments shudder at the thought of Christmas or Easter,

• the content of public school commencement addresses has become heavily scrutinized (if not censored altogether), or

• the mention of "intelligent design" renders public school administrators positively apoplectic, or

• the Pledge of Allegiance wound up embroiled in litigation over the words "under God," or

• displays that speak of our nation's heritage in terms of "God," the "Ten Commandments," or related terms spark such turmoil, or

• few Americans know the meaning of the phrase "an establishment of religion,"

. . . know that *Everson* started it all.

Almost unimaginably, the Supreme Court's 1947 decision in *Everson v. Board of Education* marked the first occasion that the Court assessed the meaning and scope of the Establishment Clause in a dispute that actually involved the Establishment Clause. Although two turn-of-the-twentieth-century Supreme Court decisions implicated the Establishment Clause in some very minor respects, neither of those decisions merits status as a true Establishment Clause decision because neither furnishes any substantive discussion of the Establishment Clause; in an 1899 decision the Supreme Court rejected the contention that a federal law that established a private corporation to construct and operate a hospital facilitated an "establishment" subject to the Establishment Clause simply because the hospital operators belonged to a particular religious group,[131] and a decade later the Supreme Court rejected the notion that the federal administration of Indian Nation trust funds used in part to provide sectarian schools for Indian pupils facilitated an "establishment" subject to the Establishment Clause.[132]

One writer offers this explanation for the dearth of Establishment Clause litigation between 1789 and 1947:

> Because the First Amendment applied only to Congress, the States were free to deal with religion as their people wished, even to maintain established churches. The [Supreme Court] decisions incorporating the First Amendment into the Fourteenth [Amendment] began in the 1920s.[133] Until then and for another two decades the Establishment Clause played little visible part in American life.[134]

Indeed, when the *Everson* litigation first began wending its way through the New Jersey state courts in 1945 "[t]here was no Establishment Clause law to speak of . . . [.]"[135]

Everson originated with a state law that authorized public school districts to reimburse students' parents for the cost of using public transportation to get to and from both public and private schools—a quintessential non-preferential funding mechanism. A disgruntled taxpayer challenged the constitutionality of one such school district's expenditures because the district had reimbursed parents for the transportation costs of sending their children to parochial (private) schools.

The New Jersey legislature had debated non-preferential public funding of transportation for both public and private schools from

1937 to 1941 without any mention of the Establishment Clause.[136] Only when the matter reached the New Jersey courts did anyone raise any federal constitutional issues, a tactic that one scholar familiar with the local New Jersey proceedings characterizes as a last gasp "afterthought":

> . . . [The attorney for Everson] listed seven grounds for holding the law void; six of them were based on the New Jersey constitution. The last of the seven reasons was a claim that the parochial school bus law violated the Fourteenth Amendment to the U.S. Constitution. This reason was something of an afterthought.[137]

Eventually, the dispute found its way to the United States Supreme Court.

Although the Supreme Court ultimately rejected the Establishment Clause challenge in *Everson* because the school district had, in fact, utilized public funds in a completely neutral fashion[138] (an almost forgotten aspect of the case—and a result that actually comports with the Establishment Clause's meaning), its opinion nevertheless wreaked permanent damage to the Establishment Clause by (1) failing altogether to report the historical events of 1789 that accord the Establishment Clause its meaning, and (2) resorting to Jefferson's 1802 letter to the Danbury Baptists as the sole source of meaning.

(1). The *Reynolds* Opinion's Gaffes Revisited in *Everson*

The *Everson* opinion veers off the path of reality at the outset when it undertakes to construe the words "Congress shall make no law respecting an establishment of religion" by examining various historical events that long *preceded* Congress's adoption of the First Amendment in 1789, while inexplicably ignoring the 1789 proceedings themselves.[139]

The opinion's historical essay begins earnestly enough, with a summary of "a vivid mental picture [in the minds of early American settlers] of conditions and practices [in England] which they fervently wished to stamp out in order to preserve liberty for themselves and for their posterity."[140] Soon, the *Everson* opinion reports, some of those very evils begin to plague settlements within the states; "[t]he imposition of taxes to pay ministers' salaries and to build and maintain churches and church property aroused their indignation" and ultimately "found expression in the First Amendment."[141]

Unfortunately, at that point the *Everson* opinion loses its grip on historical reality:

• the opinion remarks that "[t]he movement toward this end [*viz.*, the disestablishment "movement"] reached its dramatic climax in Virginia in 1785–86 when the Virginia legislative body was about to renew Virginia's tax levy for the support of the established church"[142]—events that occurred *prior* to Congress's passage of the Establishment Clause in the summer of 1789;

• the opinion remarks that "Thomas Jefferson and James Madison led the fight against this tax" during the Virginia legislative recess in 1785[143]—when Jefferson had not even been in the country for a year; and

• the opinion recites that "[w]hen the proposal [*viz.*, Patrick Henry's 1784 proposed tax] came up for consideration at that session, it not only died in committee, but the Assembly enacted the famous "Virginia Bill for Religious Liberty" [*sic;* the Bill for Establishing Religious Freedom[144]] originally written by Thomas Jefferson,"[145] when in fact Virginia never adopted Jefferson's 1779 proposal.

These historical fictions might seem familiar because they surfaced as well in the Court's *Reynolds* decision, discussed in the previous topic. Such factual errors in a Supreme Court opinion seem unfathomable, and they remain unexplained to this day.

First, as recorded history reflects with remarkable objectivity, although the events of 1785 and 1786 in the Virginia legislature certainly lend some historical perspective to the development of the Establishment Clause, what the *Everson* opinion characterizes as the "dramatic climax" of the anti-establishment movement actually occurred on *September 25, 1789,* when Congress approved the Establishment Clause and President Washington thereafter forwarded the proposed Bill of Rights to the states for ratification—a historic reality that inexplicably receives no mention whatsoever in the *Everson* opinion.

Second, as the preceding discussion of *Reynolds* explained in detail, Jefferson played no role whatsoever in Virginia's efforts in the mid-1780s to implement a church-favored tax. Thus, to say, as the Court did in *Everson,* that Jefferson "led the fight"[146] when he had no connection with the incident remains one of the oddest aspects of an exceptionally odd decision.

Third, the 1786 Virginia legislature did *not* enact any Jeffersonion proposal entitled, in the Court's words, "Virginia Bill for Religious Liberty" [*sic*].[147] For one thing, Jefferson never drafted any legislative proposal with that title. Furthermore, although in June *1779* (not 1786), Jefferson introduced a proposal in the Virginia legislature entitled A Bill for Establishing Religious Freedom,[148] the legislature never acted on that proposal.[149] And the 1786 Virginia legislature enacted only a single religious-freedom act: Madison's (not Jefferson's) proposal entitled An Act for Establishing Religious Freedom.[150] Finally, the excerpt that the *Everson* opinion offers as "the statute" in question[151]—referring to Jefferson's 1779 Bill for Establishing Religious Freedom—actually quotes from Madison's 1785 Act for Establishing Religious Freedom that the Virginia legislature enacted on January 16, 1786, *not* from Jefferson's 1779 bill.

If *Everson*'s errors ended there, the opinion would be bad enough. Indeed, *Everson* has aptly been characterized as predicated upon nothing but "mythical history,"[152] or, perhaps more comprehensively stated, "the myth and the metaphor"[153] (referencing the "myth" that Jefferson played a role in the creation of the Establishment Clause and the "metaphor" of Jefferson's "wall"). But the Supreme Court's inexplicable missteps in *Everson* continued.

(2). Fabricating Reality and Rewriting History: "It Is So Because We Say It Is"

In the *Everson* opinion the Court's lone explanation of Establishment Clause "history" appears in a few brief remarks, each of which mangles historical reality. For example, the *Everson* opinion recites that

> This Court has *previously recognized* that the provisions of the First Amendment, in the drafting and adoption of which Madison *and Jefferson* played such leading roles, *had the same objective and were intended to provide the same protection* against governmental intrusion on religious liberty as the Virginia statute.[154]

None of the emphasized passages in this excerpt bear any resemblance to historical reality.

First, the Court had not "previously recognized" any such thing. As authority for that fictional recasting of history, the *Everson* opinion cites three of its own nineteenth-century decisions.[155] Yet none of those three decisions even *involved* the Establishment Clause: in two of the cases the parties litigated the scope of the First Amendment's Free Exercise Clause[156]—scarcely an inconsequential distinction—while the opinion in the third case makes no mention of the Establishment Clause at all.[157]

Second, the excerpt from *Everson* quoted just above further misstates history by (1) perpetuating the fiction concerning Jefferson's nonexistent "role" with respect to the First Amendment, when history informs us with enduring objectivity that Jefferson played no role whatsoever; and (2) linking the Establishment Clause with "the Virginia statute," when in fact the Establishment Clause originated with the states' own constitutional assurances against an establishment. In fact, the Establishment Clause debates in the First Congress in 1789 furnish no mention of either Jefferson's draft bill or Madison's act.

But perhaps the most perplexing passage of a host of inaccuracies in the *Everson* opinion resides in the following dogmatic rhetoric—divided here into six enumerated segments:

> The "establishment of religion" clause of the First Amendment means at least this: [1] Neither a state nor the Federal Government can set up a church. [2] Neither can pass laws which aid one religion, aid all religions, or prefer one religion over another. [3] Neither can force nor influence a person to go to or to remain away from church against his will or force him to profess a belief or disbelief in any religion. [4] No person can be punished for entertaining or professing religious beliefs or disbeliefs, for church attendance or non-attendance. [5] No tax in any amount, large or small, can be levied to support any religious activities or institutions, whatever they may be called, or whatever form they may adopt to teach or practice religion. [6] Neither a state nor the Federal Government can, openly or secretly, participate in the affairs of any religious organizations or groups and vice versa.[158]

The *Everson* opinion cites no historical source for any of these six sentences because none exists; the Court simply made them all up. Worse still, this discourse never once mentions the actual target of the Establishment Clause: an "establishment," and not simply "religion" or "religious beliefs," or "religious activities," or "religious affairs."

• Although the First Amendment indeed forbids the *federal* government from "set[ting] up a church," the first of these six sentences nevertheless proves incorrect because the text of the First Amendment itself expressly limits its scope to Congress ("Congress shall make no law . . .")—at least it did until the *Everson* opinion itself declared to the contrary.[159]

• Although the government indeed cannot "prefer one religion over another," the second of these six sentences nevertheless proves incorrect because the text of the Establishment Clause only thwarts laws that would aid a *single,* dominant, government-favored *ecclesiastical institution* and not merely "religion"—hence the Establishment Clause's reference to "*an* establishment," in the singular.

• The third of these six sentences proves incorrect because it paraphrases the effects of the *Free Exercise Clause,* not the Establishment Clause.

• The fourth of these six sentences proves incorrect because the Establishment Clause says no such thing; rather, it forbids an *establishment,* absent which none of the listed effects could occur in the first place.

• The fifth of these six sentences proves incorrect because Congress designed the Establishment Clause to prohibit a *preferential* tax devoted to the support of a *single,* dominant ecclesiastical institution—a hallmark of any establishment.

• And the sixth of these six sentences proves incorrect because the text of the Establishment Clause serves only to disable Congress from implementing a national "establishment," *viz.,* a single, preferred ecclesiastical institution (or, in effect, a national church).

(3). Erecting the Folklore "Wall" as Part of Americana

The *Everson* opinion also repeats the history-altering words from *Reynolds* (discussed in the preceding topic) about Jefferson's figurative "wall," declaring that "[i]n the words of Jefferson, the clause against establishment of religion by law was intended to erect 'a wall of separation between Church and State.'"[160] Congress, of course, never "intended" any such thing, and Jefferson could not possibly have spoken for the 1789 Congress in any event.

The *Everson* opinion concludes with these oft-quoted remarks:

> The First Amendment has erected a wall between church and state. That wall must be kept high and impregnable.[161]

No one really knows what these words mean. What, for instance, does "church" mean? And what does "state" mean—especially given the reality that nothing in the First Amendment mentions "state" (and the First Amendment had no application to the states when Jefferson wrote his letter in 1802)? Indeed, as the tidal wave of post-*Everson* Establishment Clause litigation demonstrates, they can mean pretty much whatever one wants them to mean. But in reality, they mean nothing, because within the context of the historical certainties examined in the preceding chapters the Establishment Clause does not "erect a wall between church and state." To characterize the remarks made by the Supreme Court in the *Everson* opinion as fiction would be an understatement.

The late Princeton constitutional scholar and presidential advisor on constitutional issues Edward Corwin, the "dean of American constitutional scholars" during his lifetime and author of a host of highly regarded constitutional works,[162] could scarcely believe the extent to which the Supreme Court's *Everson* opinion mangled historical reality. In a commentary about *Everson* published not long after the Court's decision, Corwin wrote:

> What the "establishment of religion" clause of the First Amendment does, and *all that it does, is to forbid Congress to give any religious faith, sect, or denomination a preferred status.*[163]

⟹◆⟸

> The historical records shows beyond peradventure that the core idea of "an establishment of religion" comprises the idea of *preference;* and that any act of public authority favorable to religion in general cannot, without manifest falsification of history, be brought under the ban of that phrase. Undoubtedly the Court has the right to make history, as it has often done in the past; but it has no right to *remake* it.[164]

One scholar has subtlety mocked the Court's reliance on Jefferson's "wall" as unwarranted at the outset, observing that from 1789 until the Supreme Court's *Everson* opinion in 1947 "[t]here was *never* total separation between Church and State."[165] The Supreme Court's persistent repetition of that fiction can never make it so, anymore than the Supreme Court could alter reality with a declaration that "one plus one shall equal three," or that "east" shall now be "west."

(4). Conspicuous by Absence: The Records of the 1789 Congress

Perhaps above all else, it seems simply unimaginable that the 1947 *Everson* decision omits any discussion whatsoever of the 1789 congressional proceedings that spawned the Establishment Clause. One can scarcely pontificate about the meaning of a constitutional amendment by purposefully ignoring the history that underlies the amendment—unless, apparently, the speaker happens to be the Supreme Court.

> Conspicuous by its omission [in the *Everson* opinion] is an analysis by the Court of the recorded debates in the First Congress on the framing of the First Amendment. Conventional rules of interpretation suggest that the interpretation of a constitutional provision begin with an examination of the text and the deliberations of the body that drafted and adopted it. [The Court's *Everson* opinion] *virtually ignored* the legislative history of the First Amendment religion provisions. The interpretation of the First Amendment was, after all, at issue in *Everson. It would seem that the legislative history of the First Amendment,* not the disestablishment battles in Virginia, *should have been the focus of the Court's historical review.* Opponents speculate that the Court disregarded the text and legislative history of the First Amendment because they failed to support the Court's separationist prepossessions.[166]

In fact, the *Everson* opinion falls well shy of having "virtually ignored" the First Congress's proceedings; it *in fact* ignored them. Not until Chief Justice Rehnquist's dissenting opinion four decades later in *Wallace v. Jaffree*[167] did *anyone* on the Court examine the pertinent historical record—a record that repudiates much, if not all, of what the Supreme Court has ever said about the meaning of the Establishment Clause. The Court seems to have forgotten that it once declared:

> To determine the extent of the [words used in the Constitution], we must, therefore, place ourselves in the position of the men who framed and adopted the Constitution, and inquire what they must have understood to be the meaning and scope of those [words].[168]

If that observation holds true for the text of the 1787 Constitution, it holds equally true for the text of the Establishment Clause—which, after all, forms part of the Constitution.

(5). Just Who Did This?

Most Americans likely view the United States Supreme Court as a collection of some of the best legal minds in the nation. For roughly the past five decades or so, that view has been well warranted of the

Court as a whole, and certainly some bright stars occasionally shone before then. But, for the most part, Supreme Court justices historically have been political servants who happened to receive an appointment to the Court.

As of this writing, the individual justices on the current Supreme Court arrived with superlative academic and professional credentials. In terms of law schools alone, the Court boasts of five justices with law degrees from Harvard,[169] two with law degrees from Yale,[170] and one each from the Northwestern and Columbia Schools of Law.[171] Each of the nine justices sat on one of the eleven United States Court of Appeals,[172] three served as law clerks for prior Supreme Court justices,[173] and six taught in law schools.[174] Each has multiple law clerks with their own stellar credentials.

The 1947 version of the Court, however, bore little resemblance. For one thing, only six of the nine justices had even graduated from law school, and only four had law school pedigrees from top-ten law schools. (Few probably realize that the Constitution does not prescribe a law degree as a condition of appointment to the United States Supreme Court. "It was not until 1957 that the Supreme Court, for the first time in its history, had been composed entirely of law school graduates."[175]) And all of the justices had been active in politics at either the state or federal level, or both, and had political connections far more overt than today's Court.

The *Everson* decision represented a severe five-to-four split among the justices. The majority—which, ironically, rewrote Establishment Clause history in the *Everson* opinion yet concluded that the facts yielded no Establishment Clause violation—consisted of (in order of seniority) Justices Hugo Black (the opinion's author), Stanley Reed, William Douglas, Frank Murphy, and Fred Vinson (chief justice). The dissenting justices—who not only supported the majority's rewrite of the Establishment Clause but believed that the majority had not gone far enough—consisted of (in order of seniority) Justices Felix Frankfurter, Robert Jackson, Wiley Rutledge, and Harold Burton.

The following table summarizes some characteristics of that 1947 Supreme Court[176]:

CHARACTERISTICS OF THE 1947 *EVERSON* COURT

Justice	Appointed By	Party Affiliation	Law Degree	Prior to Appointment
Black	Pres. Roosevelt	Democrat	Univ. of Alabama[177]	Active in Democrat politics Former U.S. senator
Reed	Pres. Roosevelt	Democrat	—	Active in Kentucky politics Series of federal appointments
Douglas	Pres. Roosevelt	Democrat	Columbia Univ.	Law professor at Yale Knew Pres. Roosevelt
Murphy	Pres. Roosevelt	Democrat	Univ. of Michigan	Mayor of Detroit Governor of Michigan Knew Pres. Roosevelt
Vinson	Pres. Truman	Democrat	—[178]	Active in Democrat politics Former U.S. Congressman Knew then-vice president Truman
Frankfurter	Pres. Roosevelt	Democrat	Harvard	Law professor at Harvard Advisor to President Roosevelt Helped found the ACLU in 1920 Active in liberal politics
Jackson	Pres. Roosevelt	Democrat	—	New York lawyer[179] Series of federal appointments
Rutledge	Pres. Roosevelt	Democrat	Univ. of Colorado	Political supporter of President Roosevelt
Burton	Pres. Truman	Republican	Harvard	Knew then-senator Truman (before vice presidency)

One Supreme Court chronicler characterizes Justice Hugo Black's education as "haphazard and mediocre, an experience that would have a lasting influence on him as a judge."[180] Unfortunately, Justice Black wrote the opinion in *Everson*.

Although comparisons between different Supreme Courts, and different justices, remain fraught with imperfections and vulnerabilities, suffice it to say that the extraordinarily poor research and fundamental historical errors exemplified by *Everson* remain the product of either an incomprehensible ineptitude for the nation's top court or, as some believe, a more purposeful secularist aim driven by the political inclinations of the justices themselves.

15

The Consequences of a Rewritten History: The *Everson* Aftermath

In broad terms, the 1947 *Everson* decision animated a host of unprecedented, unhistorical novelties simultaneously, all based on nonexistent history.

First, it declared for the first time that the First Amendment's Establishment Clause burdens the states via an inherently nebulous reference to the word "liberty" in the Fourteenth Amendment—notwithstanding the twin realities that (1) alone among all constitutional amendments, the First Amendment expressly confines itself to "Congress," and (2) the records of the 1866 Congress (also the author of the Fourteenth Amendment) furnish no hint that Congress sought to enlarge the scope of the Establishment Clause.

Second, it replaced the words of the Establishment Clause with Thomas Jefferson's "wall of separation" metaphor solely on the Court's own say-so, thus not only altering the meaning of the Establishment Clause but doing so via a personal opinion voiced more than twelve years after the fact by someone who had not been a participant in either the 1787 Constitutional Convention or the inaugural Congress in 1789.

Third, and perhaps most troubling, in a move reminiscent of its momentous 1803 decision in *Marbury v. Madison* (discussed in Chapter 14), the Supreme Court ordained the courts in general as the ultimate arbiter of any dispute involving the intersection of government and "religion" in general. As such, *Everson* represents the Supreme Court's implementation of judicial review for any governmental association with "religion," "religious activities," "religious matters," and so on—whatever those terms might encompass. In practical effect, the judiciary has launched its own self-anointed practice of surveillance of federal, state, and local governmental activities that purport to implicate "religious activities." Indeed, the moniker of a "national school board" that Professor Corwin wielded in 1949[1] has proven both farsighted and apt; as of this writing, the Supreme Court has mediated dozens of school-related Establishment Clause disputes since *Everson*.[2]

Reflective of its unhistorical origins, the *Everson* opinion's "wall of separation" implicitly challenges, as violative of the Establishment Clause, many enduring aspects of our nation's heritage, including the phrase "Year of our Lord" that appears prominently in the Constitution above George Washington's signature on the Constitution itself—not to mention the host of religion-specific inscriptions on many of Washington, DC's most celebrated national monuments. Other examples abound. In one of the Supreme Court's most recent Establishment Clause decisions, in which the Court concluded that a six-foot-tall monolith inscribed with the Ten Commandments and located on the grounds of the Texas state capitol did *not* run afoul of the Establishment Clause, the Court observed that, in the Court's own words,

> . . . Such acknowledgments of the role played by the Ten Commandments in our Nation's heritage are common throughout America. We need only look within our own Courtroom. Since 1935, Moses has stood, holding two tablets that reveal portions of the Ten Commandments written in Hebrew, among other lawgivers in the south frieze. Representations of the Ten Commandments adorn the metal gates lining the north and south sides of the Courtroom as well as the doors leading into the Courtroom. Moses also sits on the exterior east facade of the building holding the Ten Commandments tablets.

> Similar acknowledgments can be seen throughout a visitor's tour of our Nation's Capital. For example, a large statue of Moses holding the Ten Commandments, alongside a statue of the Apostle Paul, has overlooked the rotunda of the Library of Congress' Jefferson Building since 1897. And the Jefferson Building's Great Reading Room contains a sculpture of a woman beside the Ten Commandments with a quote above her from the Old Testament (Micah 6:8). A medallion with two tablets depicting the Ten Commandments decorates the floor of the National Archives. Inside the Department of Justice, a statue entitled "The Spirit of Law" has two tablets representing the Ten Commandments lying at its feet. In front of the Ronald Reagan Building is another sculpture that includes a depiction of the Ten Commandments. So too a 24-foot-tall sculpture, depicting, among other things, the Ten Commandments

and a cross, stands outside the federal courthouse that houses both the Court of Appeals and the District Court for the District of Columbia. Moses is also prominently featured in the Chamber of the United States House of Representatives.[3]

⫷◆⫸

Other examples of monuments and buildings reflecting the prominent role of religion abound. For example, the Washington, Jefferson, and Lincoln Memorials all contain explicit invocations of God's importance. The apex of the Washington Monument is inscribed "Laus Deo," which is translated to mean "Praise be to God," and multiple memorial stones in the monument contain Biblical citations. The Jefferson Memorial is engraved with three quotes from Jefferson that make God a central theme. Inscribed on the wall of the Lincoln Memorial are two of Lincoln's most famous speeches, the Gettysburg Address and his Second Inaugural Address. Both inscriptions include those speeches' extensive acknowledgments of God. The first federal monument, which was accepted by the United States in honor of sailors who died in Tripoli, noted the dates of the fallen sailors as "the year of our Lord, 1804, and in the 28 year of the independence of the United States."[4]

Everson's rigid-yet-indeterminate "wall" would appear to prohibit every aspect of our nation's heritage mentioned in these excerpts. And the Supreme Court has yet to explain how it reconciles its *Everson* view of the Establishment Clause with the reality that, ever since Chief Justice Marshall's tenure,[5] the Supreme Court crier has declared the following each time the Court takes the bench: "God save the United States and this Honorable Court."[6]

Decades before the Supreme Court's folly in *Everson,* Madison presciently observed that

> [t]here has been a fallacy . . . in confounding a question whether precedents could *expound* a Constitution, with a question whether they could *alter* a Const[itution]. This distinction is too obvious to need elucidation. None will deny that precedents of a certain description fix the interpretation of a law. *Yet who will pretend that they can repeal or alter a law?*[7]

Madison, though, never anticipated the extent to which the Supreme Court of the mid-to-late twentieth century would pretty much do as it pleased insofar as constitutional text mattered. From a plainly understood, well-documented meaning and purpose in 1789, the First Amendment's Establishment Clause has spawned

Supreme Court interpretations devoid of meaning and contextual sense to the point that it has effectively been recast to mean something never envisioned by its author.

For example, in 1989 the Court decided that a local government's recurring holiday display, located on public property, consisting of a crèche that depicted the Christian Nativity scene and a Hanukkah menorah or candelabrum, yielded an "establishment" for the former because, according to the Court, the government "endorsed" a Christian message of Christmas. However, the Court concluded that no "establishment" issue existed for the latter display because, according to the Court, the government did not "endorse" a Jewish religious message.[8] And in 1977 the Court decided that a state law that authorized the provision of instructional materials and field trip transportation to students of nonpublic schools had a primary "effect" of advancing "religion" and represented an "excessive entanglement" with "religion," and thus yielded an "establishment."[9]

The most recent edition of the multivolume *History of the Supreme Court of the United States* reports that "[t]o understand the origins of Justice Black's *Everson* opinion, we might read it as an instance of creating a myth."[10]

> *Everson* . . . partakes of both legend (stories accreted around real historical personages, Thomas Jefferson and James Madison) and saga, a narrative of a historic event or struggle *embellished by fictive embroidery.*[11]

Another commentator captures the lunacy of *Everson* in just two sentences:

> *Everson* must rank as one of the worst decisions made by the Supreme Court . . . [.] It was bad law, rooted in not much more than the justices' own worldviews[.][12]

At every subsequent opportunity—and it has had literally dozens—the Supreme Court (or one of its individual justices) has unfailingly invoked the phrase "wall of separation" out of contextual reality without so much as a backward glance at the truth.

Following *Everson*, the Supreme Court found itself resolving a disparate array of Establishment Clause disputes in the next quarter century, most of which likely never would have arisen absent the Court's expansive and unhistorical reading of the Establishment Clause in *Everson* as implicating merely "religion" or "religious activities." The Court confronted Establishment Clause challenges to government programs in 1948, 1952, 1961, 1962, 1963, 1968, 1970, and 1971[13] before an alarming morass of confusion and inconsistency forced the Court to reexamine its burgeoning but undisciplined Establishment Clause jurisprudence. In effect, the Court had simply been making things up as it went along—and it showed. (A discussion of these, and other, Supreme Court decisions remains beyond the scope of this book.) But the 1971 "pause" only resulted in a bewildering series of contrived Establishment Clause "tests" that created still further chaos for decades.

A watershed moment arrived in 1985: four decades after the 1947 *Everson* decision, the Supreme Court rendered a decision that actually included a historically faithful chronicle of Establishment Clause history. Unfortunately (albeit perhaps not unexpectedly), that historical essay appeared in one of former Chief Justice William Rehnquist's dissenting opinions on the subject.[14] Thus, the Court itself—that is, a five-justice majority—opted to ignore Justice Rehnquist's history lesson. But, until that moment, *no one* on the Court had exerted any real effort to examine the historical realities detailed in the preceding chapters.

By 1985, the Court had rendered thirty decisions (beginning with *Everson*) that addressed the Establishment Clause in various contexts over a quarter century: in addition to the Court's fifteen Establishment Clause decisions from 1947 through 1971 (before the Court paused to assess itself), it rendered an additional fifteen Establishment Clause decisions from 1973 through 1984.[15] Yet *none* of these thirty decisions from 1947 to 1984 recognized (let alone discussed) the significance of the 1789 congressional proceedings during which Congress authored the Establishment Clause.

And not much has changed. The Supreme Court continues to concoct various Establishment Clause "tests" as it goes along (which yield absurd results), while at the same time it closes its eyes to historical reality. The Court has rendered an additional twenty-seven Establishment Clause decisions since 1985, and, like all other prior decisions, none acknowledges the straightforward history detailed throughout the previous chapters.[16] The morass simply thickens.

In one of its most recent excursions into its Establishment Clause labyrinth, the Court lamented that

[o]ur cases, Januslike, point in two directions in applying the

Establishment Clause. One face looks toward the strong role played by religion and religious traditions throughout our Nation's history. . . . The other face looks toward the principle that government intervention in religious matters can itself endanger religious freedom.[17]

"Januslike" references the Roman god of gates and doorways, typically depicted as a single head with two faces gazing in opposite directions. As used in the above excerpt, it aptly—and, given its author, perhaps mockingly[18]—characterizes the bizarre reality that the Court's Establishment Clause decisions depict a discombobulated *mélange* of inconsistencies, *non sequiturs,* and gobbledygook of the kind that one would expect in a "doctrine" that the Court simply made up as it went along. Indeed, when the Court characterizes its own decisions on a constitutional matter as "point[ing] in two directions," one must indeed wonder how it finds its way at all.

One can only hope that at some point at least five brave souls on the United States Supreme Court—and nine would be better still—will find themselves sufficiently moved by the remarkably objective historical record that the Court has thus far inexplicably ignored, and will for once abide by the truth that reality affords.

NOTES

Preface

1. U.S. Const., Amend. I, 1st Cong., 1st Sess., 1 Stat. 21 (1789).

2. *Newdow v. U.S. Congress*, 292 F.3d 597 (9th Cir. 2002), *opinion on rehearing*, 313 F.3d 500 (9th Cir. 2002), *order amending opinion*, 328 F.3d 466 (9th Cir. 2003), *reversed, Elk Grove Unified School District v. Newdow*, 542 U.S. 1 (2004).

The federal law that implements the Pledge of Allegiance provides:

> The Pledge of Allegiance to the Flag: "I pledge allegiance to the Flag of the United States of America, and to the Republic for which it stands, one Nation *under God,* indivisible, with liberty and justice for all.," should be rendered by standing at attention facing the flag with the right hand over the heart. When not in uniform men should remove any non-religious headdress with their right hand and hold it at the left shoulder, the hand being over the heart. Persons in uniform should remain silent, face the flag, and render the military salute.

4 USC § 4, *reaffirmed,* Act of November 13, 2002, Pub. L. 107–293, § 2, 116 Stat. 2060 (emphasis added).

3. Kurland, 839

Chapter 1

1. U.S. Const., Amend. I, 1st Cong., 1st Sess., 1 Stat. 21 (text of amendment), and 1st Cong., 1st Sess., 1 Stat. 97 (Joint House and Senate Resolution of September 25, 1789, submitting twelve proposed amendments to the states for ratification), both reproduced in *Complete Bill of Rights,* 11.

2. The First Amendment provides, in full:

> Congress shall make no law respecting an establishment of religion,

or prohibiting the free exercise thereof; or abridging the freedom of speech, or of the press; or the right of the people peaceably to assemble, and to petition the Government for a redress of grievances.

U.S. Const., Amend. I, 1st Cong., 1st Sess., 1 Stat. 21.

3. Chapter 12 explains this extraordinary transformation in detail.

4. *Black's Law Dictionary,* 847.

5. *Brown v. Allen,* 344 U.S. 443, 540 (1953) (Jackson, J., concurring).

6. Ring, 17.

7. *Wolman v. Walter,* 433 U.S. 229 (1977). (Not until a quarter of a century later did the Supreme Court declare *Wolman* an "anomaly" and "no longer good law" in *Mitchell v. Helms,* 530 U.S. 793, 808 (2000).)

8. *County of Allegheny v. ACLU,* 492 U.S. 573 (1989).

9. Thomas Sowell (Rose and Milton Friedman Senior Fellow, The Hoover Institution, Stanford University), "Supreme Farce," http://www.humanevents.com/article.php?id=18439 (December 12, 2006).

10. Ellen Hume, "Tabloids, Talk Radio, and the Future of News: Technology's Impact on Journalism," Part 4, http://www.ellen-hume.com/articles/tabloids_printable.html (Washington, DC: The Annenberg Washington Program in Communications Policy Studies of Northwestern University, 1995). In her article, Ms. Hume preceded Senator Moynihan's remark—which occurred "in a debate with his 1994 electoral opponent on WNBC in New York" (*id.*)—with her own observation that "[i]f verified facts are not part of the public discourse, then there are no reference points for accountability."

Another source who knew Senator Moynihan describes the senator's famous remark similarly:

> [Y]ou are entitled to your own opinion, but you are not entitled to your own facts.

Former Minnesota congressman Timothy Penny, "Facts Are Facts," http://www.nationalreview.com/nrof_comment/comment–penny 090403.asp (National Review Online, NRO Financial, September 4, 2003).

11. *New York Trust Co. v. Eisner,* 256 U.S. 345, 349 (1921).

Chapter 2

1. *McCreary County v. ACLU,* 545 U.S. 844, 874–75 (2005).

2. See, for instance, Pearcy, 260; Maddox, 64 (the term "establish-ment" in the Establishment Clause connotes precisely what the term had historically meant within the context of religion: "the idea that government would prefer one religion over another"); Levin, 36 ("establish" in the 1700s meant "a formal union of political and ecclesiastical authority in the hands of the state"); Cord, "Restoring the 'No Preference' Doctrine," 129; Cobb, 67; Baker, "The Establishment Clause as Intended," 41–42, 45–47; Holmes, 8 ("[A]n established or state church is the official religious organization of a country or colony."); Levy, *The Establishment Clause*, 7–8, and sources cited therein; Levy, *Original Intent*, 183–84; Levy, *Origins of the Bill of Rights*, 79.

In brief,

> The classic establishment of religion denoted a legal union between a state and a particular church that benefited from numerous privileges not shared by other churches or by the nonchurched or unbelievers.

Levy, *Original Intent*, 183–84; Levy, *Origins of the Bill of Rights*, 79.

3. Pearcy, 260; Levy, *Original Intent*, 183–84; Levy, *Origins of the Bill of Rights*, 90–91.

4. The July 1776 Declaration of Independence (1) included a num-ber of references to "states," (2) declared that "these United Colonies are, and of right ought to be, Free and Independent States," and (3) crafted the phrase "United States of America." 1 Stat. 1–3; V *Journals of the Continental Congress*, 510–15 (Proceedings of July 4, 1776); I Elliott's *Debates*, 60–63.

The Articles of Confederation (approved by the Continental Congress on July 9, 1778) included a number of references to "states" (which included "New Hampshire, Massachusetts Bay, Providence and Rhode Island Plantations, Connecticut, New York, New Jersey, Pennsylvania, Delaware, Maryland, Virginia, North Carolina, South Carolina, and Georgia") and in Article I declared the "confederacy" to be the "UNITED STATES OF AMERICA." 1 Stat. 4–9 (small caps in original); IX *Journals of the Continental Congress*, 907–25 (Proceedings of November 15, 1777); I Elliott's *Debates*, 79–84.

5. Dreisbach, *Jefferson and the Wall of Separation*, 52.

6. See, for instance, *BP America Production Co. v. Burton*, 127 S.Ct. 638, 643 (2006); *Lopez v. Gonzales*, 127 S.Ct. 625, 630 (2006); *Rapanos*

v. United States, 126 S.Ct. 2208, 2220–21 (2006); *Dunn v. Commodity Futures Trading Commission,* 519 U.S. 465, 470 (1997); *FDIC v. Meyer,* 510 U.S. 471, 476 (1994); *Arave v. Creech,* 507 U.S. 463, 472 (1993); *Reves v. Ernst & Young,* 507 U.S. 170, 179 (1993); *Estate of Cowart v. Nicklos Drilling Co.,* 505 U.S. 469, 477 (1992); *Chapman v. United States,* 500 U.S. 453, 461–62 (1991); *Dennis v. Higgins,* 498 U.S. 439, 447 incl. n. 7 (1991); *FMC Corp. v. Holliday,* 498 U.S. 52, 57 (1990); *Park 'N Fly, Inc. v. Park and Fly, Inc.,* 469 U.S. 189, 194 (1985).

7. See Chapter 5.

8. *Oxford Dictionary of Word Histories,* 185.

9. See, for instance, *Oxford Companion to the English Language,* 657 (defining "Middle English"). All references to time within this context have been obtained from the etymologies in the particular dictionaries cited.

10. V *Oxford English Dictionary,* 404.

11. Ibid.

12. Ibid., 405.

13. *New Oxford American Dictionary,* 576.

14. Ibid.

15. 1 *Shorter Oxford English Dictionary,* 860.

16. Ibid.

17. Ibid.

18. *American Heritage Dictionary,* 1111.

19. Ibid., 609.

20. Ibid.

21. Ibid.

22. *Random House Webster's Unabridged Dictionary,* 663.

23. Ibid.

24. Ibid.

25. *Random House Unabridged Dictionary,* 663.

26. Ibid.

27. Ibid.

28. *Webster's Third New International Dictionary,* 1430.

29. Ibid., 778.

30. Ibid.

31. Ibid.

32. *Funk & Wagnalls International Dictionary,* 434.

33. Ibid.

34. Ibid.

35. *Dictionary of the English Language,* unnumbered page in Volume 1.

36. Webster had earlier published the first true American dictionary in 1806: *A Compendious Dictionary of the English Language.*

37. 1 N. Webster, *American Dictionary of the English Language* (1828).

38. Brohaugh, 92.

39. Ibid., 173.

40. Ibid.

41. *Barnhart Dictionary,* 344.

42. See Chapter 3C. Patrick Henry's 1784 legislative proposal to enact a tax for religious support bore the title "A Bill Establishing a Provision for Teachers of the Christian Religion." Brant, *James Madison: The Nationalist,* 346; Ketchum, 162–63.

43. James Madison, Memorial and Remonstrance against Religious Assessments, June 20, 1785, reproduced in: 8 *Madison's Papers,* 298–304; II *Madison's Writings,* 183–91; 5 *Founders' Constitution,* 82–84 (emphasis added).

44. June 21, 1785, letter from James Madison to James Monroe (8 *Madison's Papers,* 306; II *Madison's Writings,* 146; I *Madison's Letters,* 155) (emphasis added).

45. "A Bill Establishing a Provision for Teachers of the Christian Religion." Brant, *James Madison: The Nationalist,* 346; Ketchum, 162–63 (emphasis added).

46. **New Jersey:** New Jersey Constitution of July 2, 1776, Art. XIX, reproduced in: 5 *Federal and State Constitutions,* 2597–98: 6 *Sources and Documents* 452.

Delaware: Delaware Constitution of September 20, 1776, Art. 29, reproduced in: 1 *Federal and State Constitutions,* 567; 2 *Sources and Documents,* 203.

North Carolina: North Carolina Constitution of December 18, 1776, Art. XXXIV, reproduced in: 5 *The Federal and State Constitutions,* 2793; 7 *Sources and Documents,* 406–7.

See Chapters 3E(2), 3E(3), and 3E(6) for the wording of these constitutional provisions.

47. **New York:** New York Constitution of April 20, 1777, Art. XXXV, reproduced in: 5 *The Federal and State Constitutions,* 2635–36; 7 *Sources and Documents,* 178; XIX *Documentary History . . . Ratification,* 502.

See Chapter 3E(7) for the wording of this constitutional provision.

48. **Massachusetts:** Massachusetts Constitution of March 2, 1780, Art. III, reproduced in: 3 *Federal and State Constitutions,* 1889–90; 5 *Sources and Documents,* 93–94; IV *Documentary History . . . Ratification,* 441.

New Hampshire: The New Hampshire Constitution of 1784, Declaration of Rights, Art. VI, reproduced in: 4 *Federal and State Constitutions,* 2454; 6 *Sources and Documents,* 345; *Sources of Our Liberties,* 382.

See Chapters 3E(10) and 3E(11) for the wording of these constitutional provisions.

49. In 1812, President Madison appointed Harvard Law School graduate Joseph Story to the United States Supreme Court, a position that Story held until September 1845. Only eight justices have served longer (seven of those served less than a year longer). Story, who successfully argued the first Supreme Court case in which the Court declared a state law unconstitutional (*Fletcher v. Peck,* 10 U.S. (6 Cranch) 87 (1810)), also served as professor of law at Harvard Law School from 1821 until his death in 1845 and authored the highly acclaimed multivolume *Commentaries on the Constitution of the United States,* first published in 1833 (Boston: Hilliard, Gray and Company; Cambridge: Brown, Shattuck and Company; 1833), and republished in 1851, 1858, 1873, 1891, and 1905.

50. 3 Story, *Commentaries on the Constitution* (1833 ed.), § 1867, 724 (emphasis added).

51. 3 Story, *Commentaries on the Constitution* (1833 ed.), § 1868, 726 (emphasis added).

52. A longtime law professor at the University of Michigan Law School and Michigan Supreme Court justice in the nineteenth century, Thomas Cooley rivaled Justice Story as the author of celebrated and widely used treatises on constitution law that became law library standards. See T. Cooley, *A Treatise on the Constitutional Limitations Which Rest upon the Legislative Power of the States of the American Union,* 470–71 (Boston: Little, Brown & Co., 1868); T. Cooley, *General Principles of Constitutional Law in the United States* (3d ed.; Boston: Little, Brown & Co., 1898).

53. Cooley, *General Principles of Constitutional Law,* Ch. XIII, § 1, 224 (emphasis added).

54. Levy, *The Establishment Clause,* 1; *accord* Pearcy, 260.

55. Taylor, 160; *accord* Pearcy, 260.

56. Lambert, 23, 46.

57. Taylor, 339 (italics in original).

58. 1 *Annals of America*, 87–91, 125–29, 149–53, 154–56, 157–59.

59. Cord, *Separation of Church and State*, 3.

60. **Virginia:** Cobb, 71, 74–115; Taylor, 339–40; Cord, *Separation of Church and State*, 4; Gaustad, 16; Maddox, 29, 52; I Stokes, 163–65; Holmes, 22–23; II *Dictionary of American History*, 36; VI *Dictionary of American History*, 75–76; Levy, *The Establishment Clause*, 1, 5; Greene, 91–92.

61. **New York:** Cobb, 71, 301–61; Taylor, 340; Cord, *Separation of Church and State*, 4; Gaustad, 19; I Stokes, 166–69; 1 *Annals of America*, 87–91, 125–29, 149–53, 154–56, 157–59; II *Dictionary of American History*, 36; Greene, 91–92. The Church of England existed to a lesser extent in New York than in other states. One historian reports that "[r]eligion in New York has a complicated history." II E. Channing, 435.

62. **Maryland:** Cobb, 71, 362–98; Taylor, 340; Cord, *Separation of Church and State*, 4; I Stokes, 163–65; Holmes, 21; 1 *Annals of America*, 87–91, 125–29, 149–53, 154–56, 157–59; II *Dictionary of American History*, 36; VI *Dictionary of American History*, 75–76; Levy, *The Establishment Clause*, 1, 5. Maryland began as a Catholic-dominated colony in which Lord Baltimore maintained an established church until the late 1600s, at which point the Church of England displaced Catholicism as the established church. Cobb, 71, 362–98; Taylor, 281–83; Simmons, 45–48, 92–93, 208–9; Hofstadter, 199; I Stokes, 163–65; Greene, 91–92; Holmes, 20–21.

63. **Georgia:** Cobb, 71, 418–21; Cord, *Separation of Church and State*, 4; Maddox, 52; I Stokes, 163–65; Levy, *The Establishment Clause*, 1, 5; Greene, 91–92.

64. **North Carolina:** Cobb, 71, 115–32; Taylor, 340; Cord, *Separation of Church and State*, 4; Maddox, 52; I Stokes, 163–65; II *Dictionary of American History*, 36; VI *Dictionary of American History*, 75–76; Levy, *The Establishment Clause*, 1, 5; Greene, 91–92.

65. **South Carolina:** Cobb, 71, 115–32; Taylor, 226, 340; Cord, *Separation of Church and State*, 4; Maddox, 52; I Stokes, 163–65; VI *Dictionary of American History*, 75–76; Levy, *The Establishment Clause*, 1, 5; Hofstadter, 203–4; Greene, 91–92.

66. **Pennsylvania:** Gaustad, 19; Holmes, 17. Pennsylvania quickly "disestablished" any dominant church. Cobb, 71, 440–53; Hofstadter, 198. After William Penn's arrival, Pennsylvania had "no privileged church [and] no tax-supported religious establishment," not even for Penn's Quakers. Taylor, 266.

67. **New Jersey:** Cobb, 71, 399–418; Gaustad, 19; I Stokes, 166–69; Holmes, 16. One source declares that New Jersey never had any "state church" (Hofstadter, 198), although the difference in views appears to reside in chronology.

68. **Massachusetts:** Cobb, 70, 133–238; Taylor, 165–66, 339–40; Simmons, 27–30, 38; Cord, *Separation of Church and State*, 4; Gaustad, 20; Maddox, 50–51; I Stokes, 152–63; Holmes, 9; 1 *Annals of America*, 87–91, 125–29, 149–53, 154–56, 157–59; II *Dictionary of American History*, 35; VI *Dictionary of American History*, 75–76; Levy, *The Establishment Clause*, 1–2; Greene, 83–84.

69. **Connecticut:** Cobb, 70, 238–90; Taylor, 165–66, 339–40; Simmons, 27–30, 38; Cord, *Separation of Church and State*, 4; I Stokes, 152–63; Holmes, 9; 1 *Annals of America*, 87–91, 125–29, 149–53, 154–56, 157–59; II *Dictionary of American History*, 35; Levy, *The Establishment Clause*, 1–2; Greene, 83–84.

70. **New Hampshire:** Cobb, 70, 290–301; Taylor, 340; Cord, *Separation of Church and State*, 4; I Stokes, 152–63; Holmes, 9; Levy, *The Establishment Clause*, 1–2; Greene, 83–84.

71. *Engel v. Vitale*, 370 U.S. 421 (1962). The Court's opinion also reports that "[i]n Pennsylvania and Delaware, all Christian sects were treated equally in most situations but Catholics were discriminated against in some respects. . . . In Rhode Island all Protestants enjoyed equal privileges but it is not clear whether Catholics were allowed to vote." 370 U.S. at 428 n. 10.

72. See, for instance, Pearcy, 260; Levy, *The Establishment Clause*, 5; Levy, *Origins of the Bill of Rights*, 79; Cobb, 67; Taylor, 179; Simmons, 30; Adams and Emmerich, 4–5.

73. Taylor, 357.

74. Taylor, 354; *accord* Pearcy, 260.

75. Levy, *The Establishment Clause*, 1–2; *accord* Pearcy, 260.

76. See, for instance, Levy, *Origins of the Bill of Rights*, 79; Pearcy, 260.

77. Taylor, 340–41; *accord*, Pearcy, 260. See also the Supreme Court's discussion in its opinion in *Everson v. Board of Education*, 330

U.S. 1, 10 n. 8 (1947) (identifying Virginia, North Carolina, Massachusetts, Connecticut, New York, Maryland, and New Hampshire).

78. Simmons, 30.

79. Taylor, 179; *accord* Pearcy, 260.

80. Adams and Emmerich, 4–5; *accord* Pearcy, 260.

81. Adams and Emmerich, 4.

82. A "glebe" referred to productive farmland owned by a church, and, within the establishment context, typically meant land appropriated and given to a church. McDougall, 125; *New Oxford American Dictionary*, 716; 1 *Shorter Oxford English Dictionary*, 1107; *American Heritage Dictionary*, 747; *Random House Webster's Unabridged Dictionary*, 811; *Random House Unabridged Dictionary*, 811; VI *Oxford English Dictionary*, 567; and *Webster's Third New International Dictionary*, 964.

83. Adams and Emmerich, 4; *accord* Pearcy, 260.

84. Peterson, 133; *accord* Pearcy, 260.

85. Stokes and Pfeffer, 36–37. Pennsylvania, New Jersey, and New York disestablished sooner than other states. Levy, *The Establishment Clause*, 11. The Supreme Court has reported substantially the same situation:

> Indeed, as late as the time of the Revolutionary War, there were established churches in at least eight of the thirteen former colonies and established religions in at least four of the other five.
>
> *Engel v. Vitale*, 370 U.S. 421, 427–28 (1962). The Court did not, however, explain its perceived meaning of the phrases "established *churches*" and "established *religions.*" *Id.* (emphasis added).

86. See Chapter 3A. Virginia's June 12, 1776, Declaration of Rights effectively launched the "bill of rights" disestablishment process, although the declaration itself fell short of an outright disestablishment.

87. Cord, *Separation of Church and State*, 4; Gaustad, 29; Maddox, 54–55.

88. See Chapter 3E. Virginia, the most populous state in the mid-1700s and the "oldest, largest, and most influential of the thirteen colonies" (Levy, *The Establishment Clause*, 1), had a disproportionate influence among the various states. See, for instance, the Supreme Court's observation in *Everson v. Board of Education*, 330 U.S. 1 (1947), that

Virginia, where the established church had achieved a dominant influence in political affairs and where many excesses attracted wide public attention, provided a great stimulus and able leadership for the [disestablishment] movement.

330 U.S. at 11.

89. Connecticut and New Hampshire did not disestablish the Congregational Church until the early 1800s. Cord, *Separation of Church and State*, 4. Before then, they had made it known that

[n]o Catholics, Anglicans, Baptists, or Quakers need come to New England (except to exceptional Rhode Island).

Taylor, 181.

Not until 1833 did Massachusetts become the last of the states to disestablish a state-sponsored church. Cord, *Separation of Church and State*, 4; Hofstadter, 188. Massachusetts in particular seemed loathe to acknowledge the strength of its established Congregationalist Church, preferring instead to portray it as something less. Simmons, 376.

90. See, specifically, Chapter 3.

Chapter 3

1. Hofstadter, 204; see also the discussion in Chapter 3E.

2. *Everson v. Board of Education*, 330 U.S. 1, 11 (1947).

3. Except when context demands it for some particular reason, and except for quotations, the remainder of this book will simply use the term "states" even if historical exactitude might otherwise require the use of "colonies." As noted in Chapter 2, no later than the Declaration of Independence in July 1776, the states began referring to themselves as such, and any difference would be inconsequential here.

4. IV *Journals of the Continental Congress*, 342 (Proceedings of May 10, 1776).

5. Wood, 132.

6. IV *Journals of the Continental Congress*, 357–58 (Proceedings of May 15, 1776).

7. 1 *Jefferson's Papers*, 290–91 (reproducing Virginia's May 15, 1776, resolution directing the draft of a bill of rights and state constitution); I *Madison's Writings*, 33–34; I *Mason's Papers*, 274–75; *Sources of Our Liberties*, 302; Ketchum, 71.

8. I *Madison's Writings*, 33–34; 1 *Jefferson's Papers*, 298 (reproducing

Virginia's June 7, 1776, Resolution of Independence) and 413–14; I *Jefferson's Works* ("Autobiography"), 20; *Jefferson*—"Autobiography," 13–18 (Jefferson's personal notes); *Jefferson . . . In His Own Words*, 62–63; *Sources of Our Liberties*, 302, 316; *Documents Illustrative . . . Formation of the American States*, 19–20; Ketchum, 70.

9. 1 *Jefferson's Papers*, 413–14; VI *Journals of the Continental Congress*, 1087–93 (Thomas Jefferson's personal notes, furnished to James Madison); I *Jefferson's Works* ("Autobiography"), 20; *Jefferson*— "Autobiography," 13–18 (Jefferson's personal notes); *Sources of Our Liberties*, 316.

10. VI *Journals of the Continental Congress*, 1087; *Jefferson*— "Autobiography," 13 (Thomas Jefferson's personal notes); I *Jefferson's Works* ("Autobiography"), 20.

11. 1 *Madison's Papers*, 170; I *Madison's Writings*, 34; Ketchum, 71.

12. I *Madison's Writings*, 34. Virginia's June 12, 1776, Declaration of Rights has been reproduced in: I *Madison's Writings*, 35–40; I *Madison's Letters*, 21–24; I *Mason's Papers*, 287–89; 7 *Federal and State Constitutions*, 3812–14; 10 *Sources and Documents*, 48–50; *Sources of Our Liberties*, 311–12; VIII *Documentary History . . . Ratification*, 530–31.

13. Virginia's June 29, 1776, Constitution ("Plan of Government") has been reproduced in: I *Madison's Writings*, 41–49; I *Madison's Letters*, 24–28; 1 *Jefferson's Papers*, 377–83; 7 *Federal and State Constitutions*, 3814–19; 10 *Sources and Documents*, 51–56; VIII *Documentary History . . . Ratification*, 532–37; 1 *Founders' Constitution*, 7–9.

14. 1 *Madison's Papers*, 170, 274–82 (Mason served as the "chief architect"); I *Madison's Writings*, 32 n. 1, 35 n. *; December 29, 1827, letter from James Madison to George Mason's grandson (IX *Madison's Writings*, 294; III *Madison's Letters*, 606); May 8, 1825, letter from Thomas Jefferson to Henry Lee (XVI *Jefferson's Writings* (1903 ed.), 117–18; VII *Jefferson's Writings* (1853 ed.), 407; XII *Jefferson's Works*, 408); April 3, 1825, letter from Thomas Jefferson to Augustus Woodward (XVI *Jefferson's Writings* (1903 ed.), 116; VII *Jefferson's Writings* (1853 ed.), 405–6; XII *Jefferson's Works*, 407–8).

15. See Chapter 4.

16. 1 *Madison's Papers*, 172–73 (unnumbered ¶ 9 in Mason's original draft); I *Madison's Writings*, 40; I *Mason's Papers*, 278.

17. I *Mason's Papers*, 278; 1 *Madison's Papers*, 172–73 (emphasis added).

18. I *Mason's Papers*, 284–85 (¶ 18 in Committee's revision); 1 *Madison's Papers*, 173 (¶ 18); I *Madison's Writings*, 40 (¶ 18) (emphasis added).

19. 1 *Madison's Papers*, 174; I *Madison's Writings*, 40–41 n. *; Brant, *James Madison: The Virginia Revolutionist*, 245; Ketchum, 72 (emphasis added).

20. I *Madison's Writings*, xxxvii; Brant, *James Madison: The Virginia Revolutionist*, 155.

21. I *Madison's Writings*, xxxvii; Brant, *James Madison: The Virginia Revolutionist*, 190, 272–74; *Madison and The American Nation*, 477; Wills, 13; Ketchum, 68.

22. I *Madison's Writings*, xxxvii.

23. 1 *Madison's Papers*, 171.

24. Brant, *James Madison: The Virginia Revolutionist*, 245–48; Ketchum, 72; I *Mason's Papers*, 290–91.

25. Ketchum, 72.

26. 1 *Madison's Papers*, 171.

27. 1 *Madison's Papers*, 171; I *Mason's Papers*, 290–91; Brant, *James Madison: The Virginia Revolutionist*, 190, 234–37, 241, 243–44, 245–47; Wills, 17–18.

28. 1 *Madison's Papers*, 174–75 (emphasis added).

29. Virginia's June 12, 1776, Declaration of Rights, Art. 16, reproduced in: 1 *Madison's Papers*, 175; I *Madison's Writings*, 40; I *Madison's Letters*, 24; I *Mason's Papers*, 289; 7 *Federal and State Constitutions*, 3814; 10 *Sources and Documents*, 50; *Sources of Our Liberties*, 312; VIII *Documentary History . . . Ratification*, 531.

30. Simmons, 364.

31. See Chapter 3E, identifying the various state constitutions that included disestablishment provisions modeled upon the Virginia precedent. Delaware, Pennsylvania, Maryland, North Carolina, Massachusetts, New Hampshire, and Vermont each mimicked Virginia's model of a constitution and a separate declaration of rights.

32. I *Madison's Writings*, xxxvii; Brant, *James Madison: The Virginia Revolutionist*, 313; Ketchum, 75.

33. I *Madison's Writings*, xxxvii; Brant, *James Madison: The Virginia Revolutionist*, 315; *Madison and the American Nation*, 211, 477; Wills, 13, 19; Ketchum, 78.

34. I *Mason's Papers*, 276.

35. See Mason's September 12, 1787, remarks in: III *Mason's Papers*, 981; II Farrand's *Records*, 587–88; I Elliott's *Debates*, 306; V Elliott's *Debates*, 538; *Madison's Notes*, 556–57; IV *Madison's Writings*, 442; III *Documentary History of the Constitution*, 734–35; *Documents Illustrative . . . Formation of the American States*, 716; II Madison's *Journal*, 717; and Farrand, 185–86.

36. III *Mason's Papers*, 991–93; II Farrand's *Records*, 649; I Elliott's *Debates*, 494; IV *Madison's Writings*, 470, 483; III Farrand's *Records*, 304–5 (May 26, 1788, letter from George Mason to Thomas Jefferson); IV *Documentary History of the Constitution*, 629–30 (May 26, 1788, letter from George Mason to Thomas Jefferson).

37. II Farrand's *Records*, 649; I Elliott's *Debates*, 494–96; V Elliott's *Debates*, 565; *Madison's Notes*, 583; II Madison's *Journal*, 763; Farrand, 194.

38. See "Supplement" to Farrand's *Records*, 269 ("The dating follows that in Robert Rutland, ed., *The Papers of George Mason*, 3 vols. (Chapel Hill, 1970), 3:983–85 . . . [.]").

39. II Farrand's *Records*, 637 (reported by Farrand as having been reprinted from K. Rowland, II *Life of George Mason*, 387); III *Mason's Papers*, 991; I Elliott's *Debates*, 494.

40. On June 7, 1776, the Continental Congress approved the initial resolution:

> Certain resolutions [respecting independency] being moved and seconded,
>
> Resolved, That these United Colonies are, and of right ought to be, free and independent States, that they are absolved from all allegiance to the British Crown, and that all political connection between them and the State of Great Britain is, and ought to be, totally dissolved. . . .

V *Journals of the Continental Congress*, 425–26 (Proceedings of June 7, 1776).

41. On June 8, 1776, the Continental Congress postponed consideration of the "independence" resolution until June 10, 1776. V *Journals of the Continental Congress*, 427 (Proceedings of June 8, 1776).

42. On June 10, 1776, the Continental Congress agreed to appoint a committee to prepare a declaration of "independence":

> Resolved, That the consideration of the first resolution be postponed to this day, three weeks [July 1], and in the mean while, that no time be

lost, in case the Congress agree thereto, that a committee be appointed to prepare a declaration to the effect of the said first resolution, which is in these words: "That these United Colonies are, and of right ought to be, free and independent states; that they are absolved from all allegiance to the British Crown: and that all political connexion between them and the state of Great Britain is, and ought to be, totally dissolved."

V *Journals of the Continental Congress*, 428–29 (Proceedings of June 10, 1776).

43. On June 11, 1776, the Continental Congress assigned the drafting task to a special committee. V *Journals of the Continental Congress*, 431 (Proceedings of June 11, 1776).

See also: VI *Journals of the Continental Congress*, 1087–93 (Thomas Jefferson's personal notes, furnished to James Madison); I *Jefferson's Writings* (1903 ed.) ("Autobiography") 17–27, 175–77; *Jefferson*— "Autobiography," 13–18; I *Jefferson's Works* ("Autobiography"), 20; 1 *Jefferson's Papers*, 413–14; *Jefferson . . . In His Own Words*, 62–63; I *Madison's Writings*, 33–34; *Sources of Our Liberties*, 302, 316; *Documents Illustrative . . . Formation of the American States*, 19–20; Ketchum, 70.

44. Resolved, That the committee, to prepare the declaration, consist of five members:

The members chosen, Mr. [Thomas] Jefferson, Mr. J[ohn] Adams, Mr. [Benjamin] Franklin, Mr. [Roger] Sherman, and Mr. R[obert] R. Livingston.

V *Journals of the Continental Congress*, 431 (Proceedings of June 11, 1776).

See also: VI *Journals of the Continental Congress*, 1091–92 (Thomas Jefferson's personal notes, furnished to James Madison); *Jefferson*— "Autobiography," 17 (Jefferson's personal notes): I *Jefferson's Works* ("Autobiography"), 28; 1 *Jefferson's Papers*, 414; *Jefferson . . . In His Own Words*, 62–63; *Sources of Our Liberties*, 317.

45. McDougall, 243.

46. Brodie, 108, 120; Peterson, 80; *Jefferson . . . In His Own Words*, 43–52, 54 ("his reputation as a writer had spread quickly").

47. VI *Journals of the Continental Congress*, 1092 (Thomas Jefferson's personal notes, furnished to James Madison); *Jefferson*— "Autobiography," 17 (Jefferson's personal notes); I *Jefferson's Works* ("Autobiography"), 28; 1 *Jefferson's Papers*, 414; *Jefferson . . . In His Own Words*, 63; I *Works of John Adams*, 232; *Sources of Our Liberties*, 317.

48. I *Works of John Adams*, 232.

49. Peterson, 87–88.

50. Ibid.

51. I *Jefferson's Works,* 28–29 n. 3 (reporting from Adams's biography); Brodie, 120 (citing an August 22, 1822, letter from John Adams to Timothy Pickering); I *Works of John Adams,* 232; II *Works of John Adams,* 512–14; McCullough, 119.

52. XV *Jefferson's Writings* (1903 ed.), 46.

53. VI *Journals of the Continental Congress,* 1092 (Jefferson's personal notes); *Jefferson*—"Autobiography," 17 (Jefferson's personal notes); I *Jefferson's Works* ("Autobiography"), 28.

54. McDougall, 243 ("the other members . . . had more *important* chores to perform") (italics in original).

55. VI *Journals of the Continental Congress,* 1092 (Thomas Jefferson's personal notes, furnished to James Madison); I *Jefferson's Writings* (1903 ed.) ("Autobiography"), 17–28; *Jefferson*—"Autobiography," 17–24 (Jefferson's personal notes); I *Jefferson's Works* ("Autobiography"), 28–29; July 1, 1776, letter from Jefferson to William Fleming (IV *Jefferson's Writings* (1903 ed.), 258); May 12, 1819, letter from Jefferson to Samuel Wells (XV *Jefferson's Writings* (1903 ed.), 196; VII *Jefferson's Writings* (1853 ed.), 119); August 30, 1823, letter from Jefferson to James Madison (XV *Jefferson's Writings* (1903 ed.), 461; VII *Jefferson's Writings* (1853 ed.), 304); September 16, 1825, letter from Jefferson to John Vaughan (XVI *Jefferson's Writings* (1903 ed.), 121–22; VII *Jefferson's Writings* (1853 ed.), 409); 1 *Jefferson's Papers,* 414; *Jefferson . . . In His Own Words,* 63–64; *Sources of Our Liberties,* 317.

56. The final version included eighty-six separate revisions to Jefferson's draft. 1 *Jefferson's Papers,* 414; V *Journals of the Continental Congress,* 491–502 (Proceedings of June 28, 1776) (column denoted "Reported Draft"); VI *Journals of the Continental Congress,* 1093–98 (Thomas Jefferson's working copy with Congress's changes, as furnished to James Madison).

57. VI *Journals of the Continental Congress,* 1092–93 (Thomas Jefferson's personal notes, furnished to James Madison); *Jefferson*—"Autobiography," 17–18 (Jefferson's personal notes); I *Jefferson's Works* ("Autobiography"), 29–33; 1 *Jefferson's Papers,* 414; *Jefferson . . . In His Own Words,* 64–66.

58. V *Journals of the Continental Congress,* 510–16 (Proceedings of July 4, 1776); VI *Journals of the Continental Congress,* 1093 (Thomas Jefferson's personal notes, furnished to James Madison); *Jefferson*—

"Autobiography," 24 (Jefferson's personal notes); I *Jefferson's Works* ("Autobiography"), 33–34, 43; 1 *Jefferson's Papers*, 414; II *Jefferson's Works*, 199–217; *Jefferson . . . In His Own Words*, 66.

59. VI *Journals of the Continental Congress*, 1092 (Thomas Jefferson's personal notes, furnished to James Madison); *Jefferson—* "Autobiography," 17–18 (Jefferson's personal notes); I *Jefferson's Works* ("Autobiography"), 31–32; V *Journals of the Continental Congress*, 516 n. 1 (quoting from a July 5, 1776, letter from Elbridge Gerry to General Warren) (emphasis added).

60. The New York delegates eventually added their signatures on August 2, 1776. *Jefferson . . . In His Own Words*, 70.

61. The Declaration of Independence has been reproduced in: 1 Stat. 1–3; V *Journals of the Continental Congress*, 510–16 (Proceedings of July 4, 1776); 1 *Jefferson's Papers*, 429–32; I *Jefferson's Writings* (1903 ed.), 28–38; *Jefferson—*"Autobiography," 19–24 (Jefferson's personal notes); I *Jefferson's Works* ("Autobiography"), 35–42; 1 *Sources and Documents* (2nd series), 321–26; *Documents Illustrative . . . Formation of the American States*, 22–26; *Sources of Our Liberties*, 319–22.

62. Brant, *James Madison: The Virginia Revolutionist*, 232, 241.

63. August 30, 1823, letter from Jefferson to James Madison (XV *Jefferson's Writings* (1903 ed.), 460–62; VII *Jefferson's Writings* (1853 ed.), 304); May 8, 1825, letter from Jefferson to Henry Lee (XVI *Jefferson's Writings* (1903 ed.), 117–18; VII *Jefferson's Writings* (1853 ed.), 407).

64. *Jefferson . . . In His Own Words*, 63.

65. April 3, 1825, letter from Thomas Jefferson to Augustus Woodward (XVI *Jefferson's Writings* (1903 ed.), 116; VII *Jefferson's Writings* (1853 ed.), 405–6; XII *Jefferson's Works*, 407–8).

66. Thomas Jefferson's Bill for Establishing Religious Freedom, reproduced in: 2 *Jefferson's Papers*, 305, 545–47; XI *Jefferson's Writings* (1903 ed.), 300–303; *Jefferson—*"Public Papers," 346–48; II *Jefferson's Works*, 438–41; 1 Randall, 219–20; 5 *Founders' Constitution*, 77 (periods substituted for colons and broken into separate paragraphs) (emphasis added).

67. Simmons, 377.

68. See Chapter 3D.

The respective editors of Volume 2 of *Jefferson's Papers*, Volume II of *Jefferson's Writings* (1903 ed.), and Volume 8 of *Madison's Papers*, explain in painstaking detail how the politics of the times left

Jefferson's 1776 Bill for Establishing Religious Freedom languishing in the Virginia legislature until Madison reintroduced it (in revised form) on October 31, 1785, as an Act for Establishing Religious Freedom. 2 *Jefferson's Papers,* 305–24, 547–53; II *Jefferson's Writings* (1903 ed.), 300–303; 8 *Madison's Papers,* 391–94; see also I *Jefferson's Writings* (1903 ed.), 66 ("Autobiography"), *Jefferson—* "Autobiography," 40, I *Jefferson's Works* ("Autobiography"), 71; and *Jefferson . . . In His Own Words,* 88 (each mentioning Madison's "unwearied exertions" to eventually get Jefferson's proposals passed in some form while Jefferson served as the United States' representative in Paris from 1784 to 1789).

In fact, the Virginia legislature tabled all but one of Jefferson's other legislative reforms as well. *Jefferson . . . In His Own Words,* 76–77.

69. I *Jefferson's Writings* (1903 ed.) ("Autobiography"), 74; *Jefferson—*"Autobiography," 45; I *Jefferson's Works* ("Autobiography"), 78; *Jefferson . . . In His Own Words,* 91; Malone, *Jefferson and His Time,* 301–2.

70. See XXV *Journals of the Continental Congress,* 798–99, 803 (Proceedings of November 3 and 4, 1783) (presentation of credentials from June election).

71. I *Jefferson's Writings* (1903 ed.), 90, 160–61; *Jefferson—* "Autobiography," 55, 98; I *Jefferson's Works* ("Autobiography"), 93, 158; *Jefferson's Life,* 62, 101; *Jefferson . . . In His Own Words,* 149; Malone, *Jefferson and the Rights of Man,* 209, 243; V *Dictionary of American Biography,* Pt. 2, 21–22.

72. See Madison's January 6, 1785, letter to James Madison, Sr., describing that proposal (8 *Madison's Papers,* 217); Madison's January 9, 1785, letter to Thomas Jefferson describing the same proposal (8 *Madison's Papers,* 228–29, I *Madison's Letters,* 122–24; 7 *Jefferson's Papers,* 588, 594–95).

73. Brant, *James Madison: The Nationalist,* 346; Ketchum, 162–63.

74. June 21, 1785, letter from James Madison to James Monroe (8 *Madison's Papers,* 306) (emphasis added).

75. Henry's proposed legislation included the blank spaces.

76. Patrick Henry's 1784 "Bill for Establishing a Provision for Teachers of the Christian Religion" (emphasis added), reproduced in the "Supplemental Appendix" to the Supreme Court's decision in *Everson v. Board of Education,* 330 U.S. 1, 72–74 (1947) (citing Library

of Congress, Manuscript Division, Papers of George Washington, vol. 231). The Court's replication of Henry's proposal bears the following footnote:

> This copy of the Assessment Bill is from one of the hand-bills which on December 24, 1784, when the third reading of the bill was postponed, were ordered distributed to the Virginia counties by the House of Delegates. *See* Journal of the Virginia House of Delegates, December 24, 1784; Eckenrode, 102–103. The bill is therefore in its final form, for it never again reached the floor of the House. . . .

Everson, 330 U.S. at 74 n. *.

77. Madison's notes for the "Debate on Bill for Relig. Estab. proposed by Mr. Henry" have been reproduced in: 8 *Madison's Papers,* 197–99; II *Madison's Writings,* 88–89 (same); I *Madison's Letters,* 116–17 (same).

78. Lambert 230, wielding quotes from portions of Jefferson's *Notes on the State of Virginia* that in fact bear no relationship to any such assertion.

79. See *Reynolds v. United States,* 98 U.S. (8 Otto) 145, 162–63 (1878), and *Everson v. Board of Education,* 330 U.S. 1, 11–12 (1947).

80. Brant, *James Madison: The Nationalist,* 346; Ketchum, 162–63; see also the "Supplemental Appendix" to the Supreme Court's opinion in *Everson v. Board of Education,* 330 U.S. 1, 72–74 (1947). A "broadside" (or a public notice) of Henry's proposal bears the date December 24, 1784, and it quotes from the Journal of the Virginia House of Delegates of that same date. Huston, *Religion and the State Governments.*

81. I *Jefferson's Writings* (1903 ed.), 90, 160–61; *Jefferson's Life,* 62, 101; *Jefferson . . . In His Own Words,* 149; Malone, *Jefferson and the Rights of Man,* 209, 243; and V *Dictionary of American Biography,* Pt. 2, 21–22.

82. *Jefferson—Notes on the State of Virginia,* 124; III *Jefferson's Works* (*Notes on the State of Virginia*), 335; II *Jefferson's Writings* (1903 ed.) (*Notes on the State of Virginia*), unpaginated "Introductory Notes."

83. See Huston, *Religion and the State Governments.* A "broadside" (or public notice) dated December 24, 1784, quoted the following from the Journal of the Virginia House of Delegates for December 24, 1784:

> A motion was made, and the question being put that the third reading of the engrossed Bill establishing a provision for the teachers of the

Christian religion, be *postponed until the fourth Thursday in November next,*

It was resolved in the affirmative. . . .

On a motion made, *Resolved,* That the engrossed Bill establishing a provision for the teachers of the Christian religion . . . to be published in Hand-bills, and twelve copies thereof delivered to each member of the General Assembly, to be distributed in their respective counties and that the people thereof be requested to signify their opinion respecting the adoption of such a Bill, to the *next Session* of Assembly.

Huston, *Religion and the State Governments* (emphasis added).

The Supreme Court's opinion in *Everson v. Board of Education,* 330 U.S. 1 (1947), supplies a "Supplemental Appendix" that confirms that the excerpt quoted above appeared in "one of the hand-bills which on December 24, 1784, when the third reading of the bill was postponed, were ordered distributed to the Virginia counties by the House of Delegates." 330 U.S. at 74 n. *.

84. 8 *Madison's Papers,* 136–37; II *Madison's Writings,* 89–90; I *Madison's Letters,* 108–9.

85. 9 *Madison's Papers,* 430–31.

86. 8 *Madison's Papers,* 228–29; II *Madison's Writings,* 112–13; I *Madison's Letters,* 130–31; 7 *Jefferson's Papers,* 594–95.

87. Madison's June 20, 1785, Memorial and Remonstrance against Religious Assessments, reproduced in: 8 *Madison's Papers,* 298–304; II *Madison's Writings,* 183–91; I *Madison's Letters,* 162–69; and 5 *Founders' Constitution,* 82–84 (emphasis added).

88. See Chapter 3A.

89. 1 *Madison's Papers,* 171–75.

90. Ketchum, 165.

91. Brant, *James Madison: The Nationalist,* 350; Ketchum, 165.

92. July 7, 1785, letter from George Nicholas to James Madison (8 *Madison's Papers,* 316).

93. Brant, *James Madison: The Nationalist,* 350.

94. January 22, 1786, letter from James Madison to Thomas Jefferson (8 *Madison's Papers,* 473; II *Madison's Writings,* 214; I *Madison's Letters,* 213; 9 *Jefferson's Papers,* 195–96).

95. November 1826 letter from Madison to General LaFayette (IX *Madison's Writings,* 261–66; III *Madison's Letters,* 543).

96. See Chapter 3B.

97. See Chapter 3D.

98. Ketchum, 165.

99. See Chapter 3B.

100. 8 *Madison's Papers,* 399–401.

101. 2 *Jefferson's Papers,* 305–24 and 547–53; II *Jefferson's Writings* (1903 ed.), 300–303; 8 *Madison's Papers,* 391–94; see also *Jefferson—* "Autobiography," 40, I *Jefferson's Works,* 71, and *Jefferson . . . In His Own Words,* 88 (mentioning Madison's "unwearied exertions" to eventually get Jefferson's proposals passed in some form).

102. Virginia's January 16, 1786, Act for Establishing Religious Freedom, codified in 12 Hening, *Statutes of Virginia,* 84 (1823) (emphasis added), and reproduced in: 8 *Madison's Papers,* 399–401; II *Jefferson's Writings* (1903 ed.), 300–303; 5 *Founders' Constitution,* 84–85.

103. II *Madison's Writings,* 212.

104. *Madison and the American Nation,* 13.

105. 1 *Madison's Papers,* 171.

106. Simmons, 24.

107. Levy, *The Establishment Clause,* 1.

108. Simmons, 98–100, 175–77; McDougall, 118.

109. Meinig, 247.

110. Meinig, 247; Simmons, 124.

111. *History of the United States,* 26. For reasons left unexplained, the source for this particular data does not include Delaware.

112. 5 *Historical Statistics,* 652; Simmons, 175–77, 379.

113. *History of the United States,* 58.

114. 5 *Historical Statistics,* 652; Simmons, 175–77, 379.

115. *History of the United States,* 58.

116. 5 *Historical Statistics,* 652; Simmons, 175–77, 379.

117. 5 *Historical Statistics,* 659.

118. *History of the United States,* 58.

119. 5 *Historical Statistics,* 652; Simmons, 175–77, 379.

120. 5 *Historical Statistics,* 660.

121. *History of the United States,* 58.

122. 5 *Historical Statistics,* 652; Simmons, 175–77, 379.

123. 5 *Historical Statistics,* 661.

124. 5 *Historical Statistics,* 652; Simmons, 175–77, 379.

125. *History of the United States,* 58.

126. 5 *Historical Statistics,* 652; Simmons, 175–77, 379.

127. 5 *Historical Statistics,* 663.

128. *History of the United States,* 58.

129. 5 *Historical Statistics,* 652; Simmons, 175–77, 379.

130. 5 *Historical Statistics,* 662. By 1790, New Jersey and New York combined had increased to 314,000. *History of the United States,* 58.

131. 5 *Historical Statistics,* 652; Simmons, 175–77, 379.

132. 5 *Historical Statistics,* 658.

133. *History of the United States,* 58.

134. 5 *Historical Statistics,* 652; Simmons, 175–77, 379.

135. *History of the United States,* 58.

136. 5 *Historical Statistics,* 652; Simmons, 175–77, 379.

137. *History of the United States,* 58.

138. 5 *Historical Statistics,* 652; Simmons, 175–77, 379.

139. *History of the United States,* 58.

140. 5 *Historical Statistics,* 652; Simmons, 175–77, 379.

141. *History of the United States,* 58.

142. Simmons, 177, 379.

143. Simmons, 195; Taylor, 134.

144. 5 *Historical Statistics,* 717.

145. Ibid., 672–73.

146. Ibid., 712.

147. McDougall, 45.

148. II *Jefferson's Writings* (1903 ed.), 160 (*Notes on the State of Virginia*).

149. McDougall, 234–35.

150. U.S. Const., Art. I, § 2, ¶ 3, 1 Stat. 10–11 (emphasis added).

151. XI *Documentary History . . . First Federal Congress,* 828 n. 3.

152. XI *Documentary History . . . First Federal Congress,* 828 n. 3. Connecticut's 1662 charter has been reproduced in: 1 *Federal and State Constitutions,* 529–36; 2 *Sources and Documents,* 131–36.

153. 2 *Sources and Documents,* 143.

154. 1 *Federal and State Constitutions,* 536–47; 2 *Sources and Documents,* 143.

155. XI *Documentary History . . . First Federal Congress,* 828 n. 3. Rhode Island's 1663 charter has been reproduced in: 6 *Federal and State Constitutions,* 3211–22; 8 *Sources and Documents,* 362–69.

156. 6 *Federal and State Constitutions,* 3222–35; 8 *Sources and Documents,* 386–96.

157. Virginia's June 12, 1776, Declaration of Rights has been reproduced in: I *Madison's Writings,* 35–40; I *Mason's Papers,* 287–89; I *Madison's Letters,* 21–24; 7 *Federal and State Constitutions,* 3812–14;

10 *Sources and Documents,* 48–50; *Sources of Our Liberties,* 311–12; VIII *Documentary History . . . Ratification,* 530–31; 5 *Founders' Constitution,* 7–9.

Virginia's separate June 29, 1776, Constitution, which supplied only a "Plan of Government," has been reproduced in: I *Madison's Writings,* 41–49; I *Madison's Letters,* 24–28; 1 *Jefferson's Papers,* 377–83; 7 *Federal and State Constitutions,* 3814–19; 10 *Sources and Documents,* 51–56; VIII *Documentary History . . . Ratification,* 532–37; 1 *Founders' Constitution,* 7–9.

158. Virginia's January 16, 1786, Act for Establishing Religious Freedom, codified in 12 Hening, *Statutes of Virginia,* 84 (1823), has been reproduced in: 8 *Madison's Papers,* 399–401; II *Jefferson's Writings* (1903 ed.), 300–303; 5 *Founders' Constitution,* 84–85.

159. New Jersey's July 3, 1776, Constitution has been reproduced in: 5 *Federal and State Constitutions,* 2594–98; 6 *Sources and Documents,* 449–53.

160. Delaware's September 20, 1776, Constitution has been reproduced in: 1 *Federal and State Constitutions,* 562–68; 2 *Sources and Documents,* 199–204.

161. Delaware's independently adopted September 11, 1776, Declaration of Rights has been reproduced in: 2 *Sources and Documents,* 197–99; *Sources of Our Liberties,* 338–40.

162. Pennsylvania's September 28, 1776, Constitution has been reproduced in: 5 *Federal and State Constitutions,* 3084–92; 8 *Sources and Documents,* 277–85. The Declaration of Rights within Pennsylvania's 1776 constitution has been reproduced in: 5 *Federal and State Constitutions,* 3082–84; 8 *Sources and Documents,* 278–79; *Sources of Our Liberties,* 329–31.

163. Maryland's independently adopted November 3, 1776, Declaration of Rights has been reproduced in: 3 *Federal and State Constitutions,* 1686–91; 4 *Sources and Documents,* 372–75; *Sources of Our Liberties,* 346–51.

164. Maryland's November 8, 1776, Constitution has been reproduced in: 3 *Federal and State Constitutions,* 1691–1701; 4 *Sources and Documents,* 376–83.

165. North Carolina's December 18, 1776, Constitution has been reproduced in: 5 *Federal and State Constitutions,* 2789–94; 7 *Sources and Documents,* 404–7. The Declaration of Rights within North Carolina's 1776 constitution has been reproduced in: 5 *Federal and*

State Constitutions, 2787–89; 7 *Sources and Documents,* 402–4; *Sources of Our Liberties,* 355–57.

166. New York's April 20, 1777, Constitution has been reproduced in: 5 *Federal and State Constitutions,* 2623–38; 7 *Sources and Documents,* 168–79; XIX *Documentary History . . . Ratification,* 501–4. Although New York did have a separate declaration of rights in statutory (not constitutional) form (à la Virginia), it contained no provision concerning religion. See New York's Act Concerning the Rights of the Citizens of This State, XIX *Documentary History . . . Ratification,* 504–6.

167. Georgia's February 5, 1777, Constitution has been reproduced in: 2 *Federal and State Constitutions,* 777–85; 2 *Sources and Documents,* 443–49.

Georgia's May 6, 1789, Constitution (effective October 5, 1789) has been reproduced in: 2 *Federal and State Constitutions,* 785–90; in 2 *Sources and Documents,* 452–55.

168. South Carolina's March 19, 1778, Constitution has been reproduced in: 6 *Federal and State Constitutions,* 3255–57; 8 *Sources and Documents,* 468–75.

169. Massachusetts's March 2, 1780, Constitution (effective October 25, 1780) has been reproduced in: 3 *Federal and State Constitutions,* 1893–1911; 5 *Sources and Documents,* 96–109. The Declaration of Rights within Massachusetts's 1780 constitution has been reproduced in: 3 *Federal and State Constitutions,* 1888–93; 5 *Sources and Documents,* 92–96; IV *Documentary History . . . Ratification,* 440–45.

170. New Hampshire's 1784 Constitution (effective June 2, 1784) has been reproduced in: 4 *Federal and State Constitutions,* 2458–70; 6 *Sources and Documents,* 344–57. The Declaration of Rights within New Hampshire's 1784 Constitution has been reproduced in: 4 *Federal and State Constitutions,* 2453–57; 6 *Sources and Documents,* 344–47.

171. Vermont's initial 1777 Constitution has been reproduced in: 6 *Federal and State Constitutions,* 3737–49; 9 *Sources and Documents,* 487–95. Vermont's replacement 1786 Constitution has been reproduced in: 6 *Federal and State Constitutions,* 3749–61; 9 *Sources and Documents,* 497–505.

172. Vermont's statehood occurred via Act of Congress of February 18, 1791, 1st Cong., 3rd Sess., Ch. 7, 1 Stat. 191 (1791) (reproduced in 6 *Federal and State Constitutions,* 3761; 2 *Annals of Congress,* Appendix, 2374).

173. Simmons, 364.

174. Virginia's June 12, 1776, Declaration of Rights, Art. 16 (emphasis added), reproduced in: 1 *Madison's Papers,* 175; I *Madison's Writings,* 40; I *Mason's Papers,* 289; 7 *Federal and State Constitutions,* 3814; 10 *Sources and Documents,* 50; VIII *Documentary History . . . Ratification,* 531; *Sources of Our Liberties,* 312; 5 *Founders' Constitution,* 9.

175. Virginia's 1786 Act Establishing Religious Freedom (emphasis added), codified in 12 Hening, *Statutes of Virginia,* 84 (1823), and reproduced in: 8 *Madison's Papers,* 399–401; II *Jefferson's Writings* (1903 ed.), 300–303; 5 *Founders' Constitution,* 84–85.

176. New Jersey did not have a separate Declaration of Rights.

177. New Jersey Constitution of July 3, 1776, Art. XVIII (emphasis added), reproduced in: 5 *Federal and State Constitutions,* 2597; 6 *Sources and Documents,* 452.

178. New Jersey Constitution of July 3, 1776, Art. XIX (emphasis added), reproduced in: 5 *Federal and State Constitutions,* 2597–98; 6 *Sources and Documents,* 452.

179. Delaware Constitution of September 20, 1776, Art. 29 (emphasis added), reproduced in: 1 *Federal and State Constitutions,* 567; 2 *Sources and Documents,* 203.

180. Delaware Declaration of Rights of September 11, 1776, § 2 (emphasis added), reproduced in: 2 *Sources and Documents,* 197; *Sources of Our Liberties,* 338.

181. Delaware Declaration of Rights of September 11, 1776, § 3 (emphasis added), reproduced in 2 *Sources and Documents,* 197; 5 *Founders' Constitution,* 5–6.

182. Pennsylvania's September 28, 1776, Constitution incorporated both an independent "Declaration of Rights" (5 *Federal and State Constitutions,* 3082–84; 8 *Sources and Documents,* 278–79; *Sources of Our Liberties,* 329–31) and an independent "Constitution" (5 *Federal and State Constitutions,* 3084–92; 8 *Sources and Documents,* 277–85).

183. Pennsylvania Constitution of September 28, 1776, "Declaration of Rights," Art. II (emphasis added), reproduced in: 5 *Federal and State Constitutions,* 3082; 8 *Sources and Documents,* 278; *Sources of Our Liberties,* 329.

184. Pennsylvania Constitution of September 28, 1776, § 45 (emphasis added), reproduced in: 5 *Federal and State Constitutions,*

3091; 8 *Sources and Documents,* 285.

185. Maryland's November 3, 1776, Declaration of Rights has been reproduced in: 3 *Federal and State Constitutions,* 1686–91; 4 *Sources and Documents,* 372–75; *Sources of Our Liberties,* 346–51.

186. Maryland's November 8, 1776, Constitution (devoted solely to the framework of government) has been reproduced in: 3 *Federal and State Constitutions,* 1691–1701; 4 *Sources and Documents,* 376–83.

187. Maryland's November 3, 1776, Declaration of Rights, Art. XXXI-II (emphasis added), reproduced in: 3 *Federal and State Constitutions,* 1689–90; 4 *Sources and Documents,* 374; *Sources of Our Liberties,* 349.

188. North Carolina's December 18, 1776, Constitution incorporated both an independent "Declaration of Rights" (5 *Federal and State Constitutions,* 2787–89; 7 *Sources and Documents,* 402–4; *Sources of Our Liberties,* 355–57) and an independent "Constitution" (5 *Federal and State Constitutions,* 2789–94; 7 *Sources and Documents,* 404–7).

189. A "glebe" referred to productive farmland owned by a church, and, within the establishment context, typically meant land appropriated by government authorities and given to an established ecclesiastical institution. McDougall, 125; *New Oxford American Dictionary,* 716; 1 *Shorter Oxford English Dictionary,* 1107; *American Heritage Dictionary of the English Language,* 747; *Random House Webster's Unabridged Dictionary,* 811; *Random House Unabridged Dictionary,* 811; VI *Oxford English Dictionary,* 567; *Webster's Third New International Dictionary,* 964.

190. North Carolina Constitution of December 18, 1776, Art. XXXIV (emphasis added), reproduced in: 5 *Federal and State Constitutions,* 2793; 7 *Sources and Documents,* 406–7.

191. New York did not adopt any separate Declaration of Rights.

192. New Jersey, Delaware, North Carolina, Massachusetts, and New Hampshire each had specific "no-establishment" assurances in their respective pre-1789 constitutions.

193. New York Constitution of April 20, 1777, Art. XXXV (emphasis added), reproduced in: 5 *Federal and State Constitutions,* 2635–36; 7 *Sources and Documents,* 178; XIX *Documentary History . . . Ratification,* 502.

194. New York Constitution of April 20, 1777, Art. XXXVIII (emphasis added), reproduced: in 5 *Federal and State Constitutions,* 2636–37; 7 *Sources and Documents,* 178; XIX *Documentary History . . . Ratification,* 503.

195. Georgia did not adopt a separate Declaration of Rights.

196. Georgia Constitution of February 5, 1777, Art. LVI (emphasis added), reproduced in: 2 *Federal and State Constitutions,* 784; 2 *Sources and Documents,* 449.

197. Georgia Constitution of May 6, 1789, Art. IV, § 5 (emphasis added), reproduced in: 2 *Federal and State Constitutions,* 789; 2 *Sources and Documents,* 454.

198. South Carolina did not adopt a separate Declaration of Rights.

199. South Carolina Constitution of March 19, 1778, Art. XXXVI-II (emphasis added), reproduced in: 6 *Federal and State Constitutions,* 3256–57; 8 *Sources and Documents,* 475.

200. Massachusetts's March 2, 1780, Constitution (effective October 25, 1780) incorporated both an independent "Declaration of Rights" (3 *Federal and State Constitutions,* 1889–93; 5 *Sources and Documents,* 92–96; IV *Documentary History . . . Ratification,* 440–45), and an independent "Constitution" dedicated to the framework of government (3 *Federal and State Constitutions,* 1893–1911; 5 *Sources and Documents,* 96–109).

201. Massachusetts's Constitution of March 2, 1780, "Declaration of Rights," Art. II (emphasis added), reproduced in: 3 *Federal and State Constitutions,* 1889–90; 5 *Sources and Documents,* 93; *Sources of Our Liberties,* 374.

202. Massachusetts's Constitution of March 2, 1780, "Declaration of Rights," Art. III (emphasis added), reproduced in: 3 *Federal and State Constitutions,* 1889–90; 5 *Sources and Documents,* 93–94; IV *Documentary History . . . Ratification,* 441; *Sources of Our Liberties,* 374.

203. Massachusetts's Constitution of March 2, 1780, "Declaration of Rights," Art. III (emphasis added), reproduced in: 3 *Federal and State Constitutions,* 1889–90; 5 *Sources and Documents,* 93–94; IV *Documentary History . . . Ratification,* 441; *Sources of Our Liberties,* 374.

204. New Hampshire's 1784 Constitution (effective June 2, 1784) incorporated both an independent "Declaration of Rights" (4 *Federal and State Constitutions,* 2453–57; 6 *Sources and Documents,* 344–47) and an independent "Constitution" dedicated to the framework of government (4 *Federal and State Constitutions,* 2458–70; 6 *Sources and Documents,* 347–57).

A New Hampshire convention had adopted an early constitution on January 5, 1776, during a time when the state suddenly found itself without any functioning government. That 1776 constitution consisted of a few short paragraphs, and the convention never submitted it to a vote of the state's residents. See 4 *Federal and State Constitutions*, 2451–53; 6 *Sources and Documents*, 342–43.

205. The New Hampshire Constitution of 1784, "Declaration of Rights," Art. VI (emphasis added), reproduced in: 4 *Federal and State Constitutions*, 2454; 6 *Sources and Documents*, 345; *Sources of Our Liberties*, 382.

206. Vermont had its own constitution when the First Congress assembled in 1789, but did not achieve statehood until March 4, 1791, via Act of Congress of February 18, 1791, 1st Cong., 3rd Sess., Ch. 7, 1 Stat. 191 (1791) (statute reproduced in: 6 *Federal and State Constitutions*, 3761; 2 *Annals of Congress*, Appendix, 2374).

207. The Vermont Constitution of July 8, 1777, incorporated both an independent "Declaration of Rights" (6 *Federal and State Constitutions*, 3739–42; 9 *Sources and Documents*, 489–90) and an independent "Constitution" dedicated to the framework of government (6 *Federal and State Constitutions*, 3742–49; 9 *Sources and Documents*, 490–95).

208. The Vermont Constitution of July 4, 1786, likewise incorporated both an independent "Declaration of Rights" (6 *Federal and State Constitutions*, 3751–54; 9 *Sources and Documents*, 497–99) and an independent "Constitution" dedicated to the framework of government (6 *Federal and State Constitutions*, 3754–61; 9 *Sources and Documents*, 499–505).

209. Vermont Constitution of July 8, 1777, "Declaration of Rights," Ch. I, Art. 3 (emphasis added), reproduced in: 6 *Federal and State Constitutions*, 3740; 9 *Sources and Documents*, 489; and *Sources of Our Liberties*, 365.

210. Vermont Constitution of July 4, 1786, "Declaration of Rights," Ch. I, Art. 3 (emphasis added), reproduced in: 6 *Federal and State Constitutions*, 3752; 9 *Sources and Documents*, 498.

211. **Virginia:** Virginia's 1786 Act Establishing Religious Freedom, codified in 12 Hening, *Statutes of Virginia*, 84 (1823), and reproduced in: 8 *Madison's Papers*, 399–401; II *Jefferson's Writings* (1903 ed.), 300–303; 5 *Founders' Constitution*, 84–85; **New Jersey:** New Jersey Constitution of July 3, 1776, Art. XIX, reproduced in: 5 *Federal and State Constitutions*, 2597–98; 6 *Sources and Documents*, 452; **Delaware:** Delaware Declaration of Rights of September 11,

1776, § 3, reproduced in 2 *Sources and Documents,* 197; 5 *Founders' Constitution,* 5–6; **Pennsylvania:** Pennsylvania Constitution of September 28, 1776, § 45, reproduced in: 5 *Federal and State Constitutions,* 3091; 8 *Sources and Documents,* 285; **Maryland:** Maryland Constitution of November 8, 1776, Declaration of Rights, Art. XXXI-II, reproduced in: 3 *Federal and State Constitutions,* 1689–90; 4 *Sources and Documents,* 374; *Sources of Our Liberties,* 349; **North Carolina:** North Carolina Constitution of December 18, 1776, Art. XXXIV, reproduced in: 5 *Federal and State Constitutions,* 2793; 7 *Sources and Documents,* 406–7; **New York:** New York Constitution of April 20, 1777, Art. XXXVIII, reproduced: in 5 *Federal and State Constitutions,* 2636–37; 7 *Sources and Documents,* 178; XIX *Documentary History . . . Ratification,* 503; **South Carolina:** South Carolina Constitution of March 19, 1778, Art. XXXVIII, reproduced in: 6 *Federal and State Constitutions,* 3256–57; 8 *Sources and Documents,* 475; **Massachusetts:** Massachusetts Constitution of March 2, 1780, Art. II, reproduced in: 3 *Federal and State Constitutions,* 1889–90; 5 *Sources and Documents,* 93; *Sources of Our Liberties,* 374; **New Hampshire:** The New Hampshire Constitution of 1784, Declaration of Rights, Art. VI, reproduced in: 4 *Federal and State Constitutions,* 2454; 6 *Sources and Documents,* 345; *Sources of Our Liberties,* 382; **Vermont:** Vermont Constitution of July 4, 1786, Ch. I, Art. 3, reproduced in: 6 *Federal and State Constitutions,* 3752; 9 *Sources and Documents,* 498.

212. **Virginia:** Virginia's 1786 Act Establishing Religious Freedom, codified in 12 Hening, *Statutes of Virginia,* 84 (1823), and reproduced in: 8 *Madison's Papers,* 399–401; II *Jefferson's Writings* (1903 ed.), 300–303; 5 *Founders' Constitution,* 84–85; **New Jersey:** New Jersey Constitution of July 3, 1776, Art. XVIII, reproduced in: 5 *Federal and State Constitutions,* 2597; 6 *Sources and Documents,* 452; **Delaware:** Delaware Declaration of Rights of September 11, 1776, § Section 2, reproduced in: 2 *Sources and Documents,* 197; *Sources of Our Liberties,* 338; **Pennsylvania:** Pennsylvania Constitution of September 28, 1776, Declaration of Rights, Art. II, reproduced in: 5 *Federal and State Constitutions,* 3082; 8 *Sources and Documents,* 278; *Sources of Our Liberties,* 329; **Maryland:** Maryland Constitution of November 8, 1776, Declaration of Rights, Art. XXXIII, reproduced in: 3 *Federal and State Constitutions,* 1689–90; 4 *Sources and Documents,* 374; *Sources of Our Liberties,* 349; **North Carolina:** North Carolina Constitution of December 18, 1776, Art. XXXIV,

reproduced in: 5 *Federal and State Constitutions*, 2793; 7 *Sources and Documents*, 406–7; **Georgia:** Georgia Constitution of May 6, 1789, Art. IV, § 5, reproduced in: 2 *Federal and State Constitutions*, 789; 2 *Sources and Documents*, 454; **South Carolina:** South Carolina Constitution of March 19, 1778, Art. XXXVIII, reproduced in: 6 *Federal and State Constitutions*, 3256–57; 8 *Sources and Documents*, 475; **Vermont:** Vermont Constitution of July 4, 1786, Ch. I, Art. 3, reproduced in: 6 *Federal and State Constitutions*, 3752; 9 *Sources and Documents*, 498.

The Virginia legislature enacted its ecclesiastical-specific assurances in quasi-constitutional form via Article 16 in its 1776 Declaration of Rights and in statutory form via its 1786 Act for Establishing Religious Freedom. Virginia confined its separate 1776 Constitution, labeled a "Plan of Government," to the structure and function of government. I *Madison's Writings*, 41–49; I *Madison's Letters*, 24–28; 1 *Jefferson's Papers*, 377–83; 7 *Federal and State Constitutions*, 3814–19; 10 *Sources and Documents*, 51–56; VIII *Documentary History . . . Ratification*, 532–37; 1 *Founders' Constitution*, 7–9.

213. **Massachusetts:** Massachusetts Constitution of March 2, 1780, Art. III, reproduced in: 3 *Federal and State Constitutions*, 1889–90; 5 *Sources and Documents*, 93–94; IV *Documentary History . . . Ratification*, 441; *Sources of Our Liberties*, 374; **New Hampshire:** New Hampshire Constitution of 1784, Declaration of Rights, Art. VI, reproduced in: 4 *Federal and State Constitutions*, 2454; 6 *Sources and Documents*, 345; *Sources of Our Liberties*, 382.

214. **New Jersey:** New Jersey Constitution of July 3, 1776, Art. XIX, reproduced in: 5 *Federal and State Constitutions*, 2597–98; 6 *Sources and Documents*, 452; **Delaware:** Delaware Constitution of September 20, 1776, Art. 29, reproduced in: 1 *Federal and State Constitutions*, 567; 2 *Sources and Documents*, 203; **North Carolina:** North Carolina Constitution of December 18, 1776, Art. XXXIV, reproduced in: 5 *Federal and State Constitutions*, 2793; 7 *Sources and Documents*, 406–7; **New York:** New York Constitution of April 20, 1777, Art. XXXV, reproduced in: 5 *Federal and State Constitutions*, 2635–36; 7 *Sources and Documents*, 178; XIX *Documentary History . . . Ratification*, 502; **Massachusetts:** Massachusetts Constitution of March 2, 1780, Art. III, reproduced in: 3 *Federal and State Constitutions*, 1889–90; 5 *Sources and Documents*, 93–94; IV *Documentary History . . . Ratification*, 441;

Sources of Our Liberties, 374; **New Hampshire:** The New Hampshire Constitution of 1784, Declaration of Rights, Art. VI, reproduced in: 4 *Federal and State Constitutions,* 2454; 6 *Sources and Documents,* 345; *Sources of Our Liberties,* 382.

215. **Virginia:** Virginia's June 12, 1776, Declaration of Rights, Art. 16, reproduced in: 1 *Madison's Papers,* 175; I *Madison's Writings,* 40; I *Mason's Papers,* 289; 7 *Federal and State Constitutions,* 3814; 10 *Sources and Documents,* 50; VIII *Documentary History . . . Ratification,* 531; *Sources of Our Liberties,* 312; 5 *Founders' Constitution,* 9; Virginia's 1786 Act Establishing Religious Freedom, codified in 12 Hening, *Statutes of Virginia,* 84 (1823), and reproduced in: 8 *Madison's Papers,* 399–401; II *Jefferson's Writings* (1903 ed.), 300–303; 5 *Founders' Constitution,* 84–85; **New Jersey:** New Jersey Constitution of July 3, 1776, Art. XVIII, reproduced in: 5 *Federal and State Constitutions,* 2597; 6 *Sources and Documents,* 452; **Delaware:** Delaware Declaration of Rights of September 11, 1776, § 2, reproduced in: 2 *Sources and Documents,* 197; *Sources of Our Liberties,* 338; **Pennsylvania:** Pennsylvania Constitution of September 28, 1776, Declaration of Rights, Art. II, reproduced in: 5 *Federal and State Constitutions,* 3082; 8 *Sources and Documents,* 278; *Sources of Our Liberties,* 329; **North Carolina:** North Carolina Constitution of December 18, 1776, Art. XXXIV, reproduced in: 5 *Federal and State Constitutions,* 2793; 7 *Sources and Documents,* 406–7; **Vermont:** Vermont Constitution of July 4, 1786, ·Ch. I, Art. 3, reproduced in: 6 *Federal and State Constitutions,* 3752; 9 *Sources and Documents,* 498.

The Virginia legislature enacted its ecclesiastical-specific assurances in quasi-constitutional form via Article 16 in its 1776 Declaration of Rights and in statutory form via its 1786 Act for Establishing Religious Freedom.

216. **Maryland:** Maryland Constitution of November 8, 1776, Declaration of Rights, Art. XXXIII, reproduced in: 3 *Federal and State Constitutions,* 1689–90; 4 *Sources and Documents,* 374; *Sources of Our Liberties,* 349; **Massachusetts:** Massachusetts Constitution of March 2, 1780, Art. III, reproduced in: 3 *Federal and State Constitutions,* 1889–90; 5 *Sources and Documents,* 93–94; IV *Documentary History . . . Ratification,* 441; *Sources of Our Liberties,* 374; **New Hampshire:** The New Hampshire Constitution of 1784, Declaration of Rights, Art. VI, reproduced in: 4 *Federal and State Constitutions,* 2454; 6 *Sources and Documents,* 345; *Sources of Our Liberties,* 382.

The Massachusetts and New Hampshire Constitutions authorized nonpreferential financial support, although only among "public Protestant teachers," while the Maryland Constitution authorized a statewide tax for "the support of the Christian religion."

217. South Carolina Constitution of March 19, 1778, Art. XXXVI-II, reproduced in: 6 *Federal and State Constitutions*, 3256–57; 8 *Sources and Documents*, 475.

218. The New Jersey constitution actually contained the phrase "no establishment."

219. The Delaware constitution actually contained the phrase "no establishment."

220. The Maryland Constitution confined any state financial assistance to "the Christian religion."

221. The North Carolina constitution actually contained the phrase "no establishment."

222. The New York constitution dis-"established" religion.

223. The Massachusetts constitution declared that no preference shall be "established" or tolerated.

224. The Massachusetts constitution confined any state financial assistance to "public Protestant teachers."

225. The New Hampshire constitution declared that no preference shall be "established" or tolerated.

226. The New Hampshire constitution confined any state financial assistance to "public Protestant teachers."

227. Although the Maryland, Massachusetts, and New Hampshire constitutions authorized the legislature to implement a tax to support a particular aspect of the states' ecclesiastical institutions, any such tax could only be *non*preferential and thus unavailing for establishment purposes.

Chapter 4

1. III *Mason's Papers*, 981; II Farrand's *Records*, 587–88; V Elliott's *Debates*, 538; *Madison's Notes*, 556–57; *Documents Illustrative . . . Formation of the American States*, 716; IV *Madison's Writings*, 441–42; II Madison's *Journal*, 717; III *Documentary History . . . Constitution*, 734–35; Farrand, 185–86.

The various declarations of rights have been discussed in detail in Chapter 3E.

2. See Chapter 3A.

3. III *Mason's Papers*, 981; II Farrand's *Records*, 587–88; V Elliott's *Debates*, 538; *Madison's Notes*, 556–57; IV *Madison's Writings*, 442; II Madison's *Journal*, 717; III *Documentary History . . . Constitution*, 734–35; *Documents Illustrative . . . Formation of the American States*, 716; Farrand, 185–86.

4. II Farrand's *Records*, 588; I Elliott's *Debates*, 306; V Elliott's *Debates*, 538; *Madison's Notes*, 556–57; IV *Madison's Writings*, 441–42; II Madison's *Journal*, 717; III *Documentary History . . . Constitution*, 734–35; *Documents Illustrative . . . Formation of the American States*, 716; Farrand, 185–86.

5. Labunski, 9.

6. I Elliott's *Debates*, 494–96; V Elliott's *Debates*, 565; II Farrand's *Records*, 649; *Madison's Notes*, 583; IV *Madison's Writings*, 483; II Madison's *Journal*, 763; III *Documentary History of the Constitution*, 770; *Documents Illustrative . . . Formation of the American States*, 745; Farrand, 194.

7. Labunski, 10.

8. Rakove, 288.

9. See, for instance, *Federalist No. 84;* II Elliott's *Debates*, 78 (Massachusetts Ratifying Convention) (Proceedings of January 23, 1788) (statement of Varnum), and 436, 453, 455 (Pennsylvania Ratifying Convention) (Proceedings of October 28, 1787, December 3, 1787, and December 4, 1787, respectively) (statements of Wilson); III Elliott's *Debates*, 203–4, 450, 600 (Virginia Ratifying Convention) (Proceedings of June 10, 1788, June 14, 1788, and June 24, 1788, respectively) (statements of Randolph and Nicholas); IV Elliott's *Debates*, 149, 208 (North Carolina Ratifying Convention) (Proceedings of July 26, 1788, and July 30, 1788, respectively) (statements of Iredale and Spaight), and 315–16 (South Carolina Ratifying Convention) (Proceedings of January 18, 1788) (statement of Pinckney).

10. In 1787 and 1788, Alexander Hamilton, along with James Madison and John Jay, authored a series of anonymous essays (published in New York newspapers under the name "Publius") that expressed their opinions about the nature of the new government proposed by the yet-to-be-ratified Constitution. They structured the essays to persuade the pivotal state of New York to ratify the Constitution, and the eighty-five essays have long since been known as *The Federalist Papers*. Madison later described *The Federalist Papers* as

"the most authentic exposition of the text of the Federal Constitution, as understood by the Body which prepared and the authority which accepted it." February 8, 1825, letter from James Madison to Thomas Jefferson (IX *Madison's Writings*, 218).

11. *Federalist No. 84.*

12. October 17, 1788, letter from James Madison to Thomas Jefferson (11 *Madison's Papers*, 297–300; V *Madison's Writings*, 271; 14 *Jefferson's Papers*, 18).

13. January 2, 1789, letter from James Madison to George Eve (11 *Madison's Papers*, 404–5; V *Madison's Writings*, 319; I *Madison's Letters*, 446–47).

14. See, for instance, *Federalist No. 38* and *Federalist No. 48* (last paragraph) ("a mere demarcation on parchment of the constitutional limits of the several departments is not a sufficient guard against those encroachments which lead to a tyrannical concentration of all the powers of government in the same hands").

15. Labunski, 160–61.

16. III Elliott's *Debates*, 330 (Virginia Ratifying Convention) (Proceedings of June 12, 1788) (Statement of James Madison).

17. III Elliott's *Debates*, 330 (Virginia Ratifying Convention) (Proceedings of June 12, 1788) (Statement of James Madison).

18. See, for instance: September 30, 1787, letter from James Madison to George Washington (10 *Madison's Papers*, 180–81; V *Madison's Writings*, 4; 5 *Washington's Papers, Confederation Series*, 346–47); and January 13, 1789, letter from James Madison to Thomas Randolph (11 *Madison's Papers*, 416).

19. Labunski, 9.

20. III Elliott's *Debates*, 317–18 (Virginia Ratifying Convention) (Proceedings of June 12, 1788) (Statement of Patrick Henry); October, 21, 1789, letter from James Madison to Archibald Stuart referencing Henry's opposition to ratification (10 *Madison's Papers*, 202; 5 *Founders' Constitution*, 88).

When Patrick Henry advocated as much during the Virginia Ratifying Convention in June 1788, only eight states had voted to ratify the Constitution. Likely unknown to Henry, South Carolina's eighth vote had occurred just three weeks earlier, so Henry may well have believed he could thwart ratification at that point. But just nine days after Henry's speech, New Hampshire's ninth vote served to ratify the Constitution and thus rendered Henry's argument moot insofar as he thought it might forestall ratification.

21. See, for instance, Labunski, 60, 65 ("Their [*viz.*, ratification opponents] best opportunity to successfully challenge adoption of the proposed plan would come in Virginia.")

22. December 20, 1787, letter from Thomas Jefferson to James Madison (12 *Jefferson's Papers,* 440; VI *Jefferson's Writings* (1903 ed.), 387; II *Jefferson's Writings* (1853 ed.), 327; V *Jefferson's Works,* 371; 10 *Madison's Papers,* 336). Jefferson expressed the same sentiments in a February 2, 1788, letter to John Rutledge, Jr. (12 *Jefferson's Papers,* 557; VI *Jefferson's Writings* (1903 ed.), 418; II *Jefferson's Writings* (1853 ed.), 349–50; V *Jefferson's Works,* 386).

23. Article VII of the Constitution prescribed (and actually still prescribes) a ratification of the Constitution by at least nine states:

> The ratification of the conventions of nine states, shall be suffi-cient for the establishment of this Constitution between the states so ratifying the same.

U.S. Const., Art. VII, 1 Stat. 19.

24. "The framers decided that if nine states ratified the Constitution, it would go into effect for those states, and the govern-ment would begin to operate. The other states could join the union when they approved the Constitution." Labunski, 14.

25. Malone, *Jefferson and the Rights of Man,* 171.

26. February 2, 1788, letter from Thomas Jefferson to William Stephens (12 *Jefferson's Papers,* 558; V *Jefferson's Works,* 384).

27. February 2, 1788, letter from Thomas Jefferson to John Rutledge, Jr. (12 *Jefferson's Papers,* 557; VI *Jefferson's Writings* (1903 ed.), 418; II *Jefferson's Writings* (1853 ed.), 349–50; V *Jefferson's Works,* 386).

28. February 2, 1788, letter from Thomas Jefferson to William Stephens (12 *Jefferson's Papers,* 558; V *Jefferson's Works,* 384).

29. February 7, 1788, letter from Thomas Jefferson to Alexander Donald (12 *Jefferson's Papers,* 571; VI *Jefferson's Writings* (1903 ed.), 425; II *Jefferson's Writings* (1853 ed.), 355–56).

30. February 12, 1788, letter to C. Dumas (12 *Jefferson's Papers,* 584; VI *Jefferson's Writings* (1903 ed.), 430; II *Jefferson's Writings* (1853 ed.), 357–59).

31. See, for instance, Labunski, 98.

32. The 1787 Convention installed Washington as Convention President as its first act. I Farrand's *Records,* 2 (Constitutional Convention Proceedings of May 14, 1787).

33. See, for instance, Washington's . . .

• October 15, 1787, letter to Henry Knox (29 *Washington's Writings*, 289; 5 *Washington's Papers, Confederation Series*, 375–76) ("Is there not a Constitutional door open for alterations and amendments, & is it not probable that real defects will be as readily discovered *after*, as before, trial?") (emphasis added);

• November 30, 1787, letter to David Stuart (29 *Washington's Writings*, 323; 5 *Washington's Papers, Confederation Series*, 466) ("Every attempt to amend the Constitution at this time, is, in my opinion, idly vain.");

• December 14, 1787, letter to Charles Carter (29 *Washington's Writings*, 340; 5 *Washington's Papers, Confederation Series*, 492) (". . . I am fully persuaded it is the best that can be obtained at *this* day and that it or disunion is before us—if the first is our choice [then] when the defects of it are experienced a Constitutional door is open for amendments and may be adopted in a peaceable manner without tumult or disorder") (italics in original);

• January 8, 1788, letter to Edmund Randolph (29 *Washington's Writings*, 357–58; 6 *Washington's Papers, Confederation Series*, 17–18) (". . . [I]t is more clear than ever, that an attempt to amend the Constitution which is submitted, would be productive of more heat, & greater confusion[,] than can well be conceived.");

• April 25, 1788, letter to John Armstrong (29 *Washington's Writings*, 465 (". . . [T]o make such amendments as may be proposed by the several States the condition of its adoption would, in my opinion, amount to a complete rejection of it[.]"); 6 *Washington's Papers, Confederation Series*, 225);

• April 28, 1788, letter to Marquis de Lafayette (29 *Washington's Writings*, 478; 6 *Washington's Papers, Confederation Series*, 244) (". . . [T]he Constitution ought by all means to be accepted by nine States *before* any attempt should be made to procure amendments.") (emphasis added); and,

• August 16, 1788, letter to Charles Pettit (30 *Washington's Writings*, 41; 6 *Washington's Papers, Confederation Series*, 447–48) ("The great danger, in my view, was that every thing might have been thrown into the last stage of confusion before any government whatsoever could have been established.").

34. Labunski, 60.

35. Ibid., 27.

36. On September 17, 1787, the Convention unanimously adopted the following resolution (in pertinent part):

> Resolved,
>
> That the preceding Constitution be laid before the United States in Congress assembled, and that it is the Opinion of this Convention, that it should afterwards be submitted to a Convention of Delegates, chosen in each State by the People thereof, under the Recommendation of its Legislature, for the Assent and Ratification; and that each Convention assenting to, and ratifying the Same, should give Notice thereof to the United States in Congress assembled.

II Farrand's *Records*, 665.

37. See, for instance, Rakove, 106, 116.

38. U.S. Const., Art. VII, 1 Stat. 19.

39. See, for instance, the discussion in Rakove, 106–8.

40. Opponents included political heavy-hitters from Massachusetts, New York, and Virginia. Labunski, 20.

41. Labunski, 58.

42. See, for instance, Rakove, 120.

43. Massachusetts ratification submittal dated February 7, 1788, I Elliott's *Debates*, 323.

44. February 15, 1788, letter from James Madison to George Washington (15 *Madison's Papers*, 510; 6 *Washington's Papers, Confederation Series*, 115).

45. March 2, 1788, letter from George Washington to James Madison (6 *Washington's Papers, Confederation Series*, 136; 29 *Washington's Writings*, 430–31; 15 *Madison's Papers*, 553).

46. May 27, 1788, letter from Thomas Jefferson to Edward Carrington (13 *Jefferson's Papers*, 208; VII *Jefferson's Writings* (1903 ed.), 36).

47. June 3, 1788, letter from Thomas Jefferson to William Carmichael (13 *Jefferson's Papers*, 232; VII *Jefferson's Writings* (1903 ed.), 29). The version in *Jefferson's Papers* bears a date of June 3 (*id.*, 229), while the version in *Jefferson's Writings* bears a date of May 27 (*id.*, 26).

48. Rakove, 122–28; Labunski, 121.

49. I Elliott's *Debates*, 331–33; IV Elliott's *Debates*, 243–47; *Madison's*

Notes, 674–76, 676–80; II *Documentary History . . . Constitution*, 266–76, 290; *Documents Illustrative . . . Formation of the American States*, 1044–51; XIII *Documentary History . . . Ratification*, xlii; 5 *Founders' Constitution*, 17–19.

50. IV Elliott's *Debates*, 242 (North Carolina Ratifying Convention) (Proceedings of August 1, 1788) (emphasis added).

51. I Elliott's *Debates*, 331–33; IV Elliott's *Debates*, 243–47; *Madison's Notes*, 674–80; II *Documentary History . . . Constitution*, 266–76, 290; *Documents Illustrative . . . Formation of the American States*, 1044–51; XIII *Documentary History . . . Ratification*, xlii; 5 *Founders' Constitution*, 17–19.

52. Rakove, 128.

53. I Elliott's *Debates*, 333–37; *Madison's Notes*, 680–87; II *Documentary History . . . Constitution*, 310–20; *Documents Illustrative . . . Formation of the American States*, 1052–59; XIII *Documentary History . . . Ratification*, xlii.

54. See Chapter 5D.

55. U.S. Const., Art. VII, 1 Stat. 19.

56. 1 *Senate Journal*, 1st Cong., 2nd Sess., 105, 109 (Proceedings of January 13 and 29, 1790) (North Carolina); 1 *Annals of Congress*, 1st Cong., 2nd Sess., 973, 978 (Senate Proceedings of January 13 and 29, 1790) (North Carolina); 1 *Senate Journal*, 1st Cong., 3rd Sess., 222 (Proceedings of December 15 and 17, 1790) (Rhode Island); 2 *Annals of Congress*, 1st Cong., 3rd Sess., 1777 (Senate Proceedings of December 15 and 17, 1790) (Rhode Island).

57. 1 *House Journal*, 1st Cong., 2nd Sess., 178, 182, 190, 196, 243 (Proceedings of March 19 and 24, April 6 and 19, and June 16, 1790) (North Carolina); 2 *Annals of Congress*, 1st Cong., 2nd Sess., 1514, 1525, 1572, 1584, 1696 (House of Representatives Proceedings of March 19 and 24, April 6 and 19, and June 16, 1790) (North Carolina); 1 *House Journal*, 1st Cong., 3rd Sess., 338 (Proceedings of December 17, 1790) (Rhode Island); 2 *Annals of Congress*, 1st Cong., 3rd Sess., 1859 (House of Representatives Proceedings of December 17, 1790) (Rhode Island).

58. **Delaware vote (no proposed amendments):** I Elliott's *Debates*, 319; *Madison's Notes*, 642–43; II *Documentary History . . . Constitution*, 24–26; *Documents Illustrative . . . Formation of the American States*, 1009; III *Documentary History . . . Ratification*, 105–6; XIII *Documentary History . . . Ratification*, xli.

59. **Pennsylvania vote (no proposed amendments)**: I Elliott's *Debates*, 319–20; *Madison's Notes*, 643–44; II *Documentary History . . . Constitution*, 27–45; *Documents Illustrative . . . Formation of the American States*, 1010; II *Documentary History . . . Ratification*, 600; XIII *Documentary History . . . Ratification*, xli.

60. **New Jersey vote (no proposed amendments)**: I Elliott's *Debates*, 320–21; *Madison's Notes*, 644–47; II *Documentary History . . . Constitution*, 46–64; *Documents Illustrative . . . Formation of the American States*, 1011–14; III *Documentary History . . . Ratification*, 184; XIII *Documentary History . . . Ratification*, xli.

61. **Georgia vote (no proposed amendments)**: I Elliott's *Debates*, 323–24; *Madison's Notes*, 647–49; II *Documentary History . . . Constitution*, 65–85; *Documents Illustrative . . . Formation of the American States*, 1014–15; III *Documentary History . . . Ratification*, 273–77; XIII *Documentary History . . . Ratification*, xli.

62. **Connecticut vote (no proposed amendments)**: I Elliott's *Debates*, 321–22; *Madison's Notes*, 649–51; II *Documentary History . . . Constitution*, 86–89; *Documents Illustrative . . . Formation of the American States*, 1016–17; III *Documentary History . . . Ratification*, 560; XIII *Documentary History . . . Ratification*, xli.

63. **Massachusetts vote (with proposed amendments)**: IV *Documentary History . . . First Federal Congress*, 12–13; I Elliott's *Debates*, 322–23; *Madison's Notes*, 651–53; II *Documentary History . . . Constitution*, 90–96; *Documents Illustrative . . . Formation of the American States*, 1018–20; IV *Documentary History . . . Ratification*, 1469–70; XIII *Documentary History . . . Ratification*, xli; 1 *Founders' Constitution*, 461–62.

64. **Maryland vote (no proposed amendments)**: I Elliott's *Debates*, 324–25; *Madison's Notes*, 653–54; II *Documentary History . . . Constitution*, 97–122; *Documents Illustrative . . . Formation of the American States*, 1021–22; XIII *Documentary History . . . Ratification*, xli.

65. **South Carolina vote (with proposed amendments)**: IV *Documentary History . . . First Federal Congress*, 13–14; I Elliott's *Debates*, 325; *Madison's Notes*, 655–56; II *Documentary History . . . Constitution*, 138–40; *Documents Illustrative . . . Formation of the American States*, 1022–24; XIII *Documentary History . . . Ratification*, xlii.

66. **New Hampshire vote (with proposed amendments)**: IV *Documentary History . . . First Federal Congress*, 14–15; I Elliott's *Debates*, 325–27; *Madison's Notes*, 656–59; II *Documentary History . . .*

Constitution, 141–44; *Documents Illustrative . . . Formation of the American States,* 1024–27; XIII *Documentary History . . . Ratification,* xlii.

67. XXXIV *Journals of the Continental Congress,* 281–82 (Proceedings of July 2, 1788); *Madison's Notes,* 687–88; II *Documentary History . . . Constitution,* 161–62.

68. **Virginia vote (with proposed amendments):** IV *Documentary History . . . First Federal Congress,* 15–17 (declaration of rights) and 17–19 (amendments); I Elliott's *Debates,* 327; III Elliott's *Debates,* 657–61; *Madison's Notes,* 659–62 (declaration of rights) and 662–65 (amendments); II *Documentary History . . . Constitution,* 145–46, 160, 377–85; *Documents Illustrative . . . Formation of the American States,* 1027–34; X *Documentary History . . . Ratification,* 1551–56; XIII *Documentary History . . . Ratification,* xlii; 1 *Founders' Constitution,* 472–74; 5 *Founders' Constitution,* 15–17.

69. **New York vote (with proposed amendments):** IV *Documentary History . . . First Federal Congress,* 19–26; I Elliott's *Debates,* 327–31; *Madison's Notes,* 665–69 (declaration of rights) and 669–73 (amendments); II *Documentary History . . . Constitution,* 189–203; *Documents Illustrative . . . Formation of the American States,* 1034–44; XIII *Documentary History . . . Ratification,* xlii.

70. **North Carolina vote (with proposed amendments):** I Elliott's *Debates,* 331–33; IV Elliott's *Debates,* 243–47; *Madison's Notes,* 674–76 (declaration of rights) and 676–80 (amendments); II *Documentary History . . . Constitution,* 266–76, 290; *Documents Illustrative . . . Formation of the American States,* 1044–51; XIII *Documentary History . . . Ratification,* xlii; 5 *Founders' Constitution,* 17–19.

71. **Rhode Island vote (with proposed amendments):** I Elliott's *Debates,* 333–37; *Madison's Notes,* 680–83 (declaration of rights) and 684–87 (amendments); II *Documentary History . . . Constitution,* 310–20; *Documents Illustrative . . . Formation of the American States,* 1052–59; XIII *Documentary History . . . Ratification,* xlii.

72. XXXIV *Journals of the Continental Congress,* 522–23 (Proceedings of September 13, 1788); II *Documentary History . . . Constitution,* 262–64.

73. **New Hampshire's proposed religion-specific Constitutional amendment:** IV *Documentary History . . . First Federal Congress,* 15, ¶ "Eleventh"; I Elliott's *Debates,* 326, ¶ "11th" (New Hampshire Ratifying Convention) (Proceedings of June 21, 1788); *Madison's*

Notes, 658; II *Documentary History . . . Constitution,* 143; *Documents Illustrative . . . Formation of the American States,* 1026 (emphasis added).

74. See Chapter 5A(9).

75. Brant, *James Madison: Father of the Constitution,* 271.

76. **Virginia's proposed religion-specific Constitutional amendment:** IV *Documentary History . . . First Federal Congress,* 17, ¶ "Twentieth"; III Elliott's *Debates,* 659, ¶ "20th" (Virginia Ratifying Convention) (Proceedings of June 27, 1788); *Madison's Notes,* 662; X *Documentary History . . . Ratification,* 1553; II *Documentary History . . . Constitution,* 380; *Documents Illustrative . . . Formation of the American States,* 1030–31; 1 *Founders' Constitution,* 472–73; 5 *Founders' Constitution,* 15–16 (emphasis added).

77. See Chapter 3A.

78. **New York's proposed religion–specific Constitutional amendment:** IV *Documentary History . . . First Federal Congress,* 20, unnumbered ¶; I Elliott's *Debates,* 328, unnumbered paragraph (New York Ratifying Convention) (Proceedings of July 26, 1788); *Madison's Notes,* 666; II *Documentary History . . . Constitution,* 191; *Documents Illustrative . . . Formation of the American States,* 1035; 5 *Founders' Constitution,* 12 (emphasis added).

79. **North Carolina's proposed religion-specific Constitutional amendment:** IV Elliott's *Debates,* 244, ¶ 20 (Second North Carolina Ratifying Convention) (Proceedings of November 21, 1789, ratifying the amendments proposed during the first ratifying convention proceedings of August 1, 1788 [see IV Elliott's *Debates,* 242–47]); *Madison's Notes,* 676; II *Documentary History . . . Constitution,* 269–70; *Documents Illustrative . . . Formation of the American States,* 1047; 5 *Founders' Constitution,* 18 (emphasis added).

80. Virginia's proposal included the word "particular" in front of the phrase "religious sect or society."

81. July 31, 1788, letter from Thomas Jefferson to James Madison (13 *Jefferson's Papers,* 442–43; VII *Jefferson's Writings* (1903 ed.), 96–97; II *Jefferson's Writings* (1853 ed.), 443; V *Jefferson's Works,* 426–27; 11 *Madison's Papers,* 211–12).

82. October 17, 1788, letter from James Madison to Thomas Jefferson (11 *Madison's Papers,* 297–300; V *Madison's Writings,* 271; 14 *Jefferson's Papers,* 18).

83. Labunski, 120.

84. Ibid., 133.

85. Ibid., 134.

86. Ibid., 134–36.

87. Ibid., 136–37.

88. Ibid., 137.

89. Ibid., 139–74.

90. See, for instance, Labunski, 143 ("Religious groups . . . were especially concerned about the lack of protection in the Constitution for religious freedom, and they were greatly disturbed by the news that Madison did not believe such an amendment was necessary.")

91. Labunski, 143.

92. Ibid., 158.

93. January 2, 1789, letter from James Madison to George Eve (11 *Madison's Papers,* 404–5; V *Madison's Writings,* 319; I *Madison's Letters,* 446–47) (emphasis added).

94. See, for instance: January 14, 1789, letter from James Madison to George Washington (11 *Madison's Papers,* 418; V *Madison's Writings,* 318; I *Madison's Letters,* 449–50; 1 *Washington's Papers, Presidential Series,* 244); and January 27, 1789, letter from Madison published in the January 29, 1789, edition of the Fredericksburg *Va. Herald* (11 *Madison's Papers,* 428–29).

95. Labunski, 167–71.

96. January 13, 1789, letter from James Madison to Thomas Randolph (11 *Madison's Papers,* 416).

97. January 14, 1789, letter from James Madison to George Washington (11 *Madison's Papers,* 418; V *Madison's Writings,* 318; I *Madison's Letters,* 449–50; 1 *Washington's Papers, Presidential Series,* 244).

98. January 27, 1789, letter from Madison published in the January 29, 1789, edition of the Fredericksburg *Va. Herald* (11 *Madison's Papers,* 428–29).

99. Labunski, 159.

100. Rakove, 330.

101. March 15, 1789, letter from Thomas Jefferson to James Madison (14 *Jefferson's Papers,* 659–61; VII *Jefferson's Writings* (1903 ed.), 310–12; III *Jefferson's Writings* (1853 edition), 3; VI *Jefferson's Works,* 461–63; 12 *Madison's Papers,* 14–15).

102. U.S. Const., Art. I, § 8, 1 Stat. 14 (emphasis added).

103. Brant, *James Madison: Father of the Constitution,* 266.

104. *The Federalist Papers, No. 33.*

105. Chapter 5E discusses this issue in detail. Suffice it to say at this point that on May 29, 1787, Virginia's Randolph introduced, as part of the "Virginia Plan," a fifteen-part resolution concerning "the establishment of a *national* government" in which the word "national" appeared nineteen times in relationship to a new government. I Farrand's *Records,* 20–22; I Elliott's *Debates,* 143–45; *Madison's Notes,* 23–26; I Madison's *Journal,* 61–64; V Elliott's *Debates,* 127–28; III *Documentary History . . . Constitution,* 17–20; *Documents Illustrative . . . Formation of the American States,* 116–19 (emphasis added).

On May 30, 1787, the Convention agreed to the following resolution:

> Resolved that it is the opinion of this Committee that a *national* government ought to be established consisting of a supreme Legislative [*sic;* "Legislature"], Judiciary, and Executive.

I Farrand's *Records,* 30–31, 33–35; I Elliott's *Debates,* 150–51; *Madison's Notes,* 27–29; I Madison's *Journal,* 73–75; V Elliott's *Debates,* 132–34; III *Documentary History . . . Constitution,* 20–23; *Documents Illustrative . . . Formation of the American States,* 120–22 (emphasis added).

On June 19, 1787, the Convention approved a modified nineteen-resolution version of Randolph's initial resolutions, in which the word "national" appeared twenty-six times in relationship to a new government. I Farrand's *Records,* 312, 322; I Elliott's *Debates,* 181–83; *Madison's Notes,* 127–29; I Madison's *Journal,* 196; V Elliott's *Debates,* 211–12; *Documents Illustrative . . . Formation of the American States,* 234–37.

On June 20, 1787, however, the Convention—with Madison acceding—surrendered to the concerns of the states' rights advocates and voted to strike the word "national" from any description of the new constitutional government, replacing it with "United States." I Farrand's *Records,* 334–36; I Elliott's *Debates,* 183; *Madison's Notes,* 131–32; I Madison's *Journal,* 199–200; V Elliott's *Debates,* 214; III *Documentary History . . . Constitution,* 166–67; *Documents Illustrative . . . Formation of the American States,* 240–41.

Chapter 5

1. March 19, 1823, letter from James Madison to Edward Everett (III *Madison's Letters,* 308–9; X *Madison's Writings,* 128–29).

2. III *Documentary History . . . First Federal Congress,* xvi. The pertinent provision in Article I reads:

Each House shall keep a journal of its proceedings, and from time to time publish the same, excepting such parts as may in their judgment require secrecy; and the yeas and nays of the members of either House on any question shall, at the desire of one fifth of those present, be entered on the journal.

U.S. Const., Art. I, § 5, ¶ 3.

3. III *Documentary History . . . First Federal Congress,* 74–75 (House of Representatives Proceedings of May 28, 1789); 1 *House Journal,* 1st Cong., 1st Sess., 42 (Proceedings of May 28, 1789).

4. III *Documentary History . . . First Federal Congress,* xvi–xvii.

5. I *Documentary History . . . First Federal Congress,* 50 (Proceedings of May 19, 1789); 1 *Senate Journal,* 1st Cong., 1st Sess., 27 (Proceedings of May 19, 1789).

6. I *Documentary History . . . First Federal Congress,* x–xi.

7. I *Documentary History . . . First Federal Congress,* xi n. 6. See the bibliography entries for *Journal . . . First Session . . . Senate* (Greenleaf ed.), *Journal . . . Second Session . . . Senate* (Fenno ed.), and *Journal . . . Third Session . . . Senate* (Fenno ed.).

8. I *Documentary History . . . First Federal Congress,* 50 (Proceedings of May 19, 1789); 1 *Senate Journal,* 1st Cong., 1st Sess., 27 (Proceedings of May 19, 1789) (emphasis added).

9. II *Documentary History . . . First Federal Congress,* 3 (Proceedings of May 25, 1789); 1 *Senate Executive Journal,* 1st Cong., 1st Sess., (unnumbered page) 3 (Proceedings of May 25, 1789).

10. 3 *Senate Executive Journal,* 20th Cong., 1st Sess., 603 (Proceedings of April 4, 1828) (approving March 28, 1828, proposed resolution).

11. IV *Documentary History . . . First Federal Congress,* xi.

12. IV *Documentary History . . . First Federal Congress,* xi.

13. 1 *Annals of Congress,* 1st Cong., 1st Sess., 15–96.

14. 1 *Annals of Congress,* 1st Cong., 1st Sess., 99–964.

15. 2 Byrd, 312; Amer, 2.

16. 2 *Senate Journal,* 3rd Cong., 1st Sess., 33–34 (Proceedings of February 20, 1794); 4 *Annals of Congress,* 3rd Cong., 1st Sess., 46–47 (Senate Proceedings of February 20, 1794).

17. 2 Byrd, 312.

18. Tinling, 519; Amer, 2–4; 2 Byrd, 312; X *Documentary History . . . First Federal Congress,* xv.

19. Tinling, 519–20; Amer, 2–4; 2 Byrd, 312; X *Documentary History . . . First Federal Congress,* xv.

20. III *Documentary History . . . First Federal Congress,* 3; 1 *House Journal,* 1st Cong., 1st Sess., 3 (Proceedings of March 4, 1789); 1 *Annals of Congress,* 1st Cong., 1st Sess., 99 (House of Representatives Proceedings of March 4, 1789).

21. III *Documentary History . . . First Federal Congress,* 7; 1 *House Journal,* 1st Cong., 1st Sess., 6 (Proceedings of April 1, 1789); 1 *Annals of Congress,* 1st Cong., 1st Sess., 100 (House of Representatives Proceedings of April 1, 1789).

22. See III *Documentary History . . . First Federal Congress,* 3–8, 16, 18, 25, 28, 30, 31, 43, 49, 54, 71, 83, 87, 89, 149; 1 *House Journal,* 1st Cong., 1st Sess., 3, 4, 5, 6, 7, 11, 12, 16, 18, 19, 24, 29, 31, 40, 46, 48, 49, 79; and 1 *Annals of Congress,* 1st Cong., 1st Sess., 99, 100, 101, 106, 109, 126, 167, 178, 199, 241, 242, 276, 306, 425, 440, 471, 498, 745 (each chronicling the appearances of the various representatives during the proceedings of March 4, 5, 14, 17, 18, 23, 25, and 30; April 1, 2, 3, 4, 6, 8, 9, 13, 17, 20, 22, 23, and 30; May 1, 6, 9, and 25; June 8, 15, and 17; and August 14, 1789).

23. Ketchum, 289.

24. X *Documentary History . . . First Federal Congress,* 391 (not a word-for-word replication of Madison's exact words, but a summary as reported in *Congressional Record* publisher Thomas Lloyd's notes from May 4, 1789).

For reasons left to speculation, neither the official House Journal, nor the *House Journal,* nor the *Annals of Congress* mentions this particular announcement. See III *Documentary History . . . First Federal Congress,* 44–45 (Proceedings of May 4, 1789); 1 *House Journal,* 1st Cong., 1st Sess., 26–27 (Proceedings of May 4, 1789); 1 *Annals of Congress,* 1st Cong., 1st Sess., 242–57 (House of Representatives Proceedings of May 4, 1789).

25. U.S. Const., Art. V, 1 Stat. 19 (emphasis added).

26. X *Documentary History . . . First Federal Congress,* 779–81 (New York *Daily Advertiser* edition of May 26, 1789, reporting the proceedings of May 25, 1789; *New-York Daily Gazette* edition of May 26, 1789, reporting the proceedings of May 25, 1789; *Gazette of the United States* edition of May 27, 1789, reporting the proceedings of May 25, 1789).

For reasons left to speculation, neither the official House Journal, nor the *House Journal,* nor the *Annals of Congress* mentions this particular announcement. See III *Documentary History . . . First Federal Congress,* 71–72 (Proceedings of May 25, 1789); 1 *House Journal,* 1st

Cong., 1st Sess., 40–41 (Proceedings of May 25, 1789); 1 *Annals of Congress*, 1st Cong., 1st Sess., 425–26 (House of Representatives Proceedings of May 25, 1789).

27. III *Documentary History . . . First Federal Congress*, 84 (Proceedings of June 8, 1789); 1 *House Journal*, 1st Cong., 1st Sess., 46 (Proceedings of June 8, 1789); 1 *Annals of Congress*, 1st Cong., 1st Sess., 440 (House of Representatives Proceedings of June 8, 1789) (Statement of Representative Madison); IV *Documentary History . . . First Federal Congress*, 3 incl. n. 1; XI *Documentary History . . . First Federal Congress*, 803–4 (New York *Daily Advertiser* edition of June 9, 1789, reporting the proceedings of June 8, 1789), 804 (*New-York Daily Gazette* edition of June 9, 1789, reporting the proceedings of June 8, 1789), 805 (*Gazette of the United States* edition of June 10, 1789, reporting the proceedings of June 8, 1789), and 811 (*Congressional Register* reporting the proceedings of June 8, 1789).

28. 1 *Annals of Congress*, 1st Cong., 1st Sess., 440–41 (House of Representatives Proceedings of June 8, 1789) (Statement of Representative Madison); XI *Documentary History . . . First Federal Congress*, 811 (*Congressional Register* reporting the proceedings of June 8, 1789).

29. 1 *Annals of Congress*, 1st Cong., 1st Sess., 441 (House of Representatives Proceedings of June 8, 1789) (Statement of Representative Madison); IV *Documentary History . . . First Federal Congress*, 3–4; XI *Documentary History . . . First Federal Congress*, 803–4 (New York *Daily Advertiser* edition of June 9, 1789, reporting the June 8, 1789, proceedings), 804 (*New-York Daily Gazette* edition of June 9, 1789, reporting the June 8, 1789, proceedings), 805 (*Gazette of the United States* edition of June 10, 1789, reporting the June 8, 1789, proceedings), and 811 (*Congressional Register* reporting the proceedings of June 8, 1789).

30. XI *Documentary History . . . First Federal Congress*, 806–9 (*Gazette of the United States* edition of June 10, 1789, reporting the June 8, 1789, proceedings) and 814–21 (*Congressional Register* reporting the proceedings of June 8, 1789); 1 *Annals of Congress*, 1st Cong., 1st Sess., 448–50, 453–59.

31. III *Documentary History . . . First Federal Congress*, 84 (Proceedings of June 8, 1789); 1 *Annals of Congress*, 1st Cong., 1st Sess., 441–48 (House of Representatives Proceedings of June 8, 1789); XI *Documentary History . . . First Federal Congress*, 805–10

(*Gazette of the United States* edition of June 10, 1789, reporting the June 8, 1789, proceedings), and 811–36 (*Congressional Register* reporting the proceedings of June 8, 1789).

32. 1 *Annals of Congress,* 1st Cong., 1st Sess., 448 (House of Representatives Proceedings of June 8, 1789) (Motion of Representative Madison); IV *Documentary History . . . First Federal Congress,* 3–4; XI *Documentary History . . . First Federal Congress,* 804 (New York *Daily Advertiser* edition of June 9, 1789, reporting the June 8, 1789, proceedings), 808 (*Gazette of the United States* edition of June 10, 1789, reporting the June 8, 1789, proceedings), and 818–19 (*Congressional Register* reporting the proceedings of June 8, 1789); *Complete Bill of Rights,* 57 (New York *Daily Advertiser* edition of June 9, 1789, reporting the June 8, 1789, proceedings) and 59 (*Gazette of the United States* edition of June 10, 1789, reporting the June 8, 1789, proceedings).

33. See Chapter 4.

34. 1 *Annals of Congress,* 1st Cong., 1st Sess., 448–50, 453–59 (House of Representatives Proceedings of June 8, 1789) (Statements of Representative Madison); XI *Documentary History . . . First Federal Congress,* 804 (New York *Daily Advertiser* edition of June 9, 1789, reporting the June 8, 1789, proceedings), 807–9 (*Gazette of the United States* edition of June 10, 1789, reporting the June 8, 1789, proceedings), and 813–14, 818–21 (*Congressional Register* reporting the proceedings of June 8, 1789).

35. August 19, 1789, letter from James Madison to Richard Peters (2 *Madison's Papers,* 346–47).

36. 1 *Annals of Congress,* 1st Cong., 1st Sess., 464 (House of Representatives Proceedings of June 8, 1789) (Statement of Representative Gerry); see also XI *Documentary History . . . First Federal Congress,* 809–10 (*Gazette of the United States* edition of June 10, 1789, reporting the June 8, 1789, proceedings), and 830–33 (*Congressional Register* reporting the proceedings of June 8, 1789) (Statement of Representative Gerry).

37. See Chapter 4A.

38. 1 *Annals of Congress,* 1st Cong., 1st Sess., 448–59 (House of Representatives Proceedings of June 8, 1789) (Statement of Representative Madison), with the text of the proposed amendments sandwiched at 1 *Annals of Congress,* 1st Cong., 1st Sess., 451–53; see also Madison's June 8, 1789, resolution reproduced in IV *Documentary History . . . First Federal Congress,* 9–12.

39. 1 *Annals of Congress,* 1st Cong., 1st Sess., 453–59 (House of

Representatives Proceedings of June 8, 1789) (Statement of Representative Madison); XI *Documentary History . . . First Federal Congress,* 818–27 (*Congressional Register* reporting the proceedings of June 8, 1789).

40. 1 *Annals of Congress,* 1st Cong., 1st Sess., 450–53 (House of Representatives Proceedings of June 8, 1789) (Statement of Representative Madison); IV *Documentary History . . . First Federal Congress,* 9–12 (citing the New York *Daily Advertiser* edition of June 12, 1798, reporting the June 8, 1789, proceedings). One writer claims that Madison "offered about seventy-five distinct amendments." Labunski, 199. That scarcely seems possible, given the list announced (and read) by Madison, but, again, it depends upon the manner in which the reader divides them. By comparison, the House later isolated seventeen discrete amendments. See Chapter 5A(14). The divergence of views assumes no significance.

41. Madison's notes for his June 8, 1789, introduction of proposed constitutional amendments to the First Congress have been reproduced in XVI *Documentary History . . . First Federal Congress,* 723–25.

42. 1 *Annals of Congress,* 1st Cong., 1st Sess., 451 (House of Representatives Proceedings of June 8, 1789) (Statement of Representative Madison); IV *Documentary History . . . First Federal Congress,* 9 (citing the New York *Daily Advertiser* edition of June 12, 1789, reporting the June 8, 1789, proceedings).

43. 1 *Annals of Congress,* 1st Cong., 1st Sess., 453 (House of Representatives Proceedings of June 8, 1789) (Statement of Representative Madison); IV *Documentary History . . . First Federal Congress,* 12 (citing the New York *Daily Advertiser* edition of June 12, 1789, reporting the June 8, 1789, proceedings).

44. 1 *Annals of Congress,* 1st Cong., 1st Sess., 454–55 (House of Representatives Proceedings of June 8, 1789) (Statement of Representative Madison); IV *Documentary History . . . First Federal Congress,* 10–11 (citing the New York *Daily Advertiser* edition of June 12, 1789, reporting the June 8, 1789, proceedings).

45. Article I, Section 8, ¶ 18, provides:

> The Congress shall have power . . . [t]o make all laws which shall be *necessary and proper* for carrying into execution the foregoing powers . . .[.]

U.S. Const., Art. I, § 8, 1 Stat. 14 (emphasis added).

46. Both Hamilton and Madison had written about the Constitution's "necessary and proper" clause in their *Federalist Papers* essays, Hamilton in No. 33 and Madison in No. 44. Each sought to minimize states' fears about the uncertain extent of that congressional power by advising that, as Hamilton put it,

> the constitutional operation of the intended government would be precisely the same if these clauses [referring to the "necessary and proper" clause and one other] were entirely obliterated as if they were repeated in every article,

and

> [t]hey are only declaratory of a truth which would have resulted by necessary and unavoidable implication from the very act of constituting a federal government and vesting it with certain specified powers.

The Federalist Papers, No. 33.
Madison wrote similarly, advising that

> [w]ithout the substance of this power, the whole Constitution would be a dead letter.

The Federalist Papers, No. 44 (italics in original).

47. 1 *Annals of Congress,* 1st Cong., 1st Sess., 455 (House of Representatives Proceedings of June 8, 1789) (Statement of Representative Madison); XI *Documentary History . . . First Federal Congress,* 808 (*Gazette of the United States* edition of June 10, 1789, reporting the June 8, 1789, proceedings) and 823–24 (*Congressional Register* reporting the proceedings of June 8, 1789); *Complete Bill of Rights,* 55 (citing the *Congressional Register* reporting the proceedings of June 8, 1789) and 58 (citing the *Gazette of the United States* edition of June 10, 1789, reporting the June 8, 1789, proceedings).

48. 1 *Annals of Congress,* 1st Cong., 1st Sess., 451 (House of Representatives Proceedings of June 8, 1789) (Statement of Representative Madison) (emphasis added); IV *Documentary History . . . First Federal Congress,* 10 (citing the New York *Daily Advertiser* edition of June 12, 1789, reporting the June 8, 1789, proceedings); *Complete Bill of Rights,* 1 (*Congressional Register* reporting the proceedings of June 8, 1789; New York *Daily Advertiser* edition of June 12, 1789, reporting the June 8, 1789, proceedings; *New-York Daily Gazette* edition of June 13, 1789, reporting the June 8, 1789, proceedings).

For some reason left unexplained, volume XI of *Documentary History . . . First Federal Congress* excises the text of Madison's proposals.

XI *Documentary History . . . First Federal Congress,* 821 (*Congressional Register* reporting the proceedings of June 8, 1789).

49. U.S. Const., Art. I, § 9, ¶¶ 3 and 4, 1 Stat. 15.

50. See Chapter 3E.

51. April 17, 1824, letter from Madison to Edward Livingston (IX *Madison's Writings,* 62; III *Madison's Letters,* 436; V *Documentary History . . . Constitution,* 330).

52. Madison's pertinent writings appear throughout Chapters 3 and 11.

53. Brant, *James Madison: Father of the Constitution,* 269.

54. III Elliott's *Debates,* 330 (Virginia Ratifying Convention) (Proceedings of June 12, 1788) (Comments of James Madison) (emphasis added).

For context, at the time of his speech Madison sought to convince Constitution opponents that the Constitution required no supplemental "bill" or "declaration" of rights as a condition to its acceptance, and he took that stance to prompt a swift and uncomplicated ratification process unimpeded by political objections that the First Congress could well resolve later.

55. See Chapter 2.

56. XI *Documentary History . . . First Federal Congress,* 804 (*New-York Daily Gazette* edition of June 9, 1789, reporting the June 8, 1789, proceedings) (emphasis added).

Although the *Gazette of the United States* and the *Congressional Register* also reported Representative Gerry's remarks (XI *Documentary History . . . First Federal Congress,* 809–10 [Statement of Representative Gerry] [*Gazette of the United States* edition of June 10, 1789, reporting the June 8, 1789, proceedings] and 830–33 [Statement of Representative Gerry] [*Congressional Register* reporting the proceedings of June 8, 1789]), neither of those sources contains any reference to a specific number of states in the manner of the *New-York Daily Gazette.*

57. IV *Documentary History . . . First Federal Congress,* 12–26.

An editorial footnote that accompanies a report of Representative Gerry's remarks during the August 13, 1789, proceedings, *infra,* comments that "[f]ive states—Massachusetts, South Carolina, New Hampshire, Virginia, and New York—sent constitutional amendments to Congress as part of their acts of ratification and instructed their representatives to work for adoption." XI *Documentary History . . . First Federal Congress,* 1219 n. 9.

58. See Chapter 4B.

Another source reports that Congress derived the "Religious Freedom" aspect of the First Amendment—which does not differentiate between the Establishment Clause and the Free Exercise Clause—from not only the amendments offered by the five ratifying states but from North Carolina's proposed amendments as well. E. Dumbauld, *The Bill of Rights and What It Means Today,* 160 (Norman: University of Oklahoma Press, 1957), reproduced in full in Levy, *Origins of the Bill of Rights,* 264. Although North Carolina did submit proposed amendments for the First Congress to consider, it did not participate in the First Congress. In any event, the text of North Carolina's proposed religion-specific amendment simply replicated the Virginia text. See Chapter 4B.

59. IV *Documentary History . . . First Federal Congress,* 17, ¶ "Twentieth"; III Elliott's *Debates,* 659, ¶ "20th" (Virginia Ratifying Convention) (Proceedings of June 27, 1788); *Madison's Notes,* 662; X *Documentary History . . . Ratification,* 1553; II *Documentary History . . . Constitution,* 380; *Documents Illustrative . . . Formation of the American States,* 1030–31; 1 *Founders' Constitution,* 472–73; 5 *Founders' Constitution,* 15–16.

60. IV *Documentary History . . . First Federal Congress,* 20, unnumbered ¶; I Elliott's *Debates,* 328, unnumbered paragraph (New York Ratifying Convention) (Proceedings of July 26, 1788); *Madison's Notes,* 666; II *Documentary History . . . Constitution,* 191; *Documents Illustrative . . . Formation of the American States,* 1035; 5 *Founders' Constitution,* 12.

61. Brant, *James Madison: Father of the Constitution,* 264.

The "Pennsylvania minority" proposals appeared originally in the December 18, 1787, edition of the *Pennsylvania Packet and Daily Advertiser* in a document entitled "The Address and Reasons of Dissent of the Minority of the Convention of Pennsylvania to Their Constituents." See 3 *The Complete Anti-Federalist,* 145 (Part 3.11, Introduction); 1 *Debate on the Constitution,* 526. Among its list of fourteen recommended amendments appeared the following:

> 1. The right of conscience shall be held inviolable; and neither the legislative, executive[,] nor judicial powers of the United States shall have authority to alter, abrogate, or infringe any part of the constitution of the several states, which provide for the preservation of liberty in matters of religion.

3 *The Complete Anti-Federalist,* 150–51 (Part 3.11.13); 1 *Debate on the Constitution,* 532.

The "Maryland minority" proposals consisted of a number of proposed amendments rejected by a majority vote at the Maryland Ratification Convention, and included the following:

12. That there be no national religion established by law; but that all persons be equally entitled to protection in their religious liberty.

II Elliott's *Debates,* 553 (Maryland Ratification Convention) (Proceedings of April 21, 1788).

62. Brant, *James Madison: Father of the Constitution,* 265.

63. 1 *Annals of Congress,* 1st Cong., 1st Sess., 459 (House of Representatives Proceedings of June 8, 1789) (Motion of Representative Madison); XI *Documentary History . . . First Federal Congress,* 827 (*Congressional Register* reporting the proceedings of June 8, 1789).

64. The *Annals of Congress* employs the incorrect spelling "Lawrence." Other sources employ the correct spelling of "Laurence." III *Documentary History . . . First Federal Congress,* 16 (Proceedings of April 8, 1789) (Representative Laurence's first appearance), 26 (Proceedings of April 18, 1789) (listing representatives), 152 (August 18, 1789, vote on amendments), 161–62 (August 21, 1789, vote on amendments), and 164 (August 22, 1789, vote on amendments); 1 *House Journal,* 1st Cong., 1st Sess., 17 (listing representatives); XI *Documentary History . . . First Federal Congress,* 836 (*Congressional Register* reporting the proceedings of June 8, 1789).

All quotations from the *Annals of Congress* will use the actual text, misspellings and all.

65. III *Documentary History . . . First Federal Congress,* 84 (Proceedings of June 8, 1789); 1 *House Journal,* 1st Cong., 1st Sess., 46 (Proceedings of June 8, 1789); 1 *Annals of Congress,* 1st Cong., 1st Sess., 467–68 (House of Representatives Proceedings of June 8, 1789) (Motion of Representative Laurence); IV *Documentary History . . . First Federal Congress,* 4; XI *Documentary History . . . First Federal Congress,* 804 (New York *Daily Advertiser* edition of June 9, 1789, reporting the June 8, 1789, proceedings), 804 (*New-York Daily Gazette* edition of June 9, 1789, reporting the June 8, 1789, proceedings), 810 (*Gazette of the United States* edition of June 10, 1789, reporting the June 8, 1789, proceedings), and 836 (*Congressional Register* reporting the proceedings of June 8, 1789) (Motion of Representative Laurence).

66. III *Documentary History . . . First Federal Congress,* 84 (Proceedings of June 8, 1789); 1 *House Journal,* 1st Cong., 1st Sess.,

46 (Proceedings of June 8, 1789); 1 *Annals of Congress,* 1st Cong., 1st Sess., 468 (House of Representatives Proceedings of June 8, 1789); IV *Documentary History . . . First Federal Congress,* 4; XI *Documentary History . . . First Federal Congress,* 804 (New York *Daily Advertiser* edition of June 9, 1789, reporting the June 8, 1789, proceedings), 804 (*New-York Daily Gazette* edition of June 9, 1789, reporting the June 8, 1789, proceedings), 810 (*Gazette of the United States* edition of June 10, 1789, reporting the June 8, 1789, proceedings), and 836 (*Congressional Register* reporting the proceedings of June 8, 1789).

67. Rakove, 330–31.

68. Ibid., 331.

69. III *Documentary History . . . First Federal Congress,* 117 (Proceedings of July 21, 1789); 1 *House Journal,* 1st Cong., 1st Sess., 64 (Proceedings of July 21, 1789); 1 *Annals of Congress,* 1st Cong., 1st Sess., 685–86 (House of Representatives Proceedings of July 21, 1789) (Statement of Representative Madison); IV *Documentary History . . . First Federal Congress,* 4; XI *Documentary History . . . First Federal Congress,* 1157 (New York *Daily Advertiser* edition of July 22, 1789, reporting the July 21, 1789, proceedings), 1157 (*New-York Daily Gazette* edition of July 22, 1789, reporting the July 21, 1789, proceedings), and 1158–63 (*Congressional Register* reporting the proceedings of July 21, 1789).

70. 1 *Annals of Congress,* 1st Cong., 1st Sess., 686 (House of Representatives Proceedings of July 21, 1789) (Statement of Representative Ames); XI *Documentary History . . . First Federal Congress,* 1157 (New York *Daily Advertiser* edition of July 22, 1789, reporting the July 21, 1789, proceedings), 1157 (*New-York Daily Gazette* edition of July 22, 1789, reporting the July 21, 1789, proceedings), and 1158 (*Congressional Register* reporting the proceedings of July 21, 1789).

71. 1 *Annals of Congress,* 1st Cong., 1st Sess., 687–89 (House of Representatives Proceedings of July 21, 1789) (Statements of Representatives Partridge, Jackson, and Ames); XI *Documentary History . . . First Federal Congress,* 1157 (New York *Daily Advertiser* edition of July 22, 1789, reporting the July 21, 1789, proceedings), 1157–58 (*New-York Daily Gazette* edition of July 22, 1789, reporting the July 21, 1789, proceedings), and 1158–1163 (*Congressional Register* reporting the proceedings of July 21, 1789).

72. 1 *Annals of Congress,* 1st Cong., 1st Sess., 686–87, 689–90 (House of Representatives Proceedings of July 21, 1789) (Statements of Representatives Sedgwick, White, Page, Tucker, and Gerry); XI *Documentary History . . . First Federal Congress,* 1158–63 (*Congressional Register* reporting the proceedings of July 21, 1789).

73. The reference to "three-fourths" necessarily implicated Article V of the Constitution, which provided (and still provides):

> The Congress, whenever two[-]thirds of both Houses shall deem it necessary, shall propose amendments to this Constitution, or, on the application of the legislatures of two[-]thirds of the several states, shall call a convention for proposing amendments, which, in either case, shall be valid to all intents and purposes, as part of this Constitution, *when ratified by the legislatures of three[-]fourths of the several states, or by conventions in three[-]fourths thereof,* as the one or the other mode of ratification may be proposed by the Congress[.] . . .

U.S. Const., Art. V, 1 Stat. 19 (emphasis added).

74. 1 *Annals of Congress,* 1st Cong., 1st Sess., 686 (House of Representatives Proceedings of July 21, 1789) (Statement of Representative Sherman); XI *Documentary History . . . First Federal Congress,* 1159 (*Congressional Register* reporting the proceedings of July 21, 1789) (Statement of Representative Sherman).

75. 1 *Annals of Congress,* 1st Cong., 1st Sess., 687 (House of Representatives Proceedings of July 21, 1789) (Statement of Representative Gerry); XI *Documentary History . . . First Federal Congress,* 1160 (*Congressional Register* reporting the proceedings of July 21, 1789) (Statement of Representative Gerry).

76. 1 *Annals of Congress,* 1st Cong., 1st Sess., 688 (House of Representatives Proceedings of July 21, 1789) (Statement of Representative Gerry); XI *Documentary History . . . First Federal Congress,* 1160–61 (*Congressional Register* reporting the proceedings of July 21, 1789) (Statement of Representative Gerry).

77. III *Documentary History . . . First Federal Congress,* 117 (Proceedings of July 21, 1789); 1 *House Journal,* 1st Cong., 1st Sess., 64 (Proceedings of July 21, 1789); 1 *Annals of Congress,* 1st Cong., 1st Sess., 690 (House of Representatives Proceedings of July 21, 1789); IV *Documentary History . . . First Federal Congress,* 4; XI *Documentary History . . . First Federal Congress,* 1157 (New York *Daily Advertiser* edition of July 22, 1798, reporting the July 21, 1798, proceedings), 1158 (*New-York Daily Gazette* edition of July 22,

1789, reporting the July 21, 1789, proceedings), and 1163 (*Congressional Register* reporting the proceedings of July 21, 1789).

78. III *Documentary History . . . First Federal Congress,* 117 (Proceedings of July 21, 1789); 1 *House Journal,* 1st Cong., 1st Sess., 64 (Proceedings of July 21, 1789); 1 *Annals of Congress,* 1st Cong., 1st Sess., 690 (House of Representatives Proceedings of July 21, 1789); XI *Documentary History . . . First Federal Congress,* 1157 (New York *Daily Advertiser* edition of July 22, 1798, reporting the July 21, 1798, proceedings), 1158 (*New-York Daily Gazette* edition of July 22, 1789, reporting the July 21, 1789, proceedings), and 1163 (*Congressional Register* reporting the proceedings of July 21, 1789).

79. III *Documentary History . . . First Federal Congress,* 117 (Proceedings of July 21, 1789); 1 *House Journal,* 1st Cong., 1st Sess., 64 (Proceedings of July 21, 1789); 1 *Annals of Congress,* 1st Cong., 1st Sess., 691 (House of Representatives Proceedings of July 21, 1789); IV *Documentary History . . . First Federal Congress,* 4.

80. III *Documentary History . . . First Federal Congress,* 124 (Proceedings of July 28, 1789); 1 *House Journal,* 1st Cong., 1st Sess., 67 (Proceedings of July 28, 1789); 1 *Annals of Congress,* 1st Cong., 1st Sess., 699 (House of Representatives Proceedings of July 28, 1789); IV *Documentary History . . . First Federal Congress,* 4, 27–31; *Complete Bill of Rights,* 2.

The full text of the House select committee report of July 28, 1789, accompanied by editorial footnotes that reference subsequent House votes pertaining to it, has been reproduced in IV *Documentary History . . . First Federal Congress,* 27–31, as reproduced from a printing by congressional printer Thomas Greenleaf contained in the Broadside Collection in the Rare Book Room of the Library of Congress.

81. IV *Documentary History . . . First Federal Congress,* 28 (House Committee Report); *Complete Bill of Rights,* 2 (House Committee Report) (small caps in original).

82. IV *Documentary History . . . First Federal Congress,* 28 (House Committee Report); *Complete Bill of Rights,* 2 (House Committee Report). See also the later discussions concerning the mode of actualizing any amendments at 1 *Annals of Congress,* 1st Cong., 1st Sess., 757 (House of Representatives Proceedings of August 15, 1789); XI *Documentary History . . . First Federal Congress,* 1254 (New York *Daily Advertiser* edition of August 17, 1789, reporting

the August 15, 1789, proceedings), 1257 (*Gazette of the United States* edition of August 19, 1789, reporting the August 15, 1789, proceedings), and 1260 (*Congressional Register* reporting the proceedings of August 15, 1789).

83. Brant, *James Madison: Father of the Constitution,* 270.

84. Ketchum, 192, 196.

85. I Farrand's *Records,* 20–22; I Elliott's *Debates,* 143–45; *Madison's Notes,* 23–26; I Madison's *Journal,* 61–64; V Elliott's *Debates,* 127–28; III *Documentary History . . . Constitution,* 17–20; *Documents Illustrative . . . Formation of the American States,* 116–19 (emphasis added).

86. I Farrand's *Records,* 30–31, 33–35; I Elliott's *Debates,* 150–51; *Madison's Notes,* 27–29; I Madison's *Journal,* 73–75; V Elliott's *Debates,* 132–34; III *Documentary History . . . Constitution,* 20–23; *Documents Illustrative . . . Formation of the American States,* 120–22 (emphasis added).

87. I Farrand's *Records,* 312, 322; I Elliott's *Debates,* 181–83; *Madison's Notes,* 127–29; I Madison's *Journal,* 196; V Elliott's *Debates,* 211–12; *Documents Illustrative . . . Formation of the American States,* 234–37.

88. I Farrand's *Records,* 334–36; I Elliott's *Debates,* 183; *Madison's Notes,* 131–32; I Madison's *Journal,* 199–200; V Elliott's *Debates,* 214; III *Documentary History . . . Constitution,* 166–67; *Documents Illustrative . . . Formation of the American States,* 240–41.

89. Farrand, 91.

90. I Farrand's *Records,* 336; *Madison's Notes,* 132; I Madison's *Journal,* 200; V Elliott's *Debates,* 214.

91. Ketchum, 207.

92. III *Documentary History . . . First Federal Congress,* 130 (Proceedings of August 3, 1789); 1 *House Journal,* 1st Cong., 1st Sess., 70 (Proceedings of August 3, 1789); 1 *Annals of Congress,* 1st Cong., 1st Sess., 700 (House of Representatives Proceedings of August 3, 1789); IV *Documentary History . . . First Federal Congress,* 4.

93. MR. LEE moved that the House now resolve itself into a Committee of the whole, on the report of the committee of eleven, to whom it had been referred to take the subject of amendments to the constitution of the United States generally into their consideration.

1 *Annals of Congress,* 1st Cong., 1st Sess., 730 (House of

Representatives Proceedings of August 13, 1789) (Motion of Representative Lee). (small caps in original) See also III *Documentary History . . . First Federal Congress,* 148 (Proceedings of August 13, 1789); 1 *House Journal,* 1st Cong., 1st Sess., 79 (Proceedings of August 13, 1789); IV *Documentary History . . . First Federal Congress,* 5; XI *Documentary History . . . First Federal Congress,* 1207–8 (New York *Daily Advertiser* edition of August 14, 1789, reporting the August 13, 1789, proceedings), 1211–12 (*Gazette of the United States* edition of August 15, 1789, reporting the August 13, 1789, proceedings), and 1216 (*Congressional Register* reporting the proceedings of August 13, 1789).

94. 1 *Annals of Congress,* 1st Cong., 1st Sess., 730–31, 734 (House of Representatives Proceedings of August 13, 1789) (Statements of Representatives Page [twice], Madison [twice], and Vining); XI *Documentary History . . . First Federal Congress,* 1207–8 (New York *Daily Advertiser* edition of August 14, 1789, reporting the August 13, 1789, proceedings), 1211–16 (*Gazette of the United States* edition of August 15, 1789, reporting the August 13, 1789, proceedings), and 1216–21 (*Congressional Register* reporting the proceedings of August 13, 1789).

95. 1 *Annals of Congress,* 1st Cong., 1st Sess., 731–34 (House of Representatives Proceedings of August 13, 1789) (Statements of Representatives Sedgwick [twice], Smith [twice], Hartley, Gerry, and Laurence); XI *Documentary History . . . First Federal Congress,* 1207–8 (New York *Daily Advertiser* edition of August 14, 1789, reporting the August 13, 1789, proceedings), 1211–16 (*Gazette of the United States* edition of August 15, 1789, reporting the August 13, 1789, proceedings), and 1216–21 (*Congressional Register* reporting the proceedings of August 13, 1789).

96. III *Documentary History . . . First Federal Congress,* 148 (Proceedings of August 13, 1789); 1 *House Journal,* 1st Cong., 1st Sess., 79 (Proceedings of August 13, 1789); 1 *Annals of Congress,* 1st Cong., 1st Sess., 734 (House of Representatives Proceedings of August 13, 1789); IV *Documentary History . . . First Federal Congress,* 5; XI *Documentary History . . . First Federal Congress,* 1208 (New York *Daily Advertiser* edition of August 14, 1789, reporting the August 13, 1789, proceedings), 1212 (*Gazette of the United States* edition of August 15, 1789, reporting the August 13, 1789, proceedings), and 1221 (*Congressional Register* reporting the proceedings of August 13, 1789).

97. U.S. Const., Art. V, 1 Stat. 19.

98. See III Farrand's *Records,* 587–90 (identifying the signatories).

99. 1 *Annals of Congress,* 1st Cong., 1st Sess., 737–38 (House of Representatives Proceedings of August 13, 1789) (Statement of Representative Stone); XI *Documentary History . . . First Federal Congress,* 1213 (*Gazette of the United States* edition of August 15, 1789, reporting the proceedings of August 13, 1789) and 1224 (*Congressional Register* reporting the proceedings of August 13, 1789).

100. 1 *Annals of Congress,* 1st Cong., 1st Sess., 734 (House of Representatives Proceedings of August 13, 1789) (Statement of Representative Sherman); XI *Documentary History . . . First Federal Congress,* 1208–9 (New York *Daily Advertiser* edition of August 14, 1789, reporting the proceedings of August 13, 1789), 1212 (*Gazette of the United States* edition of August 15, 1789, reporting the proceedings of August 13, 1789), and 1221 (*Congressional Register* reporting the proceedings of August 13, 1789).

101. 1 *Annals of Congress,* 1st Cong., 1st Sess., 735 (House of Representatives Proceedings of August 13, 1789) (motion of Representative Sherman) and 744 (House of Representatives Proceedings of August 13, 1789) (vote on motion); IV *Documentary History . . . First Federal Congress,* 5; XI *Documentary History . . . First Federal Congress,* 1208–10 (New York *Daily Advertiser* edition of August 14, 1789, reporting the August 13, 1789, proceedings), 1212–16 (*Gazette of the United States* edition of August 15, 1789, reporting the August 13, 1789, proceedings), and 1221 (*Congressional Register* reporting the proceedings of August 13, 1789).

102. 1 *Annals of Congress,* 1st Cong., 1st Sess., 744 (House of Representatives Proceedings of August 13, 1789); IV *Documentary History . . . First Federal Congress,* 5; XI *Documentary History . . . First Federal Congress,* 1210 (New York *Daily Advertiser* edition of August 14, 1789, reporting the August 13, 1789, proceedings), 1216 (*Gazette of the United States* edition of August 15, 1789, reporting the August 13, 1789, proceedings), and 1231 (*Congressional Register* reporting the proceedings of August 13, 1789).

For unknown reasons, neither the official House Journal nor the *House Journal* contains any reference to that particular vote. See III *Documentary History . . . First Federal Congress,* 148 (Proceedings of August 13, 1789); and 1 *House Journal,* 1st Cong., 1st Sess., 79 (Proceedings of August 13, 1789).

103. 1 *Annals of Congress,* 1st Cong., 1st Sess., 730–44 (House of Representatives Proceedings of August 13, 1789).

104. III *Documentary History . . . First Federal Congress,* 148 (Proceedings of August 13, 1789); 1 *Annals of Congress,* 1st Cong., 1st Sess., 744 (House of Representatives Proceedings of August 13, 1789); 1 *House Journal,* 1st Cong., 1st Sess., 79 (Proceedings of August 13, 1789).

105. III *Documentary History . . . First Federal Congress,* 149 (Proceedings of August 14, 1789); 1 *House Journal,* 1st Cong., 1st Sess., 79–80 (Proceedings of August 14, 1789); 1 *Annals of Congress,* 1st Cong., 1st Sess., 745 (House of Representatives Proceedings of August 14, 1789); IV *Documentary History . . . First Federal Congress,* 5; XI *Documentary History . . . First Federal Congress,* 1232–35 (New York *Daily Advertiser* edition of August 15, 1789, reporting the August 14, 1789, proceedings), 1235–40 (*Gazette of the United States* edition of August 15, 1789, reporting the August 14, 1789, proceedings), and 1240–54 (*Congressional Register* reporting the proceedings of August 14, 1789).

106. III *Documentary History . . . First Federal Congress,* 149 (Proceedings of August 14, 1789); 1 *House Journal,* 1st Cong., 1st Sess., 79–80 (Proceedings of August 14, 1789); 1 *Annals of Congress,* 1st Cong., 1st Sess., 757 (House of Representatives Proceedings of August 14, 1789); XI *Documentary History . . . First Federal Congress,* 1235 (New York *Daily Advertiser* edition of August 15, 1789, reporting the August 14, 1789, proceedings), and 1240 (*Gazette of the United States* edition of August 15, 1789, reporting the August 14, 1789, proceedings).

107. III *Documentary History . . . First Federal Congress,* 149–50 (Proceedings of August 15, 1789); 1 *House Journal,* 1st Cong., 1st Sess., 80 (Proceedings of August 15, 1789); 1 *Annals of Congress,* 1st Cong., 1st Sess., 757 (House of Representatives Proceedings of August 15, 1789); IV *Documentary History . . . First Federal Congress,* 5; XI *Documentary History . . . First Federal Congress,* 1254–57 (New York *Daily Advertiser* edition of August 17, 1789, reporting the August 15, 1789, proceedings), 1257–60 (*Gazette of the United States* edition of August 19, 1789, reporting the August 15, 1789, proceedings), and 1260–82 (*Congressional Register* reporting the proceedings of August 15, 1789); *Complete Bill of Rights,* 59 (*Congressional Register* reporting the proceedings of August 15, 1789).

108. 1 *Annals of Congress,* 1st Cong., 1st Sess., 757 (House of Representatives Proceedings of August 15, 1789); IV *Documentary History . . . First Federal Congress,* 5, 28; XI *Documentary History . . . First Federal Congress,* 1254 (New York *Daily Advertiser* edition of August 17, 1789, reporting the August 15, 1789, proceedings), 1257 (*Gazette of the United States* edition of August 19, 1789, reporting the August 15, 1789, proceedings), and 1260–62 (*Congressional Register* reporting the proceedings of August 15, 1789); *Complete Bill of Rights,* 59.

109. The *Annals* employs the incorrect spelling "Sylvester." Other sources employ the correct spelling of "Silvester." III *Documentary History . . . First Federal Congress,* 26 (Proceedings of April 18, 1789) (listing representatives), 30 (Proceedings of April 22, 1789) (Representative Silvester's first appearance), 152 (August 18, 1789, vote on amendments), 161 (August 21, 1789, vote on amendments), 164 (August 22, 1789, vote on amendments), and 229 (September 24, 1789, vote on amendments); 1 *House Journal,* 1st Cong., 1st Sess., 17 (listing representatives), 81 (August 18, 1789, vote on amendments), 86–87 (August 21, 1789, vote on amendments), 88 (August 22, 1789, vote on amendments, and 121 (September 24, 2789, vote on amendments); XI *Documentary History . . . First Federal Congress,* 1260 (*Congressional Register* reporting the proceedings of August 15, 1789).

All quotations from the *Annals* will use the actual text, misspellings and all.

110. **Silvester's remarks:** 1 *Annals of Congress,* 1st Cong., 1st Sess., 757 (House of Representatives Proceedings of August 15, 1789) (Statement of Representative Silvester) (small caps in original); XI *Documentary History . . . First Federal Congress,* 1257 (*Gazette of the United States* edition of August 19, 1789, reporting the proceedings of August 15, 1789), 1260 (*Congressional Register* reporting the proceedings of August 15, 1789); *Complete Bill of Rights,* 59 (*Congressional Register* reporting the proceedings of August 15, 1789).

111. **Vining's remarks:** 1 *Annals of Congress,* 1st Cong., 1st Sess., 757 (House of Representatives Proceedings of August 15, 1789) (Statement of Representative Vining) (small caps in original); XI *Documentary History . . . First Federal Congress,* 1260 (*Congressional Register* reporting the proceedings of August 15, 1789); *Complete Bill of Rights,* 59 (*Congressional Register* reporting the proceedings of August 15, 1789).

112. **Gerry's remarks:** 1 *Annals of Congress,* 1st Cong., 1st Sess., 757

(House of Representatives Proceedings of August 15, 1789) (Statement of Representative Gerry) (small caps in original); XI *Documentary History . . . First Federal Congress,* 1261 (*Congressional Register* reporting the proceedings of August 15, 1789); *Complete Bill of Rights,* 59 (*Congressional Register* reporting the proceedings of August 15, 1789) (emphasis added).

113. III *Documentary History . . . First Federal Congress,* xxvii, 3; 1 *House Journal,* 1st Cong., 1st Sess., (unnumbered) page 3 (Proceedings of March 4, 1789); 1 *Annals of Congress,* 1st Cong., 1st Sess., (unnumbered page) 99 (House of Representatives Proceedings of March 4, 1789) (all identifying Gerry as from Massachusetts).

114. See Chapter 2B.

115. **Sherman's remarks:** 1 *Annals of Congress,* 1st Cong., 1st Sess., 757 (House of Representatives Proceedings of August 15, 1789) (Statement of Representative Sherman) (small caps in original); XI *Documentary History . . . First Federal Congress,* 1257 (*Gazette of the United States* edition of August 19, 1789, reporting the proceedings of August 15, 1789), and 1261 (*Congressional Register* reporting the proceedings of August 15, 1789); *Complete Bill of Rights,* 59 (*Congressional Register* reporting the proceedings of August 15, 1789).

116. U.S. Const., Art. I, § 8, ¶18, 1 Stat. 14 (emphasis added).

117. **Carroll's remarks:** 1 *Annals of Congress,* 1st Cong., 1st Sess., 757 (House of Representatives Proceedings of August 15, 1789) (Statement of Representative Carroll) (small caps in original); XI *Documentary History . . . First Federal Congress,* 1261 (*Congressional Register* reporting the proceedings of August 15, 1789); *Complete Bill of Rights,* 59 (*Congressional Register* reporting the proceedings of August 15, 1789).

118. **Madison's remarks:** 1 *Annals of Congress,* 1st Cong., 1st Sess., 758 (House of Representatives Proceedings of August 15, 1789) (Statement of Representative Madison) (small caps in original); XI *Documentary History . . . First Federal Congress,* 1261 (*Congressional Register* reporting the proceedings of August 15, 1789); *Complete Bill of Rights,* 60 (*Congressional Register* reporting the proceedings of August 15, 1789) (emphasis added).

119. **Huntington's remarks:** 1 *Annals of Congress,* 1st Cong., 1st Sess., 758 (House of Representatives Proceedings of August 15, 1789) (Statement of Representative Huntington) (small caps in

original); XI *Documentary History . . . First Federal Congress,* 1261–62 (*Congressional Register* reporting the proceedings of August 15, 1789); *Complete Bill of Rights,* 60 (*Congressional Register* reporting the proceedings of August 15, 1789) (emphasis added).

120. Brant, *James Madison: Father of the Constitution,* 270.

121. One source reports these remarks by Madison as a "motion." *Complete Bill of Rights,* 2 (citing the *Congressional Register* report of the proceedings of August 15, 1789). Presumably, Madison had moved to insert the word "national" in the text of the proposed amendment. This source also reports that Madison later "withdr[ew]" his motion.

Although the *Annals* utilized the *Congressional Register* as its primary source for the proceedings of the First Congress, neither the *Annals* nor any other source quoting the *Congressional Register* characterizes Madison's remarks as a "motion." 1 *Annals of Congress,* 1st Cong., 1st Sess., 758–59 (Proceedings of August 15, 1789) (Statement of Representative Madison); XI *Documentary History . . . First Federal Congress,* 1262 (*Congressional Register* reporting the proceedings of August 15, 1789); *Complete Bill of Rights,* 60 (*Congressional Register* reporting the proceedings of August 15, 1789).

122. **Madison's remarks:** 1 *Annals of Congress,* 1st Cong., 1st Sess., 758–59 (House of Representatives Proceedings of August 15, 1789) (Statement of Representative Madison) (small caps in original); XI *Documentary History . . . First Federal Congress,* 1262 (*Congressional Register* reporting the proceedings of August 15, 1789); *Complete Bill of Rights,* 60 (*Congressional Register* reporting the proceedings of August 15, 1789) (emphasis added).

123. Some sources also report these remarks by Representative Livermore as a "motion." 1 *House Journal,* 1st Cong., 1st Sess., 80 (Proceedings of August 15, 1789); IV *Documentary History . . . First Federal Congress,* 28 n. 8; *Complete Bill of Rights,* 2 (citing [but not quoting] the *Congressional Register* reporting the proceedings of August 15, 1789; the New York *Daily Advertiser* edition of August 17, 1789, reporting the August 15, 1789, proceedings; the *New-York Daily Gazette* edition of August 18, 1789, reporting the August 15, 1789, proceedings; and the *Gazette of the United States* edition of August 19, 1789, reporting the August 15, 1789, proceedings).

Although the *Annals* utilized the *Congressional Register* as its primary source reporting the proceedings of the First Congress, neither the

Annals nor any other report quoting the *Congressional Register* characterizes Livermore's remarks as a "motion." 1 *Annals of Congress,* 1st Cong., 1st Sess., 759 (Proceedings of August 15, 1789) (Statement of Representative Livermore); XI *Documentary History . . . First Federal Congress,* 1262 (quoting *Congressional Register* reporting the proceedings of August 15, 1789).

124. **Livermore's remarks:** 1 *Annals of Congress,* 1st Cong., 1st Sess., 759 (House of Representatives Proceedings of August 15, 1789) (Statement of Representative Livermore) (small caps in original); XI *Documentary History . . . First Federal Congress,* 1254 (*Daily Advertiser* edition of August 17, 1789, reporting the August 15, 1789, proceedings), 1257 (*Gazette of the United States* edition of August 19, 1789, reporting the August 15, 1789, proceedings), and 1262 (*Congressional Register* reporting the proceedings of August 15, 1789); *Complete Bill of Rights,* 2 (*Congressional Register* reporting the proceedings of August 15, 1789; New York *Daily Advertiser* edition of August 17, 1789, reporting the August 15, 1789, proceedings; *New-York Daily Gazette* edition of August 18, 1789, reporting the August 15, 1789, proceedings; and *Gazette of the United States* edition of August 19, 1789, reporting the August 15, 1789, proceedings), and 60 (*Congressional Register* reporting the proceedings of August 15, 1789).

125. IV *Documentary History . . . First Federal Congress,* 15, ¶ "Eleventh"; I Elliott's *Debates,* 326, ¶ "11th" (New Hampshire Ratifying Convention) (Proceedings of June 21, 1788); *Madison's Notes,* 658; II *Documentary History . . . Constitution,* 143; *Documents Illustrative . . . Formation of the American States,* 1026.

126. Brant, *James Madison: Father of the Constitution,* 271.

127. XI *Documentary History . . . First Federal Congress,* 1254 (New York *Daily Advertiser* edition of August 17, 1789, on the August 15, 1789 proceedings).

128. Four sources include this reference by Representative Gerry to "the honorable gentlemen's motion" but otherwise do not identify either the movant or the motion. Gerry's remarks leave it plain enough, though, that Gerry's remark that the unidentified movant "shows that he considers it in the same light" likely referred to Livermore and not Madison; Livermore's proposal that day omitted any reference to "national," while Madison's preference for the term "national" seems at odds with Gerry's concerns. IV *Documentary*

History . . . First Federal Congress, 28 n. 8; 1 *Annals of Congress,* 1st Cong., 1st Sess., 757–59 (Proceedings of August 15, 1789); 1 *House Journal,* 1st Cong., 1st Sess., 80 (Proceedings of August 15, 1789); and XI *Documentary History . . . First Federal Congress,* 1262 (*Congressional Register* reporting the proceedings of August 15, 1789).

129. **Gerry's remarks:** 1 *Annals of Congress,* 1st Cong., 1st Sess., 759 (House of Representatives Proceedings of August 15, 1789) (Statement of Representative Gerry) (small caps in original); XI *Documentary History . . . First Federal Congress,* 1262 (*Congressional Register* reporting the proceedings of August 15, 1789); *Complete Bill of Rights,* 60–61 (*Congressional Register* reporting the proceedings of August 15, 1789) (emphasis added).

130. I Farrand's *Records,* 17; I Elliott's *Debates,* 143; III Farrand's *Records,* 588 (Appendix B) ("Attendance of Delegates"); *Madison's Notes,* 21; I Madison's *Journal,* 58; V Elliott's *Debates,* 126; III *Madison's Writings,* 13; III *Documentary History of the Constitution,* 13; *Documents Illustrative . . . Formation of the American States,* 113.

131. II Farrand's *Records,* 649; I Elliott's *Debates,* 494–96; *Madison's Notes,* 583; II Madison's *Journal,* 763; V Elliott's *Debates,* 565; IV *Madison's Writings,* 483; III *Documentary History of the Constitution,* 770; *Documents Illustrative . . . Formation of the American States,* 745; Farrand, 194.

132. Presumably, this references Madison's "motion" to insert the word "national" in the proposed amendment.

133. **Madison's remarks:** 1 *Annals of Congress,* 1st Cong., 1st Sess., 759 (House of Representatives Proceedings of August 15, 1789) (Statement of Representative Madison) (small caps in original); XI *Documentary History . . . First Federal Congress,* 1262 (*Congressional Register* reporting the proceedings of August 15, 1789); *Complete Bill of Rights,* 61 (*Congressional Register* reporting the proceedings of August 15, 1789) (emphasis added).

134. 1 *Annals of Congress,* 1st Cong., 1st Sess., 759 (House of Representatives Proceedings of August 15, 1789); IV *Documentary History . . . First Federal Congress,* 28 n. 9; XI *Documentary History . . . First Federal Congress,* 1254 (New York *Daily Advertiser* edition of August 17, 1789, reporting the August 15, 1789, proceedings), 1257 (*Gazette of the United States* edition of August 19, 1789, reporting the August 15, 1789, proceedings, and 1262 (*Congressional Register* reporting the proceedings of August 15, 1789; *Complete Bill of Rights,*

2, 61–62 (New York *Daily Advertiser* edition of August 17, 1789, reporting the August 15, 1789, proceedings; *New-York Daily Gazette* edition of August 18, 1789, reporting the August 15, 1789, proceedings; *Congressional Register* reporting the proceedings of August 15, 1789; *Gazette of the United States* edition of August 19, 1789, reporting the August 15, 1789, proceedings).

135. See IV *Documentary History . . . First Federal Congress*, 28 n. 9 (reference to the change in wording).

136. III *Documentary History . . . First Federal Congress*, 150 (Proceedings of August 17, 1789); 1 *House Journal*, 1st Cong., 1st Sess., 80 (Proceedings of August 17, 1789); 1 *Annals of Congress*, 1st Cong., 1st Sess., 778–85 (House of Representatives Proceedings of August 17, 1789); IV *Documentary History . . . First Federal Congress*, 5; XI *Documentary History . . . First Federal Congress*, 1283–85 (*Gazette of the United States* edition of August 22, 1789, reporting the August 17, 1789, proceedings), and 1285–94 (*Congressional Register* reporting the proceedings of August 17, 1789).

137. III *Documentary History . . . First Federal Congress*, 151–54 (Proceedings of August 18, 1789); 1 *House Journal*, 1st Cong., 1st Sess., 81–83 (Proceedings of August 18, 1789); 1 *Annals of Congress*, 1st Cong., 1st Sess., 785–92 (House of Representatives Proceedings of August 18, 1789); IV *Documentary History . . . First Federal Congress*, 6; XI *Documentary History . . . First Federal Congress*, 1294–95 (New York *Daily Advertiser* editions of August 19 and 20, 1789, reporting the August 18, 1789, proceedings), 1295–97 (*Gazette of the United States* editions of August 19 and 20, 1789, reporting the August 18, 1789, proceedings), and 1297–1301 (*Congressional Register* reporting the proceedings of August 18, 1789).

138. See III *Documentary History . . . First Federal Congress*, 151–54 (Proceedings of August 18, 1789), and also 150–51 n. 58 (Proceedings of August 17, 1789 [describing next day's motions]); 1 *House Journal*, 1st Cong., 1st Sess., 81–83 (Proceedings of August 18, 1789); 1 *Annals of Congress*, 1st Cong., 1st Sess., 786–88, 790–92 (House of Representatives Proceedings of August 18, 1789) (Motions of Representatives Gerry and Tucker, respectively); IV *Documentary History . . . First Federal Congress*, 6, 31–33 (reproducing Representative Gerry's motion and Representative Tucker's seventeen proposed amendments); XI *Documentary History . . . First Federal Congress*, 1294–95 (New York *Daily Advertiser* editions of August 19 and 20, 1789, reporting

the August 18, 1789, proceedings), 1295 (*Gazette of the United States* edition of August 19, 1789, reporting the August 18, 1789, proceedings), and 1297–99 (*Congressional Register* reporting the proceedings of August 18, 1789) (Motions of Representatives Gerry and Tucker, respectively).

139. In his argument in support of one of the motions, Representative Tucker declared that "[f]ive important states have plainly expressed their apprehensions." XI *Documentary History . . . First Federal Congress,* 1297 (*Congressional Register* reporting the proceedings of August 18, 1789); 1 *Annals of Congress,* 1st Cong., 1st Sess., 787 (House of Representatives Proceedings of August 18, 1789) (Statement of Representative Tucker).

140. III *Documentary History . . . First Federal Congress,* 151–54 (Proceedings of August 18, 1789); 1 *House Journal,* 1st Cong., 1st Sess., 81–83 (Proceedings of August 18, 1789); 1 *Annals of Congress,* 1st Cong., 1st Sess., 788, 792 (House of Representatives Proceedings of August 18, 1789) (votes on motions of Representatives Gerry and Tucker, respectively); IV *Documentary History . . . First Federal Congress,* 6.

141. III *Documentary History . . . First Federal Congress,* 156 (Proceedings of August 19, 1789); 1 *House Journal,* 1st Cong., 1st Sess., 83–84 (Proceedings of August 19, 1789); 1 *Annals of Congress,* 1st Cong., 1st Sess., 792–95 (House of Representatives Proceedings of August 19, 1789); IV *Documentary History . . . First Federal Congress,* 6; XI *Documentary History . . . First Federal Congress,* 1308 (*Congressional Register* reporting the proceedings of August 19, 1789).

142. See 1 *Annals of Congress,* 1st Cong., 1st Sess., 735 (House of Representatives Proceedings of August 13, 1789) (motion of Representative Sherman), and 744 (House of Representatives Proceedings of August 13, 1789) (vote on motion); IV *Documentary History . . . First Federal Congress,* 5; XI *Documentary History . . . First Federal Congress,* 1208–10 (New York *Daily Advertiser* edition of August 14, 1789, reporting the August 13, 1789, proceedings), 1212–16 (*Gazette of the United States* edition of August 15, 1789, reporting the August 13, 1789, proceedings), and 1221–31 (*Congressional Register* reporting the August 13, 1789, proceedings).

143. Mr. Sherman renewed his motion for adding the amendments to the constitution by way of supplement.

1 *Annals of Congress,* 1st Cong., 1st Sess., 795 (House of

Representatives Proceedings of August 19, 1789) (Motion of Representative Sherman); see also XI *Documentary History . . . First Federal Congress*, 1308 (*Congressional Register* reporting the proceedings of August 19, 1789).

144. 1 *Annals of Congress*, 1st Cong., 1st Sess., 795 (House of Representatives Proceedings of August 19, 1789) (Vote on motion); IV *Documentary History . . . First Federal Congress*, 6; XI *Documentary History . . . First Federal Congress*, 1308 (*Congressional Register* reporting the proceedings of August 19, 1789).

Neither the official House Journal nor the *House Journal* makes any mention of Sherman's particular motion, or the vote thereon. III *Documentary History . . . First Federal Congress*, 156–57 (Proceedings of August 19, 1789); 1 *House Journal*, 1st Cong., 1st Sess., 83–84 (Proceedings of August 19, 1789).

145. See, for instance, Labunski, 201, 218–20.

146. III *Documentary History . . . First Federal Congress*, 157 (Proceedings of August 20, 1789); 1 *House Journal*, 1st Cong., 1st Sess., 84 (Proceedings of August 20, 1789); 1 *Annals of Congress*, 1st Cong., 1st Sess., 795 (House of Representatives Proceedings of August 20, 1789); IV *Documentary History . . . First Federal Congress*, 6; XI *Documentary History . . . First Federal Congress*, 1308–9 (*Gazette of the United States* edition of August 22, 1789, reporting the August 20, 1789, proceedings).

147. 1 *Annals of Congress*, 1st Cong., 1st Sess., 796 (House of Representatives Proceedings of August 20, 1789) (motion of Representative Ames); IV *Documentary History . . . First Federal Congress*, 28 n. 9 (referencing Representative Ames's motion); XI *Documentary History . . . First Federal Congress*, 1308 (the *Gazette of the United States* edition of August 22, 1789, reporting the August 20, 1789, proceedings); *Complete Bill of Rights*, 2, 62 (citing the *Congressional Register* report of the August 20, 1789, proceedings, and the *Gazette of the United States* edition of August 22, 1789, reporting the August 20, 1789, proceedings) (emphasis added).

148. The *Annals of Congress* simply reports that "[t]his [*viz.*, Representative Ames's motion] being adopted." 1 *Annals of Congress*, 1st Cong., 1st Sess., 796 (House of Representatives Proceedings of August 20, 1789) (motion of Representative Ames).

Although the *Annals* utilized the *Congressional Register* as its primary source for its reports of the proceedings, and although the *Complete Bill of Rights* references the *Congressional Register* as well for the August 20, 1789, proceedings, the *Congressional Register* for August 20, 1789, receives no mention for that date in XI *Documentary History . . . First Federal Congress*. And neither the official House Journal nor the *House Journal* mentions that day's modification. III *Documentary History . . . First Federal Congress*, 157 (Proceedings of August 20, 1789); 1 *House Journal*, 1st Cong., 1st Sess., 84 (Proceedings of August 20, 1789).

149. U.S. Const., Amend. I, 1 Stat. 21.

150. Brant, *James Madison: Father of the Constitution*, 271.

151. III *Documentary History . . . First Federal Congress*, 158–62 (Proceedings of August 21, 1789); 1 *House Journal*, 1st Cong., 1st Sess., 85–87 (Proceedings of August 21, 1789); 1 *Annals of Congress*, 1st Cong., 1st Sess., 796–802 (House of Representatives Proceedings of August 21, 1789); IV *Documentary History . . . First Federal Congress*, 6; XI *Documentary History . . . First Federal Congress*, 1309–16 (*Congressional Register* reporting the proceedings of August 21, 1789).

152. III *Documentary History . . . First Federal Congress*, 158–60 (Proceedings of August 21, 1789) (reproducing "seventeen proposed articles of amendment"); 1 *House Journal*, 1st Cong., 1st Sess., 85–87 (Proceedings of August 21, 1789) (identifying seventeen specific articles that two-thirds of the House approved). Other sources—*viz.*, the *Annals of Congress*, XI *Documentary History . . . First Federal Congress*, and *Complete Bill of Rights*—make no mention of the House vote on August 21, 1789, presumably because those sources in turn relied upon various newspaper publications and the latter appear to have omitted any mention of that vote.

153. III *Documentary History . . . First Federal Congress*, 159 (Proceedings of August 21, 1789); 1 *House Journal*, 1st Cong., 1st Sess., 85 (Proceedings of August 21, 1789); *Complete Bill of Rights*, 3 (citing the official House Journal, 107) (emphasis added).

154. See III *Documentary History . . . First Federal Congress*, 158–62 (Proceedings of August 21, 1789); 1 *House Journal*, 1st Cong., 1st Sess., 85–87 (Proceedings of August 21, 1789); 1 *Annals of Congress*, 1st Cong., 1st Sess., 796–802 (House of Representatives Proceedings of August 21, 1789).

155. See III *Documentary History . . . First Federal Congress*, 159 (Proceedings of August 21, 1789) (quoting the text approved); and 1 *House Journal*, 1st Cong., 1st Sess., 85 (Proceedings of August 21, 1789) (quoting the text approved).

156. III *Documentary History . . . First Federal Congress*, 163–65

(Proceedings of August 22, 1789); 1 *House Journal,* 1st Cong., 1st Sess., 87–88 (Proceedings of August 22, 1789); 1 *Annals of Congress,* 1st Cong., 1st Sess., 802–8 (House of Representatives Proceedings of August 22, 1789); IV *Documentary History . . . First Federal Congress,* 6–7; XI *Documentary History . . . First Federal Congress,* 1316–18 (*Gazette of the United States* edition of August 26, 1789, reporting the August 22, 1789, proceedings) and 1319–24 (*Congressional Register* reporting the August 22, 1789, proceedings).

157. III *Documentary History . . . First Federal Congress,* 163–64 (Proceedings of August 22, 1789); 1 *House Journal,* 1st Cong., 1st Sess., 87–88 (Proceedings of August 22, 1789); 1 *Annals of Congress,* 1st Cong., 1st Sess., 803–8 (House of Representatives Proceedings of August 22, 1789); IV *Documentary History . . . First Federal Congress,* 6–7, 34; XI *Documentary History . . . First Federal Congress,* 1316–18 (*Gazette of the United States* edition of August 26, 1789, reporting the August 22, 1789, proceedings) and 1319–24 (*Congressional Register* reporting the August 22, 1789, proceedings).

158. III *Documentary History . . . First Federal Congress,* 164–65 (Proceedings of August 22, 1789); 1 *House Journal,* 1st Cong., 1st Sess., 88 (Proceedings of August 22, 1789); 1 *Annals of Congress,* 1st Cong., 1st Sess., 808 (House of Representatives Proceedings of August 22, 1789); IV *Documentary History . . . First Federal Congress,* 6–7; *Complete Bill of Rights,* 3.

159. III *Documentary History . . . First Federal Congress,* 166 (Proceedings of August 24, 1789); 1 *House Journal,* 1st Cong., 1st Sess., 89 (Proceedings of August 24, 1789); 1 *Annals of Congress,* 1st Cong., 1st Sess., 808–9 (House of Representatives Proceedings of August 24, 1789); IV *Documentary History . . . First Federal Congress,* 6–7; XI *Documentary History . . . First Federal Congress,* 1325 (*Gazette of the United States* edition of August 26, 1789, reporting the August 24, 1789, proceedings).

160. I *Documentary History . . . First Federal Congress,* 135–38 (Proceedings of August 25, 1789) (noting the Senate's next-day receipt of the proposed amendments); 1 *Senate Journal,* 1st Cong., 1st Sess., 63–64 (Proceedings of August 25, 1789) (quoting the seventeen amendments that the Senate received from the House).

161. III *Documentary History . . . First Federal Congress,* 166 (Proceedings of August 24, 1789); 1 *House Journal,* 1st Cong., 1st Sess., 89 (Proceedings of August 24, 1789); 1 *Annals of Congress,* 1st

Cong., 1st Sess., 808–9 (House of Representatives Proceedings of August 24, 1789) (resolution reproduced); IV *Documentary History* . . . *First Federal Congress*, 7, 35–39 (reproducing congressional printer Thomas Greenleaf's August 25, 1789, printing).

162. IV *Documentary History* . . . *First Federal Congress*, 36; *Complete Bill of Rights*, 3; I *Documentary History* . . . *First Federal Congress*, 135–36 (Proceedings of August 25, 1789) (Senate's next-day receipt of House transmittal); 1 *Senate Journal*, 1st Cong., 1st Sess., 63–64 (Proceedings of August 25, 1789) (Senate receipt of House transmittal).

163. 2 *Senate Journal*, 3rd Cong., 1st Sess., 33–34 (Proceedings of February 20, 1794); 4 *Annals of Congress*, 3rd Cong., 1st Sess., 46–47 (Senate Proceedings of February 20, 1794).

164. 1 *Annals of Congress*, 1st Cong., 1st Sess., 15 (prefatory note) (Senate Proceedings of March 4, 1789); 2 Byrd, 312; Amer, 2.

165. See *Maclay's Journal*.

166. Schwartz, 1145.

167. *Maclay's Journal*, 134 (notes of August 25, 1798); IX *Documentary History* . . . *First Federal Congress*, 133 (notes of August 25, 1798).

168. Compare 1 *Annals of Congress*, 1st Cong., 1st Sess., 15–96 (Senate Proceedings from March 4, 1789, to September 29, 1789), with 1 *Annals of Congress*, 1st Cong., 1st Sess., 99–964 (House of Representatives Proceedings from March 4, 1789, to September 29, 1789).

169. 1 *Senate Journal*, 1st Cong., 1st Sess.

170. 1 *Senate Journal*, 1st Cong., 1st Sess., 5–95 (Senate Proceedings from March 4, 1789, to September 29, 1789).

171. 1 *Annals of Congress*, 1st Cong., 1st Sess., 15–96 (Senate Proceedings from March 4, 1789, to September 29, 1789).

172. IV *Documentary History* . . . *First Federal Congress*, 43–45 (identifying the twenty-six separate Senate amendments approved on September 9, 1789, and returned to the House of Representatives). See also I *Documentary History* . . . *First Federal Congress*, 149–50, 151–52, 153–55, 158–59, 166–68 (Proceedings of September 2, 3, 4, 7, and 9, 1789, respectively); 1 *Senate Journal*, 1st Cong., 1st Sess., 69, 70, 70–71, 72–73, 77 (Proceedings of September 2, 3, 4, 7, and 9, 1789, respectively).

173. See IV *Documentary History* . . . *First Federal Congress*, 44.

174. See IV *Documentary History . . . First Federal Congress,* 44.

175. I *Documentary History . . . First Federal Congress,* 135–38 (Proceedings of August 25, 1789); 1 *Senate Journal,* 1st Cong., 1st Sess., 63–64 (Proceedings of August 25, 1789); 1 *Annals of Congress,* 1st Cong., 1st Sess., 73–74 (Senate Proceedings of August 25, 1789); *Maclay's Journal,* 134; IX *Documentary History . . . First Federal Congress,* 133; IV *Documentary History . . . First Federal Congress,* 7; *Complete Bill of Rights,* 3.

176. I *Documentary History . . . First Federal Congress,* 138 (Proceedings of August 25, 1789); 1 *Senate Journal,* 1st Cong., 1st Sess., 64 (Proceedings of August 25, 1789); 1 *Annals of Congress,* 1st Cong., 1st Sess., 74 (Senate Proceedings of August 25, 1789); IV *Documentary History . . . First Federal Congress,* 7.

177. I *Documentary History . . . First Federal Congress,* 138 incl. n. 92 (Proceedings of August 25, 1789); 1 *Senate Journal,* 1st Cong., 1st Sess., 64 (Proceedings of August 25, 1789).

178. I *Documentary History . . . First Federal Congress,* 149–50 (Proceedings of September 2, 1789); 1 *Senate Journal,* 1st Cong., 1st Sess., 69 (Proceedings of September 2, 1789); 1 *Annals of Congress,* 1st Cong., 1st Sess., 76–77 (Senate Proceedings of September 2, 1789); IV *Documentary History . . . First Federal Congress,* 7.

179. I *Documentary History . . . First Federal Congress,* 150–52 (Proceedings of September 3, 1789); 1 *Senate Journal,* 1st Cong., 1st Sess., 69–70 (Proceedings of September 3, 1789); IV *Documentary History . . . First Federal Congress,* 7; *Complete Bill of Rights,* 3. Although the *Annals of Congress* briefly references certain Senate proceedings on September 3, 1789, it omits any reference to the Senate's consideration of the proposed amendments. 1 *Annals of Congress,* 1st Cong., 1st Sess., 77 (Senate Proceedings of September 3, 1789).

180. I *Documentary History . . . First Federal Congress,* 151 (Proceedings of September 3, 1789); 1 *Senate Journal,* 1st Cong., 1st Sess., 70 (Proceedings of September 3, 1789); IV *Documentary History . . . First Federal Congress,* 36 n. 7; *Complete Bill of Rights,* 3–4 (reporting from the official Senate Journal).

181. I *Documentary History . . . First Federal Congress,* 151 (Proceedings of September 3, 1789); 1 *Senate Journal,* 1st Cong., 1st Sess., 70 (Proceedings of September 3, 1789) ("On motion for reconsideration: It passed in the affirmative."). The chronicle in *Complete Bill of Rights,* 3–4 (reporting from the official Senate

Journal), makes no mention of the reconsideration vote, although it reports all other votes that day on the subject.

182. I *Documentary History . . . First Federal Congress*, 151 (Proceedings of September 3, 1789); 1 *Senate Journal*, 1st Cong., 1st Sess., 70 (Proceedings of September 3, 1789); IV *Documentary History . . . First Federal Congress*, 36 n. 7; *Complete Bill of Rights*, 3–4 (reporting from the official Senate Journal).

183. I *Documentary History . . . First Federal Congress*, 151 (Proceedings of September 3, 1789); 1 *Senate Journal*, 1st Cong., 1st Sess., 70 (Proceedings of September 3, 1789); IV *Documentary History . . . First Federal Congress*, 36 n. 8; *Complete Bill of Rights*, 4 (reporting from the official Senate Journal).

184. I *Documentary History . . . First Federal Congress*, 151 (Proceedings of September 3, 1789); 1 *Senate Journal*, 1st Cong., 1st Sess., 70 (Proceedings of September 3, 1789); IV *Documentary History . . . First Federal Congress*, 36 n. 8; *Complete Bill of Rights*, 4 (reporting from the official Senate Journal).

185. The inclusion of the phrase "in preference to others" within the context of establishment proves redundant; any "establishment" necessarily implicates a *preference* for a single ecclesiastical institution (or religion, church, denomination, faith, sect, creed, or religious society), thus rendering superfluous any reference to "preference," and also rendering the terms "one" and "any" interchangeable within that context.

Furthermore, the phrases "*one* religious sect or society" and "*any* religious sect or society" remain interchangeable; within the context of establishment concerns only "one" institution (or religion, church, denomination, faith, sect, creed, or religious society) could be "established," thus the establishment of "any" such institution (or religion, church, denomination, faith, sect, creed, or religious society) would result in an establishment.

186. I *Documentary History . . . First Federal Congress*, 151 (Proceedings of September 3, 1789); 1 *Senate Journal*, 1st Cong., 1st Sess., 70 (Proceedings of September 3, 1789); IV *Documentary History . . . First Federal Congress*, 36 n. 6; *Complete Bill of Rights*, 4–5 (reporting from the official Senate Journal).

187. I *Documentary History . . . First Federal Congress*, 151 (Proceedings of September 3, 1789); 1 *Senate Journal*, 1st Cong., 1st Sess., 70 (Proceedings of September 3, 1789); IV *Documentary*

History . . . *First Federal Congress,* 36 n. 8; *Complete Bill of Rights,* 5 (reporting from the official Senate Journal).

188. I *Documentary History* . . . *First Federal Congress,* 151 (Proceedings of September 3, 1789); 1 *Senate Journal,* 1st Cong., 1st Sess., 70 (Proceedings of September 3, 1789); IV *Documentary History* . . . *First Federal Congress,* 36 n. 8; *Complete Bill of Rights,* 5 (reporting from the official Senate Journal).

189. I *Documentary History* . . . *First Federal Congress,* 151 (Proceedings of September 3, 1789); 1 *Senate Journal,* 1st Cong., 1st Sess., 70 (Proceedings of September 3, 1789).

190. I *Documentary History* . . . *First Federal Congress,* 153–55 (Proceedings of September 4, 1789); 1 *Senate Journal,* 1st Cong., 1st Sess., 70–71 (Proceedings of September 4, 1789); 1 *Annals of Congress,* 1st Cong., 1st Sess., 77 (Senate Proceedings of September 4, 1789); IV *Documentary History* . . . *First Federal Congress,* 8.

191. I *Documentary History* . . . *First Federal Congress,* 153–55 (Proceedings of September 4, 1789); 1 *Senate Journal,* 1st Cong., 1st Sess., 70–71 (Proceedings of September 4, 1789); IV *Documentary History* . . . *First Federal Congress,* 8 (reporting Senate consideration beginning with the fourth proposed amendment that day).

192. I *Documentary History* . . . *First Federal Congress,* 158–60 (Proceedings of September 7, 1789); 1 *Senate Journal,* 1st Cong., 1st Sess., 72–73 (Proceedings of September 7, 1789); 1 *Annals of Congress,* 1st Cong., 1st Sess., 78 (Senate Proceedings of September 7, 1789); IV *Documentary History* . . . *First Federal Congress,* 8, 39–40.

193. I *Documentary History* . . . *First Federal Congress,* 158–60 (Proceedings of September 7, 1789); 1 *Senate Journal,* 1st Cong., 1st Sess., 72–73 (Proceedings of September 7, 1789); 1 *Annals of Congress,* 1st Cong., 1st Sess., 78 (Senate Proceedings of September 7, 1789); IV *Documentary History* . . . *First Federal Congress,* 8, 39–40.

194. I *Documentary History* . . . *First Federal Congress,* 160–64 (Proceedings of September 8, 1789); 1 *Senate Journal,* 1st Cong., 1st Sess., 73–76 (Proceedings of September 8, 1789); 1 *Annals of Congress,* 1st Cong., 1st Sess., 79 (Senate Proceedings of September 8, 1789); IV *Documentary History* . . . *First Federal Congress,* 8, 40–43.

195. I *Documentary History* . . . *First Federal Congress,* 166–68 (Proceedings of September 9, 1789); 1 *Senate Journal,* 1st Cong., 1st Sess., 76–77 (Proceedings of September 9, 1789); 1 *Annals of Congress,* 1st Cong., 1st Sess., 80 (Senate Proceedings of September

9, 1789); IV *Documentary History . . . First Federal Congress,* 8, 43–45; *Complete Bill of Rights,* 5–6 (reporting from the official Senate Journal).

196. I *Documentary History . . . First Federal Congress,* 166 (Proceedings of September 9, 1789); 1 *Senate Journal,* 1st Cong., 1st Sess., 77 (Proceedings of September 9, 1789); IV *Documentary History . . . First Federal Congress,* 36 n. 6, 44; *Complete Bill of Rights,* 5–6 (reporting from the official Senate Journal, and also reproducing Senator Ellsworth's personal notes of those very changes). Although the *Annals of Congress* briefly references certain Senate proceedings on September 9, 1789, it omits any reference of the Senate's consideration of the proposed amendments. 1 *Annals of Congress,* 1st Cong., 1st Sess., 80 (Senate Proceedings of September 9, 1789).

197. I *Documentary History . . . First Federal Congress,* 166 (Proceedings of September 9, 1789); 1 *Senate Journal,* 1st Cong., 1st Sess., 77 (Proceedings of September 9, 1789); IV *Documentary History . . . First Federal Congress,* 36 n. 6, 44, 46; *Complete Bill of Rights,* 5–6 (reporting from the official Senate Journal, and also reproducing Senator Ellsworth's personal notes of those very changes).

198. Brant, *James Madison: Father of the Constitution,* 271–72.

199. Ibid.

200. Brant, *James Madison: Father of the Constitution,* 271, referring to Patrick Henry's unsuccessful attempt in 1784 to have the Virginia legislature enact Henry's proposal for governmental financial support for churches and religious schools entitled A Bill Establishing a Provision for Teachers of the Christian Religion (see Brant, *James Madison: The Nationalist,* 346; Ketchum, 162–63).

201. Brant, *James Madison: Father of the Constitution,* 271.

202. I *Documentary History . . . First Federal Congress,* 166–68 (Proceedings of September 9, 1789); 1 *Senate Journal,* 1st Cong., 1st Sess., 77 (Proceedings of September 9, 1789); IV *Documentary History . . . First Federal Congress,* 43–45 (specifying the twenty-six amendments); *Complete Bill of Rights,* 6. Both the official House Journal and the *House Journal* also reference the twenty-six amendments returned by the Senate, albeit in reports of later proceedings. III *Documentary History . . . First Federal Congress,* 217 (Proceedings of September 21, 1789); 1 *House Journal,* 115–16 (Proceedings of September 21, 1789).

On September 14, 1789, Senate printer Thomas Greenleaf printed a cleaned-up version of the proposed amendments—actually, proposed Articles—that included all of the Senate's various modifications. IV *Documentary History . . . First Federal Congress,* 45–47.

203. IV *Documentary History . . . First Federal Congress,* 44 (italics and strikeout in original).

204. III *Documentary History . . . First Federal Congress,* 199 (Proceedings of September 10, 1789); 1 *House Journal,* 1st Cong., 1st Sess., 106 (Proceedings of September 10, 1789); 1 *Annals of Congress,* 1st Cong., 1st Sess., 923 (House of Representatives Proceedings of September 10, 1789).

205. III *Documentary History . . . First Federal Congress,* 216–17 (Proceedings of September 19, 1789); 1 *House Journal,* 1st Cong., 1st Sess., 115 (Proceedings of September 19, 1789); 1 *Annals of Congress,* 1st Cong., 1st Sess., 937–38 (House Proceedings of September 19, 1789); IV *Documentary History . . . First Federal Congress,* 8.

206. III *Documentary History . . . First Federal Congress,* 217 (Proceedings of September 21, 1789); 1 *House Journal,* 1st Cong., 1st Sess., 115–16 (Proceedings of September 21, 1789); 1 *Annals of Congress,* 1st Cong., 1st Sess., 939 (House Proceedings of September 21, 1789); IV *Documentary History . . . First Federal Congress,* 8–9; *Complete Bill of Rights,* 6 (reporting from the official House Journal).

207. III *Documentary History . . . First Federal Congress,* 218 (Proceedings of September 21, 1789); 1 *House Journal,* 1st Cong., 1st Sess., 116 (Proceedings of September 21, 1789); I *Documentary History . . . First Federal Congress,* 181 (Proceedings of September 21, 1789); 1 *Senate Journal,* 1st Cong., 1st Sess., 83–84 (Proceedings of September 21, 1789); 1 *Annals of Congress,* 1st Cong., 1st Sess., 85–86 (Senate Proceedings of September 21, 1789); *Complete Bill of Rights,* 7 (reporting from the official Senate Journal).

208. I *Documentary History . . . First Federal Congress,* 182 (Proceedings of September 21, 1789); 1 *Senate Journal,* 1st Cong., 1st Sess., 84 (Proceedings of September 21, 1789); 1 *Annals of Congress,* 1st Cong., 1st Sess., 939 (House Proceedings of September 21, 1789); IV *Documentary History . . . First Federal Congress,* 8–9; *Complete Bill of Rights,* 7–8 (reporting from the official Senate Journal) (emphasis added).

209. I *Documentary History . . . First Federal Congress,* 166

(Proceedings of September 9, 1789); 1 *Senate Journal*, 1st Cong., 1st Sess., 77 (Proceedings of September 9, 1789); IV *Documentary History . . . First Federal Congress*, 44, 46; *Complete Bill of Rights*, 6.

210. III *Documentary History . . . First Federal Congress*, 218 (Proceedings of September 21, 1789); 1 *House Journal*, 1st Cong., 1st Sess., 116 (Proceedings of September 21, 1789); 1 *Annals of Congress*, 1st Cong., 1st Sess., 939 (House Proceedings of September 21, 1789); I *Documentary History . . . First Federal Congress*, 181 (Proceedings of September 21, 1789); 1 *Senate Journal*, 1st Cong., 1st Sess., 84 (Proceedings of September 21, 1789); 1 *Annals of Congress*, 1st Cong., 1st Sess., 85–86 (Senate Proceedings of September 21, 1789); IV *Documentary History . . . First Federal Congress*, 8–9; *Complete Bill of Rights*, 6 (reporting from the official House Journal).

211. III *Documentary History . . . First Federal Congress*, 218 (Proceedings of September 21, 1789) (appointing Representatives Madison, Sherman, and Vining); 1 *House Journal*, 1st Cong., 1st Sess., 116 (Proceedings of September 21, 1789) (appointing Representatives Madison, Sherman, and Vining); 1 *Annals of Congress*, 1st Cong., 1st Sess., 939 (House Proceedings of September 21, 1789) (appointing Representatives Madison, Sherman, and Vining).

212. I *Documentary History . . . First Federal Congress*, 182 (Proceedings of September 21, 1789) (appointing Senators Ellsworth, Carroll, and Paterson); 1 *Senate Journal*, 1st Cong., 1st Sess., 84 (Proceedings of September 21, 1789) (appointing Senators Ellsworth, Carroll, and Paterson); 1 *Annals of Congress*, 1st Cong., 1st Sess., 86 (Senate Proceedings of September 21, 1789) (appointing Senators Ellsworth, Carroll, and Paterson); *Complete Bill of Rights*, 7–8.

213. I *Documentary History . . . First Federal Congress*, 182 (Proceedings of September 21, 1789); 1 *Senate Journal*, 1st Cong., 1st Sess., 84 (Proceedings of September 21, 1789); 1 *Annals of Congress*, 1st Cong., 1st Sess., 939 (House Proceedings of September 21, 1789); IV *Documentary History . . . First Federal Congress*, 8–9.

214. III *Documentary History . . . First Federal Congress*, 226 (Proceedings of September 23, 1789); 1 *House Journal*, 1st Cong., 1st Sess., 120 (Proceedings of September 23, 1789).

215. III *Documentary History . . . First Federal Congress*, 226 n. 141 (Proceedings of September 23, 1789); 1 *House Journal*, 1st Cong., 1st Sess., 120 (Proceedings of September 23, 1789).

216. **House:** III *Documentary History . . . First Federal Congress,* 228–29 (Proceedings of September 24, 1789); 1 *House Journal,* 1st Cong., 1st Sess., 121 (Proceedings of September 24, 1789); 1 *Annals of Congress,* 1st Cong., 1st Sess., 948 (House Proceedings of September 24, 1789); IV *Documentary History . . . First Federal Congress,* 9; *Complete Bill of Rights,* 8–9 (reporting from the official House Journal).

Senate: I *Documentary History . . . First Federal Congress,* 185–86 (Proceedings of September 24, 1789); 1 *Senate Journal,* 1st Cong., 1st Sess., 86 (Proceedings of September 24, 1789); IV *Documentary History . . . First Federal Congress,* 9; *Complete Bill of Rights,* 8–9 (reporting from Senator Ellsworth's personal notes of the Conference Committee Report, and also reporting from the official Senate Journal, respectively).

The full text of the Conference Committee Report of September 24, 1789, has been reproduced in IV *Documentary History . . . First Federal Congress,* 47–48. In addition, Senator Ellsworth's personal notes of the Conference Committee Report appear in *Complete Bill of Rights,* 8.

217. See III *Documentary History . . . First Federal Congress,* 228 (Proceedings of September 24, 1789); 1 *House Journal,* 1st Cong., 1st Sess., 121 (Proceedings of September 24, 1789); 1 *Annals of Congress,* 1st Cong., 1st Sess., 948 (House of Representatives Proceedings of September 24, 1789); I *Documentary History . . . First Federal Congress,* 185–86 (Proceedings of September 24, 1789); 1 *Senate Journal,* 1st Cong., 1st Sess., 86 (Proceedings of September 24, 1789); IV *Documentary History . . . First Federal Congress,* 9; and *Complete Bill of Rights,* 8–9 (reporting from both the official House and Senate journals).

218. IV *Documentary History . . . First Federal Congress,* 47 (italics in original). Senator Ellsworth's personal notes of the Conference Committee Report identify the same wording. *Complete Bill of Rights,* 8.

219. See IV *Documentary History . . . First Federal Congress,* 43–45 (reproducing the Senate list).

220. IV *Documentary History . . . First Federal Congress,* 43–45 (identifying the twenty-six separate Senate amendments approved on September 9, 1789, and returned to the House of Representatives).

221. IV *Documentary History . . . First Federal Congress,* 47–48

(reproducing the Conference Committee Report); *Complete Bill of Rights,* 8 (reproducing the Conference Committee Report).

222. Brant, *James Madison: Father of the Constitution,* 271.

223. I Stokes, 547.

224. 12 *Madison's Papers,* 53.

225. Ketchum, 276.

226. 12 *Madison's Papers,* 53, citing a May 31, 1789, letter from Fisher Ames to George Minot (I *Works of Fisher Ames,* 35).

227. I *Jefferson's Writings* (1903 ed.) ("Autobiography"), 61–62; *Jefferson*—"Autobiography," 37; I *Jefferson's Works* ("Autobiography"), 66.

228. III *Documentary History . . . First Federal Congress,* 228 (Proceedings of September 24, 1789); 1 *House Journal,* 1st Cong., 1st Sess., 121 (Proceedings of September 24, 1789); 1 *Annals of Congress,* 1st Cong., 1st Sess., 948 (House of Representatives Proceedings of September 24, 1789); IV *Documentary History . . . First Federal Congress,* 9; *Complete Bill of Rights,* 8.

229. III *Documentary History . . . First Federal Congress,* 228 (Proceedings of September 24, 1789); 1 *House Journal,* 1st Cong., 1st Sess., 121 (Proceedings of September 24, 1789); 1 *Annals of Congress,* 1st Cong., 1st Sess., 948 (House of Representatives Proceedings of September 24, 1789).

230. III *Documentary History . . . First Federal Congress,* 228 (Proceedings of September 24, 1789); 1 *House Journal,* 1st Cong., 1st Sess., 121 (Proceedings of September 24, 1789); 1 *Annals of Congress,* 1st Cong., 1st Sess., 948 (House of Representatives Proceedings of September 24, 1789); IV *Documentary History . . . First Federal Congress,* 9; *Complete Bill of Rights,* 8.

231. Article V of the Constitution requires a two-thirds vote by Congress to approve any proposed constitutional amendment:

> The Congress, whenever two[-]thirds of both Houses shall deem it necessary, shall propose Amendments to this Constitution . . . [.]

U.S. Const., Art. V, 1 Stat. 19.

232. III *Documentary History . . . First Federal Congress,* 228 (Proceedings of September 24, 1789); 1 *House Journal,* 1st Cong., 1st Sess., 121 (Proceedings of September 24, 1789); 1 *Annals of Congress,* 1st Cong., 1st Sess., 948 (House of Representatives Proceedings of September 24, 1789); IV *Documentary History . . . First Federal Congress,* 9; *Complete Bill of Rights,* 8 (reporting from the official House Journal).

233. III *Documentary History . . . First Federal Congress*, 229 (Proceedings of September 24, 1789); 1 *House Journal*, 1st Cong., 1st Sess., 122 (Proceedings of September 24, 1789).

234. I *Documentary History . . . First Federal Congress*, 189–90 (Proceedings of September 24, 1789); 1 *Senate Journal*, 1st Cong., 1st Sess., 87 (Proceedings of September 24, 1789); IV *Documentary History . . . First Federal Congress*, 9; *Complete Bill of Rights*, 9–10 (reporting from the official Senate Journal).

235. When the Senate returned the various proposed amendments to the House on September 10, the last four clauses in "Article the Third" read:

> Congress shall make no law . . . abridging the freedom of speech, or of the press; or the right of the people peaceably to assemble, and petition the government for a redress of grievances.

I *Documentary History . . . First Federal Congress*, 166 (Proceedings of September 9, 1789); 1 *Senate Journal*, 1st Cong., 1st Sess., 77 (Proceedings of September 9, 1789); IV *Documentary History . . . First Federal Congress*, 36 n. 6, 44; *Complete Bill of Rights*, 5–6 (reporting from the official Senate Journal, and also reproducing Senator Ellsworth's personal notes of those very changes).

236. I *Documentary History . . . First Federal Congress*, 189 (Proceedings of September 24, 1789); 1 *Senate Journal*, 1st Cong., 1st Sess., 87 (Proceedings of September 24, 1789); IV *Documentary History . . . First Federal Congress*, 9; *Complete Bill of Rights*, 10.

237. I *Documentary History . . . First Federal Congress*, 190 (Proceedings of September 24, 1789); 1 *Senate Journal*, 1st Cong., 1st Sess., 87 (Proceedings of September 24, 1789); 1 *Annals of Congress*, 1st Cong., 1st Sess., 88 (Senate Proceedings of September 24, 1789).

238. III *Documentary History . . . First Federal Congress*, 229 (Proceedings of September 24, 1789); 1 *House Journal*, 1st Cong., 1st Sess., 122 (Proceedings of September 24, 1789); 1 *Annals of Congress*, 1st Cong., 1st Sess., 948 (House of Representatives Proceedings of September 24, 1789). The resolution mentions Rhode Island and North Carolina separately because, at the time, neither of them had yet voted to ratify the Constitution.

239. I *Documentary History . . . First Federal Congress*, 192 (Proceedings of September 25, 1789); 1 *Senate Journal*, 1st Cong., 1st Sess., 88 (Proceedings of September 25, 1789); 1 *Annals of Congress*, 1st Cong., 1st Sess., 90 (Senate Proceedings of September

25, 1789); IV *Documentary History . . . First Federal Congress,* 9; *Complete Bill of Rights,* 10–11 (reporting from the official Senate Journal).

240. III *Documentary History . . . First Federal Congress,* 233 (Proceedings of September 25, 1789) (receiving notice from the Senate); 1 *House Journal,* 1st Cong., 1st Sess., 124 (Proceedings of September 25, 1789) (receiving notice from the Senate); IV *Documentary History . . . First Federal Congress,* 9.

241. I *Documentary History . . . First Federal Congress,* 191–92 (Proceedings of September 25, 1789) (receiving notice from the House); 1 *Senate Journal,* 1st Cong., 1st Sess., 88 (Proceedings of September 25, 1789) (receiving notice from the House); 1 *Annals of Congress,* 1st Cong., 1st Sess., 90 (Senate Proceedings of September 25, 1789); IV *Documentary History . . . First Federal Congress,* 9.

242. I *Documentary History . . . First Federal Congress,* 198 (Proceedings of September 26, 1789); 1 *Senate Journal,* 1st Cong., 1st Sess., 90 (Proceedings of September 26, 1789); IV *Documentary History . . . First Federal Congress,* 9.

243. III *Documentary History . . . First Federal Congress,* 238 (Proceedings of September 28, 1789) (receiving notice from the Senate); 1 *House Journal,* 1st Cong., 1st Sess., 126 (Proceedings of September 28, 1789) (receiving notice from the Senate).

244. House/Senate Joint Resolution, reproduced in: 1 Stat. 97–98; IV *Documentary History . . . First Federal Congress,* 1; "Appendix" found in 1 *Senate Journal,* 1st Cong., 1st Sess., 96–97; *Madison's Notes,* 689–91; I Elliott's *Debates,* 338–39; II *Documentary History . . . Constitution,* 321–24; *Documents Illustrative . . . Formation of the American States,* 1063–65.

245. House/Senate Joint Resolution, reproduced in: 1 Stat. 97–98; IV *Documentary History . . . First Federal Congress,* 1; "Appendix" found in 1 *Senate Journal,* 1st Cong., 1st Sess., 96–97; *Madison's Notes,* 690; I Elliott's *Debates,* 338; II *Documentary History . . . Constitution,* 322; *Documents Illustrative . . . Formation of the American States,* 1063 (emphasis added).

246. Article V of the Constitution provides that any constitutional amendments "shall be valid to all intents and purposes, as part of this Constitution, when ratified by the legislatures of three[-]fourths of the several states, or by conventions in three[-]fourths thereof . . . [.]" U.S. Const., Art. V, 1 Stat. 19.

247. Act of Congress of February 18, 1791, 1st Cong., 3rd Sess.,

Ch. 7, 1 Stat. 191 (statute reproduced in 6 *Federal and State Constitutions,* 376, and 2 *Annals of Congress,* Appendix, 2374).

248. II *Documentary History . . . Constitution,* 377–90; I *Elliott's Debates,* 340; *Madison's Notes,* 691–92 n. 1; *Documents Illustrative . . . Formation of the American States,* 1065 n. 2. Although the appendix to the second volume of the *Annals of Congress* reports nine state ratification votes, it does not report the December 1791 Virginia ratification vote because the appendix terminates its coverage on March 3, 1791, the date the First Congress adjourned its third session.

249. **New Jersey:** II *Documentary History . . . Constitution,* 325–29; 2 *Annals of Congress,* Appendix, 2039–40; I *Elliott's Debates,* 340; *Madison's Notes,* 691–92 n. 1; *Documents Illustrative . . . Formation of the American States,* 1065 n. 2.

250. **Maryland:** II *Documentary History . . . Constitution,* 330–34; 2 *Annals of Congress,* Appendix, 2037; I *Elliott's Debates,* 340; *Madison's Notes,* 691–92 n. 1; *Documents Illustrative . . . Formation of the American States,* 1065 n. 2.

251. **North Carolina:** II *Documentary History . . . Constitution,* 335–39; 2 *Annals of Congress,* Appendix, 2038–39; I *Elliott's Debates,* 340; *Madison's Notes,* 691–92 n. 1; *Documents Illustrative . . . Formation of the American States,* 1065 n. 2.

252. **South Carolina:** II *Documentary History . . . Constitution,* 340–44; 2 *Annals of Congress,* Appendix, 2038; I *Elliott's Debates,* 340; *Madison's Notes,* 691–92 n. 1; *Documents Illustrative . . . Formation of the American States,* 1065 n. 2.

253. **New Hampshire:** II *Documentary History . . . Constitution,* 345–46; 2 *Annals of Congress,* Appendix, unnumbered page 2033; I *Elliott's Debates,* 339; *Madison's Notes,* 691–92 n. 1; *Documents Illustrative . . . Formation of the American States,* 1065 n. 2.

254. **Delaware:** II *Documentary History . . . Constitution,* 348–51; 2 *Annals of Congress,* Appendix, 2037; I *Elliott's Debates,* 340; *Madison's Notes,* 691–92 n. 1; *Documents Illustrative . . . Formation of the American States,* 1065 n. 2.

255. **New York:** II *Documentary History . . . Constitution,* 353–62; 2 *Annals of Congress,* Appendix, unnumbered pages 2033–34, 2035; I *Elliott's Debates,* 339; *Madison's Notes,* 691–92 n. 1; *Documents Illustrative . . . Formation of the American States,* 1065 n. 2.

256. **Pennsylvania:** II *Documentary History . . . Constitution,* 352–56, 367; 2 *Annals of Congress,* Appendix, 2036; I *Elliott's Debates,*

339; *Madison's Notes,* 691–92 n. 1; *Documents Illustrative . . . Formation of the American States,* 1065 n. 2.

257. **Rhode Island:** II *Documentary History . . . Constitution,* 363–66; 2 *Annals of Congress,* Appendix, 2039; I Elliott's *Debates,* 340; *Madison's Notes,* 691–92 n. 1; *Documents Illustrative . . . Formation of the American States,* 1065 n. 2.

Although some sources report—incorrectly—that Rhode Island ratified all of the twelve proposed amendments, Rhode Island in fact did *not* ratify proposed Article II. Rhode Island voted to ratify "all the Amendments proposed by Congress, *except the second,*" as part of its ratification vote. 2 *Annals of Congress,* Appendix, 2039; see also II *Documentary History . . . Constitution,* 364 (Rhode Island's ratification vote reproducing Articles I and III–XII, but omitting Article II) and 366 (ratifying all "except the IIth" [*sic*] article).

258. **Vermont:** II *Documentary History . . . Constitution,* 371–76; I Elliott's *Debates,* 340; *Madison's Notes,* 691–92 n. 1; *Documents Illustrative . . . Formation of the American States,* 1065 n. 2. Although the appendix to the second volume of the *Annals of Congress* reports nine state ratification votes, it does not report the November 1791 Vermont ratification vote because the appendix terminates its coverage on March 3, 1791, the date the First Congress adjourned its third session.

259. **Virginia:** II *Documentary History . . . Constitution,* 377–90; I Elliott's *Debates,* 340; *Madison's Notes,* 691–92 n. 1; *Documents Illustrative . . . Formation of the American States,* 1065 n. 2.

260. A summary of all of the states' ratification votes also appears in: I Elliott's *Debates,* 339–40; *Madison's Notes,* 691–92 n. 1; *Documents Illustrative . . . Formation of the American States,* 1065 n. 2; and II *Documentary History . . . Constitution,* 390 note.

261. Act of February 4, 1791, 1st Cong., 3rd Sess., Ch. 4, 1 Stat. 189 (reproduced in 2 *Annals of Congress,* Appendix, 2372–73).

262. Act of February 4, 1791, 1st Cong., 3rd Sess., Ch. 4, § 2, 1 Stat. 189 (reproduced in 2 *Annals of Congress,* Appendix, 2372–73).

263. See I Elliott's *Debates,* 340; *Madison's Notes,* 692 n. 1; *Documents Illustrative . . . Formation of the American States,* 1065 n. 2.

264. The United States Archivist's certification to that effect appears in F.R. Doc. 92–11951, 57 F.R. 21187, and H. Doc. 108–95, 108th Cong., 1st Sess., *The Constitution off the United States, as amended,* printed pursuant to House of Representatives Resolution 139,

June 20, 2004, 108th Cong., 1st Sess., 26–27. Illinois also ratified the amendment on May 12, 1992, although its vote proved unnecessary by that time.

265. See, for instance, Levy, *Original Intent,* 179 (" . . . [A] House select committee omitted the term 'national.' It is not a part of the First Amendment, and it should not be construed . . . as if it were still a part and as if the ban against a 'national religion' authorized nonpreferential assistance to all faiths.").

266. See Chapter 5C(6).

267. B. Adamson, "Peering over History's 'Wall of Separation,'" *The* (Portland) *Oregonian,* "Commentary," October 19, 2005.

268. Emphasis added. See Chapter 5A(3).

269. See Chapter 5A(5).

270. Emphasis added. See Chapter 5A(4).

271. See Chapter 5A(9).

272. Ibid.

273. Ibid.

274. Ibid.

275. See I Farrand's *Records,* 17; I Elliott's *Debates,* 124–25, 143; III Farrand's *Records,* 588 (Appendix B) ("Attendance of Delegates"); V Elliott's *Debates,* 126; *Madison's Notes,* 21; I Madison's *Journal,* 58; III *Madison's Writings,* 13; III *Documentary History of the Constitution,* 13; *Documents Illustrative . . . Formation of the American States,* 113.

276. Brant, *James Madison: Father of the Constitution,* 23, 30; Ketchum, 192, 196.

277. I Farrand's *Records,* 20–22; I Elliott's *Debates,* 143–45; *Madison's Notes,* 23–26; I Madison's *Journal,* 61–64; V Elliott's *Debates,* 127–28; III *Documentary History . . . Constitution,* 17–20; *Documents Illustrative . . . Formation of the American States,* 116–19 (emphasis added).

278. I Farrand's *Records,* 30–31, 33–35; I Elliott's *Debates,* 150–51; *Madison's Notes,* 27–29; I Madison's *Journal,* 73–75; V Elliott's *Debates,* 132–34; III *Documentary History . . . Constitution,* 20–23; *Documents Illustrative . . . Formation of the American States,* 120–22 (emphasis added).

279. I Farrand's *Records,* 30–31, 33–35; I Elliott's *Debates,* 150–51; *Madison's Notes,* 27–29; I Madison's *Journal,* 73–75; V Elliott's *Debates,* 132–34; III *Documentary History . . . Constitution,* 20–23; *Documents Illustrative . . . Formation of the American States,* 120–22 (emphasis added).

280. I Farrand's *Records,* 33; *Madison's Notes,* 27–28; I Madison's *Journal,* 73; V Elliott's *Debates,* 132–33; see also Farrand, 73.

> . . . [T]he third substitute resolution was taken up [on May 30, 1787], "that a *national* government ought to be established consisting of a *supreme* Legislative, Executive and Judiciary." . . . [T]he discussion which followed turned "less on its general merits than on the force and extent of the particular terms *national & supreme.* . . [.]

Farrand, 73 (italics in original).

281. I Farrand's *Records,* 34; *Madison's Notes,* 28; I Madison's *Journal,* 74; V Elliott's *Debates,* 133.

282. I Farrand's *Records,* 33–35; *Madison's Notes,* 28; I Madison's *Journal,* 73–74; V Elliott's *Debates,* 133.

283. I Farrand's *Records,* 45–46, 47–48; I Elliott's *Debates,* 152; *Madison's Notes,* 31; I Madison's *Journal,* 78; V Elliott's *Debates,* 135; III *Documentary History . . . Constitution,* 26; *Documents Illustrative . . . Formation of the American States,* 124–25 (emphasis added).

284. I Farrand's *Records,* 46, 48–50; I Elliott's *Debates,* 152–53; *Madison's Notes,* 31–33; I Madison's *Journal,* 78–80; V Elliott's *Debates,* 135–37; III *Documentary History . . . Constitution,* 26–29; *Documents Illustrative . . . Formation of the American States,* 125–27 (emphasis added).

285. I Farrand's *Records,* 46, 48–50; I Elliott's *Debates,* 152–53; *Madison's Notes,* 31–33; I Madison's *Journal,* 78–80; V Elliott's *Debates,* 135–37; III *Documentary History . . . Constitution,* 26–29; *Documents Illustrative . . . Formation of the American States,* 125–27.

286. I Farrand's *Records,* 46, 51–52; I Elliott's *Debates,* 153; *Madison's Notes,* 34–35; I Madison's *Journal,* 81–82; V Elliott's *Debates,* 137–39; III *Documentary History . . . Constitution,* 29–32; *Documents Illustrative . . . Formation of the American States,* 127–29 (emphasis added).

287. I Farrand's *Records,* 46–47, 52–54; I Elliott's *Debates,* 153; *Madison's Notes,* 35; I Madison's *Journal,* 83; V Elliott's *Debates,* 139; III *Documentary History . . . Constitution,* 32–33; *Documents Illustrative . . . Formation of the American States,* 129–30 (emphasis added).

288. I Farrand's *Records,* 62–63, 64–66; I Elliott's *Debates,* 154; *Madison's Notes,* 37–39; I Madison's *Journal,* 84–86; V Elliott's *Debates,* 140–41; III *Documentary History . . . Constitution,* 35–37; *Documents Illustrative . . . Formation of the American States,* 131–33 (emphasis added).

289. I Farrand's *Records*, 63, 66–67; I Elliott's *Debates*, 155; *Madison's Notes*, 39–40; I Madison's *Journal*, 86–88; V Elliott's *Debates*, 141–42; III *Documentary History* . . . *Constitution*, 37–38; *Documents Illustrative* . . . *Formation of the American States*, 133–34 (emphasis added).

290. I Farrand's *Records*, 93–95, 97–104; I Elliott's *Debates*, 159–60; *Madison's Notes*, 51–56; I Madison's *Journal*, 101–7; V Elliott's *Debates*, 151–55; III *Documentary History* . . . *Constitution*, 54–62; *Documents Illustrative* . . . *Formation of the American States*, 145–52 (emphasis added).

291. I Farrand's *Records*, 95, 104–5; I Elliott's *Debates*, 160; *Madison's Notes*, 56; I Madison's *Journal*, 107–8; V Elliott's *Debates*, 155; III *Documentary History* . . . *Constitution*, 62; *Documents Illustrative* . . . *Formation of the American States*, 152–53 (emphasis added).

292. The sequence on June 5 proves confusing. At the end of the day on June 4, the first clause in Randolph's ninth proposed resolution read:

> Resolved that a National judiciary be established to consist of one supreme tribunal, and of one or more inferior tribunals[.]

On June 5, the Convention first struck the words "one or more," so that the proposal then read:

> Resolved that a national judiciary be established to consist of one supreme tribunal, and of inferior tribunals[.]

Next, the Convention revised the second clause in Randolph's ninth proposed resolution ("to be chosen by the National Legislature") by striking the phrase "the National Legislature" and inserting a blank (recommended by Madison), so as to read:

> to be chosen by _____[.]

Next, the Convention approved the deletion of the phrase "and of inferior tribunals," so that the first and second clauses of Randolph's ninth proposed resolution read:

> Resolved that a national judiciary be established to consist of one supreme tribunal, to be chosen by _____[.]

Finally, the Convention approved the enlargement of the first and second clauses of Randolph's ninth proposed resolution to read:

> Resolved that a national judiciary be established to consist of one

supreme tribunal, to be chosen by _____, [and] that the national legislature be empowered to appoint inferior tribunals.

I Farrand's *Records,* 116, 118–20, 124–25; I Elliott's *Debates,* 161–63; *Madison's Notes,* 56–58; I Madison's *Journal,* 108–9, 114; V Elliott's *Debates,* 155–56, 159–60; III *Documentary History . . . Constitution,* 62–69; *Documents Illustrative . . . Formation of the American States,* 153–54, 158–59.

293. I Farrand's *Records,* 116, 118–20, 124–25; I Elliott's *Debates,* 161–63; *Madison's Notes,* 56–58; I Madison's *Journal,* 108–9, 114; V Elliott's *Debates,* 155–56, 159–60; III *Documentary History . . . Constitution,* 62–69; *Documents Illustrative . . . Formation of the American States,* 153–54, 158–59 (emphasis added).

294. I Farrand's *Records,* 116, 121–22; I Elliott's *Debates,* 161; *Madison's Notes,* 58; I Madison's *Journal,* 110; V Elliott's *Debates,* 156; III *Documentary History . . . Constitution,* 64; *Documents Illustrative . . . Formation of the American States,* 155.

295. I Farrand's *Records,* 117, 121; I Elliott's *Debates,* 161; *Madison's Notes,* 58; I Madison's *Journal,* 110; V Elliott's *Debates,* 156–57; III *Documentary History . . . Constitution,* 64; *Documents Illustrative . . . Formation of the American States,* 155 (emphasis added).

296. I Farrand's *Records,* 117, 121–22; I Elliott's *Debates,* 162; *Madison's Notes,* 58–59; I Madison's *Journal,* 110–11; V Elliott's *Debates,* 157; III *Documentary History . . . Constitution,* 64; *Documents Illustrative . . . Formation of the American States,* 155.

297. I Farrand's *Records,* 149, 156; I Elliott's *Debates,* 165; *Madison's Notes,* 74; I Madison's *Journal,* 130; V Elliott's *Debates,* 170; III *Documentary History . . . Constitution,* 87; *Documents Illustrative . . . Formation of the American States,* 173 (emphasis added).

298. I Farrand's *Records,* 192–93, 200–201; I Elliott's *Debates,* 168; *Madison's Notes,* 88; I Madison's *Journal,* 147; V Elliott's *Debates,* 181; III *Documentary History . . . Constitution,* 102, 106; *Documents Illustrative . . . Formation of the American States,* 189 (emphasis added).

299. I Farrand's *Records,* 193, 202; I Elliott's *Debates,* 169; *Madison's Notes,* 89; I Madison's *Journal,* 148; V Elliott's *Debates,* 182; III *Documentary History . . . Constitution,* 108; *Documents Illustrative . . . Formation of the American States,* 190 (emphasis added).

300. I Farrand's *Records,* 194, 203; I Elliott's *Debates,* 170; *Madison's*

Notes, 90; I Madison's *Journal,* 149; V Elliott's *Debates,* 183; III *Documentary History . . . Constitution,* 109; *Documents Illustrative . . . Formation of the American States,* 191.

301. I Farrand's *Records,* 194, 204; I Elliott's *Debates,* 170; *Madison's Notes,* 90–91; I Madison's *Journal,* 150; V Elliott's *Debates,* 183; III *Documentary History . . . Constitution,* 110; *Documents Illustrative . . . Formation of the American States,* 191–92.

302. I Farrand's *Records,* 209, 214; I Elliott's *Debates,* 170; *Madison's Notes,* 91; I Madison's *Journal,* 150–51; V Elliott's *Debates,* 183; III *Documentary History . . . Constitution,* 110; *Documents Illustrative . . . Formation of the American States,* 192.

[I Elliott's *Debates* misplaces the vote results on June 11 instead of June 12.]

303. I Elliott's *Debates,* 181–83; *Madison's Notes,* 127–29; *Documents Illustrative . . . Formation of the American States,* 234–37 (emphasis added).

304. I Farrand's *Records,* 334–36; I Elliott's *Debates,* 183; *Madison's Notes,* 131–32; I Madison's *Journal,* 199–200; V Elliott's *Debates,* 214; III *Documentary History . . . Constitution,* 166–67; *Documents Illustrative . . . Formation of the American States,* 240–41.

305. I Farrand's *Records,* 335; *Madison's Notes,* 131–32; I Madison's *Journal,* 199–200; V Elliott's *Debates,* 214.

306. I Farrand's *Records,* 336; *Madison's Notes,* 132; I Madison's *Journal,* 200; V Elliott's *Debates,* 214.

307. I Farrand's *Records,* 336; *Madison's Notes,* 132; I Madison's *Journal,* 200; V Elliott's *Debates,* 214.

308. I Farrand's *Records,* 336, 344; *Madison's Notes,* 132; I Madison's *Journal,* 200; V Elliott's *Debates,* 214.

309. See, for instance, Martin's remarks on June 20, 1787. I Farrand's *Records,* 340–41; *Madison's Notes,* 136; I Madison's *Journal,* 204–5; V Elliott's *Debates,* 217–18.

310. III Farrand's *Records,* Appendix A, 195 (document CLVIII, ¶¶ 35 and 36) (Convention Delegate Luther Martin's "Genuine Information" speech, delivered to the Maryland legislature on November 29, 1787, and printed in Dunlap's *Maryland Gazette* and *Baltimore Advertiser* from December 28, 1787, to February 8, 1788).

311. I Farrand's *Records,* 174–75; I Elliott's *Debates,* 167; *Madison's Notes,* 79; I Madison's *Journal,* 136; V Elliott's *Debates,* 174;

III *Documentary History . . . Constitution,* 94; *Documents Illustrative . . . Formation of the American States,* 179.

312. December 26, 1826, letter from Madison to Thomas Cooper (III Farrand's *Records,* Appendix A, 338 [item CCCLVII]; V *Documentary History . . . Constitution,* 338).

313. The official 1787 Convention Journal remained unpublished until 1819, after Congress authorized its publication the previous year. *Journal, Acts and Proceedings, of the Convention . . . Which Formed the Constitution of the United States* (Boston, 1819), published pursuant to Congressional Resolution of March 27, 1818, 15th Cong., 1st Sess., 3 Stat. 175 (resolution reproduced in III Farrand's *Records,* Appendix A, 425 [item CCCXXIII]).

Madison's personal Convention notes did not surface publicly for another two decades, after his death in 1836. On March 3, 1837, Congress authorized the purchase of Madison's Convention notes from Mrs. Madison, and on July 9, 1838, Congress directed their publication. Act of July 9, 1838, 25th Cong., 2d Sess., Ch. 264, 5 Stat. 309–10. The first authorized publication spanned three volumes, titled *The Madison Papers,* with H. Gilpin as editor. I *Madison's Writings,* xxiv.

In 1848, Congress authorized the acquisition of the remainder of Madison's personal papers (Act of May 31, 1848, 30th Cong., 1st Sess., Ch. 52, 9 Stat. 235; I *Madison's Writings,* xxiv), and not until 1856 did Congress authorize the actual publication of this second acquisition of Madison's papers (Act of August 18, 1856, 34th Cong., 1st Sess., Ch. 162, § 1, 11 Stat. 117; I *Madison's Writings,* xxxiv), with four volumes eventually published in 1865 titled *The Works of James Madison.*

314. Brant, *James Madison: Father of the Constitution,* 76.

315. *The Federalist Papers, No. 39.*

316. Ketchum, 207.

317. Farrand, 91. Farrand's abbreviated version of the Convention proceedings—*The Framing of the Constitution of the United States,* cited throughout as "Farrand"—seems to suggest that the deletion of "national" occurred on June 19, 1787. Farrand, 91. However, Farrand's reporting in that particular book merely condenses the late June proceedings, as all of the detailed sources—including Farrand's own *Records*—confirm that the word "national" remained until the June 20, 1787, proceedings. I Farrand's *Records,* 334–36; I Elliott's *Debates,* 183;

Madison's Notes, 131–32; I Madison's *Journal*, 199–200; V Elliott's *Debates*, 214; III *Documentary History . . . Constitution*, 166–67; *Documents Illustrative . . . Formation of the American States*, 240–41.

318. I Farrand's *Records*, 336; *Madison's Notes*, 132; I Madison's *Journal*, 200; V Elliott's *Debates*, 214.

319. March 25, 1826, letter from Madison to Andrew Stevenson (III Farrand's *Records*, Appendix A, 473 [item CCCLVI]; V *Documentary History . . . Constitution*, 332) (underscore in original).

320. March 25, 1826, letter from Madison to Andrew Stevenson (III Farrand's *Records*, Appendix A, 473 [item CCCLVI]; V *Documentary History . . . Constitution*, 332) (underscore in original).

321. Undated December, 1831, letter from Madison to N. P. Trist (III Farrand's *Records*, Appendix A, 517 [item CCCLXXXVIII]; V *Documentary History . . . Constitution*, 377–78).

322. December 26, 1826, letter from Madison to Thomas Cooper (III Farrand's *Records*, Appendix A, 474–75 [item CCCLVII]; V *Documentary History . . . Constitution*, 338) (underscore in original).

323. Undated December, 1831, letter from Madison to N. P. Trist (III Farrand's *Records*, Appendix A, 517 [item CCCLXXXVI-II]; V *Documentary History . . . Constitution*, 377) (underscore in original).

Chapter 6

1. *Chisholm v. Georgia*, 2 U.S. (2 Dall.) 419, 477 (1793) (Chief Justice Jay's opinion). Before Chief Justice Marshall's era (*viz.* prior to February, 1801). Supreme Court justices wrote individual opinions and the result became essentially a vote count; the Court rendered no single opinion designated as the judgment of the "Court." Marshall, who served as chief justice from 1801 to 1835, changed that practice, and implemented the process that the Court still uses: a single opinion embraced by a majority of the justices deemed to be the Court's judgment. In *Chisholm*, the individual opinions of Justices Jay, Blair, Wilson, and Cushing formed a four-to-one majority over the single differing opinion of Justice Iredell.

2. *South Carolina v. United States*, 199 U.S. 437, 448 (1905).

3. Levy, *Origins of the Bill of Rights*, 79 (emphasis added).

4. See, for instance, his opinions in *Gompers v. United States*, 233 U.S. 604, 610–13 (1914); *Missouri v. Holland*, 252 U.S. 416, 432–35 (1920); *International Stevedoring Co. v. Haverty*, 272 U.S. 50, 52 (1926); and

Boston Sand & Gravel Co. v. United States, 278 U.S. 41, 46–49 (1928).

5. W. Rehnquist, "The Notion of a Living Constitution," 29 *Harv. Jour. Law & Pub. Pol.* 401, 402 (Spring 2006), reprinting W. Rehnquist, "The Notion of a Living Constitution," 54 *Tex. L. Rev.* 693 (1976), citing Holmes's opinion in *Missouri v. Holland,* 252 U.S. 416, 432–35 (1920).

6. Holmes referenced a "penumbra" in his individual opinions in *Hanover Star Milling Co. v. Metcalf,* 240 U.S. 403, 426 (1916) (Holmes, J., concurring); *Schlesinger v. State of Wisconsin,* 270 U.S. 230, 241 (1926) (Holmes, J., dissenting); *Springer v. Government of the Philippine Islands,* 277 U.S. 189, 209 (1928) (Holmes, J., dissenting); and *Olmstead v. United States,* 277 U.S. 438, 469 (1928) (Holmes, J., dissenting).

7. Rakove, 342–43.

8. August 24, 1855, letter from Lincoln to Joshua Speed (2 *Lincoln's Works,* 323; Donald, 189; Sandburg, *Lincoln's Prairie Years,* 320).

9. September 15, 1821, letter from James Madison to Thomas Ritchie (III *Madison's Letters,* 228; IX *Madison's Writings,* 72; III Farrand's *Records,* 447 (Appendix A, item CCCXL); V *Documentary History . . . Constitution,* 310–11); see also December 27, 1821, letter from James Madison to John Jackson (IX *Madison's Writings,* 74) (expressing same belief).

10. See, for instance, Justice Stevens's remarks in his concurring opinion in *Roper v. Simmons,* 543 U.S. 551, 587 (2005) (Stevens, J., concurring) (urging that the meaning of one of the first ten amendments ought not be "frozen [in time] when it was originally drafted," and embracing the notion that "our understanding of the Constitution does change from time to time"); former Justice Brennan's remarks in *Marsh v. Chambers,* 463 U.S. 783, 816 (1983) (Brennan, J., dissenting) (declaring that he would not consider the Constitution as a "static" document); the Court's opinion in *Trop v. Dulles,* 356 U.S. 86, 101 (1958) (in which the Court declared that a constitutional amendment "must draw its meaning from the evolving standards of decency that mark the progress of a maturing society."); the Court's opinion in *Wolf v. Colorado,* 338 U.S. 25, 27 (1949) (declaring, in effect, that the Constitution means whatever the courts think it means at any particular time, by "the gradual and empiric process of inclusion and exclusion"); and the Court's opinion

in *Weems v. United States*, 217 U.S. 349, 373, 378 (1910) (declaring that "[a] principle, to be vital, must be capable of wider application than the mischief which gave it birth"—a notion "peculiarly true of constitutions," and that the meaning of a constitutional amendment "may acquire meaning as public opinion becomes enlightened").

Former Justice Brennan, for one, repeatedly declared that the meaning of the various parts to the Constitution necessarily change with time, and that he would never consider otherwise. W. Brennan, "The Constitution of the United States: Contemporary Ratification," 27 *South Texas Law Review* 433, 438 (Fall 1986); W. Brennan, "Construing the Constitution," 19 *Univ. Cal. Davis L. Rev.* 2, 7 (1985); W. Brennan, *The New York Times*, October 13, 1985, 36.

> 11. Where a meaning is clear, the consequences, whatever they may be, are to be admitted—where doubtful, it is fairly triable by its consequences.
>
> In controverted cases, the meaning of the parties to the instrument, if to be collected by reasonable evidence, is a proper guide.
>
> Contemporary and current expositions are a reasonable evidence of the meaning of the parties.

2 *Annals of Congress*, 1946 (House of Representatives Proceedings of February 2, 1791) (Statement of Representative Madison) (debate of the constitutionality of a national bank).

12. As explained in Chapter 5, the Senate recorded no debates, only vote results.

13. See Chapter 2, note 49.

14. See Chapter 2, note 52.

15. III Story, *Commentaries on the Constitution* (1833 ed.), § 1867, 724 (emphasis added).

16. III Story, *Commentaries on the Constitution* (1833 ed.), § 1868, 726; II Story, *Commentaries on the Constitution* (1891 ed.), 630 (emphasis added).

17. III Story, *Commentaries on the Constitution* (1833 ed.), § 1871, 728 (emphasis added).

18. III Story, *Commentaries on the Constitution* (1833 ed.), § 1873, 731 (emphasis added).

19. *Holy Trinity Church v. United States*, 143 U.S. 457, 471 (1892).

20. Cooley, *General Principles of Constitutional Law*, Ch. XIII, § 1, 224 (emphasis added).

21. *Terrett v. Taylor*, 13 U.S. (9 Cranch) 43 (1815).

22. See Chapter 3A.

23. See Chapter 3D.

24. The Court's opinion in *Terrett* quotes from Article 16 of Virginia's June 12, 1776, Declaration of Rights, which provided:

> 16. That Religion, or the duty which we owe to our Creator, and the manner of discharging it, can be directed only by reason and conviction, not by force or violence; and, therefore, all men are equally entitled to the free exercise of religion, according to the dictates of conscience; and that it is the mutual duty of all to practise [sic] Christian forbearance, love, and charity, towards each other.

1 *Madison's Papers*, 175; I *Madison's Writings*, 40; I *Mason's Papers*, 289; 7 *Federal and State Constitutions*, 3814; 10 *Sources and Documents*, 50; VIII *Documentary History . . . Ratification*, 530–31; *Sources of Our Liberties*, 312; 5 *Founders' Constitution*, 9.

25. *Terrett*, 13 U.S. (9 Cranch) at 48–49 (emphasis added).

26. See the Court's 1984 opinion in *Lynch v. Donnelly*, 465 U.S. 668, 678 (1984).

27. *Everson v. Board of Education*, 330 U.S. 1 (1947); *McCollum v. Board of Education*, 333 U.S. 203 (1948); *Zorach v. Clauson*, 343 U.S. 306 (1952); *McGowan v. Maryland*, 366 U.S. 420 (1961); *Two Guys v. McGinley*, 366 U.S. 582 (1961); *Braunfeld v. Brown*, 366 U.S. 599 (1961); *Gallagher v. Crown Kosher Market*, 366 U.S. 617 (1961); *Engel v. Vitale*, 370 U.S. 421 (1962); *Abington School District v. Schempp*, 374 U.S. 203 (1963); *Board of Education v. Allen*, 392 U.S. 236 (1968); *Epperson v. Arkansas*, 393 U.S. 97 (1968); *Walz v. Tax Commission*, 397 U.S. 664 (1970); *Gillette v. United States*, 401 U.S. 437 (1971); *Lemon v. Kurtzman*, 403 U.S. 602 (1971); *Tilton v. Richardson*, 403 U.S. 672 (1971); *Levitt v. Committee for Public Education*, 413 U.S. 472 (1973); *Hunt v. McNair*, 413 U.S. 734 (1973); *Committee for Public Education v. Nyquist*, 413 U.S. 756 (1973); *Sloan v. Lemon*, 413 U.S. 825 (1973); *Meek v. Pittenger*, 421 U.S. 349 (1975); *Roemer v. Maryland Board of Public Works*, 426 U.S. 736 (1976); *Wolman v. Walter*, 433 U.S. 229 (1977); *Committee for Public Education & Religious Liberty v. Regan*, 444 U.S. 646 (1980); *Stone v. Graham*, 449 U.S. 39 (1980); *Widmar v. Vincent*, 454 U. S. 263 (1981); *Larson v. Valente*, 456 U.S. 228 (1982); *Larkin v. Grendel's Den, Inc.*, 459 U.S. 116 (1982); *Mueller v. Allen*, 463 U.S. 388 (1983); and *Marsh v. Chambers*, 463 U.S. 783 (1983).

28. *Lynch*, 465 U.S. at 678, citing III Story, *Commentaries on the Constitution* (1833 ed.), § 1871, 728.

29. See, for instance, Powell, 948.

It is commonly assumed that the "interpretive intention" of the Constitution's framers was that the Constitution would be construed in accordance with what future interpreters could gather of the framers' own *purposes, expectations, and intentions.* Inquiry shows that assumption to be *incorrect."*

Id. (emphasis added).

30. U.S. Const., Art. V, 1 Stat. 19 (emphasis added).

31. *Chisholm v. Georgia,* 2 U.S. (2 Dall.) 419 (1793).

32. *Chisholm,* 2 U.S. (2 Dall.) at 468 (opinion of Justice Cushing).

33. June 25, 1824, letter from James Madison to Henry Lee (IX *Madison's Writings,* 191–92; III *Madison's Letters,* 442–43; III Farrand's *Records,* 464 (Appendix A, item CCCLI) (emphasis added)).

34. June 25, 1824, letter from James Madison to Henry Lee (IX *Madison's Writings,* 191–92; III *Madison's Letters,* 442–43; III Farrand's *Records,* 464 (Appendix A, item CCCLI)).

35. August 28, 1830, letter from James Madison to Edward Everett (IX *Madison's Writings,* 401; IV *Madison's Letters,* 104).

36. See Chapter 14A.

37. June 12, 1823, letter from Thomas Jefferson to Supreme Court Justice William Johnson (XV *Jefferson's Writings* (1903 ed.), 447–49; VII *Jefferson's Writings* (1853 ed.), 290; XII *Jefferson's Works,* 256–57 note; *Jefferson*—"Letters," 1474; IV *Jefferson's Memoirs,* 373).

38. The Constitution actually prescribes two ratification processes, one in Article VII for the Constitution itself (votes of at least nine states) and one in Article V for any proposed amendments (votes of at least three-fourths of the states).

39. Rakove, 17–18.

40. See, for instance, a September 15, 1821, letter from James Madison to Thomas Ritchie (III *Madison's Letters,* 228; IX *Madison's Writings,* 72; III Farrand's *Records,* 447 (Appendix A, item CCCXL); V *Documentary History . . . Constitution,* 310–11); a December 27, 1821, letter from James Madison to John Jackson (IX *Madison's Writings,* 74).

41. 5 *Annals of Congress,* 776 (House of Representatives Proceedings of April 6, 1796) (Statement of Representative Madison); 3 Farrand's *Records,* 374 (Appendix A item CCLXVI). See also 16 *Madison's Papers* 295–96.

42. See 3 Farrand's *Records,* 587–90 (Appendix B) ("Attendance of Delegates") (identifying the signatories).

43. Rakove, 18 (emphasis added).

Chapter 7

1. 2 *Annals of Congress,* 1st Cong., 3rd Sess., 1946 (House of Representatives Proceedings of February 2, 1791) (Statement of Representative Madison) (debate of the constitutionality of a national bank).

2. *Chisholm v. Georgia,* 2 U.S. (2 Dall.) 419 (1793).

[Early volumes of the "U.S." Reports of Supreme Court decisions also bore the name of the individual Supreme Court reporter: "Dall." (for Dallas) for volumes 1 through 4; "Cranch" for volumes 5 through 13; "Wheat." (for Wheaton) for volumes 14 through 25; "Pet." (for Peters) for volumes 26 through 41; "How." (for Howard) for volumes 42 through 65; "Black" for volumes 66 and 67; "Wall." (for Wallace) for volumes 68 through 90; and "Otto" for volumes 91 through 107.]

3. Act of September 24, 1789, 1st Cong., 1st Sess., Ch. 20, 1 Stat. 73–93, reproduced in 2 *Annals of Congress,* Appendix, 2239–55.

4. I *Documentary History . . . First Federal Congress,* 67 (Proceedings of June 12, 1789); 1 *Senate Journal,* 1st Cong., 1st Sess., 34 (Proceedings of June 12, 1789); 1 *Annals of Congress,* 1st Cong., 1st Sess., 47 (Senate Proceedings of June 12, 1789).

5. See, for instance: *Turner v. Bank of North America,* 4 U.S. (4 Dall.) 8, 10 (1799); *United States v. Hudson & Goodwin,* 11 U.S. (7 Cranch) 32, 33 (1812); *McIntire v. Wood,* 11 U.S. (7 Cranch) 504, 506 (1813); *Osborn v. Bank of the United States,* 22 U.S. (9 Wheat.) 738, 822–23 (1824); *Cary v. Curtis,* 44 U.S. (3 How.) 236, 244–45 (1845); *Sheldon v. Sill,* 49 U.S. (8 How.) 441, 449 (1850); and *Mayor v. Cooper,* 73 U.S. (6 Wall.) 247, 252 (1867).

6. Article III, Section 2, authorizes the federal courts to hear nine categories of "cases" and "controversies":

    (1) "all cases, in law and equity, arising under this Constitution, the laws of the United States, and treaties made, or which shall be made, under their authority";

    (2) ". . . all cases affecting ambassadors, other public ministers and consuls";

    (3) ". . . all cases of admiralty and maritime jurisdiction";

    (4) ". . . controversies to which the United States shall be a party";

(5) ". . . controversies between two or more states";

(6) ". . . [controversies] between a state and citizens of another state";

(7) ". . . [controversies] between citizens of different states";

(8) ". . . [controversies] between citizens of the same state claiming lands under grants of different states"; and

(9) ". . . [controversies] between a state, or the citizens thereof, and foreign states, citizens or Subjects."

U.S. Const., Art. III, § 2, 1 Stat. 17–18.

7. Only the individual opinion of Justice Iredell mentioned the 1789 Judiciary Act specifically. 2 U.S. (2 Dall.) at 431. Yet no doubt exists that Section 13 of that act lay at the heart of the case.

8. Senator Maclay's *Journal* confirms that Senator Ellsworth authored the Judiciary Act:

> This vile bill [viz., the Judiciary Act] is a child of his [referring to Ellsworth], and he defends it with the care of a parent, even with wrath and anger. He kindled, as he always does, when it is meddled with.

Maclay's Journal, 91–92 (notes of June 29, 1789); IX *Documentary History . . . First Federal Congress,* 91 (notes of June 29, 1789). The Supreme Court's opinion in *Myers v. United States,* 272 U.S. 52, 122 (1926), separately confirms that Sen. Ellsworth "was the author of the Judiciary Act in that Congress."

9. I *Documentary History . . . First Federal Congress,* 11 (Proceedings of April 7, 1789); 1 *Senate Journal,* 1st Cong., 1st Sess., 10 (Proceedings of April 7, 1789); 1 *Annals of Congress,* 1st Cong., 1st Sess., 18 (Senate Proceedings of April 7, 1789).

I *Documentary History . . . First Federal Congress,* 14 (Proceedings of April 13, 1789); 1 *Senate Journal,* 1st Cong., 1st Sess., 11 (Proceedings of April 13, 1789); 1 *Annals of Congress,* 1st Cong., 1st Sess., 19 (Senate Proceedings of April 13, 1789).

10. See I Elliott's *Debates,* 124–25; III Farrand's *Records,* Appendix B, 557–59 ("List of Delegates") and 587–90 ("Attendance of Delegates").

11. Eleven states—all except North Carolina and Rhode Island—had elected senators to serve during the First Session of the First Congress that began in March 1789 and adjourned in September 1789. See I *Documentary History . . . First Federal Congress,* 3, 5, 6, 7, 13, 15, 21, 51, 61, 91; 1 *Senate Journal,* 1st Cong., 1st Sess., (unnumbered

page) 5, 7, 10–11, 14, 28, 31, 44, 45; and 1 *Annals of Congress,* 1st Cong., 1st Sess., 16, 18, 19, 22, 40, 46, 53 (Senate Proceedings) (each chronicling the appearances of the various senators during the proceedings of March 4, 19, 21, 28; April 6, 13, 14, 20; May 21; June 8; July 25 and 27, 1789).

The senators from North Carolina and Rhode Island did not appear until the Second and Third Sessions, respectively, of the First Congress. 1 *Senate Journal,* 1st Cong., 2nd Sess., 105, 109 (Proceedings of January 13 and 29, 1790) (North Carolina); 1 *Annals of Congress,* 1st Cong., 2nd Sess., 973, 978 (Senate Proceedings of January 13 and 29, 1790) (North Carolina); 1 *Senate Journal,* 1st Cong., 3rd Sess., 222 (Proceedings of December 15 and 17, 1790) (Rhode Island); 2 *Annals of Congress,* 1st Cong., 3rd Sess., 1777 (Senate Proceedings of December 15 and 17, 1790) (Rhode Island).

12. Senators Bassett (DE), Butler (SC), Ellsworth (MA), Few (GA), Johnson (CT), Langdon (NH), Morris (PA), Paterson (NJ), Read (DE), and Strong (MA) had been delegates at the 1787 Constitutional Convention. I Elliott's *Debates,* 124–25; III Farrand's *Records,* Appendix B, 557–59, 587–90. All except Strong and Ellsworth signed the Constitution. (Only thirty-nine delegates signed the Constitution. III Farrand's *Records,* 587–90 (Appendix B) ("Attendance of Delegates") (identifying the signatories).)

13. Article I, Section 2, of the Constitution prescribed no more than sixty-five representatives for the inaugural Congress:

> The Number of Representatives shall not exceed one for every thirty Thousand, but each State shall have at Least one Representative; and until such enumeration shall be made, the State of New Hampshire shall be entitled to choose three, Massachusetts eight, Rhode-Island and Providence Plantations one, Connecticut five, New-York six, New Jersey four, Pennsylvania eight, Delaware one, Maryland six, Virginia ten, North Carolina five, South Carolina five, and Georgia three.

U.S. Const., Art. I, § 2, 1 Stat. 10–11. However, neither North Carolina nor Rhode Island sent representatives to the inaugural Congress, thus reducing the actual number of representatives to fifty-nine for the First Session of the First Congress in 1789. See III *Documentary History . . . First Federal Congress,* 3–8, 16, 18, 25, 28, 30, 31, 43, 49, 54, 71, 83, 87, 89, 149; 1 *House Journal,* 1st Cong., 1st Sess., (unnumbered page) 3, 4, 5, 6, 7, 11, 12, 16, 18, 19, 24, 29, 31, 40, 46, 48, 49, 79; and 1 *Annals of Congress,* 1st Cong., 1st Sess., (unnumbered page) 99, 100, 101, 106, 109, 126, 167, 178, 199, 241, 242, 276, 306, 425, 440, 471, 498, 745 (House of Representatives Proceedings) (each chronicling the appearances of the various representatives during the proceedings of March 4, 5, 14, 17, 18, 23, 25, and 30; April 1, 2, 3, 4, 6, 8, 9, 13, 17, 20, 22, 23, and 30; May 1, 6, 9, and 25, June 8, 15, and 17; and August 14, 1789).

The representatives from North Carolina and Rhode Island did not appear until the Second and Third Sessions, respectively, of the First Congress. 1 *House Journal,* 1st Cong., 2nd Sess., 178, 182, 190, 196, 243 (Proceedings of March 19 and 24, April 6 and 19, and June 16, 1790) (North Carolina); 2 *Annals of Congress,* 1st Cong., 2nd Sess., 1514, 1525, 1572, 1584, 1696 (House of Representatives Proceedings of March 19 and 24, April 6 and 19, and June 16, 1790) (North Carolina); 1 *House Journal,* 1st Cong., 3rd Sess., 338 (Proceedings of December 17, 1790) (Rhode Island); 2 *Annals of Congress,* 1st Cong., 3rd Sess., 1859 (House of Representatives Proceedings of December 17, 1790) (Rhode Island).

14. Representatives Sherman (CT), Baldwin (GA), Carroll (MD), Gerry (MA), Gilman (NH), Clymer (PA), Fitzsimons (PA), and Madison (VA) had been delegates at the 1787 Constitutional Convention. I Elliott's *Debates,* 124–25; III Farrand's *Records,* Appendix B, 557–59, 587–90. All except Gerry signed the Constitution. (Only thirty-nine delegates signed the Constitution. III Farrand's *Records,* 587–90 (Appendix B) ("Attendance of Delegates").)

15. In *Chisholm,* the individual opinions of Justices Blair, Wilson, Cushing, and Jay (2 U.S. (2 Dall.) at 450–53, 453–66, 466–69, 469–79, respectively) formed a four-to-one majority over the single differing opinion of Justice Iredell (2 U.S. (2 Dall.) at 429–50).

16. *Ames v. Kansas,* 111 U.S. at 449 (1884).

17. *Ames v. Kansas,* 111 U.S. at 464.

18. Ibid.

19. *Ames v. Kansas,* 111 U.S. at 469, referring to the 1789 Judiciary Act that implemented Article III, Section 2, of the Constitution.

20. *Wisconsin v. Pelican Insurance Co.,* 127 U.S. at 265 (1888).

21. *Wisconsin v. Pelican Insurance Co.,* 127 U.S. at 297.

22. *Myers v. United States,* 272 U.S. 52 (1926).

23. Act of July 27, 1789, 1st Cong., 1st Sess., Ch. 4, 1 Stat. 28–29 (An Act for Establishing an Executive Department).

24. *Myers,* 272 U.S. 174–75 (emphasis added).

25. 1 *Senate Journal,* 1st Cong., 1st Sess., 16 (Proceedings of April 25, 1789); I *Documentary History . . . First Federal Congress,* 25 (Proceedings of April 25, 1789).

26. 1 *House Journal,* 1st Cong., 1st Sess., 26 (Proceedings of May 1, 1789); III *Documentary History . . . First Federal Congress,* 44 (Proceedings of May 1, 1789).

27. "An Act for Allowing Compensation to the Members of the Senate and House of Representatives of the United States, and to the Officers of Both Houses," 1 *House Journal,* 1st Cong., 1st Sess., 75–76 (Proceedings of August 10, 1789); III *Documentary History . . . First Federal Congress,* 141–42 (Proceedings of August 10, 1789); 1 *Annals of Congress,* 1st Cong., 1st Sess., 714–15 (House of Representatives Proceedings of August 10, 1789).

Although the *House Journal* does not contain the text of the bill (HB 19 [see 1 *House Journal,* 1st Cong., 1st Sess., 746] [list of House bills]), the subsequent Senate debates—as well as the text of the eventual legislation itself—identify "each [congressional] chaplain" as included within the compensation bill. 1 *Senate Journal,* 1st Cong., 1st Sess., 67 (Proceedings of August 28, 1789); I *Documentary History . . . First Federal Congress,* 144 (Proceedings of August 28, 1789).

28. 1 *Senate Journal,* 1st Cong., 1st Sess., 68 (Proceedings of August 31, 1789); I *Documentary History . . . First Federal Congress,* 146 (Proceedings of August 31, 1789); 1 *Annals of Congress,* 1st Cong., 1st Sess., 75 (Senate Proceedings of August 31, 1789).

29. 1 *Senate Journal,* 1st Cong., 1st Sess., 80 (Proceedings of September 14, 1789); I *Documentary History . . . First Federal Congress,* 174 (Proceedings of September 14, 1789); 1 *House Journal,* 110 (Proceedings of September 14, 1789); III *Documentary History . . . First Federal Congress,* 205 (Proceedings of September 14, 1789).

30. Act of September 22, 1789, 1st Cong., 1st Sess., Ch. 17, § 4, 1 Stat. 71 ("That there shall be allowed to each chaplain of Congress, at the rate of five hundred dollars per annum during the session of Congress[.]"). Congress renewed the chaplain compensation measure in 1796 (Act of March 10, 1796, 4th Cong., 1st Sess., Ch. 5, § 3, 1 Stat. 449) and again in 1816 (Act of April 30, 1816, 14th Cong., 1st Sess., Ch. 170, 3 Stat. 334).

31. See 2 USC § 61d (Senate Chaplain) and 2 USC § 84–2

(House Chaplain), prescribing current House and Senate Chaplains' salaries.

32. Senate Rule IV provides, in pertinent part (as of this writing):

> 1(a)The Presiding Officer having taken the chair, *following the prayer of the Chaplain*, . . . the Journal of the preceding day shall be read . . . [.]
>
> 2. During a session of the Senate when that body is in continuous session, the Presiding Officer shall temporarily suspend the business of the Senate at noon each day *for the purpose of having the customary daily prayer by the Chaplain.*

Senate Rule IV, paragraphs 1(a) and 2, Standing Rules of the Senate, S. Doc. No. 106–15, 106th Cong., 2nd Sess. (emphasis added).

House of Representative Rule II provides, in pertinent part (as of this writing):

> 1. There shall be elected at the commencement of each Congress, . . . *a Chaplain.* . . .
>
> 5. *The Chaplain shall offer a prayer at the commencement of each day's sitting of the House.*

House of Representatives Rule II, Clauses 1 and 5, The Rules of the House of Representatives, H. Doc. No. 107–284, 107th Cong., 2nd Sess. (emphasis added).

33. *Marsh v. Chambers*, 463 U.S. 783 (1983).

34. *Marsh*, 463 U.S. at 786.

35. Ibid.

36. Ibid., at 788.

37. *Marsh*, 463 U.S. at 788–90, quoting from *Wisconsin v. Pelican Ins. Co.*, 127 U.S. 265, 297 (1888), discussed earlier in this chapter.

38. Act of September 22, 1789, 1st Cong., 1st Sess., Ch. 17, § 4, 1 Stat. 71.

The Senate concurred in the House's final revisions to the Establishment Clause (and other amendments) just three days earlier, on September 25, 1789—thus concluding congressional consideration of the first set of constitutional amendments. I *Documentary History* . . . *First Federal Congress,* 192 (Proceedings of September 25, 1789); 1 *Senate Journal,* 1st Cong., 1st Sess., 88 (Proceedings of September 25, 1789); 1 *Annals of Congress,* 1st Cong., 1st Sess., 90 (Senate Proceedings of September 25, 1789); IV *Documentary History* . . . *First Federal Congress,* 9; *Complete Bill of Rights,* 10–11 (reporting from the official Senate Journal). A day later, the Senate separately concurred in the House's proposed joint resolution that the finalized set of amendments be sent to the states for ratification. I *Documentary History . . . First Federal Congress,* 198 (Proceedings of September 26, 1789); 1 Senate Journal, 1st Cong., 1st Sess., 90 (Proceedings of September 26, 1789); IV *Documentary History . . . First Federal Congress,* 9. On September 28, 1789, the president transmitted the proposed amendments to the states for ratification, pursuant to the House/Senate Joint Resolution reproduced in: 1 Stat. 97–98; IV *Documentary History . . . First Federal Congress,* 1; "Appendix" in 1 *Senate Journal,* 96–97; *Madison's Notes,* 689–91; I Elliott's *Debates,* 338–39; II *Documentary History . . . Constitution,* 321–24; *Documents Illustrative . . . Formation of the American States,* 1063–65.

39. *Marsh,* 463 at 790.

40. *Marsh,* 463 at 789 n. 9. See Chapter 7D.

41. An Act to Establish the Judicial Courts of the United States, Act of September 24, 1789, 1st Cong., 1st Sess., Ch. 20, 1 Stat. 73–93, reproduced in 2 *Annals of Congress,* Appendix, 2239–55.

42. Act of September 24, 1789, 1st Cong., 1st Sess., Ch. 20, §§ 7 and 8, 1 Stat. 76 (emphasis added).

> 43. Each justice or judge of the United States shall take the following oath or affirmation before performing the duties of his office: "I, ___ XXX, do solemnly swear (or affirm) that I will administer justice without respect to persons, and do equal right to the poor and to the rich, and that I will faithfully and impartially discharge and perform all the duties incumbent upon me as ___ under the Constitution and laws of the United States. *So help me God.*"

28 USC § 453 (emphasis added).

44. XXXI *Journals of the Continental Congress,* 667 n. 1 (Proceedings of September 18, 1786).

45. XXXI *Journals of the Continental Congress,* 669–72 (Proceedings of September 19, 1786).

46. XXXI *Journals of the Continental Congress,* 669 (Proceedings of September 19, 1786).

47. **September 21, 1786** (XXXI *Journals of the Continental Congress,* 686 n. 1 (Proceedings of September 21, 1786)); **April 26, 1787** (XXXII *Journals of the Continental Congress,* 242 (Proceedings of April 26, 1787)); **May 9, 1787** (XXXII *Journals of the Continental Congress,* 275 (Proceedings of May 9, 1787)); **May 10, 1787** (XXXII *Journals of*

the Continental Congress, 281–83 (Proceedings of May 10, 1787)); **July 9, 1787** (XXXII *Journals of the Continental Congress,* 310 n. 3 (Proceedings of July 9, 1787)); **July 11, 1787** (XXXII *Journals of the Continental Congress,* 314–20 (Proceedings of July 11, 1787)); **July 12, 1787** (XXXII *Journals of the Continental Congress,* 333 n. 1 (Proceedings of July 12, 1787)); and **July 13, 1787** (XXXII *Journals of the Continental Congress,* 334–43 (Proceedings of July 13, 1787)).

48. XXXII *Journals of the Continental Congress,* 314 (Proceedings of July 11, 1787) and 334 (Proceedings of July 13, 1787).

49. XXXII *Journals of the Continental Congress,* 318 (Proceedings of July 11, 1787) (emphasis added).

50. See XXXII *Journals of the Continental Congress,* 334–43 (Proceedings of July 13, 1787); *Documents Illustrative . . . Formation of the American States,* 47–54; 1 *Sources and Documents* (2nd series), 383–90; *Sources of Our Liberties,* 392–97.

51. XXXII *Journals of the Continental Congress,* 340 (Proceedings of July 13, 1787); *Documents Illustrative . . . Formation of the American States,* 52; 1 *Sources and Documents* (2nd series), 388; *Sources of Our Liberties,* 396 (emphasis added).

52. XXXII *Journals of the Continental Congress,* 342 (Proceedings of July 13, 1787) (emphasis added).

53. III *Documentary History . . . First Federal Congress,* 113, 114, 116 (Proceedings of July 16, 17, and 20, 1789); 1 *House Journal,* 1st Cong., 1st Sess., 61, 62, 63 (Proceedings of July 16, 17, and 20, 1789); 1 *Annals of Congress,* 1st Cong., 1st Sess., 667, 684, 685 (House of Representatives Proceedings of July 16, 17, and 20, 1789); VI *Documentary History . . . First Federal Congress,* 1560.

54. III *Documentary History . . . First Federal Congress,* 116–17 (Proceedings of July 21, 1789); 1 *House Journal,* 1st Cong., 1st Sess., 63 (Proceedings of July 21, 1789); 1 *Annals of Congress,* 1st Cong., 1st Sess., 685 (House of Representatives Proceedings of July 21, 1789); VI *Documentary History . . . First Federal Congress,* 1560–61.

55. I *Documentary History . . . First Federal Congress,* 89, 103, 104 (Proceedings of July 21, July 31, and August 3, 1789); 1 *Senate Journal,* 1st Cong., 1st Sess., 44, 51 (Proceedings of July 21, July 31, and August 3, 1789); 1 *Annals of Congress,* 1st Cong., 1st Sess., 52, 56 (Senate Proceedings of July 21, July 31, and August 3, 1789); VI *Documentary History . . . First Federal Congress,* 1560–61.

56. I *Documentary History . . . First Federal Congress,* 105–6

(Proceedings of August 4, 1789); 1 *Senate Journal*, 1st Cong., 1st Sess., 52 (Proceedings of August 4, 1789); 1 *Annals of Congress*, 1st Cong., 1st Sess., 57 (Senate Proceedings of August 4, 1789); VI *Documentary History . . . First Federal Congress*, 1561.

57. III *Documentary History . . . First Federal Congress*, 133–34 (Proceedings of August 5, 1789); 1 *House Journal*, 1st Cong., 1st Sess., 71–72 (Proceedings of August 5, 1789); 1 *Annals of Congress*, 1st Cong., 1st Sess., 702 (House of Representatives Proceedings of August 5, 1789); VI *Documentary History . . . First Federal Congress*, 1561.

58. I *Documentary History . . . First Federal Congress*, 108 (Proceedings of August 5, 1789); 1 *Senate Journal*, 1st Cong., 1st Sess., 53 (Proceedings of August 5, 1789); 1 *Annals of Congress*, 1st Cong., 1st Sess., 57–58 (Senate Proceedings of August 5, 1789); VI *Documentary History . . . First Federal Congress*, 1561.

59. III *Documentary History . . . First Federal Congress*, 135–36 (Proceedings of August 6, 1789); 1 *House Journal*, 1st Cong., 1st Sess., 72 (Proceedings of August 6, 1789); VI *Documentary History . . . First Federal Congress*, 1561.

See also I *Documentary History . . . First Federal Congress*, 110 (Proceedings of August 6, 1789) (Senate informed of preparation of final bill); 1 *Senate Journal*, 1st Cong., 1st Sess., 54 (Proceedings of August 6, 1789) (Senate informed of preparation of final bill); VI *Documentary History . . . First Federal Congress*, 1561.

60. III *Documentary History . . . First Federal Congress*, 137 (Proceedings of August 7, 1789); 1 *House Journal*, 1st Cong., 1st Sess., 73 (Proceedings of August 7, 1789); VI *Documentary History . . . First Federal Congress*, 1561.

61. III *Documentary History . . . First Federal Congress*, 139 (Proceedings of August 7, 1789); 1 *House Journal*, 1st Cong., 1st Sess., 74 (Proceedings of August 7, 1789); VI *Documentary History . . . First Federal Congress*, 1561; I *Documentary History . . . First Federal Congress*, 114 (Proceedings of August 8, 1789) (Senate informed by House of president's signature); 1 *Senate Journal*, 1st Cong., 1st Sess., 56 (Proceedings of August 8, 1789) (Senate informed by House of president's signature); VI *Documentary History . . . First Federal Congress*, 1561.

62. An Act to Provide for the Government of the Territory Northwest of the River Ohio, Act of August 7, 1789, 1st Cong., 1st Sess., Ch. 8, 1 Stat. 52 n. "(a)" (reproducing the text of the Third

Article of the 1787 Northwest Ordinance) (emphasis added). See also *Documents Illustrative . . . Formation of the American States,* 47–54; 1 *Sources and Documents* (2nd series), 383–90; *Sources of Our Liberties,* 392–97.

63. Act of August 7, 1789, 1st Cong., 1st Sess., Ch. 8, 1 Stat. 52 n. "(a)" (reproducing the text of the Third Article of the 1787 Northwest Ordinance as enacted by the Continental Congress, XXXII *Journals of the Continental Congress,* 342) (Proceedings of July 13, 1787) (emphasis added). See also *Documents Illustrative . . . Formation of the American States,* 47–54; 1 *Sources and Documents* (2nd series), 383–90; *Sources of Our Liberties,* 392–97.

64. See *Everson v. Board of Education,* 330 U.S. 1 (1947); *McCollum v. Board of Education,* 333 U.S. 203 (1948); *Zorach v. Clauson,* 343 U.S. 306 (1952); *McGowan v. Maryland,* 366 U.S. 420 (1961); *Two Guys v. McGinley,* 366 U.S. 582 (1961); *Braunfeld v. Brown,* 366 U.S. 599 (1961); and *Gallagher v. Crown Kosher Market,* 366 U.S. 617 (1961).

65. *Engel v. Vitale,* 370 U.S. 421 (1962).

66. *Engel v. Vitale,* 370 U.S. 421, 443 n. 9 (1962) (Douglas, J., concurring).

67. Following the Supreme Court's 1962 decision in *Engel,* the Court rendered an additional twenty-two decisions up to 1985 that involved the Establishment Clause without once mentioning the Northwest Ordinance: *Abington School District v. Schempp,* 374 U.S. 203 (1963); *Board of Education v. Allen,* 392 U.S. 236 (1968); *Epperson v. Arkansas,* 393 U.S. 97 (1968); *Walz v. Tax Commission,* 397 U.S. 664 (1970); *Gillette v. United States,* 401 U.S. 437 (1971); *Lemon v. Kurtzman,* 403 U.S. 602 (1971); *Tilton v. Richardson,* 403 U.S. 672 (1971); *Levitt v. Committee for Public Education,* 413 U.S. 472 (1973); *Hunt v. McNair,* 413 U.S. 734 (1973); *Committee for Public Education v. Nyquist,* 413 U.S. 756 (1973); *Sloan v. Lemon,* 413 U.S. 825 (1973); *Meek v. Pittenger,* 421 U.S. 349 (1975) (later declared an "anomaly" and "no longer good law" in *Mitchell v. Helms,* 530 U.S. 793, 808 (2000)); *Roemer v. Maryland Board of Public Works,* 426 U.S. 736 (1976); *Wolman v. Walter,* 433 U.S. 229 (1977) (later declared an "anomaly" and "no longer good law" in *Mitchell v. Helms,* 530 U.S. 793, 808 (2000)) *Committee for Public Education & Religious Liberty v. Regan,* 444 U.S. 646 (1980); *Stone v. Graham,* 449 U.S. 39 (1980); *Widmar v. Vincent,* 454 U.S. 263 (1981); *Larson v. Valente,* 456 U.S. 228

(1982); *Larkin v. Grendel's Den, Inc.*, 459 U.S. 116 (1982); *Mueller v. Allen*, 463 U.S. 388 (1983); *Marsh v. Chambers*, 463 U.S. 783 (1983); and *Lynch v. Donnelly*, 465 U.S. 668 (1984).

68. *Wallace v. Jaffree*, 472 U.S. 38, 100 (Rehnquist, C. J., dissenting).

69. Following the Supreme Court's 1985 decision in *Wallace*, the Court rendered an additional fifteen decisions up to 1995 that involved the Establishment Clause without once mentioning the Northwest Ordinance: *Estate of Thornton v. Caldor, Inc.*, 472 U.S. 703 (1985); *Grand Rapids School District v. Ball*, 473 U.S. 373 (1985) (overruled by *Agostini v. Felton*, 521 U.S. 203 (1997)); *Aguilar v. Felton*, 473 U.S. 402 (1985) (overruled by *Agostini v. Felton*, 521 U.S. 203 (1997)); *Witters v. Washington Dep't. of Social Services*, 474 U.S. 481 (1986); *Edwards v. Aguillard*, 482 U.S. 578 (1987); *Corporation of Presiding Bishop v. Amos*, 483 U.S. 327 (1987); *Bowen v. Kendrick*, 487 U.S. 589 (1988); *Texas Monthly, Inc. v. Bullock*, 489 U.S. 1 (1989); *County of Allegheny v. ACLU*, 492 U.S. 573 (1989); *Westside Community Schools v. Mergens*, 496 U.S. 226 (1990); *Lee v. Weisman*, 505 U.S. 577 (1992); *Lamb's Chapel v. Center Moriches Union Free School District*, 508 U.S. 384 (1993); *Zobrest v. Catalina Foothills School District*, 509 U.S. 1 (1993); *Board of Education of Kiryas Joel School District v. Grumet*, 512 U.S. 687 (1994); and *Capitol Square Review and Advisory Board v. Pinette*, 515 U.S. 753 (1995).

70. *Rosenberger v. University of Virginia*, 515 U.S. 819, 862 (1995) (Thomas, J., concurring).

71. *Permoli v. Municipality No. 1 of City of New Orleans*, 44 U.S. (3 How.) 589, 609 (1845) (emphasis added).

72. *Coyle v. Smith*, 221 U.S. 559, 568 (1910).

73. Fifth Article, Northwest Ordinance, as enacted by the Continental Congress, XXXII *Journals of the Continental Congress*, 342 (Proceedings of July 13, 1787) (emphasis added), as enacted as a federal law by the First Congress. Act of August 7, 1789, 1st Cong., 1st Sess., Ch. 8, 1 Stat. 52 n. "(a)" (reproducing the text of the Third Article of the 1787 Northwest Ordinance). See also *Documents Illustrative . . . Formation of the American States*, 47–54; 1 *Sources and Documents* (2nd series), 383–90; *Sources of Our Liberties*, 392–97.

74. III *Documentary History . . . First Federal Congress*, 232 (Proceedings of September 25, 1789); 1 *House Journal*, 1st Cong., 1st Sess., 123 (Proceedings of September 25, 1789); 1 *Annals of Congress*, 1st Cong., 1st Sess., 949–50 (House of Representatives

Proceedings of September 25, 1789); XI *Documentary History* . . . *First Federal Congress,* 1500–1501 (*Congressional Register* reporting the proceedings of September 25, 1789) (emphasis added).

75. I *Documentary History* . . . *First Federal Congress,* 192 (Proceedings of September 26, 1789); 1 *Senate Journal,* 1st Cong., 1st Sess., 90, 92 (Proceedings of September 26, 1789); 1 *Annals of Congress,* 1st Cong., 1st Sess., 92 (Senate Proceedings of September 26, 1789); see also III *Documentary History* . . . *First Federal Congress,* 238 (Proceedings of September 28, 1789) (House advised of Senate concurrence); 1 *House Journal,* 1st Cong., 1st Sess., 126 (Proceedings of September 28, 1789) (House advised of Senate concurrence).

76. XI *Documentary History* . . . *First Federal Congress,* 1501 n. 40.

77. 1 *Annals of Congress,* 1st Cong., 1st Sess., 949–50 (House of Representatives Proceedings of September 25, 1789) (Statement of Representative Sherman); XI *Documentary History* . . . *First Federal Congress,* 1501 (*Congressional Register* reporting the proceedings of September 25, 1789).

78. 30 *Washington's Writings,* 427–28.

Chapter 8

1. See, for instance, the Supreme Court's remarks to that effect in *United States v. X-Citement Video, Inc.,* 513 U.S. 64, 77 n. 6 (1994) (Congress's views of statute enacted years earlier by a different Congress entitled to scant significance); *Weinberger v. Rossi,* 456 U.S. 25, 35 (1982) ("*post hoc*" comments of Congress entitled to minimal consideration); *County of Washington v. Gunther,* 452 U.S. 161, 176 n. 16 (1981); *Consumer Product Safety Commission v. GTE Sylvania,* 447 U.S. 102, 118 n. 13 (1980) (Congress's subsequent informal opinion concerning earlier legislation entitled to little weight); *United States v. Clark,* 445 U.S. 23, 33 n. 9 (1980) (Congress's views of statute enacted years earlier by a different Congress entitled to scant significance); *Teamsters v. United States,* 431 U.S. 324, 354 n. 39 (1977) (Court gives minimal, if any, consideration to post-enactment comments of congressional legislators); *United States v. Southwestern Cable Co.,* 392 U.S. 157, 170 (1968) (Congress's views of statute enacted years earlier by a different Congress entitled to little weight); *United States v. Price,* 361 U.S. 304, 314 (1960), and *United States v. United Mine Workers,* 330 U.S.

258, 281–82 (1947) (views of a subsequent Congress cannot supply any substantive inference concerning the meaning accorded a law by a prior Congress); and *Rainwater v. United States,* 356 U.S. 590, 593 (1958) (Congress's views of statute enacted years earlier by a different Congress entitled to marginal significance).

2. Act of April 22, 1864, 38th Cong., 1st Sess., Ch. 66, § 1, 13 Stat. 54, 54–55.

3. Act of March 3, 1865, 38th Cong., 2nd Sess., Ch. 100, § 5, 13 Stat. 517, 518.

4. Act of February 12, 1873, 42nd Cong., 3rd Sess., Ch. 131, § 18, 17 Stat. 424, 427.

5. Act of May 18, 1908, 60th Cong., 1st Sess., Ch. 173, § 1, 35 Stat. 164.

6. Act of July 11, 1955, 84th Cong., 1st Sess., Ch. 303, 60 Stat. 290, initially codified as part of 31 U.S.C. §§ 324 and 324a, respectively, and later moved to 31 U.S.C. §§ 5112(d)(1) and 5114(b), respectively. Federal law still requires that those words appear on all coins and currency. 31 USC §§ 5112(d)(1), 5112(e), and 5114(b).

7. *Newdow v. Congress, et al.,* 435 F. Supp. 2d 1066 (E.D. Cal. 2006), appeal pending in the Ninth Circuit Court of Appeals, *Newdow v. Congress,* 9th Cir. No. 06–16344.

8. Act of June 22, 1942, Pub. L. 77–623, Ch. 435, § 7, 77th Cong., 2nd Sess., 56 Stat. 377, 380, codified at the time as *former* 36 USC § 172.

9. Act of June 14, 1954, Pub. L. 83–396, Ch. 297, 83rd Cong., 2nd Sess., 68 Stat. 249, codified at the time as *former* 36 USC § 172, and currently codified as 4 USC § 4. (Congress revised and recodified Title 36 of the United States Code via Act of August 12, 1998, Pub. L. 105–225, § 2(a), 112 Stat. 1494. *Former* 36 USC § 172 became 4 USC § 4.)

10. 4 USC § 4, as amended by Act of Nov. 13, 2002, Pub. L. 107–293, § 2, 107th Cong., 2nd Sess., 116 Stat. 2060.

11. H. R. Rep. No. 1693, 83rd Cong., 2d Sess., 2 (1954), reproduced in 2 U.S. *Code Cong. & Admin. News,* 83rd Cong., 2d Sess., 2339, 2340.

12. *Newdow v. U.S. Congress,* 292 F.3d 597 (9th Cir. 2002), *opinion on rehearing,* 313 F.3d 500 (9th Cir. 2002), *order amending opinion,* 328 F3d 466 (9th Cir. 2003), *reversed, Elk Grove Unified School District v. Newdow,* 542 U.S. 1 (2004).

13. *Newdow,* 292 F.3d at 601 (emphasis added).

14. See Chapter 15.

15. *Elk Grove Unified School District v. Newdow,* 542 U.S. 1 (2004), reversing the Court of Appeals' ruling.

16. *Newdow v. Congress, et al.,* 383 F. Supp. 2d 1229 (E.D. Cal. 2005), appeal pending in the Ninth Circuit Court of Appeals, *Roe v. Rio Linda Union School District* and *Newdow v. Carey,* 9th Cir. Nos. 05–17257, 05–17344, and 06–15093.

17. **SEC. 2.ONE NATION UNDER GOD.**

(a) REAFFIRMATION.—Section 4 of title 4, United States Code, is amended to read as follows:

§ 4. Pledge of allegiance to the flag; manner of delivery.

The Pledge of Allegiance to the Flag "I pledge allegiance to the Flag of the United States of America, and to the Republic for which it stands, one Nation under God, indivisible, with liberty and justice for all.," should be rendered by standing at attention facing the flag with the right hand over the heart. When not in uniform men should remove any non-religious headdress with their right hand and hold it at the left shoulder, the hand being over the heart. Persons in uniform should remain silent, face the flag, and render the military salute.

(b) CODIFICATION.—In codifying this subsection, the Office of the Law Revision Counsel shall show in the historical and statutory notes that the 107th Congress reaffirmed the exact language that has appeared in the Pledge for decades.

Act of Nov. 13, 2002, Pub. L. 107–293, §§ 2(a) and (b), 107th Cong., 2nd Sess., 116 Stat. 2057–60 ("An act to reaffirm the reference to one Nation under God in the Pledge of Allegiance").

The Senate approved the bill 99–0 on June 27, 2002, and the House of Representatives approved it 401–5 on October 8, 2002.

18. The unexplained reference to July 21, 1798, seems odd (not to mention incorrect), since no substantive action occurred with respect to the Establishment Clause on that date. See Chapter 5A(4).

The date error appeared in the original bill (Senate Bill 2690) and survived in the lengthy House of Representatives analysis as well (H.R. Rep. 107–659, 107th Cong., 2nd Sess., 6, 10). It seems that the legislative process suffered somewhat from Congress's desire to act far quicker than usual following the Ninth Circuit's decision in *Newdow.* The House Report also contains the term "absurg" [*sic*] instead of "absurd." *Id.* 13. See the next two notes as well, each identifying other minor errors.

19. Similar to the preceding note, the reference to June "15" proves incorrect; Congress enacted the 1954 amendment to the Pledge law on June *14,* 1952. See Act of June 14, 1954, Pub. L. 83–396, Ch. 297, 83rd Cong., 2nd Sess., 68 Stat. 249, codified at the time as *former* 36 USC § 172, and currently codified as 4 USC § 4.

20. Similar to the preceding note, the reference to July "20" proves incorrect; Congress enacted the 1956 national motto on July *30,* 1956. See Act of July 30, 1956, Pub. L. 84–851, Ch. 795, 84th Cong., 2nd Sess., 70 Stat. 732, codified as 36 USC § 302 (*formerly* 36 USC § 186).

21. *Newdow v. U.S. Congress,* 292 F.3d 597 (9th Cir. 2002), *opinion on rehearing,* 313 F.3d 500 (9th Cir. 2002), *order amending opinion on rehearing and denying rehearing en banc,* 328 F3d 466 (9th Cir. 2003), *reversed sub nom, Elk Grove Unified School District v. Newdow,* 542 U.S. 1 (2004).

22. Act of Nov. 13, 2002, Pub. L. 107–293, Sec. 1, 107th Cong., 2nd Sess., 116 Stat. 2057–60 (emphasis added).

23. Act of July 30, 1956, Pub. L. 84–851, Ch. 795, 84th Cong., 2nd Sess., 70 Stat. 732, codified as 36 USC § 302 (*formerly* 36 USC § 186).

24. In 2002, Congress reenacted the national motto without change and included the following mandate as part of that reaffirmation:

SEC. 3.REAFFIRMING THAT GOD REMAINS IN OUR MOTTO.

(a)REAFFIRMATION.—Section 302 of title 36, United States Code, is amended to read as follows:

§ 302. National Motto.

"In God we trust" is the national motto.

(b)CODIFICATION.—In codifying this section, the Office of the Law Revision Counsel shall make no change in section 302, title 36, United States Code, but shall show in the historical and statutory notes that the 107th Congress reaffirmed the exact language that has appeared in the Motto for decades.

Act of Nov. 13, 2002, Pub. L. 107–293, § 3, 107th Cong., 2nd Sess., 116 Stat. 2060–61 (bold in original).

25. *Newdow v. Congress, et al.,* 435 F. Supp. 2d 1066 (E.D. Cal. 2006), appeal pending in the Ninth Circuit Court of Appeals, *Newdow v. Congress,* 9th Cir. No. 06–16344.

26. Act of March 3, 1931, 71st Cong., 3rd Sess., Ch. 436, 46 Stat. 1508. The codification of "The Star-Spangled Banner" as the nation's national anthem appears in 36 USC § 301(a) ("The composition consisting of the words and music known as the Star-Spangled Banner is the national anthem.").

27. Key happened to have been aboard a neutral prisoner-exchange vessel, not an uncommon feature of the war, as capable seamen on both sides remained in dire need. When the British fleet arrived in the harbor to attack Fort McHenry, it prevented all vessels from leaving.

28. Act of April 17, 1952, Pub. L. 82–324, Ch. 216, 82nd Cong., 2nd Sess., 66 Stat. 64.

29. Act of August 12, 1998, Pub. L. 105–225, 105th Cong., 2nd Sess., 112 Stat. 1258, codified as 36 USC § 119 (*formerly* 36 USC § 169h).

Chapter 9

1. See Chapter 3E.

2. The New Jersey constitution actually contained the phrase "no establishment."

3. The Delaware constitution actually contained the phrase "no establishment."

4. The North Carolina constitution actually contained the phrase "no establishment."

5. The New York constitution specifically dis-"established" religion.

6. The Massachusetts constitution declared that no preference shall be "established" or tolerated.

7. The New Hampshire constitution declared that no preference shall be "established" or tolerated.

8. See Chapters 4 and 10.

Chapter 10

1. See Chapters 4 and 9.

2. See Chapter 5A(3).

3. See Chapter 4B.

4. See Chapter 5A(13).

Chapter 11

1. 1 *Madison's Papers*, 106; Wills, 15; Brant, *James Madison: The Virginia Revolutionist*, 52; Ketchum, 58.

2. Wills, 15.

3. Brant, *James Madison: The Virginia Revolutionist*, 68.

4. Ketchum, 25–38.

5. Brant, *James Madison: The Virginia Revolutionist*, 67; Ketchum, 25.

6. Ketchum, 38.

7. Madison graduated in 1771 after only three years. I *Madison's Writings*, xxxvii; *Madison and the American Nation*, 477; Wills, 16; Ketchum, 28, 35.

8. Ketchum, 45.

9. December 1, 1773, letter from Madison to Bradford (1 *Madison's Papers*, 101).

10. January 24, 1774, letter from Madison to Bradford (1 *Madison's Papers*, 105; I *Madison's Writings*, 18–19; I *Madison's Letters*, 10–11).

11. April 1, 1774, letter from Madison to Bradford (1 *Madison's Papers*, 108–10; I *Madison's Writings*, 22–25; I *Madison's Letters*, 13–15).

12. See Chapters 3A and 3D.

13. See Chapters 4C and 5.

14. For instance, Massachusetts Representative Gerry sought to reduce Madison's proposal to embrace mere "religious doctrine." 1 *Annals of Congress*, 1st Cong., 1st Sess., 757 (House of Representatives Proceedings of August 15, 1789) (Statement of Representative Gerry); XI *Documentary History . . . First Federal Congress*, 1261 (*Congressional Register* reporting the proceedings of August 15, 1789); *Complete Bill of Rights*, 59 (*Congressional Register* reporting the proceedings of August 15, 1789) (emphasis added). Gerry also railed against the term "national" as it rekindled the anti-"national" concerns that beset the 1787 Constitution Convention. 1 *Annals of Congress*, 1st Cong., 1st Sess., 759 (House of Representatives Proceedings of August 15, 1789) (Statement of Representative Gerry); XI *Documentary History . . . First Federal Congress*, 1262 (*Congressional Register* reporting the proceedings of August 15, 1789); *Complete Bill of Rights*, 60–61 (*Congressional Register* reporting the proceedings of August 15, 1789).

New Hampshire representative Livermore urged a debilitating revision that would have substituted the cryptic and elusive phrase "touching religion." 1 *Annals of Congress*, 1st Cong., 1st Sess., 759 (House of Representatives Proceedings of August 15, 1789) (Statement of Representative Livermore); XI *Documentary History . . . First Federal*

Congress, 1254 (New York *Daily Advertiser* edition of August 17, 1789, reporting the August 15, 1789, proceedings), 1257 (*Gazette of the United States* edition of August 19, 1789, reporting the August 15, 1789, proceedings), and 1262 (*Congressional Register* reporting the proceedings of August 15, 1789); *Complete Bill of Rights,* 2 (*Congressional Register* reporting the proceedings of August 15, 1789; New York *Daily Advertiser* edition of August 17, 1789, reporting the August 15, 1789, proceedings; *New-York Daily Gazette* edition of August 18, 1789, reporting the August 15, 1789, proceedings; and *Gazette of the United States* edition of August 19, 1789, reporting the August 15, 1789, proceedings), and 60 (*Congressional Register* reporting the proceedings of August 15, 1789).

And New England senators, in concert with Virginia senator Lee (a supporter of Patrick Henry's ill-fated 1784 establishment tax in Virginia), had provoked the Senate's September 9 retreat on the establishment issue that sought to limit Madison's proposal to "articles of faith or a mode of worship." Brant, *James Madison: Father of the Constitution,* 271–72.

15. *Madison's remarks:* 1 *Annals of Congress,* 1st Cong., 1st Sess., 758 (House of Representatives Proceedings of August 15, 1789) (Statement of Representative Madison) (small caps in original); XI *Documentary History . . . First Federal Congress,* 1261 (*Congressional Register* reporting the proceedings of August 15, 1789); *Complete Bill of Rights,* 60 (*Congressional Register* reporting the proceedings of August 15, 1789) (emphasis added).

16. See Chapter 5A(13).

17. See Chapter 5B(7).

18. See Chapter 5C(5).

19. See Chapters 5A(3) and 5A(9).

20. 1 *Annals of Congress,* 1st Cong., 1st Sess., 451 (House of Representatives Proceedings of June 8, 1789) (Statement of Representative Madison); IV *Documentary History . . . First Federal Congress,* 10 (citing the New York *Daily Advertiser* edition of June 12, 1789, reporting the June 8, 1789, proceedings); *Complete Bill of Rights,* 1 (*Congressional Register* reporting the proceedings of June 8, 1789; New York *Daily Advertiser* edition of June 12, 1789, reporting the June 8, 1789, proceedings; *New-York Daily Gazette* edition of June 13, 1789, reporting the June 8, 1789, proceedings).

21. Brant, *James Madison: Father of the Constitution,* 155; Ketchum, 229; Wills, 37.

22. Brant, *James Madison: Father of the Constitution,* 155.

23. Wills, 37.

24. Wood, 472.

25. Rakove, 42.

26. Malone, *Jefferson and the Rights of Man,* 87, 163; Brant, *James Madison: The Nationalist,* 410–11.

27. Malone, *Jefferson and the Rights of Man,* 87.

28. Rakove, 42.

29. Malone, *Jefferson and the Rights of Man,* 162.

30. Ibid., 162–63.

31. Ketchum, 45.

32. I *Jefferson's Writings* (1903 ed.) ("Autobiography"), 61–62; *Jefferson*—"Autobiography," 37; I *Jefferson's Works* ("Autobiography"), 66.

33. Rakove, 331.

34. Brant, *James Madison: Father of the Constitution,* 271.

35. 12 *Madison's Papers,* 53, citing a May 31, 1789, letter from Fisher Ames to George Minot (I *Works of Fisher Ames,* 35).

36. 12 *Madison's Papers,* 53.

37. Wills, 25–35; Ketchum, 190–230; Rakove, 330; Labunski, 2.

38. Rakove, 330.

39. Ibid., 331.

40. Brant, *James Madison: Secretary of State,* 35.

41. Brant, *James Madison: The President,* 11.

42. Undated 1832 letter from James Madison to Rev. Adams (IX *Madison's Writings,* 485–86) (emphasis added).

43. Act of Dec. 19, 2000, Pub. L. 106–550, 106th Cong., 2nd Sess., 114 Stat. 2745–46, codified as a note preceding 36 USC § 101.

Chapter 12

1. III Story, *Commentaries on the Constitution* (1833 ed.), § 1871, 728 (emphasis added).

2. *Barron v. Baltimore,* 32 U.S. (7 Pet) 243 (1833).

3. *Barron,* 32 U.S. (7 Pet) at 247 (emphasis added).

4. *Barron,* 32 U.S. (7 Pet) at 250 (emphasis added).

5. *Permoli v. Municipality No. 1 of the City of New Orleans,* 44 U.S. (3 How) 589 (1845).

6. *Permoli,* 44 U.S. (3 How) at 609 (emphasis added).

7. Rice, 12 (emphasis added).

8. *Dred Scott v. Sandford,* 60 U.S. (19 How.) 393 (1857).

9. U.S. Const., Art. IV, § 2.

10. U.S. Const., Amend. XIV, § 1,. 15 Stat. 710–11 (Appendix) (enumeration and emphasis added).

11. For clarity's sake, the Fourteenth Amendment in fact replicated two provisions that already existed in both Article IV of the Constitution and the Fifth Amendment.

Article IV, Section 2, of the Constitution provides:

> The citizens of each State shall be entitled to all *privileges and immunities* of citizens in the several States.

U.S. Const., Art. IV, § 2, 1 Stat. 18 (emphasis added).

The Fifth Amendment provides, in part:

> No person shall . . . be deprived of life, liberty, or property, without due process of law[.] . . .

U.S. Const., Amend. V, 1 Stat. 21 (emphasis added).

12. See, for instance, *The Slaughter-House Cases,* 83 U.S. (16 Wall) 36, 74–79 (1873) (concluding that the Fourteenth Amendment's "privileges or immunities" clause neither created any new "rights" nor burdened the states with any portion of the Bill of Rights that otherwise burdens only Congress), and *United States v. Cruikshank,* 92 U.S. (2 Otto) 542, 554–55 (1876) (concluding that the Fourteenth Amendment's "due process" and "equal protection" clauses neither created any new "rights" nor burdened the states with any portion of the Bill of Rights that otherwise burdens only Congress).

13. The Latin term "*ipse dixit*" means, literally, "he himself said it." *Black's Law Dictionary,* 847. More colloquially, it insinuates the truth of a declaration solely on the basis of the speaker having declared it (*viz.,* "because I say so").

14. *The Slaughter-House Cases,* 83 U.S. (16 Wall) 36 (1873), and *United States v. Cruikshank,* 92 U.S. (2 Otto) 542 (1876).

15. *Twining v. State of New Jersey,* 211 U.S. 78, 92 (1908) (emphasis added).

16. *Jacobellis v. Ohio,* 378 U.S. 184 (1964).

17. *Jacobellis,* 378 U.S. at 197 (Stewart, P., concurring) (emphasis added).

18. *Palko v. Connecticut,* 302 U.S. 319 (1937).

19. *Palko,* 302 U.S., at 323. The Court declared that "[t]here is no such general rule." *Id.*

20. *Palko,* 302 U.S., at 324–25 (emphasis added).

21. Rice, 12.

22. Amar, *Bill of Rights,* 7 (emphasis added).

23. *Cantwell v. Connecticut,* 310 U.S. 296 (1940).

24. The First Amendment contains six discrete assurances:

> Congress shall make no law respecting [1] an establishment of religion, or [2] prohibiting the free exercise thereof; or [3] abridging the freedom of speech, or [4] of the press; or [5] the right of the people peaceably to assemble, and [6] to petition the Government for a redress of grievances.

U.S. Const., Amend. I, 1st Cong., 1st Sess., 1 Stat. 21 (enumeration added).

25. *Cantwell,* 310 U.S., at 303 (emphasis added).

26. *Schneider v. State,* 308 U.S. 147, 160 (1939).

27. *Everson v. Board of Education,* 330 U.S. 1 (1947). See the discussion of *Everson* in Chapter 14C.

28. *Everson,* 330 U.S. at 8.

29. *Everson,* 330 U.S. at 8, citing *Murdock v. Commonwealth of Pennsylvania,* 319 U.S. 105 (1943).

30. *Palko,* 302 U.S., at 324–25.

31. See, for instance, C. Fairman, "Does the Fourteenth Amendment Incorporate the Bill of Rights?," 2 *Stan. L. Rev.* 5 (1949), which has been described as the "definitive" analysis of that legislative history (Rice, 13). See, as well, F. Shapiro, "The Most-Cited Law Review Articles," 73 *Cal. L. Rev.* 1540, 1550 (1985) (referencing Fairman's famous article).

32. See, for instance, Amar, *Bill of Rights,* 137–230.

33. *Adamson v. California,* 332 U.S. 46, 59–68 (1947) (Frankfurter, J., concurring), and 68–91 (Black, J., dissenting). (The Court's decision in *Malloy v. Hogan,* 378 U.S. 1 (1964), later overruled *Adamson* in part on other grounds.)

34. In its celebrated 1803 decision in *Marbury v. Madison,* 5 U.S. (1 Cranch) 137 (1803), the Supreme Court declared that the Constitution impliedly bestowed upon the courts the inherent and absolute authority to assess and declare whether or not congressional legislation conflicted with the Constitution—authority known as the power of "judicial review." Chapter 14A explains *Marbury v. Madison* in detail.

Chapter 13

1. *Tiller v. Atlantic Coast Line R. Co.,* 318 U.S. 54, 68 (1943) (Frankfurter, J., concurring).

Justice Frankfurter also wrote, again in a concurring opinion, that the invocation of uncritical "judicial history" in matters of constitutional law serves as

> a striking illustration of an occasional tendency to encrust unwarranted interpretations upon the Constitution and thereafter to consider merely what has been judicially said about the Constitution, rather than to be primarily controlled by a fair conception of the Constitution. . . . *But the ultimate touchstone of constitutionality is the Constitution itself and not what we have said about it.*"

Graves v. People of State of New York, 306 U.S. 466, 491–92 (1939) (Frankfurter, J., concurring) (emphasis added).

2. Maddox, 25.

3. See Chapter 14.

4. I *Jefferson's Writings* (1903 ed.), 90, 160–61; *Jefferson's Life,* 62, 101; *Jefferson . . . In His Own Words,* 149; Malone, *Jefferson and the Rights of Man,* 209, 243; V *Dictionary of American Biography,* Pt. 2, 21–22.

5. 12 *Jefferson's Papers,* 136; 10 *Madison's Papers,* 169.

6. 12 *Jefferson's Papers,* 218; VI *Jefferson's Writings* (1903 ed.), 335; II *Jefferson's Writings* (1853 ed.), 292; V *Jefferson's Works,* 355; 10 *Madison's Papers,* 187.

7. 12 *Jefferson's Papers,* 438; VI *Jefferson's Writings* (1903 ed.), 385; II *Jefferson's Writings* (1853 ed.), 327; V *Jefferson's Works,* 368; 10 *Madison's Papers,* 335.

8. 12 *Jefferson's Papers,* 568; V *Jefferson's Works,* 387; 10 *Madison's Papers,* 473.

9. 12 *Jefferson's Papers,* 656; 11 *Madison's Papers,* 1.

10. 13 *Jefferson's Papers,* 121; 11 *Madison's Papers,* 31.

11. 13 *Jefferson's Papers,* 129; VI *Jefferson's Writings* (1903 ed.), 455; II *Jefferson's Writings* (1853 ed.), 375; 11 *Madison's Papers,* 33.

12. 13 *Jefferson's Papers,* 201; VII *Jefferson's Writings* (1903 ed.), 39; II *Jefferson's Writings* (1853 ed.), 406; V *Jefferson's Works,* 394; 11 *Madison's Papers,* 54.

13. 13 *Jefferson's Papers,* 440; VII *Jefferson's Writings* (1903 ed.), 93; II *Jefferson's Writings* (1853 ed.), 443; V *Jefferson's Works,* 424; 11 *Madison's Papers,* 210.

14. 13 *Jefferson's Papers,* 469; 11 *Madison's Papers,* 220.

15. 14 *Jefferson's Papers,* 187; VII *Jefferson's Writings* (1903 ed.), 183; II *Jefferson's Writings* (1853 ed.), 505; V *Jefferson's Works,* 433; 11 *Madison's Papers,* 353.

16. 14 *Jefferson's Papers,* 436; VII *Jefferson's Writings* (1903 ed.), 267; II *Jefferson's Writings* (1853 ed.), 563; V *Jefferson's Works,* 444; 11 *Madison's Papers,* 412.

17. 14 *Jefferson's Papers,* 659; VII *Jefferson's Writings* (1903 ed.), 309; III *Jefferson's Writings* (1853 ed.), 3; V *Jefferson's Works,* 461; 12 *Madison's Papers,* 13.

18. 15 *Jefferson's Papers,* 121; VII *Jefferson's Writings* (1903 ed.), 353; III *Jefferson's Writings* (1853 ed.), 33; 12 *Madison's Papers,* 151.

19. 15 *Jefferson's Papers,* 194; VII *Jefferson's Writings* (1903 ed.), 386; 12 *Madison's Papers,* 241.

20. 15 *Jefferson's Papers,* 299; VII *Jefferson's Writings* (1903 ed.), 424; III *Jefferson's Writings* (1853 ed.), 82; 12 *Madison's Papers,* 303.

21. 15 *Jefferson's Papers,* 315; V *Jefferson's Works,* 485; 12 *Madison's Papers,* 315.

22. 15 *Jefferson's Papers,* 364; VII *Jefferson's Writings* (1903 ed.), 444; III *Jefferson's Writings* (1853 ed.), 96; V *Jefferson's Works,* 487; 12 *Madison's Papers,* 360.

23. 15 *Jefferson's Papers,* 392; VII *Jefferson's Writings* (1903 ed.), 454; III *Jefferson's Writings* (1853 ed.), 102; VI *Jefferson's Works,* 3; 12 *Madison's Papers,* 382.

24. 15 *Jefferson's Papers,* 438; 12 *Madison's Papers,* 408.

25. I *Jefferson's Writings* (1903 ed.), "Autobiography," 134–60; *Jefferson*—"Autobiography," 82–98.

26. 10 *Madison's Papers,* 163; 12 *Jefferson's Papers,* 102.

27. 10 *Madison's Papers,* 205; V *Madison's Writings,* 17; I *Madison's Letters,* 343; 12 *Jefferson's Papers,* 270.

28. 10 *Madison's Papers,* 310; V *Madison's Writings,* 62; I *Madison's Letters,* 362; 12 *Jefferson's Papers,* 408.

29. 10 *Madison's Papers,* 331; V *Madison's Writings,* 74; 12 *Jefferson's Papers,* 443.

30. 10 *Madison's Papers,* 518; V *Madison's Writings,* 100; I *Madison's Letters,* 376; 12 *Jefferson's Papers,* 607.

31. 10 *Madison's Papers,* 526; 12 *Jefferson's Papers,* 611.

32. 11 *Madison's Papers,* 27; V *Madison's Writings,* 120; I *Madison's Letters,* 387; 13 *Jefferson's Papers,* 98.

33. 11 *Madison's Papers,* 196; V *Madison's Writings,* 240; I *Madison's Letters,* 404; 13 *Jefferson's Papers,* 412.

34. 11 *Madison's Papers,* 225; V *Madison's Writings,* 244; I *Madison's Letters,* 407; 13 *Jefferson's Papers,* 497.

35. 11 *Madison's Papers*, 238; V *Madison's Writings*, 254; I *Madison's Letters*, 410; 13 *Jefferson's Papers*, 539.

36. 11 *Madison's Papers*, 257; V *Madison's Writings*, 262; I *Madison's Letters*, 417; 13 *Jefferson's Papers*, 624.

37. 11 *Madison's Papers*, 276; I *Madison's Letters*, 420; 14 *Jefferson's Papers*, 3.

38. 11 *Madison's Papers*, 295; V *Madison's Writings*, 269; I *Madison's Letters*, 421; 14 *Jefferson's Papers*, 16.

39. 11 *Madison's Papers*, 381; V *Madison's Writings*, 309; I *Madison's Letters*, 441; 14 *Jefferson's Papers*, 339.

40. 11 *Madison's Papers*, 390; I *Madison's Letters*, 446; 14 *Jefferson's Papers*, 352.

41. 12 *Madison's Papers*, 37; V *Madison's Writings*, 333; I *Madison's Letters*, 457; 15 *Jefferson's Papers*, 5.

42. 12 *Madison's Papers*, 142; V *Madison's Writings*, 355 n.; I *Madison's Letters*, 465; 15 *Jefferson's Papers*, 114.

43. 12 *Madison's Papers*, 182; V *Madison's Writings*, 369 n.; I *Madison's Letters*, 470; 15 *Jefferson's Papers*, 147.

44. 12 *Madison's Papers*, 185; V *Madison's Writings*, 370 n.; I *Madison's Letters*, 471; 15 *Jefferson's Papers*, 153.

45. 12 *Madison's Papers*, 217; I *Madison's Letters*, 475; 15 *Jefferson's Papers*, 180.

46. 12 *Madison's Papers*, 267; I *Madison's Letters*, 479; 15 *Jefferson's Papers*, 224.

47. 15 *Jefferson's Papers*, 324.

48. See Chapter 2B.

49. Malone, *Jefferson The President*, 190–91.

50. Malone, *Jefferson and the Ordeal of Liberty*, 478–83; Brodie, 325–26; Lambert, 265–75.

51. Malone, *Jefferson The President*, 191.

52. Ibid., 190.

53. Malone, *Jefferson and the Ordeal of Liberty*, 479.

54. Malone, *Jefferson The President*, 191; Dreisbach, *Jefferson and the Wall of Separation*, 25.

55. Dreisbach, *Jefferson and the Wall of Separation*, 26–30, 38–40.

56. Malone, *Jefferson The President*, 109.

57. January 23, 1808, letter from Jefferson to Rev. Samuel Miller (XI *Jefferson's Writings* (1903 ed.), 428; V *Jefferson's Writings* (1853 ed.), 237) (emphasis added).

58. The "ancient charter" references Connecticut's "Constitutional Ordinance of 1776," which adopted Connecticut's 1662 Charter as its "Civil Constitution." 2 *Sources and Documents,* 143. Connecticut did not adopt its own constitution until 1818. 1 *Federal and State Constitutions,* 536–37; 2 *Sources and Documents,* 143.

Although Connecticut's 1662 charter ensured the maintenance of the "Christian Faith," it furnished Connecticut residents no religious rights that resembled those in the various state constitutions and bills of rights adopted by other states.

59. The Danbury Baptists' letter to Jefferson can be found in: Jefferson's original papers maintained in the Manuscript Division, Library of Congress; Dreisbach, *Jefferson and the Wall of Separation,* 31–32 and *id.* Appendix 6, 142–44. It appears as well on various Internet sites, including http://memory.loc.gov/ammem/ mtjhtml/mtjhome.html.

60. The excellent research reported by Daniel Dreisbach reports that "[m]ost published collections of Jefferson's writings incorrectly transcribe this word as 'legislative'," and Dreisbach cites both *Jefferson's Writings* (1853 ed.) and *Jefferson's Writings* (1903 ed.), among other sources, as examples that have perpetuated the mis-transcription of the Danbury Baptist letter. Dreisbach, *Jefferson and the Wall of Separation,* 48 n. 71. (See also *Jefferson*—"Addresses, Messages, and Replies," 510 [same error].)

It seems plain enough from an enlargement of Jefferson's actual handwriting that Jefferson indeed used the term "legitimate," not "legislative": *the legitimate powers of government*

See Dreisbach, *Jefferson and the Wall of Separation,* 36, 37; http://www.loc.gov/exhibits/religion/rel06-2.html; http://www.loc.gov/exhibits/religion/danburys.jpg.

No one seems to have noticed that Jefferson used the identical reference to "legitimate" two decades earlier in his 1781 publication *Notes on the State of Virginia,* when he wrote, as part of "Query XVII" (Religion):

> The *legitimate* powers of government extend to such acts only as are injurious to others.

Jefferson—*Notes on the State of Virginia,* 285; IV *Jefferson's Works* (*Notes on the State of Virginia*), 78; II *Jefferson's Writings* (1903 ed.) (*Notes on the State of Virginia*), 221 (emphasis added).

61. Dreisbach, *Jefferson and the Wall of Separation,* 48; VIII *Jefferson's*

Writings (1853 ed.), 113; XVI *Jefferson's Writings* (1903 ed.), 281–82; *Jefferson*—"Addresses, Messages, and Replies," 510; IX *Jefferson's Works*, 346–47 (emphasis added). The various sources do not necessarily replicate the handwritten letter precisely but depict certain editorial changes.

62. January 1, 1802, letter from Jefferson to Attorney General Lincoln (X *Jefferson's Writings* (1903 ed.), 305; IV *Jefferson's Writings* (1853 ed.), 427; X *Jefferson's Works*, 346–47) (emphasis added).

63. Dreisbach, *Jefferson and the Wall of Separation*, 25–26, 29–30; Malone, *Jefferson The President*, 109, 190; Peterson, 672.

64. Malone, *Jefferson The President*, 191.

65. Lincoln, along with Postmaster General Granger, remained Jefferson's "chief consultants on New England." Malone, *Jefferson The President*, 109.

66. Dreisbach, *Jefferson and the Wall of Separation*, 46–47.

67. Ibid., Dreisbach, *Jefferson and the Wall of Separation*, 47.

68. January 1, 1802, letter from Jefferson to Attorney General Lincoln (X *Jefferson's Writings* (1903 ed.), 305; IV *Jefferson's Writings* (1853 ed.), 427; X *Jefferson's Works*, 346–47) (emphasis added).

69. Huston, *A Wall of Separation*, reproduced online at http://www.loc.gov/loc/lcib/9806/danpost.html (accessible via http://www.loc.gov/loc/lcib/9806/danbury.html); see also Dreisbach, *Jefferson and the Wall of Separation*, 35–38 (explaining the sequence of Jefferson's revisions); http://www.loc.gov/exhibits/religion/rel06–2.html; and http://www.loc.gov/exhibits/religion/danburys.jpg, each of which depicts a photocopy of Jefferson's actual draft letter with the changes that Jefferson made after receiving Attorney General Lincoln's comments. This version depicts both the text that Jefferson obliterated by hand and his other alterations.

70. Dreisbach, *Jefferson and the Wall of Separation*, 48. VIII *Jefferson's Writings* (1853 ed.), 113; XVI *Jefferson's Writings* (1903 ed.), 281–82; Dreisbach, *Jefferson and the Wall of Separation*, 48 (emphasis added); see also Dreisbach, *Jefferson and the Wall of Separation*, 37; http://www.loc.gov/exhibits/religion/rel06–2.html; and http://www.loc.gov/exhibits/religion/danburys.jpg. The various sources do not necessarily replicate the handwritten letter precisely but depict certain editorial changes.

71. Huston, *A Wall of Separation*, reproduced online at http://www.loc.gov/loc/lcib/9806/danpost.html (accessible via

http://www.loc.gov/loc/lcib/9806/danbury.html); Dreisbach, *Jefferson and the Wall of Separation*, 35–41.

72. Huston, *Religion and the Federal Government,* reproduced at http://www.loc.gov/exhibits/religion/rel06–2.html (accessible only via http://www.loc.gov/exhibits/religion/).

73. Ibid.

74. *Reynolds v. United States,* 98 U.S. (8 Otto) 145, 164 (1878). The Court reiterated that historical falsehood in *Everson v. Board of Education,* 330 U.S. 1 (1947), and forever ensconced Jefferson's "wall" in judicial lore. See the discussions in Chapter 14, specifically Chapters 14B and 14C.

75. Malone, *Jefferson The President,* 108.

76. See, for instance, Chapter 3B.

77. Brodie, 129.

78. Dreisbach, *Jefferson and the Wall of Separation,* 29 (emphasis added).

79. Dreisbach, *Jefferson and the Wall of Separation,* 30 (emphasis added), quoting from Huston, *A Wall of Separation,* 137.

80. Dreisbach, *Jefferson and the Wall of Separation,* 30, quoting from Huston, *A Wall of Separation,* 163.

81. Dreisbach, *Jefferson and the Wall of Separation,* 27.

82. Dreisbach, *Jefferson and the Wall of Separation,* 27, quoting from Edward Corwin, "The Supreme Court as a National School Board," in *A Constitution of Powers in a Secular State,* 106 (Charlottesville: Michie, 1951).

83. Corwin wrote: the seminal *The Constitution and What It Means Today* (first published in 1920, 3rd edition 1928, thirteen revised editions since); *National Supremacy—Treaty Power vs. State Power* (1913); *The Doctrine of Judicial Review* (1914); *The President's Control of Foreign Relations* (1917); *John Marshall and the Constitution* (1919); *The President's Removal Power under the Constitution* (1927); *The Twilight of the Supreme Court* (1935); *Commerce Power Versus State Rights—Back to the Constitution* (1936); *Court Over Constitution* (1938); *The President: Office and Power* (1940); *Constitutional Revolution* (1941); *The Constitution and World Organization* (1944); *Total War and the Constitution* (1947); *Liberty against Government* (1948); *The Constitution of the United States of America: Analysis and Interpretation* (1949); and *A Constitution of Power in a Secular State* (1951).

84. Dreisbach, *Jefferson and the Wall of Separation,* 27.

85. See, as well, discussions of Corwin in: 5 *American National Biography*, 547–48; *Dictionary of American Biography*, Supp. 7, 146–47; IV *Who Was Who in America*, 204.

86. The Danbury Baptists' letter and Jefferson's response quickly appeared in the following newspapers: (New York) *American Citizen and General Advertiser*, edition of January 18, 1802, 2; (Boston) *Independent Chronicle*, edition of January 25, 1802, 2–3; (Boston) *Constitutional Telegraphe*, edition of January 27, 1802, 2; *Salem Register*, edition of January 28, 1802, 1; (Hartford) *American Mercury*, edition of January 28, 1802, 3; (Newport) *Rhode-Island Republican*, edition of January 30, 1802, 2; (Portsmouth) *New Hampshire Gazette*, edition of February 9, 1802, 2; and (Pittsfield, Mass.) *The Sun*, edition of February 15, 1802, 4.

See also Dreisbach, *Jefferson and the Wall of Separation*, 24 n. 71 (identifying the (New York) *American Citizen and General Advertiser*, January 18, 1802, edition 2; the (Hartford) *American Mercury*, January 28, 1802, edition, 3; the (Newark) *The Centinel* [*sic*] *of Freedom*, February 16, 1802, edition, 2–3, 23; the (Boston) *Constitutional Telegraphe*, January 27, 1802, edition, 2; the (Boston) *Independent Chronicle*, January 25, 1802, edition, 2–3; the (Portsmouth) *New Hampshire Gazette*, February 9, 1802, edition, 2; the (Newport) *Rhode-Island Republican*, January 30, 1802, edition, 2; the *Salem Register*, January 28, 1802, edition, 1; and the (Pittsfield, MA) *The Sun*, February 15, 1802, edition, 4.

87. See VIII *Jefferson's Writings* (1853 ed.), 113.

88. See Chapter 12. Not until the twentieth century did the Supreme Court embrace the *ipse dixit* notion that, via the Fourteenth Amendment, various provisions within the Constitution's Bill of Rights burdened the states as well as the federal government. And not until its 1947 decision in *Everson v. Board of Education*, 330 U.S. 1 (1947), did the Supreme Court declare that the Establishment Clause itself burdened the various states. 330 U.S. at 8. The Court, however, simply made up that decision, as the history of the Fourteenth Amendment suggests no such thing.

89. See Chapter 3E.

90. **Massachusetts's 1780 Constitution:** 3 *Federal and State Constitutions*, 1888–1911; 5 *Sources and Documents*, 92–109. See Chapter 3E(10).

91. Atypical among the various states, Massachusetts's 1780 Constitution included a "compelled-financial-support" authorization for the legislature:

. . . [T]he people of this commonwealth have a right to invest their legislature with power to authorize and require, and the *legislature shall,* from time to time, authorize and require the several towns, parishes, and other bodies politic, or religious societies, to *make suitable provision, at their own expense, for the institution of the public worship of God, and for the support and maintenance of public Protestant teachers . . .[.]*

1780 Constitution, Art. III, reproduced in: 3 *Federal and State Constitutions,* 1889–90; 5 *Sources and Documents,* 93–94 (emphasis added).

92. **Pennsylvania's 1790 Constitution:** 5 *Federal and State Constitutions,* 3092–103; 8 *Sources and Documents,* 286–95.

93. Pennsylvania's 1790 Constitution, Art. IX, § 3, reproduced in: 5 *Federal and State Constitutions,* 3100; 8 *Sources and Documents,* 292. See also Chapter 3E(4).

94. **Pennsylvania's 1838 Constitution:** 5 *Federal and State Constitutions,* 3104–17; 8 *Sources and Documents,* 296–306.

95. **South Carolina's 1790 Constitution:** 6 *Federal and State Constitutions,* 3258–65; 8 *Sources and Documents,* 476–84.

96. See Chapter 3E(9).

97. South Carolina's 1790 Constitution, Art. VIII, § 1, reproduced in: 6 *Federal and State Constitutions,* 3264; 8 *Sources and Documents,* 480–81.

98. **South Carolina's 1865 Constitution:** 6 *Federal and State Constitutions,* 3269–79; 8 *Sources and Documents,* 485–93. [In 1861 a South Carolina state convention adopted a new constitution, seemingly as part of an ordinance of secession from the United States. 6 *Federal and State Constitutions,* 3269 n. a; 8 *Sources and Documents,* 485 n. *. South Carolina repealed its secession ordinance in September 1865 (*id.*), and the legality of that 1861 Constitution remains doubtful.]

99. **Delaware's 1792 Constitution:** 1 *Federal and State Constitutions,* 568–81; 2 *Sources and Documents,* 205–15.

100. See Chapter 3E(3).

101. Delaware's 1792 Constitution, Art. I, § 1, reproduced in 1 *Federal and State Constitutions,* 568.

102. **Delaware's 1831 Constitution:** 1 *Federal and State Constitutions,* 582–600; 2 *Sources and Documents,* 217–30.

103. **New Hampshire's 1792 Constitution:** 4 *Federal and State Constitutions,* 2471–90.

104. See Chapter 3E(11).

105. New Hampshire's 1792 Constitution, "Part First (Bill of Rights)," Art. VI, reproduced in: 4 *Federal and State Constitutions*, 2471–72 (emphasis added).

106. **New Hampshire's 1902 Constitution:** 4 *Federal and State Constitutions*, 2494–2513.

107. **Vermont's 1793 Constitution:** 6 *Federal and State Constitutions*, 3762–78; 9 *Sources and Documents*, 507–14.

108. Vermont's 1793 Constitution, Ch. I, Art. 3, reproduced in: 6 *Federal and State Constitutions*, 3762; 9 *Sources and Documents*, 507–8.

109. See Chapter 3E(12).

110. **Georgia's 1798 Constitution:** 2 *Federal and State Constitutions*, 791–802; 2 *Sources and Documents*, 458–66.

111. See Chapter 3E(8).

112. Georgia's 1798 Constitution, Art. IV, § 10, reproduced in: 2 *Federal and State Constitutions*, 800–801; 2 *Sources and Documents*, 465.

113. **Georgia's 1865 Constitution:** 2 *Federal and State Constitutions*, 809–22; 2 *Sources and Documents*, 487–96. [In 1861 Georgia adopted a new constitution as part of an "Ordinance of Secession" from the United States. 2 *Federal and State Constitutions*, 809; 2 *Sources and Documents*, 475–86. The legality of that 1861 constitution remains doubtful.]

114. **New York's 1821 Constitution:** 5 *Federal and State Constitutions*, 2639–51; 7 *Sources and Documents*, 181–89.

115. See Chapter 3E(7).

116. **Virginia's 1829 Constitution:** 7 *Federal and State Constitutions*, 3819–29; 10 *Sources and Documents*, 57–66.

117. See Chapter 3E(1).

118. **New Jersey's 1844 Constitution:** 5 *Federal and State Constitutions*, 2599–2614; 6 *Sources and Documents*, 453–64.

119. See Chapter 3E(2).

120. **Maryland's 1851 Constitution:** 3 *Federal and State Constitutions*, 1712–41; 4 *Sources and Documents*, 393–415.

121. See Chapter 3E(5).

122. **North Carolina's 1868 Constitution:** 5 *Federal and State Constitutions*, 2800–2822; 7 *Sources and Documents*, 414–30. [In 1861 North Carolina adopted a new constitution as part of an "Ordinance of Secession" from the United States. 5 *Federal and State Constitutions*, 2799; 7 *Sources and Documents*, 412. The legality of that 1861 constitution remains doubtful.]

123. See Chapter 3E(6).

124. See Chapter 14C.

125. VIII *Jefferson's Writings* (1853 ed.), 113; XVI *Jefferson's Writings* (1903 ed.), 281–82; Dreisbach, *Jefferson and the Wall of Separation*, 48 (emphasis added).

126. Dreisbach, *Jefferson and the Wall of Separation*, 53 (italics in original).

127. See Chapter 14B.

128. *Reynolds v. United States*, 98 U.S. (8 Otto) 145 (1878), discussed in detail in Chapter 14B.

129. Dreisbach, *Jefferson and the Wall of Separation*, 53 (italics in original).

130. Ibid.

131. In an introduction at the beginning of his *Notes on the State of Virginia*, Jefferson wrote that "[t]he following Notes were written in Virginia in the year 1781, and somewhat corrected and enlarged in the winter of 1782 . . . [.]" *Jefferson—Notes on the State of Virginia*, 124; III *Jefferson's Works* (*Notes on the State of Virginia*), 335; II *Jefferson's Writings* (1903 ed.) (*Notes on the State of Virginia*), unpaginated "Introductory Notes."

132. II *Jefferson's Writings* (1903 ed.) (*Notes on the State of Virginia*) 221; *Jefferson—Notes on the State of Virginia*, 285; IV *Jefferson's Works* (*Notes on the State of Virginia*), 78—all within "Query XVII" (Religion).

133. "Most published collections of Jefferson's writings incorrectly transcribe this word in the Danbury Baptist letter as 'legislative.'" Dreisbach, *Jefferson and the Wall of Separation*, 48 n. 71.

134. VIII *Jefferson's Writings* (1853 ed.), 113; XVI *Jefferson's Writings* (1903 ed.), 281–82; Dreisbach, *Jefferson and the Wall of Separation*, 48 (emphasis added).

135. *Everson v. Board of Education*, 330 U.S. 1 (1947). See the discussions in Chapters 14 and 14C.

136. See: *Everson v. Board of Education*, 330 U.S. 1 (1947); *McCollum v. Board of Education*, 333 U.S. 203 (1948); *Zorach v. Clauson*, 343 U.S. 306 (1952); *McGowan v. Maryland*, 366 U.S. 420 (1961); *Braunfeld v. Brown*, 366 U.S. 599 (1961); *Engel v. Vitale*, 370 U.S. 421 (1962); *Abington School District v. Schempp*, 374 U.S. 203 (1963); *Board of Education v. Allen*, 392 U.S. 236 (1968); *Epperson v. Arkansas*, 393 U.S. 97 (1968); *Committee for Public Education v. Nyquist*, 413 U.S. 756 (1973); *Wolman v. Walter*, 433 U.S. 229 (1977); *Larkin v. Grendel's Den*,

Inc., 459 U.S. 116 (1982); *Marsh v. Chambers*, 463 U.S. 783 (1983); *Lynch v. Donnelly*, 465 U.S. 668 (1984); *Wallace v. Jaffree*, 472 U.S. 38 (1985); *County of Allegheny v. ACLU*, 492 U.S. 573 (1989); *Lee v. Weisman*, 505 U.S. 577 (1992); *Capitol Square Review and Advisory Board v. Pinette*, 515 U.S. 753 (1995); *Mitchell v. Helms*, 530 U.S. 793 (2000); and *Van Orden v. Perry*, 545 U.S. 677 (2005).

137. 1 *Jefferson's Papers*, 530.

138. Peterson, 137.

139. Malone, *Jefferson The President*, 191.

140. Peterson, 133.

141. 1 *Jefferson's Papers*, 363; *Jefferson*—"Public Papers," 344; II *Jefferson's Works*, 180.

142. *Jefferson . . . In His Own Words*, 91.

143. Virginia's June 29, 1776, Constitution, dedicated solely to a "plan of government," has been reproduced in: 1 *Jefferson's Papers*, 377–83; 7 *Federal and State Constitutions*, 3814–19; 10 *Sources and Documents*, 51–56; VIII *Documentary History . . . Ratification*, 532–37; and 1 *Founders' Constitution*, 7–9.

144. Jefferson's November 30, 1776, Draft of Bill Exempting Dissenters from Contributing to the Support of the Church (broken into separate paragraphs), reproduced in: 1 *Jefferson's Papers*, 532–33; I *Jefferson's Works*, 63 incl. n. 1; 5 *Founders' Constitution*, 74–75.

145. I *Jefferson's Writings* (1903 ed.), 58 ("Autobiography"); I *Jefferson's Works* ("Autobiography"), 63 incl. n. 1 (Virginia legislature enacted the bill on January 1, 1778); *Jefferson*— "Autobiography," 35 ("[W]e prevailed so far only as to . . . exempt dissenters from contributions to the support of the established church"); Simmons, 377.

146. See the discussion of *Everson v. Board of Education* in Chapter 14C.

147. Madison first wrote Jefferson on March 27, 1780 (2 *Madison's Papers*, 5; I *Madison's Writings*, 59; 3 *Jefferson's Papers*, 335), and Jefferson first wrote Madison on July 26, 1780 (3 *Jefferson's Papers*, 506; IV *Jefferson's Writings* (1903 ed.), 316; 2 *Madison's Papers*, 48).

148. See Chapter 5D.

149. Jefferson, born in Albemarle County, Virginia, on April 13, 1743 (Malone, *Jefferson and His Time*, 1), died—ironically—on July 4, 1826, fifty years to the day after Congress approved the Declaration of Independence that Jefferson had written. (And both John Adams

and James Monroe likewise died on July 4, in 1826 and 1831, respectively. Labunski, 263.)

150. Malone, *Jefferson and His Time*, 49, 65.

151. *Jefferson . . . In His Own Words*, 17–22; Peterson, 11–13, 16–28; Malone, *Jefferson and His Time*, 64–65.

152. *Jefferson . . . In His Own Words*, 40–53; Peterson, 33–34; Malone, *Jefferson and His Time*, 129–42, 170–72.

153. *Jefferson . . . In His Own Words*, 53–54; Malone, *Jefferson and His Time*, 198–201.

154. *Jefferson . . . In His Own Words*, 61–62.

155. *Jefferson . . . In His Own Words*, 72; Malone, *Jefferson and His Time*, 247–85.

156. See Chapter 3A.

157. *Jefferson . . . In His Own Words*, 75.

158. Peterson, 80.

159. Brodie, 129; Simmons, 377.

160. See Chapter 3B.

161. I *Jefferson's Writings* (1903 ed.), "Autobiography," 74; *Jefferson*—"Autobiography", 45; *Jefferson . . . In His Own Words*, 91; Malone, *Jefferson and His Time*, 301–2.

162. *Jefferson . . . In His Own Words*, 75–76; Malone, *Jefferson and His Time*, 306–7; Brant, *James Madison: The Virginia Revolutionist*, 272–74, 354; October 1, 1812, letter from Thomas Jefferson to Thomas Flournoy (XIII *Jefferson's Writings* (1903 ed.), 190; VI *Jefferson's Writings* (1853 ed.), 82); September 1830 letter from Madison to Margaret H. Smith (IX *Madison's Writings*, 404; IV *Madison's Letters*, 111).

163. Malone, *Jefferson and His Time*, 307; September 1830 letter from Madison to Margaret H. Smith (IX *Madison's Writings*, 404 ["The acquaintance then made with him was very slight."]; IV *Madison's Letters*, 111).

164. Jefferson set sail for Paris on July 5, 1784, and did not return to the United States until November 23, 1789. I *Jefferson's Writings* (1903 ed.), 90, 160–61; *Jefferson*—"Autobiography," 55, 98; I *Jefferson's Works* ("Autobiography"), 93, 158; *Jefferson's Life*, 62, 101; *Jefferson . . . In His Own Words*, 149; Malone, *Jefferson and the Rights of Man*, 209, 243; V *Dictionary of American Biography*, Pt. 2, 21–22.

165. *Jefferson . . . In His Own Words*, 209; see also II *Documentary History . . . First Federal Congress*, 49 (Proceedings of September 26,

1789); 1 *Senate Executive Journal,* 32 (Proceedings of September 26, 1789); 1 *Annals of Congress,* 93 (Senate Proceedings of September 26, 1789) (Senate's receipt of Jefferson's nomination; Senate confirmation that same day).

166. Madison, born in Orange County, Virginia, on March 16, 1751 (*Madison and the American Nation,* 477), died on June 28, 1836. Just prior to his passing, friends reminded Madison that Jefferson had died on July 4, and hinted that perhaps that bit of irony might well repeat itself.

> During the last week of June, when it was obvious that he was dying, his doctor offered him medicine that might have prolonged his life until July 4. . . . But Madison said no.

Ketchum, 669–70; Labunski, 263.

167. September 1830 letter from Madison to Margaret H. Smith (IX *Madison's Writings,* 404 ["the distance between our ages being considerable, and other distances much more so."]; IV *Madison's Letters,* 111).

168. Ketchum, 25–38.

169. I *Madison's Writings,* xxxvii; *Madison and the American Nation,* 477; Wills, 16; Ketchum, 28, 35.

170. Ketchum, 45.

171. I *Madison's Writings,* xxxvii; Brant, *James Madison: The Virginia Revolutionist,* 155; Ketchum, 63.

172. I *Madison's Writings,* xxxvii; Brant, *James Madison: The Virginia Revolutionist,* 190, 272–74; *Madison and the American Nation,* 477; Wills, 13; Ketchum, 68.

173. I *Madison's Writings,* xxxvii.

174. I *Madison's Writings,* xxxviii; Brant, *James Madison: The Virginia Revolutionist,* 272–74; *Madison and the American Nation,* 211; Wills, 18.

> 175. I was a stranger to Mr. Jefferson [till] the year 1776, when he took his seat in the first Legislature under the Constitution of Virginia, then newly formed; being at that time myself a member of that Body, and for the first time, a member of any public Body.

September 1830 letter from Madison to Margaret H. Smith (IX *Madison's Writings,* 404; IV *Madison's Letters,* 111).

176. Brant, *James Madison: The Virginia Revolutionist,* 272–74, 354; *Madison and the American Nation,* 211; Ketchum, 84; October 1, 1812, letter from Thomas Jefferson to Thomas Flournoy (XIII *Jefferson's*

Writings (1903 ed.), 190; VI *Jefferson's Writings* (1853 ed.), 82).

177. I *Madison's Writings*, xxxvii; Brant, *James Madison: The Virginia Revolutionist*, 313; Ketchum, 75.

178. I *Madison's Writings*, xxxvii; Brant, *James Madison: The Virginia Revolutionist*, 315; *Madison and the American Nation*, 211, 477; Wills, 13, 19; Ketchum, 78.

179. Brant, *James Madison: The Virginia Revolutionist*, 315.

180. I *Madison's Writings*, xxxvii; 8 *Madison's Papers*, xxvii–xxviii; Brant, *James Madison: The Virginia Revolutionist*, 360; *Madison and the American Nation*, 477; Wills, 19, 24; Ketchum, 85, 142–44.

181. II *Madison's Writings*, xv–xvi; *Madison and the American Nation*, 478; Wills, 24; Ketchum, 158.

182. II *Madison's Writings*, xvii.

183. II *Madison's Writings*, xvii; *Madison and the American Nation*, 478.

184. II *Madison's Writings*, xv; *Madison and the American Nation*, 478.

185. *Madison and the American Nation*, 478; Ketchum, 277.

186. Brant, *James Madison: Secretary of State*, 35.

187. Brant, *James Madison: The President*, 11.

Chapter 14

1. B. Adamson, "Would That Make It So?," *Oregon State Bar Bulletin*, October 2005 issue, 62.

2. See Wood, 291–305, 453–63.

3. Amar, *America's Constitution*, 207.

4. *Brown v. Allen*, 344 U.S. 443, 540 (1953) (Jackson, J., concurring).

5. *Black's Law Dictionary*, 1443.

6. *Wallace v. Jaffree*, 472 U.S. 38, 99 (1985) (Rehnquist, C. J., dissenting).

7. 1 *Debate on the Constitution*, 17 (quoting from the September 26, 1787, edition of the Philadelphia *Freeman's Journal*).

8. *Lynch v. Donnelly*, 465 U.S. 668, 673 (1984).

9. Amar, *America's Constitution*, 60–63, 179–81.

Modern Americans associate enforcement of the Constitution with the doctrine of judicial review, under which judges refuse to enforce federal statutes that they deem inconsistent with the supreme law of the Constitution. At the Founding, however, the Constitution integrated several enforcement devices in its general system of separated powers. Broadly speaking, the Constitution enabled and in some cases obliged each of the three main departments . . . to thwart schemes that it, and it alone, deemed unconstitutional.

Id., 60,

10. Rehnquist, *The Supreme Court,* 21.

11. Act of February 13, 1801, 6th Cong., 2nd Sess., Ch. 4, 2 Stat. 89–100.

12. Act of February 27, 1801, 6th Cong., 2nd Sess., Ch. 15, § 11, 2 Stat. 107, *as amended by* Act of March 3, 1801, 6th Cong., 2nd Sess., Ch. 24, 2 Stat. 115–16.

13. 1 *Senate Executive Journal,* 6th Cong., 2nd Sess., 381–90 (Proceedings of February 18, 20, 23, 24, 25, 26, 27, and 28; March 2 and 3, 1801).

14. 1 *Senate Executive Journal,* 6th Cong., 2nd Sess., 388 (Proceedings of March 2, 1801).

15. Levy, *Original Intent,* 78.

16. 1 *Senate Executive Journal,* 6th Cong., 2nd Sess., 390 (Proceedings of March 3, 1801).

17. Jefferson took the oath of the office of the presidency on March 4, 1801.

18. January 16, 1811, letter from Thomas Jefferson to Dr. Benjamin Rush (3 *Jefferson's Retirement Papers,* 306–7; XIII *Jefferson's Writings* (1903 ed.), 7; V *Jefferson's Writings* (1853 ed.), 561–62; XI *Jefferson's Works,* 171; *Jefferson*—"Letters," 1237–38).

19. January 16, 1811, letter from Thomas Jefferson to Dr. Benjamin Rush (3 *Jefferson's Retirement Papers,* 306–7; XIII *Jefferson's Writings* (1903 ed.), 7; V *Jefferson's Writings* (1853 ed.), 561; XI *Jefferson's Works,* 171; *Jefferson*—"Letters," 1237–38) ("scenes of midnight appointment"); June 12, 1823, letter from Thomas Jefferson to Judge William Johnson (XV *Jefferson's Writings* (1903 ed.), 447; VII *Jefferson's Writings* (1853 ed.), 295; XII *Jefferson's Works,* 256–57 note 1; *Jefferson*—"Letters," 1474; IV *Jefferson's Memoirs,* 373) ("the midnight appointments of Mr. Adams"); see also Rehnquist, *The Supreme Court,* 27.

Although one of former Chief Justice John Marshall's biographers acknowledges the story of the "midnight judges" (II Beveridge, 561), he describes the time characterization of "midnight" as a "legend" (*id.,* 562).

20. Adams had nominated Marshall as his new secretary of state less than a year earlier, on May 12, 1800. 1 *Senate Executive Journal,* 6th Cong., 1st Sess., 353 (Proceedings of May 12, 1800). The Senate consented the next day—one day prior to the adjournment of that

session of Congress. 1 *Senate Executive Journal,* 6th Cong., 1st Sess., 354 (Proceedings of May 13, 1800).

21. III Beveridge, 553–57; Baker, *Marshall,* 349–54.

22. 1 *Senate Executive Journal,* 6th Cong., 2nd Sess., 370–71 (Proceedings of January 20, 1801).

23. 1 *Senate Executive Journal,* 6th Cong., 2nd Sess., 374 (Proceedings of January 27, 1801).

24. Baker, *Marshall,* 394; Rehnquist, *The Supreme Court,* 26.

25. June 12, 1823, letter from Thomas Jefferson to Judge William Johnson (XV *Jefferson's Writings* (1903 ed.), 447; VII *Jefferson's Writings* (1853 ed.), 295; XII *Jefferson's Works,* 256–57 note 1; *Jefferson—* "Letters," 1474.

26. Rehnquist, *The Supreme Court,* 27.

27. III Beveridge, 110.

28. *Black's Law Dictionary,* 980.

29. *Marbury v. Madison,* 5 U.S. (1 Cranch) 137 (1803).

30. Amar, *America's Constitution,* 223.

31. Act of September 24, 1789, 1st Cong., 1st Sess., Ch. 20, § 13, 1 Stat. 80–81; 2 *Annals of Congress,* Appendix, 2245. Section 13 of the Act provided:

> *And be it further enacted,* That the Supreme Court shall have *exclusive jurisdiction* of all controversies of a civil nature, where a state is a party, except between a state and its citizens; and except also between a state and citizens of other states, or aliens, in which latter case it shall have *original but not exclusive jurisdiction.* And [the Supreme Court] shall have exclusively all such jurisdiction of suits or proceedings against ambassadors, or other public ministers, or their domestics, or domestic servants, as a court of law can have or exercise consistently with the law of nations; and *original, but not exclusive jurisdiction* of all suits brought by ambassadors, or their public ministers, or in which a consul, or vice consul, shall be a party. And the trial of issues in fact in the Supreme Court, in all actions at law against citizens of the United States, shall be by jury. The Supreme Court shall also have *appellate jurisdiction* from the circuit courts and courts of the several states, in the cases herein after [sic] specially provided for; and shall have power to issue writs of prohibition to the district courts, when proceeding as courts of admiralty and maritime jurisdiction, and writs of mandamus, in cases warranted by the principles and usages of law, to any courts appointed, or persons holding office, under the authority of the United States.

Id. (emphasis added).

32. Act of September 24, 1789, 1st Cong., 1st Sess., Ch. 20, § 13, 1 Stat 81, reproduced in 2 *Annals of Congress,* Appendix, 2245 (emphasis added).

33. The Constitution contains a provision known, appropriately enough, as the Supremacy Clause:

> This Constitution, and the laws of the United States which shall be made in pursuance thereof; and all treaties made, or which shall be made, under the authority of the United States, *shall be the supreme law of the land;* and the judges in every state shall be bound thereby, any thing in the constitution or laws of any state to the contrary notwithstanding.

U.S. Const., Art. VI, Clause (or Paragraph) 2, 1 Stat. 19 (emphasis added).

34. Since 1789, the first paragraph in Article III, Section 2, of the Constitution has authorized the federal courts to resolve only nine categories of "cases" or "controversies."

U.S. Const., Art. III, § 2, ¶ 1, 1 Stat. 17–18.

35. The second paragraph in Article III, Section 2, of the Constitution provides:

> In all cases affecting ambassadors, other public ministers and consuls, and those in which a state shall be party, the Supreme Court shall have *original* jurisdiction. In all the other cases before mentioned, the Supreme Court shall have *appellate* jurisdiction, both as to law and fact, with such exceptions, and under such regulations as the Congress shall make.

U.S. Const., Art. III, § 2, ¶ 2, 1 Stat. 18 (emphasis added).

36. See, for instance: *Turner v. Bank of North America,* 4 U.S. (4 Dall.) 8, 10 (1799); *United States v. Hudson & Goodwin,* 11 U.S. (7 Cranch) 32, 33 (1812); *McIntire v. Wood,* 11 U.S. (7 Cranch) 504, 506 (1813); *Osborn v. Bank of the United States,* 22 U.S. (9 Wheat.) 738, 822–23 (1824); *Cary v. Curtis,* 44 U.S. (3 How.) 236, 244–45 (1845); *Sheldon v. Sill,* 49 U.S. (8 How.) 441, 449 (1850); and *Mayor v. Cooper,* 73 U.S. (6 Wall.) 247, 252 (1867).

37. The Senate began consideration of the Judiciary Act on June 12, 1789, just two months after it first attained a quorum on April 6, 1789. I *Documentary History . . . First Federal Congress,* 67 (Proceedings of June 12, 1789); 1 *Senate Journal,* 1st Cong., 1st Sess., 34 (Proceedings of June 12, 1789); 1 *Annals of Congress,* 1st Cong., 1st Sess., 47 (Senate Proceedings of June 12, 1789).

38. Senator Maclay's journal of the First Congress's Senate proceedings confirms that Senator Ellsworth authored the Judiciary Act:

This vile bill [*viz.*, the Judiciary Act] is a child of his [referring to Ellsworth], and he defends it with the care of a parent, even with wrath and anger. He kindled, as he always does, when it is meddled with.

Maclay's Journal, 91–92 (notes of June 29, 1798); IX *Documentary History . . . First Federal Congress*, 91 (notes of June 29, 1798). The Supreme Court's opinion in *Myers v. United States*, 272 U.S. 52, 122 (1926), separately confirms that Sen. Ellsworth "was the author of the Judiciary Act in that Congress."

39. I *Documentary History . . . First Federal Congress*, 11, 14 (Proceedings of April 7 and 13, respectively, 1789); 1 *Senate Journal*, 1st Cong., 1st Sess., 10, 11 (Proceedings of April 7 and 13, respectively, 1789); 1 *Annals of Congress*, 1st Cong., 1st Sess., 18, 19 (Senate Proceedings of April 7 and 13, respectively, 1789).

40. See I Elliott's *Debates*, 124–25; III Farrand's *Records*, Appendix B, 557–59 ("List of Delegates") and 587–90 ("Attendance of Delegates").

41. Eleven states—all except North Carolina and Rhode Island—had elected senators to serve during the First Session of the First Congress that began in March 1789 and adjourned in September 1789. See I *Documentary History . . . First Federal Congress*, 3, 5, 6, 7, 13, 15, 21, 51, 61, 91; 1 *Senate Journal*, 1st Cong., 1st Sess., 5, 7, 10–11, 14, 28, 31, 44, 45; and 1 *Annals of Congress*, 1st Cong., 1st Sess., 16, 18, 19, 22, 40, 46, 53 (each chronicling the appearances of the various senators during the proceedings of March 4, 19, 21, 28; April 6, 13, 14, 20; May 21; June 8; July 25 and 27, 1789). Although neither North Carolina nor Rhode Island had ratified the Constitution by the time the First Congress convened, the Constitution had in fact been ratified by the requisite nine states and had become effective, but only as to the ratifying states.

42. Senators Bassett (DE), Butler (SC), Ellsworth (CT), Few (GA), Johnson (CT), Langdon (NH), Morris (PA), Paterson (NJ), Read (DE), and Strong (MA) had been delegates at the 1787 Constitutional Convention. I Elliott's *Debates*, 124–25; III Farrand's *Records*, Appendix B, 557–59, 587–90.

43. Article I, Section 2, of the Constitution prescribed no more than sixty-five representatives for the inaugural Congress:

The Number of Representatives shall not exceed one for every thirty Thousand, but each State shall have at Least one Representative; and until such enumeration shall be made, the State of New Hampshire shall be entitled to choose three, Massachusetts eight, Rhode-Island and Providence Plantations one, Connecticut five, New-York six, New Jersey four, Pennsylvania eight, Delaware one, Maryland six, Virginia ten, North Carolina five, South Carolina five, and Georgia three.

U.S. Const., Art. I, § 2, 1 Stat. 10–11.

However, neither North Carolina nor Rhode Island sent representatives to the inaugural Congress, thus reducing the actual number of representatives to fifty-nine for the First Session of the First Congress in 1789. See III *Documentary History . . . First Federal Congress,* 3–8, 16, 18, 25, 28, 30, 31, 43, 49, 54, 71, 83, 87, 89, 149; 1 *House Journal,* 3, 4, 5, 6, 7, 11, 12, 16, 18, 19, 24, 29, 31, 40, 46, 48, 49, 79; and 1 *Annals of Congress,* 99, 100, 101, 106, 109, 126, 167, 178, 199, 241, 242, 276, 306, 425, 440, 471, 498, 745 (each chronicling the appearances of the various representatives during the proceedings of March 4, 5, 14, 17, 18, 23, 25, and 30; April 1, 2, 3, 4, 6, 8, 9, 13, 17, 20, 22, 23, and 30; May 1, 6, 9, and 25; June 8, 15, and 17; and August 14, 1789).

44. Representatives Sherman (CT), Baldwin (GA), Carroll (MD), Gerry (MA), Gilman (NH), Clymer (PA), Fitzsimons (PA), and Madison (VA) had been delegates at the 1787 Constitutional Convention. I Elliott's *Debates,* 124–25; III Farrand's *Records,* Appendix B, 557–59, 587–90.

45. Baker, *Marshall,* 94–96.

46. II Beveridge, 77–80, 97–99, 123; Baker, *Marshall,* 160–61, 168, 188–89, 196–97, 298–99, 315–16.

47. II Beveridge, 81–91, 165.

48. II Beveridge, 77–80, 97–99, 123; Baker, *Marshall,* 169, 201–2, 316.

49. Baker, *Marshall,* 345.

50. Ibid., 401.

51. Ibid., 400.

52. More than a century and a half later, another Supreme Court justice had the same thoughts. During the Supreme Court's consideration of the "Watergate Tapes" case in the summer of 1974, *United States v. Nixon,* 418 U.S. 683 (1974) (when President Nixon challenged a special prosecutor's authority to subpoena Oval Office recordings), Justice Potter Stewart (and probably many other people) feared at one point that "if the President were to defy the

Supreme Court that would cripple the Court, perhaps forever." Woodward and Armstrong, 365. The Court ruled unanimously that the president enjoyed no "Executive Privilege" to withhold evidence under the circumstances, and President Nixon resigned seventeen days later. Woodward and Armstrong, 421.

53. Rehnquist, *The Supreme Court,* 29.

54. Ibid., 28.

55. Baker, *Marshall,* 400. Marshall purposefully altered his consideration of the legal issues, such that the question whether the Supreme Court had the authority to hear the matter in the first place—always the initial issue in any judicial decision—got bumped to the back of the line. *Id.*

56. In a roughly 10,000-word opinion, the actual ruling appears only in the final segment. Marshall spent at least three-fourths of his opinion criticizing the Jefferson administration's handling of the affair—neatly couched in legal rhetoric but technically meaningless.

57. *Marbury,* 5 U.S. (1 Cranch) at 177–80.

58. Amar, *America's Constitution,* 232 (emphasis added).

59. Rehnquist, *The Supreme Court,* 35.

60. In *Myers v. United States,* 272 U.S. 52 (1926), the Court examined the extent of the president's constitutional authority to remove a presidential appointee without congressional approval. In the course of its opinion, the Court discussed Justice Marshall's 1803 *Marbury* opinion as an example of a narrative that needlessly opined on issues not actually before the Court:

> . . . The [petition for the writ of mandamus] was discharged by the Supreme Court, for the reason that the court had no jurisdiction in such a case to issue a writ of mandamus.

> The court had therefore *nothing before it* calling for a judgment upon the merits of the question of issuing the mandamus.

272 U.S. at 140 (emphasis added). Yet, in the Court's words in *Myers,* "[n]otwithstanding this" (*viz.,* the absence of jurisdiction to do anything except dismiss Marbury's case), Marshall nevertheless proceeded to discuss other issues solely to animate an ulterior motive. *Id.*

61. *Marbury,* 5 U.S. (1 Cranch) at 139.

62. Ibid., at 162–68.

63. Baker, *Marshall,* 401.

64. Konefsky, 82.

65. Baker, *Marshall*, 395.

66. June 12, 1823, letter from Thomas Jefferson to Judge William Johnson (XV *Jefferson's Writings* (1903 ed.), 447–48; VII *Jefferson's Writings* (1853 ed.), 295; XII *Jefferson's Works*, 256–57 note 1; *Jefferson*—"Letters," 1474) (italics in original).

67. *Marbury*, 5 U.S. (1 Cranch) at 171–72 (emphasis added).

68. Marshall spoke of the pension-related Act of February 27, 1793, 2nd Cong., 2nd Sess., Ch. 17, 1 Stat. 324–25, which partially amended and partially repealed the similar Act of March 23, 1792, 2nd Cong., 1st Sess., Ch. 11, 1 Stat. 243–45.

Section 3 of the 1793 legislation provided that "it shall be the duty of the Secretary of War . . . to take such measures as may be necessary to obtain an adjudication of the Supreme Court of the United States, on the validity of any such rights claimed . . . [.]" Act of February 27, 1793, 2nd Cong., 2nd Sess., Ch. 17, § 3, 1 Stat. 325. The Court's issuance of the writ of mandamus in the 1793 matter had occurred in accordance with that specific provision.

69. Levy, *Original Intent*, 75. Professor Levy also describes the *Marbury* decision as "an opinion of slight merit, distorted reasoning, and galloping activism" (*id.*, 77), an opinion that "oozed politics and spewed Marshallian misrepresentations" (*id.*, 77)—referring to its author, Chief Justice Marshall.

70. Levy, *Original Intent*, 75.

71. In *Scott v. Sandford*, 60 U.S. (19 How.) 393 (1857), in addition to deciding that freed slaves did not qualify as "persons" within the Constitution, the Court also decided that Congress's Missouri Compromise, which prohibited slavery within the Louisiana Territory north of 36° 30' except Missouri, had not been warranted as a regulation of territory belonging to the United States.

72. III Elliott's *Debates*, 553 (Virginia Ratifying Convention) (Proceedings of June 20, 1788) (Statement of John Marshall); I Beveridge, 452.

73. Before Chief Justice Marshall's era, the Supreme Court rendered its decisions via individual opinions of each of the justices.

74. *Calder v. Bull*, 3 U.S. (3 Dall.) 386, 399 (1798).

75. *Calder*, 3 U.S. (3 Dall.) at 392.

76. *Cooper v. Telfair*, 4 U.S. (4 Dall.) 14, 19 (1800).

77. Baker, *Marshall*, 401.

78. Article I in the Constitution implements the "legislative"

power (*viz.*, congressional lawmaking authority) while Article II in the Constitution implements the "executive" power (*viz.*, presidential authority). The "judicial" power appears in Article III—not an unintended or purely fortuitous chronological arrangement in the eyes of the 1787 Constitutional Convention.

79. *The Federalist Papers, No. 78* (attributed to Alexander Hamilton) (emphasis added).

80. *Dred Scott v. Sandford,* 60 U.S. (19 How.) 393 (1857).

81. President Abraham Lincoln's Inaugural address, March 4, 1861, *Inaugural Addresses,* 194; I Sandburg, *Lincoln's War Years,* 132; *Lincoln's Life,* 86.

82. *Cherokee Nation v. Georgia,* 30 U.S. (5 Pet.) 1 (1831), and *Worcester v. Georgia,* 31 U.S. (6 Pet.) 515 (1832).

83. Konefsky, 235.

84. Baker, *Marshall,* 745 ("Although a recent study challenges that report [of Jackson's remarks], the evidence is that if Jackson did not say that, he certainly meant it.")

85. Woodward and Armstrong, 420–21. See *United States v. Nixon,* 418 U.S. 683 (1974).

86. Woodward and Armstrong, 421.

87. Konefsky, 2.

88. Ibid., 87.

89. September 6, 1819, letter from Thomas Jefferson to Judge Spencer Roane (XV *Jefferson's Writings* (1903 ed.), 213; VII *Jefferson's Writings* (1853 ed.), 134; XII *Jefferson's Works,* 137; *Jefferson*—"Letters," 1426).

90. June 27, 1823, letter from James Madison to Thomas Jefferson (IX *Madison's Writings,* 142–43; III *Madison's Letters,* 326–27) (emphasis added).

91. *Wallace v. Jaffree,* 472 U.S. 38, 107 (1985) (Rehnquist, C. J., dissenting).

92. *New York Trust Co. v. Eisner,* 256 U.S. 345, 349 (1921).

93. References to Justice Holmes's observation appear in, for instance, the Supreme Court's opinion in *Committee for Public Education v. Nyquist,* 413 U.S. 756, 777 n. 33 (1973); in Supreme Court Justice Scalia's dissenting opinion in *Lee v. Weisman,* 505 U.S. 577, 632 (1992) (Scalia, J., dissenting, joined by Chief Justice Rehnquist and Justices White and Thomas); in (former) Supreme Court Justice O'Connor's concurring opinion in *Wallace v. Jaffree,*

472 U.S. 38, 79 (1985) (O'Connor, J., concurring); and in (former) Supreme Court Justice Brennan's concurring opinion in *Walz v. Tax Commission*, 397 U.S. 664, 681 (1970) (Brennan, J., concurring).

94. *Reynolds v. United States*, 98 U.S. (8 Otto) at 145 (1878).

95. *Reynolds*, 98 U.S. (8 Otto) 164.

96. The 1853 publication of Jefferson's writings included Jefferson's famous letter. VIII *Jefferson's Writings* (1853 ed.), 113. An earlier (1829) publication of Jefferson's letters—*Jefferson's Memoirs*—made no mention of it.

97. *Reynolds*, 98 U.S. (8 Otto), at 161–62.

98. *Reynolds*, 98 U.S. (8 Otto), at 162 (emphasis added).

99. See Dreisbach, *Jefferson and the Wall of Separation*, 98 n. 17, citing: S. Safranek, "Can Science Guide Legal Argumentation?: The Role of Metaphor In Constitutional Cases," 25 *Loy. Univ. Chi. L. Jour.*, 375–76 (1994); C. Mousin, "Confronting the Wall of Separation: A New Dialogue Between Law and Religion," 42 *DePaul L. Rev.*, 3–5 (1992); C. Haynes, *Religion in American History: What to Teach and How*, 53 (Alexandria, Virginia: Association for Supervision and Curriculum Development, 1990); R. Healey, "Thomas Jefferson's 'Wall': Absolute Or Serpentine?," in 30 *Journal of Church and State*, 443 (1988); C. Mooney, *Public Virtue: Law and the Social Character of Religion*, 30 (South Bend, Indiana: University of Notre Dame Press, 1986); R. Hutchins, "The Future of the Wall," in *The Wall Between Church and State*, 17 (C. Mooney, Ed., Chicago: University of Chicago Press, 1963).

100. See Chapter 13B for a discussion of the historical mistranscription of the word "legislative" in Jefferson's letter.

101. VIII *Jefferson's Writings* (1853 ed.), 113; XVI *Jefferson's Writings* (1903 ed.), 281–82.

102. *Reynolds*, 98 U.S. (8 Otto), at 164 (emphasis added). For those interested in the full context of the Court's opinion, it reads, in pertinent part (and with Jefferson's remarks within the Court's 428-word paragraph segregated for ease of reading):

> . . . Accordingly, at the first session of the first Congress the amendment now under consideration was proposed with others by Mr. Madison. It met the views of the advocates of religious freedom, and was adopted. Mr. Jefferson afterwards, in reply to an address to him by a committee of the Danbury Baptist Association . . . , took occasion to say:
>
> > "Believing with you that religion is a matter which lies solely between man and his God; that he owes account to none other

for his faith or his worship; that the legislative powers of the government reach actions only, and not opinions, I contemplate with sovereign reverence that act of the whole American people which declared that their legislature should 'make no law respecting an establishment of religion or prohibiting the free exercise thereof,' thus building a wall of separation between church and State. Adhering to this expression of the supreme will of the nation in behalf of the rights of conscience, I shall see with sincere satisfaction the progress of those sentiments which tend to restore man to all his natural rights, convinced he has no natural right in opposition to his social duties."

Coming as this does from an acknowledged leader of the advocates of the measure, it may be accepted almost as an authoritative declaration of the scope and effect of the amendment thus secured. Congress was deprived of all legislative power over mere opinion, but was left free to reach actions which were in violation of social duties or subversive of good order.

Id.

103. R. Hutchins, "The Future of the Wall," in *The Wall Between Church and State,* 17 (C. Mooney, Ed., Chicago: University of Chicago Press, 1963) (emphasis added), quoted in Dreisbach, *Jefferson and the Wall of Separation,* 98.

104. *Reynolds,* 98 U.S. (8 Otto), at 164 (emphasis added).

105. In an introduction at the beginning of his *Notes on the State of Virginia,* Jefferson wrote that "[t]he following Notes were written in Virginia in the year 1781, and somewhat corrected and enlarged in the winter of 1782 . . . [.]" *Jefferson—Notes on the State of Virginia,* 124; III *Jefferson's Works* (*Notes on the State of Virginia*), 335; II *Jefferson's Writings* (1903 ed.) (*Notes on the State of Virginia*), unpaginated "Introductory Notes."

106. II *Jefferson's Writings* (1903 ed.) (*Notes on the State of Virginia*) 221; *Jefferson—Notes on the State of Virginia,* 285; IV *Jefferson's Works,* 78 (*Notes on the State of Virginia*) (emphasis added).

107. *Reynolds,* 98 U.S. (8 Otto), at 164 (emphasis added).

108. Jefferson's various letters to Madison between the adjournment of the Constitutional Convention on September 17, 1787, and the adjournment of the First Congress at the end of September 1789 have already been detailed in Chapter 13.

109. Madison's various letters to Jefferson between the adjournment of the Constitutional Convention on September 17, 1787, and

the adjournment of the First Congress at the end of September 1789 have already been detailed in Chapter 13.

110. Madison wrote Jefferson on **June 13, 1789** (12 *Madison's Papers,* 217; I *Madison's Letters,* 475; 15 *Jefferson's Papers,* 180), **June 30, 1789** (12 *Madison's Papers,* 267; I *Madison's Letters,* 479; 15 *Jefferson's Papers,* 224), and **August 2, 1789** (15 *Jefferson's Papers,* 324).

111. May 27, 1789, letter from Madison to Jefferson (12 *Madison's Papers,* 186; V *Madison's Writings,* 370 n.; I *Madison's Letters,* 472; 15 *Jefferson's Papers,* 154).

112. June 30, 1789, letter from Madison to Jefferson (12 *Madison's Papers,* 272; 15 *Jefferson's Papers,* 229).

113. Malone, *Jefferson and the Rights of Man,* 169.

114. 15 *Jefferson's Papers,* 325.

115. *Reynolds,* 98 U.S. (8 Otto), at 164.

116. Ibid.

117. For instance, the *Reynolds* opinion recites, accurately enough:

> Before the adoption of the Constitution, attempts were made in some of the colonies and States to legislate not only in respect to the establishment of religion, but in respect to its doctrines and precepts as well. The people were taxed, against their will, for the support of religion, and sometimes for the support of particular sects to whose tenets they could not and did not subscribe. Punishments were prescribed for a failure to attend upon public worship, and sometimes for entertaining heretical opinions. The controversy upon this general subject was animated in many of the States, but seemed at last to culminate in Virginia. In 1784, the House of Delegates of that State having under consideration "a bill establishing provision for teachers of the Christian religion," postponed it until the next session, and directed that the bill should be published and distributed, and that the people be requested "to signify their opinion respecting the adoption of such a bill at the next session of assembly."

Reynolds, 98 U.S. (8 Otto), at 162–63.

118. For the details of Patrick Henry's proposed "establishment" tax, see Chapter 3C.

119. *Reynolds,* 98 U.S. (8 Otto), at 162–63.

120. See Chapter 3D.

121. Lambert, 230, citing a particular edition of Jefferson's *Notes on the State of Virginia.* (Lambert utilized a particular version of Jefferson's *Notes.* The excerpts that he quotes can also be found in *Jefferson—Notes*

on the State of Virginia, 287 (Peterson's 1984 edition of Jefferson's *Notes*), and in IV *Jefferson's Works,* 81–82 (Ford's turn-of-the-century twelve-volume limited "Federal Edition" of *The Works of Thomas Jefferson*).) Immediately following his declaration that "Jefferson opposed the bill," Lambert quotes segments of the final dozen or so sentences in Jefferson's "Query XVII." Lambert, 230.

122. Brant, *James Madison: The Nationalist,* 346; Ketchum, 162–63; see also the "Supplemental Appendix" to the Supreme Court's opinion in *Everson v. Board of Education,* 330 U.S. 1, 72–74 (1947). A "broadside" (or a public notice) of Henry's proposal bears the date December 24, 1784, and it quotes from the Journal of the Virginia House of Delegates of that same date. Huston, *Religion and the State Governments.*

123. *Jefferson—Notes on the State of Virginia,* 124; III *Jefferson's Works* (*Notes on the State of Virginia*), 335; II *Jefferson's Writings* (1903 ed.) (*Notes on the State of Virginia*), unpaginated "Introductory Notes."

124. February 8, 1786, letter from Thomas Jefferson to James Madison (9 *Jefferson's Papers,* 264; V *Jefferson's Writings* (1903 ed.), 278; V *Jefferson's Works,* 78; 8 *Madison's Papers,* 45).

125. 1 *Jefferson's Papers,* 363; *Jefferson—*"Public Papers," 344; II *Jefferson's Works,* 180.

126. Thomas Jefferson, Draft of Bill Exempting Dissenters from Contributing to the Support of the Church, November 30, 1776, reproduced in: 1 *Jefferson's Papers,* 552–53; I *Jefferson's Works,* 63 incl. n. 1; 5 *Founders' Constitution,* 74–75.

127. See Chapter 3B.

128. *Engel v. Vitale,* 370 U.S. 421, 428 n. 10 (1962).

129. See, for instance, *County of Washington v. Gunther,* 452 U.S. 161, 176 n. 16 (1981), and *Teamsters v. United States,* 431 U.S. 324, 354 n. 39 (1977) (Court gives scant, if any, consideration to post-enactment comments of congressional legislators).

130. *Everson v. Board of Education,* 330 U.S. 1 (1947).

131. *Bradfield v. Roberts,* 175 U.S. 291 (1899).

132. *Reuben Quick Bear v. Leupp,* 210 U.S. 50 (1908).

133. The Supreme Court first declared that the First Amendment's Free Exercise Clause applied to the states (via the Fourteenth Amendment) in 1937 (*Cantwell v. Connecticut,* 310 U.S. 296 (1937)) and first declared that the First Amendment's Establishment Clause applied to the states (again, via the Fourteenth

Amendment) in 1947 (*Everson v. Board of Education*, 330 U.S. 1 (1947)).

134. Cox, 198–99.

135. XII *History of the Supreme Court*, 250.

136. Fair, 1–7.

137. Fair, 8. However, Fair's unadorned reference to the "Fourteenth Amendment" leaves it uncertain whether in the early stages of the New Jersey litigation Everson specifically contended that the Establishment Clause—which, by its terms, applied only to Congress—applied to the states as well, or whether he urged some other legal argument predicated upon the Fourteenth Amendment. (At the time, the Supreme Court had yet to declare that the Establishment Clause applied to the states via the Fourteenth Amendment; it did not make that declaration until its subsequent decision in *Everson* itself.)

138. *Everson*, 330 U.S. at 18.

139. Ibid., at 8–14.

140. *Everson*, 330 U.S. at 8. The Court explained that

> A large proportion of the early settlers of this country came here from Europe to escape the bondage of laws which compelled them to support and attend government favored churches. . . . In efforts to force loyalty to whatever religious group happened to be on top and in league with the government of a particular time and place, men and women had been fined, cast in jail, cruelly tortured, and killed. Among the offenses for which these punishments had been inflicted were such things as speaking disrespectfully of the views of ministers of government-established churches, nonattendance at those churches, expressions of non-belief in their doctrines, and failure to pay taxes and tithes to support them.

Everson, 330 U.S. at 8–9.

141. These practices of the old world were transplanted to and began to thrive in the soil of the new America. The very charters granted by the English Crown to the individuals and companies designated to make the laws which would control the destinies of the colonials authorized these individuals and companies to erect religious establishments which all, whether believers or non-believers, would be required to support and attend. . . . These practices became so commonplace as to shock the freedom-loving colonials into a feeling of abhorrence. The imposition of taxes to pay ministers' salaries and to build and maintain churches and church property aroused their indignation. . . .

Everson, 330 U.S. at 9–11.

142. *Everson,* 330 U.S. at 11.

143. Ibid., at 11–12.

144. See Chapter 3B.

145. *Everson,* 330 U.S. at 12.

146. Ibid., at 11.

147. Ibid., at 12.

148. See Chapter 3B.

149. 2 *Jefferson's Papers,* 305–24, 547–53; 8 *Madison's Papers,* 391–94.

150. See Chapter 3D.

151. The *Everson* opinion remarks:

And the statute itself [viz., Jefferson's 1779 bill] enacted

"That no man shall be compelled to frequent or support any religious worship, place, or ministry whatsoever, nor shall be enforced, restrained, molested, or burthened, in his body or goods, nor shall otherwise suffer on account of his religious opinions or belief. . . ."

Everson, 330 U.S. at 13.

152. Baker, "The Establishment Clause as Intended," 44.

153. Ibid., 41.

The [Court's] then-accepted history of the original understanding of the [E]stablishment [C]lause focused not on the actual drafting of the religious clauses but on earlier events surrounding the struggle over establishment in the state of Virginia. The Court relied on the statements of Thomas Jefferson and James Madison and assumed that Madison must have had the same intention when he proposed the First Amendment. . . . [T]he myth and [Jefferson's] metaphor determined what was doctrinally orthodox and accepted in argument.

Id.

154. *Everson,* 330 U.S. at 13 (emphasis added). The excerpted sentence from *Everson* replicates the *Reynolds* opinion's same factual miscue.

155. *Everson,* 330 U.S. at 13, citing *Reynolds v. United States,* 98 U.S. (8 Otto) 145 (1878), *Watson v. Jones,* 80 U.S. (13 Wall) 679 (1872), and *Davis v. Beason,* 133 U.S. 333 (1890).

156. *Reynolds v. United States* and *Davis v. Beason.*

157. *Watson v. Jones.*

158. *Everson,* 330 U.S. at 15–16 (enumeration added).

159. *Everson,* 330 U.S. at 8. See, as well, Chapter 12.

160. *Everson*, 330 U.S. at 16.

161. Ibid., at 18.

162. Dreisbach, "*Everson* and the Command of History," 28.

Longtime Princeton professor of jurisprudence, Edward Corwin, has authored the following books on the Constitution: the seminal *The Constitution and What It Means Today* (first published in 1920, 3rd edition 1928, thirteen revised editions since); *National Supremacy— Treaty Power vs. State Power* (1913); *The Doctrine of Judicial Review* (1914); *The President's Control of Foreign Relations* (1917); *John Marshall and the Constitution* (1919); *The President's Removal Power under the Constitution* (1927); *The Twilight of the Supreme Court* (1935); *Commerce Power Versus State Rights—Back to the Constitution* (1936); *Court Over Constitution* (1938); *The President: Office and Power* (1940); *Constitutional Revolution* (1941); *The Constitution and World Organization* (1944); *Total War and the Constitution* (1947); *Liberty against Government* (1948); *The Constitution of the United States of America: Analysis and Interpretation* (1949); and *A Constitution of Power in a Secular State* (1951).

Professor Dreisbach's description of Corwin as the "dean of American constitutional scholars" (Dreisbach, "*Everson* and the Command of History," 28) proves well-warranted. See, as well, discussions of Corwin in 5 *American National Biography*, 547–48; *Dictionary of American Biography*, Supp. 7, 146–47; IV *Who Was Who in America*, 204.

163. Corwin, 10 (italics in original).

164. Ibid., 20 (italics in original).

165. Cox, 199 (emphasis added).

166. Dreisbach, "*Everson* and the Command of History," 30.

167. *Wallace v. Jaffree*, 472 U.S. 38, 91–114 (1985) (Rehnquist, C. J., dissenting).

168. *South Carolina v. United States*, 199 U.S. 437, 450 (1905).

169. Justices Roberts, Scalia, Kennedy, Souter, and Breyer each graduated from Harvard Law School.

170. Justices Thomas and Alito each graduated from Yale Law School.

171. Justice Stevens graduated from Northwestern University School of Law, and Justice Ginsburg graduated from Columbia University School of Law.

172. Chief Justice Roberts, Justice Scalia, Justice Thomas, and

Justice Ginsburg sat on the DC Circuit Court of Appeals, Justice Souter and Justice Breyer sat on the First Circuit Court of Appeals, Justice Alito sat on the Third Circuit Court of Appeals, Justice Stevens sat on the Seventh Circuit Court of Appeals, and Justice Kennedy sat on the Ninth Circuit Court of Appeals.

173. Chief Justice Roberts clerked for former (Chief) Justice Rehnquist, Justice Stevens clerked for former Justice Rutledge, and Justice Breyer clerked for former Justice Goldberg.

174. Justices Alito, Breyer, Ginsburg, Kennedy, and Scalia each taught as professors at various law schools. Justice Stevens taught as a lecturer at two law schools.

175. *Supreme Court Justices*, 3197.

176. The data for the 1947 *Everson* Court: **Justice Black**—*Oxford Companion to the Supreme Court*, 84–87; III *Supreme Court Justices*, 2321–27, 3198; Paddock, 291; **Justice Reed**—*Oxford Companion to the Supreme Court*, 829–30; III *Supreme Court Justices*, 2373–76, 3198; Paddock, 291; **Justice Douglas**—*Oxford Companion to the Supreme Court*, 270–72; IV *Supreme Court Justices*, 2447–55, 3198; Paddock, 291; **Justice Murphy**—*Oxford Companion to the Supreme Court*, 659–60; IV *Supreme Court Justices*, 2493–501, 3198; Paddock, 291; **Justice Vinson**—*Oxford Companion to the Supreme Court*, 1050–51; IV *Supreme Court Justices*, 2639–42, 3198; Paddock 291; **Justice Frankfurter**—*Oxford Companion to the Supreme Court*, 364–67; III *Supreme Court Justices*, 2401–5, 3198; Paddock, 291; **Justice Jackson**—*Oxford Companion to the Supreme Court*, 512–14; IV *Supreme Court Justices*, 2543–70, 3198; Paddock, 291; **Justice Rutledge**—*Oxford Companion to the Supreme Court*, 877–78; IV *Supreme Court Justices*, 2593–98, 3198; Paddock, 291; and **Justice Burton**—*Oxford Companion to the Supreme Court*, 125–26; IV *Supreme Court Justices*, 2617–19, 3198; Paddock, 291.

177. Justice Black attended a two-year *undergraduate* law program; whether he obtained a law degree has only been assumed here. *Oxford Companion to the Supreme Court*, 84–87; *Supreme Court Justices*, 3198.

178. One source reports that Justice Vinson apparently obtained a law degree from a "Centre College." *Supreme Court Justices*, 3198. Another source leaves it unclear whether Vinson had a law degree. *Oxford Companion to the Supreme Court*, 1050–51.

179. Not until the mid-to-late twentieth century did states require a law degree as a condition of admission to practice law; many states

gave credit for legal experience (such as clerking in a law firm) or self-study.

180. *History of the Supreme Court,* 73.

Chapter 15

1 Professor Corwin authored "The Supreme Court as National School Board," 14 *Law and Contemporary Problems* 3 (Duke University School of Law, 1949), cited periodically throughout as simply "Corwin."

2. School-related programs have spawned Establishment Clause decisions by the Supreme Court in *Everson v. Board of Education,* 330 U.S. 1 (1947); *McCollum v. Board of Education,* 333 U.S. 203 (1948); *Zorach v. Clauson,* 343 U.S. 306 (1952); *Engel v. Vitale,* 370 U.S. 421 (1962); *Abington School District v. Schempp,* 374 U.S. 203 (1963); *Board of Education v. Allen,* 392 U.S. 236 (1968); *Epperson v. Arkansas,* 393 U.S. 97 (1968); *Lemon v. Kurtzman,* 403 U.S. 602 (1971); *Tilton v. Richardson,* 403 U.S. 672 (1971); *Levitt v. Committee for Public Education,* 413 U.S. 472 (1973) (decided concurrently with two other related cases: *Anderson v. Committee for Public Education & Religious Liberty* and *Cathedral Academy v. Committee for Public Education & Religious Liberty*); *Hunt v. McNair,* 413 U.S. 734 (1973); *Committee for Public Education v. Nyquist,* 413 U.S. 756 (1973) (decided concurrently with three other related cases: *Anderson v. Committee for Public Education & Religious Liberty, Nyquist v. Committee for Public Education & Religious Liberty,* and *Cherry v. Committee for Public Education & Religious Liberty*); *Sloan v. Lemon,* 413 U.S. 825 (1973) (decided concurrently with one other related case: *Crouter v. Lemon*); *Meek v. Pittenger,* 421 U.S. 349 (1975) (later declared an "anomaly" and "no longer good law" in *Mitchell v. Helms,* 530 U.S. 793, 808 (2000)); *Roemer v. Maryland Board of Public Works,* 426 U.S. 736 (1976); *Wolman v. Walter,* 433 U.S. 229 (1977) (later declared an "anomaly" and "no longer good law" in *Mitchell v. Helms,* 530 U.S. 793, 808 (2000)); *Committee for Public Education & Religious Liberty v. Regan,* 444 U.S. 646 (1980); *Stone v. Graham,* 449 U.S. 39 (1980); *Widmar v. Vincent,* 454 U. S. 263 (1981); *Mueller v. Allen,* 463 U.S. 388 (1983); *Wallace v. Jaffree,* 472 U.S. 38 (1985); *Grand Rapids School District v. Ball,* 473 U.S. 373 (1985) (overruled in part by *Agostini v. Felton,* 521 U.S. 203 (1997)); *Aguilar v. Felton,* 473 U.S. 402 (1985) (overruled in part by *Agostini v. Felton,* 521 U.S. 203 (1997)); *Edwards v. Aguillard,*

482 U.S. 578 (1987); *Westside Community Board of Education v. Mergens,* 496 U.S. 226 (1990); *Lee v. Weisman,* 505 U.S. 577 (1992); *Lamb's Chapel v. Center Moriches Union Free School District,* 508 U.S. 384 (1993); *Zobrest v. Catalina Foothills School District,* 509 U.S. 1 (1993); *Board of Education of Kiryas Joel School District v. Grumet,* 512 U.S. 687 (1994) (decided concurrently with two other related cases, *Board of Education of Monroe-Woodbury Central School District v. Grumet* and *Attorney General of New York v. Grumet*); *Rosenberger v. University of Virginia,* 515 U.S. 819 (1995); *Agostini v. Felton,* 521 U.S. 203 (1997); *Santa Fe Independent School District v. Doe,* 530 U.S. 290 (2000); *Mitchell v. Helms,* 530 U.S. 793 (2000); *Good News Club v. Milford Central School,* 533 U.S. 98 (2001); *Zelman v. Simmons-Harris,* 536 U.S. 639 (2002); and *Elk Grove Unified School District v. Newdow,* 542 U.S. 1 (2004).

3. *Van Orden v. Perry,* 545 U.S. 677, 688–89 (2005).

4. *Van Orden v. Perry,* 545 U.S. 677, 689 n. 9 (2005).

5. Marshall became chief justice in February 1801. For more details, see Chapter 14A.

6. See *Marsh v. Chambers,* 463 U.S. 783, 786 (1983), and *Zorach v. Clauson,* 343 U.S. 306, 313 (1952) (both recalling that historical practice); see also *McCreary County v. ACLU,* 545 U.S. 844, 886, and 888 (2005) (Scalia, J., dissenting) (referencing the Court's practice instigated by Justice Marshall, and reminding the reader that "[t]he sessions of this Court continue to open with the prayer 'God save the United States and this Honorable Court'").

7. Undated December 1831 letter from James Madison to N. P. Trist (IX *Madison's Writings,* 477; IV *Madison's Letters,* 211) (emphasis added).

8. *County of Allegheny v. ACLU,* 492 U.S. 573 (1989).

9. *Wolman v. Walter,* 433 U.S. 229 (1977). The Supreme Court later characterized the rationale expressed in *Wolman* as an "anomaly" and thus "no longer good law." *Mitchell v. Helms,* 530 U.S. 793, 808 (2000).

10. XII *History of the Supreme Court,* 261.

11. XII *History of the Supreme Court,* 261 (emphasis added).

12. Monsma, 123.

13. **From 1948 to 1971:** *McCollum v. Board of Education,* 333 U.S. 203 (1948); *Zorach v. Clauson,* 343 U.S. 306 (1952); *McGowan v. Maryland,* 366 U.S. 420 (1961); *Two Guys v. McGinley,* 366 U.S. 582 (1961); *Braunfeld v. Brown,* 366 U.S. 599 (1961); *Gallagher v. Crown Kosher*

Market, 366 U.S. 617 (1961); *Engel v. Vitale,* 370 U.S. 421 (1962); *Abington School District v. Schempp,* 374 U.S. 203 (1963); *Board of Education v. Allen,* 392 U.S. 236 (1968); *Epperson v. Arkansas,* 393 U.S. 97 (1968); *Walz v. Tax Commission,* 397 U.S. 664 (1970); *Gillette v. United States,* 401 U.S. 437 (1971); *Lemon v. Kurtzman,* 403 U.S. 602 (1971); and *Tilton v. Richardson,* 403 U.S. 672 (1971).

14. *Wallace v. Jaffree,* 472 U.S. 38, 91 (Rehnquist, C. J., dissenting).

15. **From 1973 to 1984:** *Levitt v. Committee for Public Education,* 413 U.S. 472 (1973); *Hunt v. McNair,* 413 U.S. 734 (1973); *Committee for Public Education v. Nyquist,* 413 U.S. 756 (1973); *Sloan v. Lemon,* 413 U.S. 825 (1973); *Meek v. Pittenger,* 421 U.S. 349 (1975) (later declared an "anomaly" and "no longer good law" in *Mitchell v. Helms,* 530 U.S. 793, 808 (2000)); *Roemer v. Maryland Board of Public Works,* 426 U.S. 736 (1976); *Wolman v. Walter,* 433 U.S. 229 (1977) (later declared an "anomaly" and "no longer good law" in *Mitchell v. Helms,* 530 U.S. 793, 808 (2000)); *Committee for Public Education & Religious Liberty v. Regan,* 444 U.S. 646 (1980); *Stone v. Graham,* 449 U.S. 39 (1980); *Widmar v. Vincent,* 454 U.S. 263 (1981); *Larson v. Valente,* 456 U.S. 228 (1982); *Larkin v. Grendel's Den, Inc.,* 459 U.S. 116 (1982); *Mueller v. Allen,* 463 U.S. 388 (1983); *Marsh v. Chambers,* 463 U.S. 783 (1983); and *Lynch v. Donnelly,* 465 U.S. 668 (1984).

16. **From 1985 to date:** *Wallace v. Jaffree,* 472 U.S. 38 (1985); *Estate of Thornton v. Caldor, Inc.,* 472 U.S. 703 (1985); *Grand Rapids School District v. Ball,* 473 U.S. 373 (1985) (overruled by *Agostini v. Felton,* 521 U.S. 203 (1997)); *Aguilar v. Felton,* 473 U.S. 402 (1985) (overruled by *Agostini v. Felton,* 521 U.S. 203 (1997)); *Witters v. Washington Dep't. of Social Services,* 474 U.S. 481 (1986); *Edwards v. Aguillard,* 482 U.S. 578 (1987); *Corporation of Presiding Bishop v. Amos,* 483 U.S. 327 (1987); *Bowen v. Kendrick,* 487 U.S. 589 (1988); *Texas Monthly, Inc. v. Bullock,* 489 U.S. 1 (1989); *County of Allegheny v. ACLU,* 492 U.S. 573 (1989); *Westside Community Schools v. Mergens,* 496 U.S. 226 (1990); *Lee v. Weisman,* 505 U.S. 577 (1992); *Lamb's Chapel v. Center Moriches Union Free School District,* 508 U.S. 384 (1993); *Zobrest v. Catalina Foothills School District,* 509 U.S. 1 (1993); *Board of Education of Kiryas Joel School District v. Grumet,* 512 U.S. 687 (1994); *Capitol Square Review and Advisory Board v. Pinette,* 515 U.S. 753 (1995); *Rosenberger v. University of Virginia,* 515 U.S. 819 (1995); *Agostini v. Felton,* 521 U.S. 203 (1997); *Santa Fe Independent School District v. Doe,* 530 U.S. 290 (2000); *Mitchell v. Helms,* 530 U.S. 793 (2000); *Good News Club v. Milford Central School,* 533 U.S.

98 (2001); *Zelman v. Simmons-Harris,* 536 U.S. 639 (2002); *Locke v. Davey,* 540 U. S. 712 (2004); *Elk Grove Unified School District v. Newdow,* 542 U.S. 1 (2004); *Cutter v. Wilkinson,* 544 U.S. 709, (2005); *McCreary County v. ACLU,* 545 U.S. 844, (2005); and *Van Orden v. Perry,* 545 U.S. 677, (2005).

17. *Van Orden v. Perry,* 545 U.S. 677, 683 (2005).

18. The opinion's author, former Chief Justice Rehnquist, regularly lambasted the Court's convoluted array of Establishment Clause decisions as predicated upon an utter disregard of historical reality. Typically, though, he did so in dissent, in the nature of an ineffective rudder straining without success to steer an otherwise directionless juggernaut. Perhaps his best-known Establishment Clause exposition remains his oft-cited dissent in *Wallace v. Jaffree,* 472 U.S. 38, 91–114 (1985) (Rehnquist, C. J. dissenting), in which he delved into the same historical materials that this book discusses in detail in earlier chapters—a fundamental historical narrative that had never appeared in any of the Court's Establishment Clause decisions to that point.

Bibliography

1. The *"Debates"* comprise Madison's personal notes of the 1787 Constitutional Convention (17–583), republished as well in:
   - *Journal of the Federal Convention* [not the official 1787 Convention *Journal*], vol. I, 53–390, and vol. II, 391–763 (E. Scott, Ed., Chicago: Albert, Scott & Co., 1893) (originally published in 1840 as *The Papers of James Madison* pursuant to Act of Congress of July 9, 1838, 25th Cong., 2d Sess., Ch. 264, 5 Stat. 309–10 (1838) (H. Gilpin, Ed., Washington, DC: Langtree and O'Sullivan, 1840));
   - V *The Debates in the Several State Conventions on the Adoption of the Federal Constitution,* 123–565 (J. Elliott, Ed., Philadelphia: J. B. Lippincott and Company, 2d ed., 1845);
   - III *Documentary History of the Constitution of the United States of America, 1786–1870,* 7–771 (Department of State, Washington, DC. 1900);
   - *The Writings of James Madison,* Volumes III and IV (G. Hunt, Ed., New York: G. P. Putnam & Sons, 1902 and 1903, respectively); and,
   - *Documents Illustrative of the Formation of the Union of the American*

States, 109–745 (C. Tansill, Ed., House Document No. 398, printed per House Concurrent Resolution No. 23, May 10, 1926, 69th Cong., 1st Sess., 44 Stat. 1980–81, reprinted per House Concurrent Resolution No. 400, July 7, 1965, 89th Cong., 1st Sess., 79 Stat. 1430–31 (1965) (Government Printing Office, Washington, DC, 1927).

Madison's personal 1787 Convention notes also appear interspersed with other materials throughout Volumes I and II of *The Records of the Federal Convention of 1787,* both the revised edition (4 vols. [I–IV]; M. Farrand, Ed., New Haven, Connecticut, and London: Yale University Press, rev. ed., 1937, as augmented by the *Supplement to Max Farrand's The Records of the Federal Convention of 1787* (J. Hutson, Ed., New Haven, Connecticut, and London: Yale University Press, 1987)) and the original edition (3 vols. [I–III]; M. Farrand, Ed., New Haven, Connecticut, and London: Yale University Press, 1911).

2. Citations from Elliott's *Debates* do not reference the first edition—*The Debates in the Several State Conventions on the Adoption of the Federal Constitution* (4 vols. [I–IV]; J. Elliott, Ed., Philadelphia: J. B. Lippincott and Company, 1827–30)—unless specified as such.

3. *Documentary History of the Constitution:*
- vol. I 1894
- vol. II 1894
- vol. III 1900
- vol. IV 1905
- vol. V 1905

4. Each volume bears a different title and publication data. The following volumes have been referenced:

- I *Documentary History of the First Federal Congress of the United States of America: March 4, 1789–March 3, 1791,* "Senate Legislative Journal" (L. De Pauw, Ed., Baltimore and London: The Johns Hopkins University Press, 1972);
- II *Documentary History of the First Federal Congress of the United States of America: March 4, 1789–March 3, 1791,* "Senate Executive Journal and Related Documents" (L. De Pauw, Ed., Baltimore and London: The Johns Hopkins University Press, 1974);
- III *Documentary History of the First Federal Congress of the United States of America: March 4, 1789–March 3, 1791,* "House of Representatives [Legislative] Journal" (L. De Pauw, Ed.,

Baltimore and London: The Johns Hopkins University Press, 1977);

• IV *Documentary History of the First Federal Congress of the United States of America: March 4, 1789–March 3, 1791,* "Legislative Histories—Amendments to the Constitution" (C. Bickford and H. Veit, Ed., Baltimore and London: The Johns Hopkins University Press, 1986);

• VI *Documentary History of the First Federal Congress of the United States of America: March 4, 1789–March 3, 1791,* "Legislative Histories—Northwest Territories Act of 1789" (C. Bickford and H. Veit, Ed., Baltimore and London: The Johns Hopkins University Press, 1986);

• IX *Documentary History of the First Federal Congress of the United States of America: March 4, 1789–March 3, 1791,* "The Diary of William Maclay and Other Notes on Senate Debates" (K. Bowling and H. Veit, Ed., Baltimore and London: The Johns Hopkins University Press, 1988);

• X *Documentary History of the First Federal Congress of the United States of America: March 4, 1789–March 3, 1791,* "Debates in the House of Representatives—First Session: April–May, 1789" (C. Bickford, K. Bowling, and H. Veit, Ed., Baltimore and London: The Johns Hopkins University Press, 1992);

• XI *Documentary History of the First Federal Congress of the United States of America: March 4, 1789–March 3, 1791,* "Debates In the House of Representatives—First Session: June–September, 1789" (C. Bickford, K. Bowling, and H. Veit, Ed., Baltimore and London: The Johns Hopkins University Press, 1992); and

• XVI *Documentary History of the First Federal Congress of the United States of America: March 4, 1789–March 3, 1791,* "Correspondence: First Session: June–August[,] 1789" (C. Bickford, K. Bowling, H. Veit, and W. DiGiacomantonio, Ed., Baltimore and London: The Johns Hopkins University Press, 2004).

5. *The Documentary History of the Ratification of the Constitution:*
   • vol. I M. Jensen, Ed., 1976
   • vol. II M. Jensen, Ed., 1976
   • vol. III M. Jensen, Ed., 1978
   • vol. IV J. Kaminski and G. Saladino, Ed., 1997
   • vol. V J. Kaminski and G. Saladino, Ed., 1998
   • vol. VI J. Kaminski and G. Saladino, Ed., 2000

- vol. VII J. Kaminski and G. Saladino, Ed., 2001
- vol. VIII J. Kaminski and G. Saladino, Ed., 1988
- vol. IX J. Kaminski and G. Saladino, Ed., 1990
- vol. X J. Kaminski and G. Saladino, Ed., 1993
- vol. XI [not yet published]
- vol. XII [not yet published]
- vol. XIII J. Kaminski and G. Saladino, Ed., 1981
- vol. XIV J. Kaminski and G. Saladino, Ed., 1983
- vol. XV J. Kaminski and G. Saladino, Ed., 1984
- vol. XVI J. Kaminski and G. Saladino, Ed., 1986
- vol. XVII J. Kaminski and G. Saladino, Ed., 1995
- vol. XVIII J. Kaminski and G. Saladino, Ed., 1995
- vol. XIX J. Kaminski, G. Saladino, R. Leffler, and C Schoenleber, Ed., 2003
- vol. XX J. Kaminski, G. Saladino, R. Leffler, and C Schoenleber, Ed., 2004
- vol. XXI J. Kaminski, G. Saladino, R. Leffler, and C Schoenleber, Ed., 2005

The bibliographical information page in Volume XX reflects the absence of Volumes XI or XII. The series, which is planned to contain twenty-five volumes when completed, has reserved Volumes XI, XII, and XXII–XXV for, among other topics, the ratification proceedings in Maryland, South Carolina, New Hampshire, North Carolina, and Rhode Island, none of which has thus far been reported in the series.

6. Somewhat misnamed, the two–volume *Journal of the Federal Convention* does not contain the official 1787 Constitutional Convention *Journal* first published in 1818 and republished in Volume I of *The Debates in the Several State Conventions on the Adoption of the Federal Constitution,* 139–318 (J. Elliott, Ed., Philadelphia: J. B. Lippincott and Company, 2d ed., 1836) (Elliott's *Debates*).

Instead, this "Journal"—Madison's *Journal*—includes a republication of Madison's personal notes (vol. I, 53–390, and vol. II, 391–763) originally published in 1840 as *The Papers of James Madison* pursuant to Act of Congress of July 9, 1838, 25th Cong., 2d Sess., Ch. 264, 5 Stat. 309–10 (1838) (H. Gilpin, Ed., Washington, DC: Langtree and O'Sullivan, 1840)), and republished in:

- V *The Debates in the Several State Conventions on the Adoption of the Federal Constitution,* 123–565 (J. Elliott, Ed., Philadelphia:

J. B. Lippincott and Company, 2d ed., 1845);

- III *Documentary History of the Constitution of the United States of America, 1786–1870,* 7–771 (Department of State, Washington, DC, 1900);

- *The Writings of James Madison,* Volumes III and IV (G. Hunt, Ed., New York: G. P. Putnam & Sons, 1902 and 1903, respectively);

- *The Debates in the Federal Convention of 1787 Which Framed the Constitution of the United States of America, Reported by James Madison,* 17–583 (G. Hunt & J. Scott, Ed., New York: Oxford University Press, 1920); and

- *Documents Illustrative of the Formation of the Union of the American States,* 109–745 (C. Tansill, Ed., House Document No. 398, printed per House Concurrent Resolution No. 23, May 10, 1926, 69th Cong., 1st Sess., 44 Stat. 1980–81, reprinted per House Concurrent Resolution No. 400, July 7, 1965, 89th Cong., 1st Sess., 79 Stat. 1430–31 (1965) (Government Printing Office, Washington, DC, 1927).

Madison's personal 1787 Convention notes also appear interspersed with other materials throughout Volumes I and II of *The Records of the Federal Convention of 1787,* both the revised edition (4 vols. [I–IV]; M. Farrand, Ed., New Haven, Connecticut, and London: Yale University Press, rev. ed., 1937, as augmented by the *Supplement to Max Farrand's The Records of the Federal Convention of 1787* (J. Hutson, Ed., New Haven, Connecticut, and London: Yale University Press, 1987)) and the original edition (3 vols. [I–III]; M. Farrand, Ed., New Haven, Connecticut, and London: Yale University Press, 1911).

7. The entirety of Chapter 4 in Levy's 1999 *Origins of the Bill of Rights* actually replicates *verbatim* the entirety of Chapter 9 in Levy's 1988 *Original Intent and the Framers' Constitution.*

8. *The Papers of George Washington:*

Colonial Series:

vol. 1 W. Abbot, Ed., 1983	vol. 6 W. Abbot, Ed., 1988
vol. 2 W. Abbot, Ed., 1983	vol. 7 W. Abbot and D. Twohig, Ed., 1990
vol. 3 W. Abbot, Ed., 1984	vol. 8 W. Abbot and D. Twohig, Ed., 1993
vol. 4 W. Abbot, Ed., 1984	vol. 9 W. Abbot and D. Twohig, Ed., 1994

vol. 5 W. Abbot, Ed., 1988

Confederation Series:
vol. 1 W. Abbot, Ed., 1992
vol. 2 W. Abbot, Ed., 1992
vol. 3 W. Abbot, Ed., 1994

Revolutionary Series:
vol. 1 P. Chase, Ed., 1985
vol. 2 P. Chase, Ed., 1987
vol. 3 P. Chase, Ed., 1988
vol. 4 P. Chase, Ed., 1991

vol. 5 P. Chase, Ed., 1993
vol. 6 P. Chase/F. Grizzard, Ed., 1994
vol. 7 P. Chase, Ed., 1997

Presidential Series:
vol. 1 D. Twohig, Ed., 1987
vol. 2 D. Twohig, Ed., 1987
vol. 3 D. Twohig, Ed., 1989
vol. 4 D. Twohig, Ed., 1993

vol. 5 D. Twohig/
M. Mastromarino/
J. Warren, Ed., 1996
vol. 6 M. Mastromarino,

vol. 10 W. Abbot and D. Twohig, Ed., 1995

vol. 4 W. Abbot, Ed., 1995
vol. 5 W. Abbot, Ed., 1997
vol. 6 W. Abbot, Ed., 1997

vol. 8 F. Grizzard, Ed. 1998
vol. 9 P. Chase, Ed., 1999
vol. 10 F. Grizzard, Ed., 2000
vol. 11 P. Chase and E. Lengel, Ed., 2001
vol. 12 F. Grizzard, Ed., 2002
vol. 13 E. Lengel, Ed., 2003

vol. 14 D. Hoth, Ed., 2004

vol. 7 J. Warren, Ed., 1998
vol. 8 M. Mastromarino, Ed., 1999
vol. 9 M. Mastromarino, Ed., 2000
vol. 10 R. Haggard/M. Mastromarino, Ed., 2002
vol. 11 C. Patrick, Ed. 2002
vol. 12 C. Patrick and J. Pinheiro, Ed., 1996 Ed., 2005

9. The University of Virginia has arranged Madison's Papers—not to be confused with Madison's personal notes originally published in 1840 as *The Papers of James Madison* (H. Gilpin, Ed., Washington, DC: Langtree and O'Sullivan, 1840)—in four series: the *Congressional Series,* spanning 1785 to 1801 (17 vols., all published), the *Secretary of State Series,* spanning 1801 to 1809 (5 vols. published [all University Press of Virginia, 1986, 1993, 1995, 1998, and 2000, respectively], 16 planned), the *Presidential Series,* spanning 1809 to 1817 (4 vols. published [all University Press of Virginia, 1984, 1992, 1996, and 1999, respectively], 12 planned), and the *Retirement Series,* spanning 1817 to 1836 (none yet

published). See http://www.virginia.edu/pjm/description1.htm, and http://www.virginia.edu/pjm/volumes1.htm.

The *Congressional Series* comprises:
vol. 1 W. Hutchinson and W. Rachal, Ed., Chicago: University of Chicago Press, 1962
vol. 2 W. Hutchinson and W. Rachal, Ed., Chicago: University of Chicago Press, 1962
vol. 3 W. Hutchinson and W. Rachal, Ed., Chicago: University of Chicago Press, 1963
vol. 4 W. Hutchinson and W. Rachal, Ed., Chicago: University of Chicago Press, 1965
vol. 5 W. Hutchinson and W. Rachal, Ed., Chicago: University of Chicago Press, 1967
vol. 6 W. Hutchinson and W. Rachal, Ed., Chicago: University of Chicago Press, 1969
vol. 7 W. Hutchinson and W. Rachal, Ed., Chicago: University of Chicago Press, 1971
vol. 8 R. Rutland and W. Rachal, Ed., Chicago: University of Chicago Press, 1973
vol. 9 R. Rutland and W. Rachal, Ed., Chicago: University of Chicago Press, 1975
vol. 10 R. Rutland/C. Hobson/W. Rachal/F. Teute, Ed., Chicago: University of Chicago Press, 1977
vol. 11 R. Rutland/C. Hobson, Ed., Charlottesville: University Press of Virginia, 1977
vol. 12 C. Hobson/R. Rutland, Ed., Charlottesville: University Press of Virginia, 1979
vol. 13 C. Hobson/R. Rutland, Ed., Charlottesville: University Press of Virginia, 1981
vol. 14 R. Rutland/T. Mason, Ed., Charlottesville: University Press of Virginia, 1983
vol. 15 R. Mason/R. Rutland/J. Sisson, Ed., Charlottesville: University Press of Virginia, 1985
vol. 16 J. Stagg, T. Mason/J. Sisson, Ed., Charlottesville: University Press of Virginia, 1989
vol. 17 D. Mattern/J. Stagg/J. Cross/S. Perdue, Ed., Charlottesville: University Press of Virginia,1991
   10. *The Papers of Thomas Jefferson:*

vols. 1 and 2 J. Boyd, Ed., 1950	vol. 21 C. Cullen, Ed., 1984
vols. 3 and 4 J. Boyd, Ed., 1951	vol. 22 C. Cullen, Ed., 1986
vols. 5 and 6 J. Boyd, Ed., 1952	vol. 23 C. Cullen, Ed., 1990
vols. 7 and 8 J. Boyd, Ed., 1953	vol. 24 J. Catanzariti, Ed., 1990
vols. 9 and 10 J. Boyd, Ed., 1954	vol. 25 J. Catanzariti, Ed., 1993
vols. 11 and 12 J. Boyd, Ed., 1955	vol. 26 J. Catanzariti, Ed., 1995
vol. 13 J. Boyd, Ed., 1956	vol. 27 J. Catanzariti, Ed., 1997
vols. 14 and 15 J. Boyd, Ed., 1958	vol. 28 J. Catanzariti, Ed., 2000
vol. 16 J. Boyd, Ed., 1961	vol. 29 B. Oberg, Ed., 2001
vol. 17 J. Boyd, Ed., 1965	vol. 30 B. Oberg, Ed., 2003
vol. 18 J. Boyd, Ed., 1972	vol. 31 B. Oberg, Ed., 2004
vol. 19 J. Boyd, Ed., 1974	vol. 32 B. Oberg, Ed., 2005
vol. 20 J. Boyd, Ed., 1982	vol. 33 B. Oberg, Ed., 2006

11. This particular book includes the following Jefferson writings:
- "Autobiography," 1–101;
- "A Summary View of the Rights of British America," 103–22;
- *Notes on the State of Virginia*, 123–325;
- "Public Papers," 327–486;
- "Addresses, Messages, and Replies," 487–566;
- "Miscellany," 567–707;
- "Letters," 709–1517.

12. Congress first authorized private publication by Little, Brown & Company of Boston via congressional resolution. J. Res. of March 3, 1845, 28th Cong., 2nd Sess., 5 Stat. 798–99. Congress later transferred all printing of congressional enactments and resolutions to the Congressional Printer via Act of March 9, 1868, Ch. 22, §§ 1–4, 40th Cong., 2nd Sess., 15 Stat. 40.

13. *The Writings of George Washington:*

vols. 1, 2, 3, 4 1931	vols. 24, 25, 26, 27, 28 1938
vols. 5, 6, 7 1932	vols. 29, 30, 31, 32 1939
vols. 8, 9, 10 1933	vols. 33, 34, 35 1940
vols. 11, 12 1934	vols. 36, 37 1941
vols. 13, 14, 15 1936	vols. 38, 39 1944
vols. 16, 17, 18, 19, 20, 21, 22, 23 1937	

14. *The Writings of James Madison:*
- vol. I 1900
- vol. IV 1903
- vol. VII 1908

- vol. II 1901   • vol. V 1904   • vol. VIII 1908
- vol. III 1902   • vol. VI 1906   • vol. IX 1910

Volumes III and IV of *The Writings of James Madison* contain only Madison's personal notes, republished as well in:

- *The Papers of James Madison* (H. Gilpin, Ed., Washington, DC: Langtree and O'Sullivan, 1840) (published pursuant to Act of Congress of July 9, 1838, 25th Cong., 2d Sess., Ch. 264, 5 Stat. 309–10 (1838));

- V *The Debates in the Several State Conventions on the Adoption of the Federal Constitution*, 1–565 (J. Elliott, Ed., Philadelphia: J. B. Lippincott and Company, 2d ed., 1845);

- *Journal of the Federal Convention* [not the official 1787 Convention *Journal*], vol. I, 53–390, and vol. II, 391–763 (E. Scott, Ed., Chicago: Albert, Scott & Co., 1893);

- III *Documentary History of the Constitution of the United States of America, 1786–1870*, 7–771 (Department of State, Washington, DC, 1900);

- *The Debates in the Federal Convention of 1787 Which Framed the Constitution of the United States of America, Reported by James Madison*, 17–583 (G. Hunt & J. Scott, Ed., New York: Oxford University Press, 1920); and

- *Documents Illustrative of the Formation of the Union of the American States*, 109–745 (C. Tansill, Ed., House Document No. 398, printed per House Concurrent Resolution No. 23, May 10, 1926, 69th Cong., 1st Sess., 44 Stat. 1980–81, reprinted per House Concurrent Resolution No. 400, July 7, 1965, 89th Cong., 1st Sess., 79 Stat. 1430–31 (1965) (Government Printing Office, Washington, DC, 1927).

Bibliography

Amar, A. *America's Constitution: A Biography*. New York: Random House, 2005.

———. *The Bill of Rights*. New Haven, Connecticut: Yale University Press, 1998.

Amer, M. "The Congressional Record: Content, History, and Issues," *CRS Report* 93–60, Congressional Record Service, Library of Congress (January 14, 1993).

American Heritage Dictionary of the English Language. 4th ed. New York: Houghton Mifflin, 2000.

American National Biography. 24 vols. [1–24]. J. Garraty and M. Carnes, Ed. New York and Oxford: Oxford University Press, 1999.

Annals of America. 21 vols. Encyclopædia Britannica, Inc., 1968.

Annals of Congress. 42 vols. from the 1st Cong., 1st Sess. (1789) to the 18th Cong., 2nd Sess. (1824). Washington, DC: Gales & Seaton, 1834–56.

Baker, J., Jr. "The Establishment Clause as Intended: No Preference Among Sects and Pluralism in a Large Commercial Republic," in *The Bill of Rights: Original Meaning and Current Understanding*. E. Hickok, Jr., Ed. Charlottesville, Virginia, and London: University Press of Virginia, 1991.

Baker, L. *John Marshall: A Life in Law*. New York: Macmillan Publishing Co., Inc., 1974.

Barnhart Dictionary of Etymology. R. Barnhart, Ed. New York: The H. W. Wilson Company, 1988.

Beveridge, A. *Life of John Marshall*. 4 vols. [I–IV]. Boston: Houghton Mifflin Company, 1916–19.

Black's Law Dictionary. 8th ed. B. Garner, Ed. Minneapolis: Thomsen/West, 2004.

Brant, I. *James Madison: Father of the Constitution, 1787–1800*.

Indianapolis and New York: The Bobbs-Merrill Company, Inc., 1950.

————.*James Madison: The Nationalist, 1780–1787*. Indianapolis and New York: The Bobbs-Merrill Company, Inc., 1948.

————.*James Madison: The President, 1809–1812*. Indianapolis and New York: The Bobbs-Merrill Company, Inc., 1956.

————.*James Madison: Secretary of State, 1800–1809*. Indianapolis and New York: The Bobbs-Merrill Company, Inc., 1953.

————.*James Madison: The Virginia Revolutionist, 1751–1780*. Indianapolis and New York: The Bobbs-Merrill Company, Inc., 1941.

Brodie, F. *Thomas Jefferson: An Intimate History*. New York: W. W. Norton & Company, Inc., 1974.

Brohaugh, W. *English Through the Ages*. Cincinnati: Writer's Digest Books, 1998.

Byrd, R. *The Senate 1789–1989: Addresses on the History of the United States Senate*. 4 vols. Senate Document No. 100–20, 100th Cong., 1st Sess. Washington, DC: U.S. Government Printing Office, 1991.

Channing, E. *A History of the United States*. New York: The Macmillan Company, 1921.

Cobb, S. *The Rise of Religious Liberty in America*. New York: The Macmillan Company, 1902.

The Collected Works of Abraham Lincoln. 9 vols. R. Basler, Ed. New Brunswick, New Jersey: Rutgers University Press, 1953–55.

The Complete Anti-Federalist. 7 vols. J. Storing, Ed. Chicago: University of Chicago Press, 1981.

The Complete Bill of Rights: The Drafts, Debates, Sources, and Origins. N. Cogan, Ed. New York and Oxford: Oxford University Press, 1997.

Cooley, T. *General Principles of Constitutional Law in the United States*. 3d ed. Boston: Little, Brown & Co., 1898.

————.*A Treatise on the Constitutional Limitations Which Rest upon the Legislative Power of the States of the American Union*. Boston: Little, Brown & Co., 1868.

Cord, R. "Church-State Separation: Restoring the 'No Preference' Doctrine of the First Amendment," 9 *Harv. J. L. & Pub. Pol.* 129 (1986).

————.*Separation of Church and State: Historical Fact and Current Fiction*. New York: Lambeth Press, 1982.

Corwin, E. "The Supreme Court as National School Board," 14 *Law and Contemporary Problems*, 3 Duke University School of Law (1949).

Cox, A. *The Court and the Constitution*. Boston: Houghton Mifflin Company, 1987.

The Debate on the Constitution. Parts 1 and 2. B. Bailyn, Ed. New York: Literary Classics of the United States, 1993.

The Debates in the Federal Convention of 1787 Which Framed the Constitution of the United States of America, Reported by James Madison. G. Hunt & J. Scott, Ed. New York: Oxford University Press, 1920.[1]

The Debates in the Several State Conventions on the Adoption of the Federal Constitution. 5 vols. [I–V]. J. Elliott, Ed. Philadelphia: J. B. Lippincott and Company, 2nd ed., 1836 [vols. I–IV] and 1845 [vol. V]).[2]

Dictionary of American Biography. 10 vols. D. Malone, Ed. New York: Charles Scribner's Sons, 1932.

Dictionary of American History. 7 vols. [I–VII], rev. ed. New York: Charles Scribner's Sons, 1976.

Documentary History of the Constitution of the United States of America, 1786–1870. 5 vols. [I–V]. Department of State. Washington, DC: 1894–1905.[3]

Documentary History of the First Federal Congress of the United States of America: March 4, 1789–March 3, 1791. 17 vols. [I–XVII]. Various editors. Baltimore and London: The Johns Hopkins University Press, 1972–2004.[4]

The Documentary History of the Ratification of the Constitution. 21 vols. [I–XXI]. Various editors. Madison: State Historical Society of Wisconsin, 1976–2005.[5]

Documents Illustrative of the Formation of the Union of the American States. C. Tansill, Ed. House Document No. 398, printed per House Concurrent Resolution No. 23, May 10, 1926, 69th Cong., 1st Sess., 44 Stat. 1980–81, reprinted per House Concurrent Resolution No. 400, July 7, 1965, 89th Cong., 1st Sess., 79 Stat. 1430–31 (1965). Government Printing Office, Washington, DC, 1927.

Donald, D. *Lincoln.* New York: Simon & Schuster, 1995.

Dreisbach, D. "*Everson* and the Command of History: The Supreme Court, Lessons of History, and Church-State Debate in America," in *Everson Revisited: Religion, Education, and Law at the Crossroads.* J. Formicola and J. Morken, Ed. Lanham, Maryland: Rowman & Littlefield Publishers, Inc., 1997.

———. *Thomas Jefferson and the Wall of Separation Between Church and State.* New York and London: New York University Press, 2002.

Elliott's *Debates*—see *The Debates in the Several State Conventions on the Adoption of the Federal Constitution.*

Fair, D. "The *Everson* Case in the Context of New Jersey Politics," in *Everson Revisited: Religion, Education, and Law at the Crossroads.* J. Formicola and J. Morken, Ed. Lanham, Maryland: Rowman & Littlefield Publishers, Inc., 1997.

Farrand, M. *The Framing of the Constitution of the United States.* New Haven, Connecticut: Yale University Press, 1913.

Farrand's *Records*—see *The Records of the Federal Convention of 1787.*

"FBI Helps Restore Jefferson's Obliterated Draft," *Library of Congress Information Bulletin,* vol. 57, no. 5 (May 1998).

The Federal and State Constitutions, Colonial Charters, and Other Organic Laws of the States, Territories, and Colonies Now or Heretofore Forming the United States of America. 7 vols. Compiled and edited under Act of June 30, 1906, 59th Cong., 1st Sess., Ch. 3914, 34 Stat. 759; F. Thorpe, Ed. Washington, DC: Government Printing Office, 1909.

The Federalist Papers refers to either . . .

• *The Federalist (Papers).* B. Wright, Ed. New York: Barnes & Noble Books, 2004; or

• *The Federalist Papers.* C. Rossiter, Ed. New York: Signet Classic [Penguin Group (USA)], 2003; or

• *The Federalist Papers.* I. Kramnick, Ed. London and New York: Penguin Books, 1987.

Fenno's *Senate Journal* (Second Session)—see *Journal of the Second Session of the Senate of the United States of America.*

Fenno's *Senate Journal* (Third Session)—see *Journal of the Third Session of the Senate of the United States of America.*

The Founders' Constitution. 5 vols. P. Kurland and R. Lerner, Ed. Chicago and London: University of Chicago Press, 1987.

Funk & Wagnalls Comprehensive Standard International Dictionary. Chicago: J. G. Ferguson Publishing Company, 1971.

Gaustad, E. *Church and State in America.* New York and Oxford: Oxford University Press, 1999.

Greene, E. "Provincial America: 1690–1740," in *The American Nation: A History.* A. Hart, Ed. New York and London: Harper & Brothers Publishers, 1907.

Greenleaf's *Senate Journal* (First Session)—see *Journal of the First Session of the Senate of the United States of America.*

Historical Statistics of the United States. Millennial Edition. 5 vols. Various editors. New York: Cambridge University Press, 2006.

The History of the Supreme Court of the United States. vol. XII. *The Birth of the Modern Constitution.* W. Wiecek, Ed. New York: Cambridge University Press, 2006.

A History of the United States. P. Jenkins, Ed. New York: St. Martin's Press, 1997.

Hofstadter, R. *America at 1750: A Social Portrait.* New York: Alfred A. Knopf, 1972.

Holmes, D. *The Faiths of the Founding Fathers.* New York: Oxford University Press, 2006.

House Journal—see *Journal of the House of Representatives of the United States.*

Huston, J. (Chief, Manuscript Division, Library of Congress). *Religion and the Federal Government: A Wall of Separation,* from Library of Congress Exhibition "Religion and the Founding of the American Republic," Exhibition Catalogue, Section VI, Part 2. Washington, DC: Library of Congress. Web site http://www.loc.gov/exhibits/religion/rel06–2.html, accessed through Web site via http://www.loc.gov/exhibits/religion/.

————.*Religion and the State Governments: The Church-State Debate: Virginia,* from Library of Congress Exhibition "Religion and the Founding of the American Republic," Exhibition Catalogue, Part V. Washington, DC: Library of Congress. Web site http://www.loc.gov/exhibits/religion/rel05.html, accessed through Web site via http://www.loc.gov/exhibits/religion/.

————."'A Wall of Separation': FBI Helps Restore Jefferson's Obliterated Draft." *Library of Congress Information Bulletin,* vol. 57, no. 6 (June 1998).

The Inaugural Addresses of the Presidents. J. Hunt, Ed. New York: Gramercy Books/Random House Value Publishing, 1997.

James Madison and the American Nation: 1751–1836. R. Rutland, Ed. New York: Simon & Schuster, 1994.

Jefferson—"Addresses, Messages, and Replies"—see *Thomas Jefferson: Writings,* "Addresses, Messages, and Replies."

Jefferson—"Autobiography"—see *Thomas Jefferson: Writings,* "Autobiography."

Jefferson . . . In His Own Words—see *Thomas Jefferson: A Biography in His Own Words.*

Jefferson—"Letters"—see *Thomas Jefferson: Writings,* "Letters."

Jefferson—*Notes on the State of Virginia*—see *Thomas Jefferson: Writings, Notes on the State of Virginia.*

Jefferson—"Public Papers"—see *Thomas Jefferson: Writings*, "Public Papers."

Jefferson's Life—see *The Life and Selected Writings of Thomas Jefferson.*

Jefferson's Memoirs—see *Memoir [sic], Correspondence, and Miscellanies, from the Papers of Thomas Jefferson.*

Jefferson's Papers—see *The Papers of Thomas Jefferson.*

Jefferson's Retirement Papers—see *The Papers of Thomas Jefferson, Retirement Series.*

Jefferson's Works—see *The Works of Thomas Jefferson.*

Jefferson's Writings (1853 edition)—see *The Writings of Thomas Jefferson.* 10 vols. [I–X]. H. A. Washington, Ed. New York: Taylor & Maury, 1853–54.

Jefferson's Writings (1903 edition)—see *The Writings of Thomas Jefferson.* 20 vols. [I–XX]. A. Lipscomb and A. Bergh, Ed. Washington, DC: Thomas Jefferson Memorial Association, 1903.

Johnson, S. *A Dictionary of the English Language.* 2 vols. London: printed by W. Strahan,1755.

Journal of the Executive Proceedings of the Senate. Senate Executive Proceedings from 1st Cong., 1st Sess., through 19th Cong., 2nd Sess. Washington, DC: Duff Green, 1828.

Journal of the Federal Convention [not the official Journal], a republication of Madison's notes of the 1787 Convention. 2 vols. [I and II]. E. Scott, Ed. Chicago: Albert, Scott & Co., 1893. Reprinted from the 1840 edition published by the United States government pursuant to Act of Congress of July 9, 1838, 25th Cong., 2d Sess., Ch. 264, 5 Stat. 309–10 (1838).[6]

*Journal of the First Session of the Senate of the United States of America.*1st Cong., 1st Sess. New York: Thomas Greenleaf, 1789.

Journal of the House of Representatives of the United States [not the official Journal]. 75 vols. From the 1st Cong., 1st Sess. (1789), through the 43rd Cong., 2nd Sess. (1875); Washington, DC: Various publishers, 1826–75.

Journal of the Second Session of the Senate of the United States of America. 1st Cong., 2nd Sess. New York: John Fenno, 1790.

Journal of the Senate of the United States [not the official Journal]. 70 vols. From the 1st Cong., 1st Sess. (1789), through the 43rd Cong., 2nd Sess. (1875). Washington, DC: Various publishers, 1820–74.

Journal of the Third Session of the Senate of the United States of America. 1st Cong., 3rd Sess. Philadelphia: John Fenno, 1791.

Journal of William Maclay, United States Senator from Pennsylvania, 1789–1791. E. Maclay, Ed. New York: D. Appleton and Company, 1890.

Journals of the Continental Congress: 1774–1789. 34 vols. [I–XXXIV]. From 1774 to 1789. Various editors. Washington, DC: Government Printing Office, 1904–37.

Justices of the United States Supreme Court 1789–1969: Their Lives and Major Opinions. 5 vols. [I–V]. L. Friedman and F. Israel, Ed. New York and London: Chelsea House Publishers and R. R. Bowker Company, 1969.

Ketchum, R. *James Madison: A Biography.* Charlottesville, Virginia: University Press of Virginia, 1990.

Konefsky, S. *John Marshall and Alexander Hamilton: Architects of the American Constitution.* New York: The Macmillan Company, 1964.

Kurland, P. "The Origins of the Religion Clauses of the Constitution," 27 *William & Mary Law Review* 839 (1986).

Labunski, R. *James Madison and the Struggle for the Bill of Rights.* New York: Oxford University Press, 2006.

Lambert, F. *The Founding Fathers and the Place of Religion in America.* Princeton, New Jersey: Princeton University Press, 2003.

Letters and Other Writings of James Madison. 4 vols [I–IV]. R. Worthington, Ed. New York: J. B. Lippincott and Company, 1884.

Levin, M. *Men in Black.* Washington, DC: Regnery Publishing, Inc., 2005.

Levy, L. *The Establishment Clause: Religion and the First Amendment.* 2d ed. rev. Chapel Hill, North Carolina, and London: The University of North Carolina Press, 1994.

———.*Original Intent and the Framers' Constitution.* New York: Macmillan Publishing Company, 1988.

———.*Origins of the Bill of Rights.* New Haven, Connecticut, and London: Yale University Press, 1999.[7]

The Life and Selected Writings of Thomas Jefferson. A Koch and W. Peden, Ed. New York: Random House, Inc., 1998.

Lincoln in the Times: The Life of Abraham Lincoln, as Originally Reported in The New York Times. D. Donald and H. Holzer, Ed. New York: St. Martin's Press, 2005.

Lincoln's Works—see *The Collected Works of Abraham Lincoln.*

Maclay's Journal—see *Journal of William Maclay.*

Maddox, R. *Separation of Church and State: Guarantor of Religious*

Freedom. New York: The Crossroad Publishing Company, 1987.

Madison and the American Nation—see *James Madison and the American Nation: 1751–1836.*

Madison's Letters—see *Letters and Other Writings of James Madison.*

Madison's *Journal*—see *Journal of the Federal Convention.*

Madison's Notes—see *The Debates in the Federal Convention of 1787 Which Framed the Constitution of the United States of America, Reported by James Madison.*

Madison's Papers—see *The Papers of James Madison, Congressional Series.*

Madison's Writings—see *The Writings of James Madison.*

Malone, D. *Jefferson and His Time: Jefferson the Virginian.* Boston: Little, Brown and Company, 1948.

————.*Jefferson and the Ordeal of Liberty.* Boston: Little, Brown and Co., 1962.

————.*Jefferson and the Rights of Man.* Boston: Little, Brown and Co., 1951.

————.*Jefferson The President: First Term, 1801–1805.* Boston: Little, Brown and Co., 1970.

Mason's Papers—see *The Papers of George Mason, 1725–1792.*

McCullough, D. *John Adams.* New York: Simon & Schuster, 2001.

McDougall, W. *Freedom Just Around the Corner: A New American History 1585–1828.* New York: HarperCollins Publishers, 2004.

Meinig, D. *The Shaping of America: A Geographical Perspective on 500 Years of History.* vol. 1: *Atlantic America: 1492–1800.* New Haven, Connecticut, and London: Yale University Press, 1986.

Memoir [sic], Correspondence, and Miscellanies, from the Papers of Thomas Jefferson. 4 vols. Thomas Jefferson Randolph, Ed. London: H. Colburn and R. Bentley, 1829; Charlottesville: F. Carr and Co., 1829.

Monsma, S. "The Wrong Road Taken," in *Everson Revisited: Religion, Education, and Law at the Crossroads.* J. Formicola and J. Morken, Ed. Lanham, Maryland: Rowman & Littlefield Publishers, Inc., 1997.

A Nation Dedicated to Religious Liberty: The Constitutional Heritage of the Religion Clauses. A. Adams and C. Emmerich, Ed. Philadelphia: University of Pennsylvania Press, 1990.

New Oxford American Dictionary. 2d ed. New York: Oxford University Press, 2005.

The Oxford Companion to the English Language. T. McArthur, Ed. Oxford and New York: Oxford University Press, 1992.

The Oxford Companion to the Supreme Court of the United States. 2d ed. K.

Hall, J. Ely, Jr., and J. Grossman, Ed. New York and Oxford: Oxford University Press, 2005.

Oxford Dictionary of Word Histories. G. Chantrell, Ed. Oxford and New York: Oxford University Press, 2002.

Oxford English Dictionary. 2d ed. New York: Oxford University Press, 1991.

Paddock, L. *Facts about the Supreme Court of the United States.* New York: The H. W. Wilson Company, 1996.

The Papers of George Mason, 1725–1792. 3 vols. [I–III]. R. Rutland, Ed. Chapel Hill: University of North Carolina Press, 1970.

The Papers of George Washington. 4 different series spanning 42 vols. Various editors. Charlottesville: University Press of Virginia, various years according to series.[8]

The Papers of James Madison, Congressional Series. 17 vols. Various editors. Chicago: University of Chicago Press, 1962 to 1977; Charlottesville: University Press of Virginia, 1977 to 1991.[9]

The Papers of Thomas Jefferson. Currently 33 vols. Various editors. Princeton, New Jersey: Princeton University Press, 1950–2006.[10]

The Papers of Thomas Jefferson, Retirement Series. Currently 3 vols. J. Jefferson Looney, Ed. Princeton, New Jersey: Princeton University Press, 2004–6.

Pearcy, N. *Total Truth: Liberating Christianity from Its Cultural Captivity.* 2d ed. Wheaton, Illinois: Crossway Books, 2005.

Peterson, M. *Thomas Jefferson and the New Nation.* New York: Oxford University Press, 1970.

Powell, H. "The Original Understanding of Original Intent," 98 *Harv. L. Rev.* 885 (1985).

Rakove, J. *Original Meaning: Politics and Ideas in the Making of the Constitution.* New York: Vintage Books/Random House, 1997.

Randall, H. *The Life of Thomas Jefferson.* 3 vols. New York: Derby and Jackson, 1858; Philadelphia: J. B. Lippincott, 1888.

Random House Unabridged Dictionary. 2d ed. New York: Random House, 1993.

Random House Webster's Unabridged Dictionary. 2d ed. New York: Random House, 1998.

The Records of the Federal Convention of 1787. 4 vols. M. Farrand, Ed. New Haven, Connecticut, and London: Yale University Press, rev. ed. 1937, as augmented by *Supplement to Max Farrand's Records of the Federal Convention of 1787.* J. Hutson, Ed. New Haven, Connecticut, and London: Yale University Press, 1987. 3 vols. M. Farrand, Ed., New Haven, Connecticut, and London: Yale University Press, 1911.

Rehnquist, W. "The Notion of a Living Constitution," 29 *Harv. Jour. Law & Pub. Pol.* 401 (Spring 2006), reprinting W. Rehnquist, "The Notion of a Living Constitution," 54 *Tex. L. Rev.* 693 (1976).

————.*The Supreme Court.* New York: Alfred A. Knopf, 2004.

Rice, C. "The Bill of Rights and the Doctrine of Incorporation," in *The Bill of Rights: Original Meaning and Current Understanding.* E. Hickok, Jr., Ed. Charlottesville, Virginia, and London: University Press of Virginia, 1991.

Ring, K. *Scalia Dissents: Writings of the Supreme Court's Wittiest, Most Outspoken Justice.* Washington, DC: Regnery Publishing Co., 2004.

Sandburg, C. *Abraham Lincoln: The Prairie Years.* New York: Harcourt, Brace & Company, 1926.

————.*Abraham Lincoln: The War Years.* 4 vols. [I–IV]. New York: Harcourt, Brace & Company, 1939.

Schwartz, B. *The Roots of the Bill of Rights.* 5 vols. New York: Chelsea House, 1980.

Senate Executive Journal—see *Journal of the Executive Proceedings of the Senate.*

Senate Journal—see *Journal of the Senate of the United States.*

Shorter Oxford English Dictionary. 2 vols. 5th ed. New York: Oxford University Press, 2002.

Simmons, R. C. *The American Colonies: From Settlement to Independence.* New York: David McKay Company, Inc., 1976.

Sources and Documents of United States Constitutions. 10 vols. W. Swindler, Ed. Dobbs Ferry, New York: Oceana Publications, 1973–79.

Sources and Documents of United States Constitutions. Second Series. 5 vols. W. Swindler, Ed. London, Rome, New York: Oceana Publications, Inc., 1982–87.

Sources of Our Liberties. R. Perry, Ed. Chicago: American Bar Foundation, 1978.

Stokes, A. *Church and State in the United States.* 3 vols. [I–III]. New York: Harper & Brothers, 1950.

Stokes, A. and L. Pfeffer. *Church and State in the United States.* New York: Harper & Row, rev. ed., 1964.

Story, J. *Commentaries on the Constitution of the United States.* 3 vols. [I–III]. Boston: Hilliard, Gray and Co.; Cambridge, Massachusetts: Brown, Shattuck and Co., 1833.

————.*Commentaries on the Constitution of the United States.* 2 vols. [I–II]. Boston: Little, Brown & Co., 5th ed., 1891.

Supreme Court Justices—see *The Justices of the United States Supreme Court: 1789–1969.*

Taylor, A. *American Colonies.* New York: Viking Penguin, 2001.

Thomas Jefferson: A Biography in His Own Words. J. Gardner, Ed. New York: Newsweek, 1974.

Thomas Jefferson: Writings. M. Peterson, Ed. New York: Literary Classics of the United States/Library of America, 1984.[11]

Tinling, M. "Thomas Lloyd's Reports of the First Federal Congress," 18 *William & Mary Quarterly* 519 (1961).

United States Statutes at Large (or Stat.), the official source of congressional enactments and resolutions, as first authorized to be published privately by Little, Brown & Company of Boston via congressional resolution.[12]

Washington's Papers—see *The Papers of George Washington.*

Washington's Writings—see *The Writings of George Washington from the Original Manuscript Sources, 1745–1799.*

Webster's Third New International Dictionary. New York: G. & C. Merriam Co., 1961.

Who Was Who in America. 5 vols. [I–V]. Chicago: Marquis–Who's Who, Inc., 1968.

Wills, G. *James Madison.* New York: Henry Holt and Company, 2002.

Wood, G. *The Creation of the American Republic, 1776–1787.* Chapel Hill: University of North Carolina Press, 1969, 1998.

Woodward, B. and S. Armstrong. *The Brethren: Inside the Supreme Court.* New York: Simon & Schuster, 2005 ed.

Works of Fisher Ames. Seth Ames, Ed. Boston: Little, Brown & Co., 1854.

The Works of John Adams. 10 vols. [I–X]. C. F. Adams, Ed. Boston: Little, Brown & Co., 1856.

The Works of Thomas Jefferson. 12 vols. [I–XII]. P. Ford, Ed. Federal Edition. New York and London: G. P. Putnam's Sons, 1904–5.

The Writings of George Washington from the Original Manuscript Sources, 1745–1799. 39 vols. J. Fitzpatrick, Ed. Washington, DC: United States Government Printing Office, 1931–44.[13]

The Writings of James Madison. 9 vols. [I–IX]. G. Hunt, Ed. New York: G. P. Putnam & Sons, 1900–1910.[14]

The Writings of Thomas Jefferson. 10 vols. [I–X]. H. A. Washington, Ed. New York: Taylor & Maury, 1853–54.

The Writings of Thomas Jefferson. 20 vols. [I–XX]. A. Lipscomb and A. Bergh, Ed. Washington, DC: Thomas Jefferson Memorial Association, 1903.

Index

414 FREEDOM OF RELIGION

rec
8/11

DATE DUE